EIGHTH EDITION

Discovering the American Past

A Look at the Evidence

VOLUME I: TO 1877

William Bruce Wheeler
University of Tennessee

Lorri Glover
Saint Louis University

CENGAGE
Learning®

Australia • Brazil • Mexico • Singapore • United Kingdom • United States

CENGAGE
Learning®

Discovering the American Past: A Look at the Evidence, Volume I: To 1877, **Eighth Edition**

William Bruce Wheeler and Lorri Glover

Product Director: Paul Banks

Product Manager: Clint Attebery

Content Developer: Anais Wheeler

Product Assistant: Andrew Newton

Marketing Manager: Kyle Zimmerman

IP Analyst: Alexandra Ricciardi

IP Project Manager: Farah J Fard

Manufacturing Planner: Fola Orekoya

Art and Design Direction, Production Management, and Composition: Lumina Datamatics, Inc.

Cover Image: © Everett Historical / Shutterstock (Illustration of 1770 battle)

© Yiming Chen / Getty Images (State House building in Boston)

© Historic Map Works LLC and Osher Map Library / Getty Images (Bottom Map)

Library of Congress Control Number: 2015948802

Student Edition: ISBN: 978-1-305-63042-0

Cengage Learning
20 Channel Center Street
Boston, MA 02210
USA

Cengage Learning is a leading provider of customized learning solutions with employees residing in nearly 40 different countries and sales in more than 125 countries around the world. Find your local representative at **www.cengage.com**.

Cengage Learning products are represented in Canada by Nelson Education, Ltd.

To learn more about Cengage Learning Solutions, visit **www.cengage.com.**

Purchase any of our products at your local college store or at our preferred online store **www.cengagebrain.com.**

Printed in the United States of America
Print Number: 01 Print Year: 2015

Contents

Contents

CHAPTER **6**

Church, State, and Democracy: The Sunday Mail Controversy, 1827–1831

CHAPTER **7**

Land, Growth, and Justice: The Removal of the Cherokees

CHAPTER **11**

Reconstructing Reconstruction: The Political Cartoonist and American Public Opinion

CHAPTER **12**

History Skills in Action: Designing Your Own Project

Preface

In his 1990 State of the Union Address, President George Herbert Walker Bush set forth a set of National Education Goals, one of which was the objective that by the year 2000 "American students will leave grades four, eight, and twelve having demonstrated competency in . . . English, mathematics, science, history, and geography."[1]

Almost immediately large committees were established in each of the above disciplines, including the National Council for History Standards, composed of history professors, pre-college teachers, members of numerous organizations, educators, and parents. For two years the Council worked to draft a voluntary set of National History Standards that would provide teachers, parents, and American history textbook publishers with guidelines regarding what students ought to know about the U.S. past.

Yet even before the Standards were released to the general public, a storm of controversy arose, in which the Council was accused of a "great hatred of traditional history," of giving in to "political correctness," and of jettisoning the Founding Fathers, the Constitution, and people and events that have made the nation great in favor of individuals and events that portrayed the United States in a less complimentary light. Finally, in January 1995, the U.S. Senate, by a vote of 99–1, approved a "sense-of-the-Senate" resolution condemning the standards developed by the National Council for History Standards and urging that any future guidelines for history should not be based on them.[2]

This was not the first time that American history standards and textbooks had been the sources of bitter controversy. In the late nineteenth century, northern and southern whites had radically different ideas about the Civil War and Reconstruction and demanded that public school textbooks reflect those notions. As a result, publishers created separate chapters on these periods for northern and southern schools. At the same time, Roman Catholic leaders in the United States complained about Protestant control of public education and of history textbooks, resulting in Catholics writing their own textbooks for their parochial schools.[3]

Then, in the 1940s, the popular American history textbooks of Professor Harold Rugg of Columbia University were assaulted as being too radical, mainly because Rugg had discussed subjects such as economic classes, inequality, and what he called the apparent failure of laissez-faire economics. By 1944, sales of his public school

1. Transcript, State of the Union Address, January 31, 1990, in C-SPAN.org/Transcripts /SOTU-1990.aspx. See also U.S. Department of Education, *National Goals for Education* (Washington: Dept. of Education, 1990), p. 1.
2. The Senate proceedings are summarized in Gary B. Nash, Charlotte Crabtree, and Ross E. Dunn, *History on Trial: Culture Wars and the Teaching of the Past* (New York: Alfred A. Knopf, 1997), pp. 231–235. The lone senator who voted against the resolution was Bennett Johnston of Louisiana.
3. Joseph Moreau, *Schoolbook Nation: Conflicts over American History Textbooks from the Civil War to the Present* (Ann Arbor: University of Michigan Press, 2003), pp. 15–20.

textbooks had dropped 90 percent, and by 1951 they had totally disappeared from American classrooms. The Cold War and the fear of communism extended this controversy and led to the removal from most textbooks of the sensitive subjects that had gotten Rugg into so much trouble.[4]

By the 1960s, scholars in many American colleges and universities had begun to view the nation's past in decidedly different ways, due in part to the gradual inclusion of African Americans, women, Native Americans, laborers, immigrants, and the "common folk" in the story of America's past. As these individuals took their places alongside the nation's founders, presidents, generals, corporate leaders, and intellectuals (almost all male and white), the texture and shape of American history began to change. At the same time, the Vietnam War prompted some scholars to look at the U.S. overseas record in new, less laudable ways.[5]

Some parents, school officials, and politicians, however, objected to what was being called the "new history." In the mid-1960s, distinguished historians John W. Caughey, John Hope Franklin, and Ernest R. May collaborated on a new eighth-grade American history textbook that raised a storm of protest in California and other states. Critics attacked the textbook as "very distasteful, slanted, and objectionable [and] stressed one-world government, quoted accused communists, portrayed the United States as a bully, [and] distorted history by putting American forefathers in a bad light." The authors made revisions, but "citizen groups" increased their attacks, pointing out that a speech by Patrick Henry was labeled "a tirade," that the military exploits of Generals George Patton and Omar Bradley were eliminated, and that Nathan Hale and Davy Crockett were not mentioned. Several school districts in California refused to adopt the book and some parents refused to allow their children to read it. In 1968, *Time* magazine reported that the textbook showed up on a list of 335 books that some groups demanded be banned. It seems as if both sides agreed with George Orwell when he wrote (in *1984*), "He who controls the past controls the future." Conflicts continue, over textbooks, Common Core, and what America's young men and women ought to know about their past upon their graduation.[6]

How can students hope to come to *their own* understanding of America's past? One way to do this is to go directly to the sources themselves, the "raw material" of history. In *Discovering the American Past,* we have included an engaging and at the same time challenging mixture of types of evidence, ranging from more traditional sources such as letters, newspapers, public documents, speeches, and oral reminiscences to more innovative evidence such as photographs, art, statistics, cartoons, and interviews. In each chapter students will use this varied evidence to solve the problem or answer the central question that each chapter poses.

4. *Ibid.*, pp. 219–221. Frances Fitzgerald, *America Revised: History Schoolbooks in the Twentieth Century* (Boston: Atlantic Monthly Press, 1979), pp. 36–37. For one attack on textbooks, see E. Merrill Root, *Brainwashing in the High Schools: An Examination of Eleven American History Textbooks* (New York: The Devin-Adair Co., 1958).
5. On the inclusion movements of the 1960s and 1970s, see Joyce Appleby, Lynn Hunt, and Margaret Jacob, *Telling the Truth About History* (New York: W.W. Norton, 1994), pp. 147–198.
6. John Hope Franklin, *Mirror to America: The Autobiography of John Hope Franklin* (New York: Farrar, Straus, and Giroux, 2005), pp. 227–231; Nicholas J. Karolides, *Banned Books: Literature Suppressed on Political Grounds* (New York: Facts on File, rev. ed. 2006), pp. 300–302. On Common Core see *Huffington Post*, January 30, 2014.

Soon they will understand that the historian operates in much the same way as a detective in novels, films, or television programs does when solving a crime.[7]

As much as possible, we have tried to "let the evidence speak for itself" and have avoided (we hope) leading students toward one particular interpretation or another. *Discovering the American Past*, then, is a sort of historical sampler that we believe will help students learn the methods and skills all educated people must be able to master, as well as help them learn the historical content. In the words of an old West African saying, "However far the stream flows, it never forgets its source." Nor, we trust, will you.[8]

◆

Format of the Book

Each chapter is divided into six parts: The Problem, Background, The Method, The Evidence, Questions to Consider, and Epilogue. Each part builds upon the others, creating a uniquely integrated chapter structure that helps guide the reader through the analytical process. The Problem section begins with a brief discussion of the central issues of the chapter and then states the questions students will explore. A Background section follows, designed to help students understand the historical context of the problem. The Method section gives students suggestions for studying and analyzing the evidence. The Evidence section is the heart of the chapter, providing a variety of primary source material on the particular historical event or issue described in the chapter's Problem section. Questions to Consider, the section that follows, focuses students' attention on specific evidence and on linkages among different evidence material. The Epilogue section gives the aftermath or the historical outcome of the evidence—what happened to the people involved, who won an election, how a debate ended, and so on.

◆

Changes in the Eighth Edition

Each chapter in this edition has had to pass three important screening groups: (1) the authors (and some of our graduate students) who used the chapters to teach our students, (2) student evaluators who used *Discovering the American Past* in class, and (3) instructors who either used the book or read and assessed the new and revised chapters. With advice from our screeners, we have made the following alterations that we believe will make this edition of *Discovering the American Past* even more useful and contemporary.

Volume I contains four entirely new chapters. Chapter 1, "The Beginning of the World," concentrates on Native American and Judeo-Christian accounts of creation and what they tell us about the people who embraced them; Chapter 3, "From English Servants to African Slaves," allows students to explore the evolution of racial slavery in late seventeenth- and early eighteenth-century Virginia; Chapter 10, on Civil War nurses of the Union and Confederacy, uses women's letters, diaries, and memoirs to understand the conflict through their eyes; and Chapter 12, which makes

7. See the exciting Robin W. Winks, ed., *The Historian as Detective: Essays on Evidence* (New York: Harper & Row, 1968), esp. pp. xiii–xxiv.
8. For the saying, see Nash, *History on Trial*, p. 8.

a new turn in the volume by closing with a chapter that guides students toward designing their own research projects. In addition, the evidence in Chapters 5, 6, 7, and 8 has been streamlined, and in Chapter 9 (on the "Peculiar Institution") we replaced the excerpt from Frederick Douglass with some of the writings of Solomon Northup (students perhaps will know about Northup's ordeals from the Academy Award–winning film *Twelve Years a Slave*). The chapter retains many of the materials from the WPA ex-slave interviews, but it also has been further revised to include freedom suits from antebellum St. Louis. These depositions allow students to see another way in which slaves told their own stories.

Volume II contains five entirely new chapters: Chapter 2 brings to life the transformative experience of immigration in the late nineteenth and early twentieth centuries by using the autobiography of a Russian Jewish girl who came of age in New York City working in the garment industry. Chapter 3 introduces students to environmental history by having them enter early twentieth-century debates about the damming of the Tuolumne River and the flooding of the Hetch Hetchy Valley in Yosemite National Park to provide safe and reliable water to the city of San Francisco. Chapter 10 surveys the rise of religious conservatism in the 1950s and 1960s and its role in American politics. A new Chapter 11 turns to the War on Drugs in the 1980s and the consequent rise of the prison state to try to untangle why the United States has the highest rate of incarceration in the world. Chapter 12, "History Skills in Action," offers students the opportunity to undertake their own individual research projects. In addition, all of the other chapters have been revised, Chapters 5 and 9 in a major way.

In all, we have paid close attention to students, fellow instructors, and reviewers in our efforts to keep *Discovering the American Past* fresh, challenging, and relevant. Earlier editions have shown clearly students' positive responses to the challenge of being, as Robin Winks put it, "historical detectives" who use historical evidence to reach their own conclusions.

◆

Instructor's Resource Manual

Because we value the teaching of American history and yet fully understand how difficult it is to do well, we have written our own Instructor's Resource Manual to accompany *Discovering the American Past*. In this manual, we explain our specific content and skills objectives for each chapter. In addition, we include an expanded discussion of the Method and Evidence sections. We also answer some of our students' frequently asked questions about the material in each problem. Our suggestions for teaching and evaluating student learning draw not only upon our own experiences but also upon the experiences of those of you who have shared your classroom ideas with us. Finally, we wrote updated bibliographic essays for each problem.

◆

Acknowledgments

We would like to thank all the students and instructors who have helped us in developing and refining our ideas for this edition. In addition, we extend deep thanks to those reviewers who offered us candid and enormously helpful advice and saved us from more than a few errors.

At Saint Louis University, Ivy McIntyre and Joshua Mather provided invaluable research assistance, and Torrie Hester, Stefan Bradley, and Flannery Burke generously shared their expertise and advice. Mike Everman showed us the rich potential of the St. Louis, Missouri, freedom suits. In Richmond, Virginia, Livia Marrs offered invaluable help in locating Civil War nurses and their memoirs. In Tennessee, Laura Vaught helped us through the maze of court records regarding Japanese internment suits, and SFC Darrell Rowe, Dr. Ed Caudill, and Joe and Justin Distretti helped us to understand the complicated legacy of Vietnam. Linda Claire Wheeler read almost every word and offered enlightened suggestions and gentle flogging. Dan Smith discussed, read, and encouraged, always with good cheer. Will Fontanez of the University of Tennessee Cartography Department created important maps for three chapters.

Finally, we owe a great deal to the members of the publishing team who worked together to make our ideas and words into a well-organized and attractive book. And to Jean Woy, who was present at the creation of the first edition of *Discovering the American Past* and who offered her steady and helpful guidance, we owe intellectual debts that can never be repaid. Also at Cengage, Clint Attebery represented this edition as the current U.S. History product manager. Prashanth Kamavarapu at Lumina Datamatics, guided the project through the production process. Lastly, we'd like to especially thank Anais Wheeler at Cengage, who kindly shared her wisdom on more matters than we can list.

And last, this edition is dedicated to Linda Claire Wheeler and Dan Smith, who kept the ship afloat when the waters all around us were considerably less than calm.

Any errors that do appear in any of the chapters are ours, not theirs.

The Beginning of the World: Creation Accounts and Cultural Values in the Americas and Europe

The Problem

When European explorers, conquerors, priests, and eventually settlers stepped ashore onto what they mistakenly called the "New World," they were astounded to find peoples who spoke a variety of different languages and who belonged to a plethora of religions, almost all of which possessed accounts concerning how the world and its creatures were made. Convinced that these were false, "pagan" religions, Europeans tried to convert all these peoples to Christianity while at the same time stamping out all traces of these beliefs of native peoples. In what later was referred to as Central America, Spanish priests and *conquistadors* attempted to destroy all Native American writings so that these peoples' religions and creation accounts would be totally obliterated.[1]

And yet, in spite of all the European efforts, Native American religions and creation accounts remained remarkably durable. Indeed, even today remnants of what once were large and powerful peoples still cling to creation accounts that continue to satisfy what psychologist Rollo May referred to as "a hunger for community." As early as the first generations that were overwhelmed by Europeans, a group of Aztec scholars criticized Franciscan missionaries by saying

> You said that our gods are not true gods. New words are these that you speak; because of them we are disturbed, . . . For our ancestors before us, who lived upon the earth. . . . [f]rom them we have inherited our pattern of life which in truth did they hold, in reverence they held, they honoured our gods.[2]

---

1. For one example of book burnings see Bishop Diego de Landa in Jared Diamond, *Collapse: How Societies Choose to Fail or Succeed* (New York: Viking, 2005), p. 159. The result was that today only four such books exist.

2. For Rollo May's comment see his *The Cry for Myth* (New York: W.W. Norton, 1991), p. 45. For the Aztec scholars see Karl Taube, *The Legendary Past: Aztec and Maya Myths* (Austin, TX: Univ. of Texas Press, 1993), p. 31.

✦ CHAPTER 1

The Beginning
of the World:
Creation Accounts
and Cultural
Values in the
Americas and
Europe

Why have these creation accounts survived in spite of energetic efforts to destroy them? For one thing, such accounts gave to some the power to bind people together by giving them a shared history, a united worldview, and even a shared *cosmology* (a branch of philosophy that deals with the origin, process, and structure of the universe). At the same time, these accounts offer believers an interpretive framework to understand not only the past but also its present and even future. For societies that possessed systems of writing, creation accounts were one of the first things that rulers or their scribes committed to writing. But even among nonliterate peoples, creation accounts could survive by being passed from one generation to another orally. As Everett Fox, professor of Judaic and Biblical Studies at Clark University remarked in his introduction to *The Five Books of Moses* (1995), "All peoples are interested in their own beginnings, picturing them in a way which validates their present existence."[3]

Your task in this chapter will require you to use all your analytical reading skills plus a good deal of historical imagination. In the Evidence section of this chapter, you will find five creation accounts—one from the *Book of Genesis* in the *Torah* of the Israelites and venerated by both Christians and Muslims; one from the *Popol Vuh* of the Maya civilization of Central America; one from the Aztec (or Mexican) civilization of the Central Valley of Central America; one from the Cherokee ("principal people") of southeastern North America; and one from the Iroquois (or Haudenosaunee) of the northeastern section of North America.

Carefully read each account to learn how each of these peoples sought to explain the creation of the world. Then, use your historical imagination as well as clues from this chapter and your instructor to show what each creation account tells us about the people who thought it important enough either to write it down or pass it orally from generation to generation. **What does their cosmology tell us about a people's value system; their belief in the place of humans in the world; their relationship to the universe, to other creatures, as well as to a god or gods; their own views of history; etc?** In essence, then, you will be explaining the cosmologies of five ancient peoples, an extremely important exercise for historians.[4]

3. Everett Fox, ed. and trans., *The Five Books of Moses* (New York: Schocken Books, 1995), vol. 1, p. 3.

4. On views of history, to a particular people is the process of history linear (resembling a straight line from event to event), cyclical (circular, with patterns recurring), of another form, or formless (with events occurring purely at random, or by chance)?

Background

About the time that the Indo-Aryans were moving into northern India (1500 BCE) and the Shang dynasty in China was in the process of controlling the eastern half of the Yellow River Valley (1500–1000 BCE), in Mesopotamia and the Arabian peninsula groups of homeless nomads (referred to in Mesopotamian and Egyptian sources as "Habiru") were wandering across the semiarid landscape grazing their herds. One of these groups came to be known as "Hebrews," or "Israelites" or "Jews."[5] Sometime after 1550 BCE, the Jews voluntarily migrated to Egypt to escape a drought but soon were enslaved. Around 1200 BCE, the Jews either abandoned or escaped from Egypt. The declines of both the Egyptian and Hittite empires left a power vacuum along the eastern coast of the Mediterranean Sea, and it was here that the Israelites ultimately settled, fighting off Philistines and other peoples to seize and hold the land. Sometime after 925 BCE (the traditional death of King Solomon), the Israelites broke into two kingdoms, the northern one being destroyed by Assyrian invaders while the southern kingdom (Judah) survived for another 150 years until the Babylonian Captivity.

The *Torah* contains the Israelites' creation accounts, history, and laws. Traditional authorship is credited to Moses, although a majority of biblical scholars assert the *Torah* comes from far more that a single source. According to ancient tradition, Joshua had the *Torah* "engraved upon the stones of the altar" of the tabernacle sometime before 1100 BCE, a claim that most scholars dispute as much too early (the fifth century BCE is more likely). The stabilization of the Jews' creation accounts were around 720 BCE.

In the year 587 BCE, Babylonians crushed the kingdom of Judah and carried several Jews into exile in Babylonia. During their comparatively short time in exile, the Jews appropriated the Babylonian calendar, learned the Aramaic language, and appropriated the Babylonian account of creation and of the massive flood. After less than fifty years in exile, Persian king Cyrus permitted around 40,000 exiles to return to Jerusalem and for several years that practice was continued. The Babylonian Captivity, as it came to be called, had a profound effect on the Jewish people, especially in the unification and standardization of their religious faith.[6]

About the same time, the Israelites left Egypt, groups of nomadic peoples began to coalesce and establish sedentary villages and even towns in what

---

5. At the time, "Hebrew" referred to a social category whereas "Israelite" was used to describe all the people of the group. "Jews" derived from the southern kingdom's surviving tribe of Judah.

6. Charles Pfeiffer, *Old Testament History* (Grand Rapids, MI: Baker Book House, 1973), pp. 425–474. For the Babylonian accounts of creation and the flood, see W. G. Lambert and A. R. Millard, *Atra-hasis: The Babylonian Story of the Flood* (Oxford, UK: Oxford Univ. Press, 1969).

◆ CHAPTER 1

The Beginning
of the World:
Creation Accounts
and Cultural
Values in the
Americas and
Europe

later was called Central America. No longer an exclusively hunter-gatherer society, these peoples who became the Maya were raising *maize* (corn, which constituted roughly 70 percent of their diet and can be stored for a comparatively long time), beans, squash, pumpkins, and tomatoes and were supplementing that diet with hunted deer, turkey, and wild birds as well as with fish. The population soared until by around 800 CE well over four million people were living in the Maya Lowlands. Agricultural surpluses supported the growth of several urban centers (probably well over 50), which boasted of magnificent stone temples, palaces, and monuments. It was in these urban centers that a regional economy and extensive trade networks were created and flourished and where urban elites developed a system of writing and an accurate calendar. According to expert Michael Coe, the Mayan civilization had "reached intellectual and artistic heights which no others in the New World, and few in the Old, could match at that time."[7]

The celebrated Mayan calendar (which was appropriated with variations by the Aztecs) consisted of two interactive wheels, one with 13 numbers and the other with 20 day names that moved together to form a cycle of 260 days. At the same time, the Maya and Aztecs each had a 365-day circular solar calendar which, when fit together with the other calendar, resulted in 18,980 separate combinations, or 52 years. To go through the entire cycle of numbers, day names, and solar days

took 5,130 years, after which all things would come to an end and would have to be recreated by the gods.

And yet, while the Maya civilization appeared to be both advanced and robust, at the same time it was extremely fragile. The key to Mayan survival was access to water. Systems of water storage and irrigation were only temporary solutions and a drought would result in widespread famine. For example, in the year 536 CE, an almost worldwide dense fog (perhaps the result of a major volcanic eruption in Asia) caused major changes in the weather, which led to massive starvation in Ireland, the Northern Kingdom of China (where the death toll was between 70 and 80 percent of the population), Carthage, Mesopotamia, Constantinople, Italy, the Middle East, and the Mayan Lowlands.[8] Then a series of devastating droughts between 800 and 1000 CE brought on the collapse of the Classic Mayan Civilization. By the time the Spanish—and their diseases—arrived, the Maya, in the words of historian Richardson Gill, were "overwhelmed by the brutal forces of nature."[9]

7. Michael D. Coe, *The Maya*, 7th ed. (London: Thames and Hudson, 2005), p. 81.

8. For the 536 CE event see Bruce Dahlin and Arlen Chase, "A Tale of Three Cities: Effects of the AD 536 Event in the Lowland Maya Heartland," in Gyles Iannone, ed., *The Great Mayan Droughts in Cultural Context* (Boulder: Univ. Press of Colorado, 2014), pp. 127–129; Richardson Benedict Gill, *The Great Maya Droughts: Water, Life, and Death* (Albuquerque: Univ. of New Mexico Press, 2000), pp. 227–229.

9. For droughts see Gill, *The Great Maya Droughts*, p. 363; Iannone, *The Great Mayan Droughts in Cultural Context*, p. 74; David Webster, *The Fall of the Ancient Maya: Solving the Mystery of the Maya Collapse* (London: Thames and Hudson, 2002), p. 241.

No original Mayan text of the *Popol Vuh* exists. But in the late 1600s, Dominican priest Francisco Ximenez (1666–1729?) completed a translation of the *Popol Vuh* (which he called "The Book of the People"). Whether Fr. Ximenez altered the original in any way is unknown. An English translation of the *Popol Vuh* was not published until 1950.[10]

As the Lowland Maya civilization was in decline, a new group was moving southward into the basin of what later would be called Mexico. According to their legends, they had originated in a place called Aztlan (from which the name Aztec was derived) located somewhere north of the Central Valley of Mexico. Led by a person named Huitzil, from around 1100 to 1250 CE they had wandered across the landscape in search of a new homeland. Arriving in the Central Valley, they found many of the good homesites already occupied by remnants of the Maya and by other Native American groups and were forced to continue their quest. By this time, according to legend, Huitzil had died and immediately had become one of their gods.[11]

At last the Aztecs (who referred to themselves as Mexica) settled on a few unoccupied small islands in Lake Texcoco and enlarged their new homesite by constructing artificial islands. In 1372 CE, they finished building a magnificent city, which they named Tenochtitlan, the population of which eventually reached between 150,000 and 250,000 and was the largest city ever to flourish in the pre-Hispanic New World.[12] In 1519, Hernando Cortés and his fellow *conquistadors* were awed by it. By that time, the Mexica dominated several surrounding Native American groups and extended their domination into thirty provinces, which stretched for one hundred miles to the north and south to present-day Guatemala.

The Mexica borrowed a great deal of religion, agricultural practices, culture, architecture, and art from neighboring groups, especially the weakened Maya. The Mexica calendar was modeled after the circular Maya calendar, and writing and architecture were also copied. They believed in a soul ("yolia") that lived after a person's death, leaving the body as a "bird of the heart." The practice of human sacrifice, which Cortés mentioned in his report to Emperor Charles V of Spain, was done to assuage their gods who were angered by the slaying and dismemberment of Tlaltecuhtli, the Earth Goddess. The Mexica believed that the origin of the earth proceeded from that event.[13]

10. A good history of the *Popol Vuh* may be found in the introduction to the first English translation. See Delia Goetz and Sylvanus G. Morley, *Popol Vuh: The Sacred Book of the Ancient Quich Maya* (Norman: Univ. of Oklahoma Press, 1950), pp. 3–75.
11. For excellent background on the Aztecs, see Michael L. Smith, *The Aztecs* (Chichester, UK: Wiley-Blackwell, 3rd ed. 2012) and Dirk R. Van Tuerenhout, *The Aztecs: New Perspectives* (Santa Barbara, CA: ABC-CLIO, 2005).
12. The present Mexico City was built atop the ruins of Tenochtitlan.
13. On the Mexica belief in the soul see Jill Leslie McKeever Furst, *The Natural History of the Soul in Ancient Mexico* (New Haven: Yale Univ. Press, 1995), pp. 12–13, 21–25. On human sacrifice see Karl Taube, *Aztec and Maya Myths* (Austin, TX: Univ. of Texas Press, 1993), pp. 36–37. On Cortés see Francis Augustus MacNutt, trans. *Fernando Cortés: His Five Letters of Relation to the Emperor Charles V* (Cleveland: Arthur H. Clark Co., 1908), vol. 1, pp. 161–166.

✦ CHAPTER 1

The Beginning
of the World:
Creation Accounts
and Cultural
Values in the
Americas and
Europe

The Cherokee's history is shrouded in myth and mystery. No one knows the origins of the Cherokee people, where they came from, why they chose to settle in the southern Appalachians, or even why they are called "Cherokees." The fact that their language is similar to that of the Iroquois suggests that they originally lived in what is now the northeastern United States and eastern Canada, that they moved southward voluntarily or were driven out of that homeland, and, like the Mexica, that they wandered in search of a place that was habitable and unoccupied. Archaeology suggests that they lived in the present homeland of those who refer to themselves as "the Eastern Band of the Cherokee Nation" for at least 1,000 years, and only numbered around 20,000 to 25,000 by the time of European contact. Calling themselves the "principal people," the Cherokee settled in small autonomous units with no overarching government or even any leaders in the European sense of the term.[14]

As with other Native American peoples who relied on raising crops, women played an important role in Cherokee society. Their society was matrilineal and matrilocal, which meant that women "owned their residences and the fields they worked" and until the Cherokee Constitution of 1827 were allowed to speak and vote in local councils. As a result, Europeans believed that the Cherokees were "uncivilized" because women had so much authority *and* because they were not Christians. And although the Cherokees had no system of writing until the syllabary of Sequoyah in 1821, they possessed a strong oral tradition, which included their interpretation of the origin of the world and of humans.[15]

The Native Americans known as Iroquois (or Haudenosaunee) left early archaeological footprints in northeastern North America around 500 to 800 CE. They lived in small summer villages of around 100–400 people where they raised maize. When the crop was harvested, these small groups became migratory in search of food and skins. Infant mortality was distressingly high, but the Iroquois believed that if a dead infant's body was buried along a path, its soul would rise up and enter a passing woman and be reborn.[16]

By around 1300 CE, the populations of these villages had become so large (approximately 1,400–1,500 people) that the Iroquois were forced to establish more permanent communities where maize, beans, squash, gourds, and pumpkins were raised, using fire to clear the fields. About this time, the communities were fortified, perhaps due to semi-nomadic peoples attacking the villages for food or even due to

14. John R. Finger, *The Eastern Band of the Cherokees, 1819–1900* (Knoxville: Univ. of Tennessee Press, 1984), pp. 3–4. The title "Eastern Band" was adopted after a majority of the Cherokees were removed to Arkansas and Oklahoma in the "Trail of Tears."

15. See Carolyn Ross Johnston, ed., *Voices of Cherokee Women* (Winston-Salem, NC: John F. Blair, 2013), x–xi. See also Dhyani Ywahoo, *Voices of Our Ancestors: Cherokee Teachings from the Wisdom Fire* (Boston: Shambhala Publishing, 1987).

16. Brian M. Fagan, *Ancient North America: The Archaeology of a Continent* (New York: Thames and Hudson, 1995 ed.), pp. 461–468. For the belief in the rebirth of deceased infants see William Engelbrecht, *Iroquoia: The Development of a Native World* (Syracuse: Syracuse Univ. Press, 2003), p. 60.

intratribal warfare between the Iroquois communities. Evidence suggests that these communities split into separate tribes, groups that around 1451 CE reunified into the Iroquois Confederacy of Five Nations (Seneca, Cayuga, Onondaga, Oneida, and Mohawk). These groups had common religious beliefs and notions about the origin of the world and of humans. They used pipes and tobacco as part of their religious ceremonies.[17]

What do the creation accounts of each of the peoples excerpted in the Evidence section of this chapter tell us about the people themselves? What can we discover about how they viewed the universe, themselves, the relationship between humans and their god or gods, and the unfolding of history itself?

◆

The Method

Whenever people today consult the *Torah,* the *Popol Vuh,* the Aztec religious documents such as the Codex Borgia or the Florentine Codes, or the oral traditions of the Cherokee or Iroquois, most do so either as part of their religious worship or as an inspirational guide. Each of these religious traditions, however, also can serve as a historical document that can be examined and analyzed for what that written or oral account can tell us about those who created it and those who preserved, venerated, and passed it along to later generations.

As you might expect, historians approach the religious accounts of the Israelites, the Maya, the Aztec, the Cherokee, and the Iroquois in quite different ways from those for whom the traditions are part of their creed or philosophy. To begin with, whenever it is possible, historians prefer to study the account in its oldest version and in its original language (more difficult for the oral accounts than the written ones). In that way, errors in copying, translating, or orally handing down, as well as purposeful additions to or deletions from the original account, will not lead historians into errors of judgment. Second, it is important for historians to know as closely as possible the date (or dates) of the document's creation. This information is valuable to historians because it enables them to study the context and understand more about the people who were living during that period, the events taking place, and the ideas in circulation. Historians call this process learning about the "climate of opinion" of a particular time period. Unfortunately, very early documents (such as the ones you will be working with in this chapter) or ancient oral accounts cannot be dated very precisely because

17. William W. Canfield, *The Legends of the Iroquois Told by "The Cornplanter"* (New York: A. Wessels Co., 1904), p. 9; William Englebrecht, *Iroquoia: The Development of a Native World* (Syracuse, N.Y.: Syracuse Univ. Press, 2003), pp. 5–27. It is possible that the division into separate—and conflicting—groups prompted the Cherokees to move southward.

✦ CHAPTER 1

The Beginning
of the World:
Creation Accounts
and Cultural
Values in the
Americas and
Europe

the written accounts were written down only after a long period of oral transmission and the oral accounts cannot be dated at all. Two of the oral accounts in the Evidence section of this chapter (Cherokee and Iroquois) are from oral traditions that were told to white men who transcribed what they thought they heard. The Cherokee creation accounts were told to James Mooney (1861–1921) of the U.S. Bureau of American Ethnology,[18] who published his results in 1891, centuries after the account's creation. As for the Iroquois, their creation account was passed to Major John Norton (1760–1831), a British officer whose journal resided in the library of Alnwick Castle in Northumberland and was not published until 1970. Although both men were sympathetic to the Native American people they interviewed, we cannot be sure that what you will be reading was exactly what the storytellers related.[19]

After completing these initial steps, historians then are prepared to examine the creation account of each people. When analyzing these pieces of evidence, historians ask of each account a series of questions: How does the account explain the creation of the universe, the world, human beings, and other flora and fauna? Was the creation divinely inspired—in other words, did a god or gods play an active role in the creation process, and for

what purpose? Since all the peoples surveyed depended on agriculture for their survival, how did that process affect the names and roles of the peoples' gods? In return for creation and survival, did human beings have any obligations to their creator(s)? Finally, is the creation process in each account lineal (proceeding sequentially along a line from one event to another), cyclical (circular), or another pattern, or without pattern (formless)? Having subjected each creation account to this series of questions, historians then are ready to ask what each document reveals about the people who created it. This will take some reading in your text about the people under scrutiny, as well as a considerable amount of historical imagination. For example, if each creation account can be seen as a life guide for those who venerate it, what does the account encourage or compel (or forbid) the true believers to do? Is the creation process *reproduced* in the lives of true believers (from birth to death)? What does that process tell you about the people who created the account?

Finally, you are ready to compare the six creation accounts and the people who committed them to memory and, for some, later to writing. Historians call this process *comparative textual analysis,* and it is one of the most basic methods of investigation used throughout all the humanities (literature, philosophy, linguistics, history, and the like). As you compare these accounts and their creators, using the questions above as initial guides, be careful *not* to fall into the habit of thinking of certain cultures or peoples as "inferior" or "superior" on the basis

18. The term "ethnology" refers to the anthropological study of primitive socio-economic systems.
19. In 1897 Mooney married the twenty-year-old Cherokee Ione Lee Gaut, who accompanied him on numerous research trips. As for Major Norton, he was the son of a Cherokee father and a Scottish mother.

of how far or near a particular group's beliefs are to your own beliefs or philosophy. This is a common trap, and you must make every effort to avoid it. After all, each of the creation accounts you will be examining and analyzing was preserved by a people or peoples for hundreds of years. All have become the foundation for one or more current religions or philosophies and as such have been deemed satisfying by a group or groups for many, many generations. Historians, therefore, approach these sources with great sensitivity and respect.

As you read the Evidence, be sure to take notes. One effective way of organizing your thoughts is to divide your note pages into two parts. On the left side of the page, summarize the creation account you are reading. Then, on the right side, summarize your thoughts (and questions) about the value system, the view of history, and the relationship between beings that you are able to infer from the creation account.

◆

The Evidence

Source 1 from *The Torah: A Modern Commentary* (New York: Union of American Hebrew Congregations, 1981), pp. 18–20, 29–30, 59, 116. Reprinted by permission of Union for Reformed Judaism.

1. From the First Book of Moses, called Genesis

CHAPTER 1

1] When God began to create the heaven and the earth—2] the earth being unformed and void, with darkness over the surface of the deep[20] and a wind[21] from God sweeping over the water—3] God said, "Let there be light"; and there was light. 4] God saw the light was good, and God separated the light from the darkness. 5] God called the light Day, and the darkness He called Night. And there was evening and there was morning, a first day.

6] God said, "Let there be an expanse in the midst of the water, that it may separate water from water." 7] God made the expanse, and it separated the water which was below the expanse from the water which was above the expanse. And it was so. 8] God called the expanse Sky. And there was evening and there was morning, a second day.

20. Some Hebraic scholars point out that this phrase ("surface of the deep") echoes a "Mesopotamian creation account where it is told that heaven and earth were formed from the carcass of the sea dragon Tiamat." *The Torah: A Modern Commentary*, p. 18.
21. "Wind" is also translated as "spirit."

◆ CHAPTER 1

The Beginning
of the World:
Creation Accounts
and Cultural
Values in the
Americas and
Europe

9] God said, "Let the water below the sky be gathered into one area, that the dry land may appear." And it was so. 10] God called the dry land Earth, and the gathering of waters He called Seas. And God saw that this was good. 11] And God said, "Let the earth sprout vegetation: seed-bearing plants, fruit trees of every kind on earth that bear fruit with the seed in it." And it was so. 12] The earth brought forth vegetation: seed-bearing plants of every kind, and trees of every kind bearing fruit with the seed in it. And God saw that this was good. 13] And there was evening and there was morning, a third day.

14] God said, "Let there be lights in the expanse of the sky to separate day from night; they shall serve as signs for the set times—the days and the years; 15] and they shall serve as lights in the expanse of the sky to shine upon the earth." And it was so. 16] God made the two great lights, the greater light to dominate the day and the lesser light to dominate the night, and the stars. 17] And God set them in the expanse of the sky to shine upon the earth, 18] to dominate the day and the night, and to separate light from darkness. And God saw that this was good. 19] And there was evening and there was morning, a fourth day.

20] God said, "Let the waters bring forth swarms of living creatures, and birds that fly above the earth across the expanse of the sky." 21] God created the great sea monsters, and all the living creatures of every kind that creep, which the waters brought forth in swarms; and all the winged birds of every kind. And God saw that this was good. 22] God blessed them, saying, "Be fertile and increase, fill the waters in the seas, and let the birds increase on the earth." 23] And there was evening and there was morning, a fifth day.

24] God said, "Let the earth bring forth every kind of living creature: cattle, creeping things, and wild beasts of every kind." And it was so. 25] God made wild beasts of every kind and cattle of every kind, and all kinds of creeping things of the earth. And God saw that this was good. 26] And god said, "Let us make man in our image, after our likeness. They shall rule the fish of the sea, the birds of the sky, the cattle, the whole earth, and all the creeping things that creep on earth." 27] And God created man in His image, in the image of God He created him; male and female He created them. 28] God blessed them and God said to them, "Be fertile and increase, fill the earth and master it; and rule the fish of the sea, the birds of the sky, and all the living things that creep on earth." 29] God said, "See, I give you every seed-bearing plant that is upon all the earth, and every tree that has seed-bearing fruit; they shall be yours for food. 30] And to all the animals on land, to all the birds of the sky, and to everything that creeps on earth, in which there is the breath of life, [I give] all the green plants for food." And it was so.[22] **31]** And God saw all that He had made, and found it very good. And there was evening and there was morning, the sixth day.

CHAPTER 2

1] The heaven and the earth were finished, and all their array. **2]** On the seventh day God finished the work which He had been doing, and He ceased on the seventh day from all the work which He had done. **3]** And God blessed the seventh day and declared it holy, because on it God ceased from all the work of creation which He had done.

4] Such is the story of heaven and earth when they were created. When the Lord God made earth and heaven—**5]** when no shrub of the field was yet on earth and no grasses of the field had yet sprouted, because the Lord God had not sent rain upon the earth and there was no man to till the soil, **6]** but a flow would well up from the ground and water the whole surface of the earth—**7]** the Lord God formed man from the dust of the earth. He blew into his nostrils the breath of life, and man became a living being. **8]** The Lord God planted a garden in Eden, in the east, and placed there the man whom He had formed. **9]** And from the ground the Lord God caused to grow every tree that was pleasing to the sight and good for food, with the tree of life in the middle of the garden, and the tree of knowledge of good and bad. . . . **15]** The Lord God took the man and placed him in the garden of Eden, to till it and tend it. **16]** And the Lord God commanded the man, saying, "Of every tree of the garden you are free to eat; **17]** but as for the tree of knowledge of good and bad, you must not eat of it; for as soon as you eat of it, you shall die." **18]** The Lord God said, "It is not good for man to be alone; I will make a fitting helper for him." **19]** And the Lord God formed out of the earth all the wild beasts and all the birds of the sky, and brought them to the man to see what he would call them; and whatever the man called each living creature, that would be its name. **20]** And the man gave names to all the cattle and to the birds of the sky and to all the wild beasts; but for Adam no fitting helper was found. **21]** So the Lord God cast a deep sleep upon the man; and, while he slept, He took one of his ribs and closed up the flesh at that spot. **22]** And the Lord God fashioned the rib that He had taken from the man into a woman; and He brought her to the man. **23]** Then the man said, "This one at last / Is bone of my bones / And flesh of my flesh. / This one shall be called

22. Many biblical scholars assert that humans and other animals were herbivores (exclusively vegetarian) until after the Flood, when they became omnivores (eating all kinds of food, including the flesh of other animals). See Genesis 9:3 and Isaiah 11:7.

✦ CHAPTER 1

The Beginning
of the World:
Creation Accounts
and Cultural
Values in the
Americas and
Europe

Woman, / For from man was she taken." **24]** Hence a man leaves his father and mother and clings to his wife, so that they become one flesh.

[Disobeying God's command, Adam and Eve ate the forbidden fruit, were cursed by God, and were banished from the Garden. Their first two children were Cain and Abel. Out of jealousy, Cain murdered Abel and was even further banished. Adam and Eve had many more children. After several generations, humans had become corrupt, and God determined to punish them by flooding the land. He warned righteous Noah, who gathered his family and all species in an ark, which survived the flood. Many generations later people attempted to build a tower to reach heaven, but were confounded by God, who caused them to begin speaking different languages. Many generations later, God appeared to Abram, offering to make a covenant (contract) with him.]

CHAPTER 17

1] When Abram was ninety-nine years old, the Lord appeared to Abram and said to him, "I am El Shaddai.[23] Walk in My ways and be blameless. **2]** I will establish My covenant between Me and you, and I will make you exceedingly numerous." **3]** Abram threw himself on his face, as God spoke to him further, **4]** "As for Me, this is My covenant with you; You shall be the father of a multitude of nations. **5]** And you shall no longer be called Abram, but your name shall be Abraham, for I make you the father of a multitude of nations. **6]** I will make you exceedingly fertile, and make nations of you; and kings shall come forth from you. **7]** I will maintain My covenant between Me and you, and your offspring to come, as an everlasting covenant throughout the ages, to be God to you and to your offspring to come. **8]** I give the land you sojourn in to you and your offspring to come, all the land of Canaan, as an everlasting possession. I will be their God."

Source 2 from Delia Goetz and Sylvanus Morley, trans., *Po pol Vuh: The Sacred Book of the Ancient Quiche Maya* (Norman: Univ. of Oklahoma Press, 1950), pp. 81, 83–86, 89, 165–168.

2. From Popul Vuh, "The Book of the People"

This is the first account, the first narrative. There was neither man, nor animal, birds, fishes, crabs, trees, stones, caves, ravines, grasses, nor forests; there was only the sky.

23. The term "El Shaddai" means God Almighty.

The surface of the earth had not appeared. There was only the calm sea and the great expanse of the sky.

There was nothing brought together, nothing which could make a noise, nor anything which might move, or tremble, or could make noise in the sky.

There was nothing standing; only the calm water, the placid sea, alone and tranquil. Nothing existed.

There was only immobility and silence in the darkness in the night. Only the Creator, the Maker, Tepeu,[24] Gucumatz,[25] the Forefathers,[26] were in the water surrounded with light. . . .

Then Tepeu and Gucumatz came together; then they conferred about life and light, what they would do so that there would be light and dawn, who it would be who would provide food and sustenance.

Thus let it be done! Let the emptiness be filled! Let the water recede and make a void, let the earth appear and become solid; let it be done. Thus they spoke. Let there be light, let there be dawn in the sky and on the earth! There shall be neither glory nor grandeur in our creation and formation until the human being is made, man is formed. So they spoke.

Then the earth was created by them. So it was, in truth, that they created the earth. Earth! they said, and instantly it was made.

Like the mist, like a cloud, and like a cloud of dust was the creation, when the mountains appeared from the water; and instantly the mountains grew.

Only by a miracle, only by magic art were the mountains and valleys formed; and instantly the groves of cypresses and pines put forth shoots together on the surface of the earth. . .

[Then animals, birds, and serpents were created. But since they could not speak like humans and thus were unable to praise and worship their creators, the Creator, the Maker, and the Forefathers condemned them to be eaten.]

"Let us try again! Already dawn draws near: Let us make him who shall nourish and sustain us! What shall we do to be invoked, in order to be remembered on earth? We have already tried with our first creations, our first creatures; but we could not make them praise and venerate us. So, then, let us try to make obedient, respectful beings who will nourish and sustain us." Thus they spoke.

Then was the creation and the formation. Of earth, of mud, they made [man's] flesh. But they saw that it was not good. It melted away, it was soft, did not move, had no strength, it fell down, it was limp, it could not move its head, its face fell to one side, its sight was blurred, it could not look behind.

24. "Tepeu" means king, or conqueror.
25. Gucumatz is the feathered serpent creator deity.
26. The word translated as "forefathers" here means literally, "those who beget children."

◆ CHAPTER 1

The Beginning
of the World:
Creation Accounts
and Cultural
Values in the
Americas and
Europe

At first it spoke, but had no mind. Quickly it soaked in the water and could not stand.

And the Creator and the Maker said: "Let us try again because our creatures will not be able to walk nor multiply. Let us consider this," they said.

Then they broke up and destroyed their work. . . .

[The second attempt was to carve a man out of wood.]

And instantly the figures were made of wood. They looked like men, talked like men, and populated the surface of the earth.

They existed and multiplied; they had daughters, they had sons, these wooden figures; but they did not have souls, nor minds, they did not remember their Creator, their Maker; they walked on all fours, aimlessly.

They no longer remembered the Heart of Heaven and therefore they fell out of favor. It was merely a trial, an attempt at man. At first they spoke, but their face was without expression; their feet and hands had no strength; they had no blood, nor substance, nor moisture, nor flesh; their cheeks were dry, their feet and hands were dry, and their flesh was yellow.

Therefore, they no longer thought of their Creator nor their Maker, nor of those who made them and cared for them.

These were the first men who existed in great numbers on the face of the earth.

[Because these wooden men and women did not honor or worship their creator, they were destroyed in a flood. Their descendants, monkeys, lived in the forest and resembled humans. But the forefathers, Creator, and Maker realized that their next attempt to create a man must also provide that creation with food, so they created four beasts (the mountain cat, the coyote, the small parrot, and the crow) to show man where yellow and white corn could be found.]

And thus they found the food, and this was what went into the flesh of created man, the made man; this was his blood; of this the blood of man was made. So the corn entered [into the formation of man] by the work of the Forefathers.

And in this way they were filled with joy, because they had found a beautiful land, full of pleasures, abundant in ears of yellow corn and ears of white corn, and abundant . . . in all sorts of delicious food. . . . and from this food came the strength and the flesh, and with it they created the muscles and the strength of man. This the Forefathers did, Tepeu and Gucumatz, as they were called.

After that they began to talk about the creation and the making of our first mother and father; of yellow corn and of white corn they made their flesh; of corn-meal dough they made the arms and the legs of man. Only dough of corn meal went into the flesh of our first fathers, the four men, who were created. . . .

[The first men talked, heard, walked, and were endowed with intelligence, and they saw all the things around them.]

Then the Creator and the Maker asked them: "What do you think of your condition? Do you not see? Do you not hear? Are not your speech and manner of walking good? Look, then! Contemplate the world, look [and see] if the mountains and the valleys appear! Try, then, to see!" they said to [the four first men].

And immediately they [the four first men] began to see all that was in the world. Then they gave thanks to the Creator and the Maker: "We really give you thanks, two and three times! We have been created, we have been given a mouth and a face, we speak, we hear, we think, and walk; we feel perfectly, and we know what is far and what is near. We also see the large and the small in the sky and on earth. We give you thanks, then, for having created us, oh, Creator and Maker! for having given us being, oh, our grandmother! oh, our grandfather!" they said, giving thanks for their creation and formation.

Source 3 from Michel E. Smith, *The Aztecs* (Chichester, UK: Wiley-Blackwell, 3rd ed., 2012), pp. 198–200.

3. The Aztec creation account

At the beginning of creation there was an original high god, Ometeotl ("Two-Deity"), who existed in both a male form, Ometecuhtli ("Two-Lord"), and a female form, Omecihuatl ("Two-Lady"). This couple produced four sons: Tezcatlipoca, Xipe Totec, Quetzalcoatl, and Huitzilopochtli. The latter two were given the task of creating the earth, other gods, and people. With the births of these four gods, a cycle of creation and destruction began that continues to the present day.

There have been four previous ages or "suns," each controlled by a different god and peopled by a distinctive race. Each sun was destroyed by a different cataclysm. The god Tezcatlipoca presided over the first sun, when a race of giants roamed the earth. This sun was destroyed by jaguars who ate the giants and destroyed the earth. During the second sun, presided over by Quetzalcoatl, humans who lived on acorns populated the earth. This sun was destroyed by hurricanes, and the people were transformed into monkeys. People of the third sun, under the god Tlaloc, ate aquatic seeds.

◆ CHAPTER 1

The Beginning
of the World:
Creation Accounts
and Cultural
Values in the
Americas and
Europe

The world was destroyed by a fiery rain, and humans were turned into dogs, turkeys, and butterflies. The fourth sun, presided over by Chalchiuhtlicue, was a time of gatherers who ate wild seeds. They were turned into fish in a great flood. . . .

The creation of the fifth sun, the current age, fell to Quetzalcoatl and Tezcatlipoca. In one version of this myth, the two gods found the earth completely covered with water from the flood that ended the fourth sun. The giant earth monster Tlaltecuhtli ("Earth Lord"), a crocodile-like creature, swam in the sea searching for flesh to eat. The gods turned themselves into serpents, entered the sea, and tore Tlaltecuhtli in half. The upper part of her body became the land, and the lower part was thrown into the sky to become the stars and heavens. Plants and animals grow from the back of Tlaltecuhtli and rivers pour from her body. . . .

With the land and sky in place, the gods were ready to create people. They sent Quetzalcoatl to the underworld, Mictlan ("Place of the dead"), to retrieve the bones of the people from the fourth sun:

> And then Quetzalcoatl went to Mictlan. He approached Mictlantecuhtli and Mict-lancihuatl [Lord and Lady of the underworld]; at once he spoke to them: "I come in search of the precious bones in your possession. I have come for them."
>
> And Mictlantecuhtli asked of him, "What shall you do with them, Quetzalcoatl?"
>
> And once again Quetzalcoatl said, "The gods are anxious that someone should inhabit the earth."
>
> And Mictlantecuhtli replied, "Very well, sound my shell horn and go around my circular realm four times."
>
> But his shell horn had no holes.

The false conch horn was the first of several tricks that Mictlantecuhtli used to block Quetzalcoatl's mission. Quetzalcoatl called upon worms to drill a hole in the shell, and bees to make the horn play. When Mictlantecuhtli heard the horn, he at first allowed Quetzalcoatl to gather the bones, but later changed his mind. His helper spirits dug a hole, and a quail appeared and startled Quetzalcoatl, who tripped and lost consciousness. The bones were scattered and broken, and the quail chewed on them. Quetzalcoatl finally rose, gathered up the bones, and escaped from Mictlan.

Quetzalcoatl carried the bones to Tamoanchan, a place of paradise. The old goddess Cihuacoatl ("Woman Serpent") ground them on a *metate* and placed the powder in a jade bowl. Quetzalcoatl and the other gods gathered around and shed their blood upon the ground bones, and the first people of the fifth sun were made.

Once the earth, people, and maize had been created, the gods gathered in the darkness at Teotihuacan to bring forth the sun. Two gods were chosen for the task: Tecciztecatl, a rich, powerful, and haughty lord, and Nanahuatzin, a weak, poor, scab-covered god. A huge pyre was built for a fire sacrifice. The gods called upon Tecciztecatl to throw himself into the fire. Four times he attempted to do their bidding, only to stop short. Then Nanahuatzin gathered his resolve, ran, and leaped into the flames, where his body was quickly burned up. Shamed at his earlier timidity, Tecciztecatl also jumped into the fire, followed by an eagle and a jaguar. For their bravery, these two animals became warriors, patrons of the two major Aztec military orders.

A great light appeared as Nanahuatzin rose in the east as Tonatiuh, the sun god. Then Tecciztecatl also rose as a second sun. The gods worried that the world would be too bright, so they threw a rabbit at Tecciztecatl to dim his light. He became the moon, on whose surface a rabbit can still be seen today. But the sun did not move in the sky. The gods sent a falcon to ask Tonatiuh why he did not move. He replied, "Why? Because I'm asking for their blood, their color, their precious substance." The gods realized they must sacrifice themselves to make the sun move across the sky. Quetzalcoatl performed the deed, cutting open the chests of the gods and removing their hearts to offer up to Tonatiuh. And so the sun assumed its correct path across the sky. The Aztecs believed that just as these gods sacrificed themselves for the sun, so too people had to provide blood and hearts to keep the sun going.

Source 4 from James Mooney, *The Sacred Formulas of the Cherokees, Seventh Annual Report of the Bureau of Ethnology to the Secretary of the Smithsonian Institution, 1885–1886* (Washington, DC: Government Printing Office, 1891).

4. Cherokees' How the World Was Made

The earth is a great island floating in a sea of water, and suspended at each of the four cardinal points by a cord hanging down from the sky vault, which is of solid rock. When the world grows old and worn out, the people will die and the cords will break and let the earth sink down into the ocean, and all will be water again. The Indians are afraid of this.

When all was water, the animals were above in Gălûñ'lătĭ, beyond the arch; but it was very much crowded and they were wanting more room. They wondered what was below the water, and at last Dâyuni'sĭ, "Beaver's Grandchild," the little Water-beetle, offered to go and see if it could learn.

[17]

✦ CHAPTER 1

The Beginning
of the World:
Creation Accounts
and Cultural
Values in the
Americas and
Europe

It darted in every direction over the surface of the water, but could find no firm place to rest. Then it dived to the bottom and came up with some soft mud, which began to grow and spread on every side until it became the island which we call the earth. It was afterward fastened to the sky with four cords, but no one remembers who did this.

At first the earth was flat and very soft and wet. The animals were anxious to get down, and sent out different birds to see if it was yet dry, but they found no place to alight and came back again to Gălûñ′lătĭ. At last it seemed to be time, and they sent out the Buzzard and told him to go and make ready for them. This was the Great Buzzard, the father of all the buzzards we see now. He flew all over the earth, low down near the ground, and it was still soft. When he reached the Cherokee country, he was very tired, and his wings began to flap and strike the ground, and wherever they struck the earth there was a valley, and where they turned up again there was a mountain. When the animals above saw this, they were afraid that the whole world would be mountains, so they called him back, but the Cherokee country remains full of mountains to this day.

When the earth was dry and the animals came down, it was still dark, so they got the sun and set it in a track to go every day across the island from east to west, just overhead. It was too hot this way, and Tsiska′gĭlĭ′, the Red Crawfish, had his shell scorched a bright red, so that his meat was spoiled; and the Cherokee do not eat it. The conjurers put the sun another hand-breadth higher in the air, but it was still too hot. They raised it another time, and another, until it was seven handbreadths high and just under the sky arch. Then it was right, and they left it so. This is why the conjurers call the highest place Gûlkwâ′gine Di′gălûñ′lătiyûñ′, "the seventh height," because it is seven hand-breadths above the earth. Every day the sun goes along under this arch, and returns at night on the upper side to the starting place.

There is another world under this, and it is like ours in everything— animals, plants, and people—save that the seasons are different. The streams that come down from the mountains are the trails by which we reach this underworld, and the springs at their heads are the doorways by which we enter it, but to do this one must fast and go to water and have one of the underground people for a guide. We know that the seasons in the underworld are different from ours, because the water in the springs is always warmer in winter and cooler in summer than the outer air.

When the animals and plants were first made—we do not know by whom— they were told to watch and keep awake for seven nights, just as young men now fast and keep awake when they pray to their medicine. They tried to do this, and nearly all were awake through the first night, but the next night several dropped off to sleep, and the third night others were asleep, and then others, until, on the seventh night, of all the animals only the owl, the panther, and one or two more were still awake. To these were given the power to see and to go about in the dark, and to make prey of the birds and animals which must sleep at night. Of the trees only the cedar, the pine, the spruce, the holly, and the laurel were awake to the end, and to them it was given to be always green and to be greatest for medicine, but to the others it was said: "Because you have not endured to the end you shall lose your hair every winter."

Men came after the animals and plants. At first there were only a brother and sister until he struck her with a fish and told her to multiply, and so it was. In seven days a child was born to her, and thereafter every seven days another, and they increased very fast until there was danger that the world could not keep them. Then it was made that a woman should have only one child in a year, and it has been so ever since. . . .

[In the beginning the world was without fire, and was cold. Then Thunders sent their lightning "and put fire into the bottom of a hollow sycamore tree which grew on the island." Many animals tried unsuccessfully to go after the fire until a water spider wove a bowl, fastened it on her back, and returned with one little coal of fire in the bowl. Ever since humans have had fire.]

In the old days the beasts, birds, fishes, insects, and plants could all talk, and they and the people lived together in peace and friendship. But as time went on the people increased so rapidly that their settlements spread over the whole earth, and the poor animals found themselves beginning to be cramped for room. This was bad enough, but to make it worse Man invented bows, knives, blowguns, spears, and hooks, and began to slaughter the larger animals, birds, and fishes for their flesh or their skins, while the smaller creatures, such as the frogs and worms, were crushed and trodden upon without thought, out of pure carelessness or contempt. So the animals resolved to consult upon measures for their common safety.

[All the creatures met for a conference on how to protect themselves from humans. For their part the Bears tried to fashion bows and arrows to fight humans with their own medicine, but this proved unsuccessful. At a subsequent council of Deer, Reptiles, Fishes, Squirrels, Grubworms and other small creatures, it was decided to invent a series of diseases that would hurt or even kill humans. "I'm glad some more of them will die," said the Grubworm, "for they are getting so thick that they tread on me." The thought fairly made him shake with joy, so that he fell over backward and could not get to his feet again, but had to wriggle on his back, as the Grubworm has done ever since.]

✦ CHAPTER 1

The Beginning
of the World:
Creation Accounts
and Cultural
Values in the
Americas and
Europe

When the Plants, who were friendly to Man, heard what had been done by the animals, they determined to defeat the latters' evil designs. Each Tree, Shrub, and Herb, down even to the Grasses and Mosses, agreed to furnish a cure for some one of the diseases named, and each said: "I shall appear to help Man when he calls upon me in his need." Thus came medicine; and the plants, every one of which has its use if we only knew it, furnish the remedy to counteract the evil wrought by the revengeful animals. Even weeds were made for some good purpose, which we must find out for ourselves. When the doctor does not know what medicine to use for a sick man the spirit of the plant tells him.

Source 5 from Carl F. Krinck and James J. Talman, eds., *The Journal of Major John Norton, 1816,* in The Publications of the Champlain Society (Toronto: The Champlain Society, 1970), vol. 46, pp. 88–91.

5. The Iroquois Formation of the World

The tradition of the Nottowegui or Five Nations says, "that in the beginning before the formation of the earth; the country above the sky was inhabited by Superior Beings, over whom the Great Spirit presided. His daughter having become pregnant by an illicit connection, he pulled up a great tree by the roots, and threw her through the Cavity thereby formed; but, to prevent her utter destruction, he previously ordered the Great Turtle, to get from the bottom of the waters, some slime on its back, and to wait on the surface of the water to receive her on it. When she had fallen on the back of the Turtle, with the mud she found there, she began to form the earth, and by the time of her delivery had encreased it to the extent of a little island. Her child was a daughter, and as she grew up the earth extended under their hands. When the young woman had arrived at the age of discretion, the Spirits who roved about, in human forms, made proposals of marriage for the young woman: the mother always rejected their offers, until a middle aged man, of a dignified appearance, his bow in his hand, and his quiver on his back, paid his addresses. On being accepted, he entered the house, and seated himself on the birth of his intended spouse; the mother was in a birth on the other side of the fire. She observed that her son-in-law did not lie down all night; but taking two arrows out of his quiver, he put them by the side of his bride: at the dawn of day he took them up, and having replaced them in his quiver, he went out.

"After some time, the old woman perceived her daughter to be pregnant, but could not discover where the father had gone, or who he was. At the time of delivery, the twins disputed which way they should go out of the womb; the wicked one said, let us go out of the side; but the other said, not so, lest we kill our mother; then the wicked one pretending to acquiesce, desired his brother to go out first: but as soon as he was delivered, the wicked one, in attempting to go out at her side, caused the death of his mother."

[The mother was buried, and from her grave grew maize, beans and squash, referred to as the "three sisters."][27]

"The twin brothers were nurtured and raised by their Grandmother; the eldest was named Teharonghyawago, or the Holder of Heaven; the youngest was called Tawiskaron, or Flinty rock, from his body being entirely covered with such a substance. They grew up, and with their bows and arrows, amused themselves throughout the island, which encreased in extent, and they were favoured with various animals of Chace. Tawiskaron was the most fortunate hunter, and enjoyed the favour of his Grandmother. Teharonghyawago was not so successful in the Chace, and suffered from their unkindness. When he was a youth, and roaming alone, in melancholy mood, through the island, a human figure, of noble aspect, appearing to him, addressed him thus. 'My son, I have seen your distress, and heard your solitary lamentations; you are unhappy in the loss of a mother, in the unkindness of your Grandmother and brother. I now come to comfort you, I am your father, and will be your Protector; therefore take courage, and suffer not your spirit to sink. Take this (giving him an ear of *maize*) plant it, and attend it in the manner, I shall direct; it will yield you a certain support, independent of the Chace, at the same time that it will render more palatable the viands, which you may thereby obtain. I am the Great Turtle which supports the earth, on which you move. Your brother's ill treatment will increase with his years; bear it with patience till the time appointed, before which you shall hear further.'

"After saying this, and directing him how to plant the corn, he disappeared. Teharonghyawago planted the corn, and returned home. When its verdant sprouts began to flourish above the ground, he spent his time in clearing from it all growth of grass and weeds, which might smother it or retard its advancement while yet in its tender state, before it had acquired sufficient grandeur to shade the ground. He now discovered that his wicked brother caught the timid deer, the stately elk with branching horns, and all the

27. Engelbrecht, *Iroquoia*, pp. 22, 27.

[21]

◆ CHAPTER 1

The Beginning
of the World:
Creation Accounts
and Cultural
Values in the
Americas and
Europe

harmless inhabitants of the Forest; and imprisoned them in an extensive cave, for his own particular use, depriving mortals from having the benefit of them that was originally intended by the Great Spirit. Teharonghyawago discovered the direction his brother took in conducting these animals captive to the Cave; but never could trace him quite to the spot, as he eluded his sight with more than common dexterity!"

[For a long time Teharonghyawago searched for the cave where his brother had imprisoned all the animals of the forest, and when he ultimately found the cave he set them free. When Tawiskaron discovered what his brother had one, he swore revenge. But Teharonghyawago met a fawn in the forest who told him that his brother had killed their mother and warned him of his brother's attack. In the fight Teharonghyawago killed his brother.]

This tradition, with some variation in the relation, is generally received by the Five Nations and Wyandots. They say that Teharonghyawago always assisted them in their wars, when they were undertaken with just cause: and many anecdotes are related of his being present in the battles they fought, spreading dismay through the ranks of the enemy, by his gigantic appearance, and by the havoc he made: also in attracting their notice, by his lofty stature, to cause them to aim their arrows at him, whom they could not wound, and thereby to overshoot the warriors of his favourite host. Even many of the Christian part of these people do not discredit this tradition; but endeavour to accommodate it to the Scriptural account of our Blessed Lord. Some of the old men, who have not embraced Christianity, but who have been made acquainted with some part of its doctrine, allege, as a reason for their remaining in their ancient state, that the Great spirit had taken the same pains to instruct the Aboriginal Americans that he had done to inform the Europeans: that as they were very different in their manners and customs, as well as in their situation, he had given them religions apparently indifferent, though essentially the same, as they both lead us to reverence and obey the Creator, and to love like brethren our fellow creatures. . . .[28]

---

28. Norton claimed that some old Iroquois men "had had much conversation with Roman Catholic Priests" who asked the old men whether any of them recalled the name of Teharong-hyawago's and Tawiskaron's mother. They answered, "Not in our language, but in that of the Europeans, she is called Maria." *Norton's Journal,* p. 91. This is but one of many examples of the mixing of two faith traditions by the Native Americans.

Questions to Consider

The five creation accounts in this chapter are but a tiny fraction of the many such accounts that have been found in Mesopotamia, India, Egypt, China, the Western Hemisphere, and nearly countless other places. Moreover, there probably were dozens of such accounts that have been lost, destroyed, or not yet found, for example, the rich and advanced Maya civilization of Central America was overtaken by the jungle and was not rediscovered until 1837 by American John Stephens and Britain Frederick Catherwood.[29]

Although creation accounts are different in a number of ways, the questions we can ask these accounts are very similar. In order to compare and contrast the five accounts in this chapter, it would be very helpful if you could devise a chart to use as you analyze the accounts. For example:

	Israelites	Maya	Aztec	Cherokee	Iroquois
GOD OR GODS 1. Possess human traits, emotions, personalities? 2. Role(s) in the creation of the world 3. Why did god/gods decide to create humans? 4. How were humans constructed? 5. Why were gods dissatisfied with humans and other creatures?					
WATER 1. Why did water play such a prominent role in the creation of the world and humans?					
HUMANS 1. What was the *purpose* of humans? 2. In what ways must humans reciprocate for their own creation? 3. What "lessons" were humans supposed to learn from the creation accounts? 4. In sum, what did it *mean* to be human?					
OTHER CREATURES 1. What were the roles other creatures were required to play in creation accounts?					
MANY ACCOUNTS 1. Why do some of the five peoples have more than one creation account? Explain.					

29. For Stephens and Catherwood see Jared Diamond, *Collapse: How Societies Choose to Fail or Succeed* (New York: Viking, 2005), pp. 157–158. For one tragically unsuccessful quest see David Grann, *The Lost City of Z: A Tale of Deadly Obsession in the Amazon* (New York: Vintage, 2010).

✦ CHAPTER 1

The Beginning
of the World:
Creation Accounts
and Cultural
Values in the
Americas and
Europe

Finally, what *additional questions* would you like to ask of these creation accounts?

As you examine and analyze the five creation accounts in this chapter, you will come to understand that while our *answers* to the questions in this chart are dramatically different from our own, in many ways the *questions* are not dissimilar. Even in our modern scientific/technological age, men and women still ask questions such as:

1. Why am I here?
2. Is there some activity that would give more meaning or purpose to my life?
3. What should my relations be to other humans, especially those not like me? to other creatures?
4. Is there *anything* in *any* of the ancient creation accounts that can teach me something worthwhile?

✦

Epilogue

It is not known precisely when creation accounts first began to appear. It is highly possible, however, that these accounts appeared about the time that various peoples abandoned their migratory ways and took up more sedentary lifestyles so they could grow more food for increasing populations and construct villages, towns, and even cities with more permanent housing and other structures (temples, meeting places, government buildings, etc.).[30] Over time, these societies began to appreciate their own uniqueness as a people and how they differed from their other sedentary and nomadic neighbors. Their realization of their own separateness led them to search for their own origins, a process that combined their remembered or created history with their belief in a

god or gods that participated in the creation process as well as offered their prosperity and protection. As historian Fernand Braudel put it, "religion is the strongest feature of civilizations, at the heart of both their present and their past."[31]

Most of the early religious traditions were polytheistic (the belief in more than one god) and peoples invested their gods and goddesses with human forms and emotions (love, anger, jealousy, etc.).[32] Many of those figures were connected to something important in peoples' lives: rain, bountiful harvests, victory in battle, protection from floods, droughts, diseases, and so on. And gradually a separate caste of religious leaders emerged who presided

30. Some people who lived in regions with shorter growing seasons that prevented enjoying large harvests were forced to maintain semi-nomadic lives so that they resided in villages for part of the year and then followed migrating beasts and birds for dietary supplements.

31. Fernand Braudel, *A History of Civilization,* trans. Richard Mayne (New York: Penguin Group, 1994), p. 22.
32. Jewish people claim a long tradition of monotheism, although the struggle to accept Yahweh as the one and only god was a long one that may not have been settled until as late as 587 BCE.

over rituals and ceremonies, often interpreted natural phenomena, and led the worship of the gods—and sometimes themselves.

Beginning in the late seventeenth century, in the West some intellectuals, philosophers, and scientists began to challenge the authority of various peoples' religious beliefs, including creation accounts. These challenges became increasingly widespread in universities as well as in societies of individuals who proudly called themselves "independent thinkers." Indeed, some went so far as to predict that science and the scientific method of thinking would actually *replace* religions, especially as new scientific discoveries and theories increasingly cast doubts on religious teachings such as the creation accounts. Especially threatening were the findings of naturalists Charles Darwin (1809–1882) and Alfred Russel Wallace (1823–1913). In Darwin's *The Origin of Species* (1859), he argued that species of plants and animals evolved over time through a process which he called "natural selection," the claim that variations in a species appeared at random and thereby increased that organism's ability to survive and reproduce and ultimately form a new species. Controversies between the attackers and defenders of Darwin's theory went on for over a century, although carbon dating has proven Darwin correct in his hypothesis that the time frame for all biological life is far longer than most persons believed.[33]

In spite of the continued research by a host of anthropologists, biologists, and other scientists, the ancient creation accounts continue to possess considerable strength among some contemporary followers of those religious traditions. Why is this so? For many people, creation accounts may well be myths, but at the same time they maintain that these accounts contain within them important moral and ethical lessons as well as a continued sense of unity among fellow believers, qualities that should be retained and passed on to future generations. Therefore, it would be not at all unusual for recent scientific discoveries to stand side-by-side with ancient stories of the beginning of the world and human beings, accounts that for many individuals still have much to teach.[34]

To Our Readers

For some of you, learning about various creation accounts can be an interesting and exciting experience. Many academic fields, including history, religious studies, cultural anthropology, social psychology, and philosophy can contribute to a study of creation accounts.

33. At the time that Darwin was working on *The Origin of Species,* fellow naturalist Alfred Russel Wallace (1823–1913) had reached similar conclusions, but he withdrew in favor of Darwin. Not long after his death, a rumor was circulated that on his deathbed Darwin recanted his theories. The rumor was as appalling as it was untrue. See Edward Caudill, *Darwinian Myths: The Legends and Misuses of Theory* (Knoxville: Univ. of Tennessee Press, 1997).

34. For one view of the functions of creation accounts and of religion in general see Jared Diamond, *The World Until Yesterday: What Can We Learn from Traditional Societies?* (New York: Viking, 2012), chapter 9.

✦ CHAPTER 1

The Beginning
of the World:
Creation Accounts
and Cultural
Values in the
Americas and
Europe

The University of Georgia has collected selections from over 20 creation stories titled "Creation Stories from Around the World" at www.gly.uga.edu /railsback/CS/CSIndex/html. Equally valuable is the Library of Congress's "World Treasures: Beginnings" in *World Treasures of the Library of Congress*, at www.loc.gov/exhibits/world/accounts .html. Also helpful is en.wikipedia.org /wiki/Creation-myth.

Of special interest may be the Atra-hasis of ancient Babylonia (W. G. Lambert and A. R. Millard, *Atra-hasis: The Babylonian Story of the Flood* [1969]); the Rig Veda of ancient India (Franklin Egerton, trans., *The Beginnings of Indian Philosophy* [1969]); the I Ching of ancient China (Princeton: Princeton Univ. Press, 3rd ed. 1967); and the Japanese *Tales from the Kojiki*, trans. Yaichiro Isobe, 1928.

2

The Threat of Anne Hutchinson

The Problem

On the first day of April 1638, Anne Hutchinson, accompanied by nine of her children and three grandchildren, fled the Puritan colony of Massachusetts Bay. She joined her husband, William, and a small band of their friends in Rhode Island. Just a year before, Anne and William had been respected members of the First Church of Boston. But in November 1637, she was tried by the Massachusetts Bay General Court and banished from the colony; she was kept under house arrest that winter, awaiting a separate church trial that would result in her excommunication and final exile.

What had Anne Hutchinson done? Why did Massachusetts leaders find her "a woman not fit for our society"? **Why was Anne Hutchinson too dangerous to remain in the Puritan colony?**

Background

Anne and William Hutchinson left their home in England as part of the "Great Migration" of the 1630s. During that decade, some 14,000 Puritans moved to the New World, principally to New England. These colonists sought, as did Anne, a place to practice what they believed was "true" Christianity, purified of the corruptions they saw running amuck in the Church of England.

"Puritan" was, in fact, a disparaging term in the early seventeenth century. Leaders of the Church of England (Anglican Church) used the word to dismiss reformers who objected to the course the established church was pursuing. Nevertheless, it remains a term that historians (intending no judgment at all) nearly universally use to designate the English Protestant migrants who came to colonial New England.

Puritans in England in the early 1600s generally believed that the Protestant Reformation had not gone far enough in their country; too many Roman Catholic influences remained. Puritans did not, for example, approve of high church liturgy, and they rejected priests' authority to administer sacraments. To Puritans, the ceremonialism within the Church of England seemed too similar to Catholicism—and so a heresy. Any Roman influences in the architecture, teachings, or rituals of the Church of England the Puritans scornfully labeled "popery." And since the Puritans believed that "popery" actually obstructed the ties between God and humankind, it had to be eliminated.[1]

The contempt that Puritans felt for the Roman Church is hard to overestimate. Puritans believed "papists" (another term Protestants used to denigrate Roman Catholics) were deluded if not actually in league with the devil. Puritans even referred to the Roman Church as the "Great Whore of Babylon." While the Church of England differed in many and profound ways from the Roman Church, Puritans did not necessarily see it that way.

In addition to the outward appearances and practices of the established Anglican Church, Puritans held theological differences with Anglican leaders, particularly regarding the nature of salvation. After the ascension of King James in 1606, Puritans began to worry about the Anglican Church drifting toward a theology known as Arminianism. This theology emerged from the teachings of Jacobus Arminius, a Dutch preacher. Arminius believed that God wanted to save all people but that God's design could be resisted by the free will of individuals.[2] In other words, people could reject the salvation God offered. Puritans, on the other hand, followed the teachings of John Calvin. Calvinists believed that God chose only some people for "election"—eternal salvation—and that his will was irresistible. Individuals could do nothing to alter God's plan for their eternal soul. One of the main theological disagreements, then, between Arminians and Calvinists centered on predestination: whether or not God alone decided who was saved and who was damned.

Puritans considered themselves, in the tradition of Abraham, bound to God by a "covenant of grace." They submitted to God's laws and sought His will, and in return, God would not afflict them unjustly. But they also believed that good works in this world offered no assurance of salvation in the next: eternal salvation came only through God's grace, which even the most pious of believers could neither know nor influence. Puritans claimed that Arminianism promoted what they called a "covenant of works"—the misguided and arrogant assumption that individuals could earn salvation through good behavior. This, in the

1. For an introduction to the evolution of religious values in early modern England, see Christopher Haigh, *English Reformations: Religion, Politics, and Society Under the Tudors* (New York: Oxford University Press, 1993).

2. The famous Methodist minister George Whitefield embraced Arminian teaching, as did most Baptists in the seventeenth and eighteenth centuries.

eyes of Puritans, was little better than the heretical "popery" of the Roman Church.

Despite these important theological disagreements, during the reign of King James, Anglicans and Puritans tolerated one another without too much open conflict. (James's commission of an English Bible remains extraordinarily influential among modern-day evangelical Christians). Under James, Puritan ministers led many Anglican parishes and the Church of England relaxed some of its ceremonial practices.

The death of King James and the accession of King Charles in 1625 ended all of that. Charles wanted to restore the ceremonialism his father, James, had allowed to erode, and to that end in 1628 he installed as the Bishop of London William Laud, a strong advocate of high church ritual. In 1633, he promoted Laud to Archbishop of the Church of England. Laud wanted to return the "beauty of holiness" to the Anglican Church: to institute across England uniform religious services, to make churches more attractive, to insert more ceremonialism into the liturgy, and to convey an image of elegance and order. The latter point suited King Charles's interests, too. He wanted to preside over a stable, peaceful social hierarchy. But the changes Laud promoted struck Puritans as even more dangerous than Arminianism: they seemed like a return to the diabolical "popery" of the Catholic Church.

By the time Charles appointed Laud Archbishop, Puritan ministers who resisted and even overtly condemned these policy changes were being fired from their church positions. Church courts were also prosecuting Puritans who refused to renounce their beliefs. Puritans first sought relief from Parliament. But in 1629, shortly after the House of Commons passed a resolution making the practice of either "popery" or Arminianism a capital offense, King Charles dissolved Parliament. By 1629, a growing number of Puritans believed their country and their souls in such peril that they made the radical decision to leave England. Deciding it was impossible to effect their reforms in England, some Puritans sought "voluntary banishment," as one of them called it, to the New World. There they imagined building a model godly community, based solely on their understanding of God's laws and commandments. "We shall be as a city upon a hill," proclaimed Puritan leader and colonial governor John Winthrop, "the eyes of all people are upon us." The earliest migrants to Massachusetts Bay intended to create an example of Christian goodness so compelling that their countrymen in England would be inspired to reform. The Puritans would save the Church of England from diabolical "popish" influences by living in that model community. The stakes for the colonists, then, were extraordinarily high. Puritan leaders expected every man and woman in the settlement to focus on making this vision of the Massachusetts Bay Colony a reality.

Anne and William Hutchinson remained in England until 1634. William was a wealthy merchant, and Anne the mother of twelve children; a perilous Atlantic crossing was not to be undertaken lightly. Besides, even in the early 1630s, despite the crackdown on Puritan dissenters, the Hutchinsons were still able to attend church services led by two Puritan ministers they greatly admired: the Reverend John Cotton and the Reverend John Wheelwright, the latter the husband of William Hutchinson's youngest sister, Mary. But in 1633, Cotton's preaching and teaching caught the attention of Archbishop Laud. Summoned to London to answer for his unsanctioned behavior, Cotton fled to Massachusetts Bay instead. Wheelwright was banned from preaching around the same time, and Anne concluded "there was none in England that I durst heare." She and William soon departed for New England with eleven of their children.

William, Anne, and their family, along with some 200 other passengers, arrived in Boston on September 18, 1634. John Cotton had been there nearly a year, and in that time had acquired a reputation for excellent preaching; Governor John Winthrop numbered among his admirers. Anne quickly reconnected with John Cotton. She was particularly drawn to his very strong defense of the covenant of grace.

While all New England Puritans believed that salvation came through God's grace alone, divisions were already appearing in the early 1630s about how exactly to live that theology. Some ministers stressed to their congregations the importance of preparing to receive God's grace—of living just, ordered lives so as to be ready should God decide to grant them faith and salvation. And many Puritans read events in this world—productive crops, respectful children, ordered communities—

as signs of their election. God, after all, smiled on his chosen people. John Cotton and his protégée Anne Hutchinson roundly rejected all of this. From the pulpit, Cotton condemned this drift toward Arminianism and embracing of a covenant of works. Hutchinson, who was extraordinarily intelligent and deeply pious, expanded on these ideas in meetings she hosted at her home.

In addition to being highly regarded as a devout Christian, Anne Hutchinson gained respect in Boston for her skills as a midwife. In the early seventeenth century, caring for pregnant women and delivering infants were totally female centered. Midwives like Anne were also healers of a sort, greatly needed and therefore esteemed by women. Anne's skills gave her special authority within the female world of Massachusetts Bay. Men in the community respected her talents and knowledge, too. From that valued position as a midwife, Anne began to conduct religious discussions in her home. Her concerns in these meetings echoed those of her spiritual advisor Reverend Cotton: particularly the tendency of Bostonians to slide into Arminianism when they should focus instead on the omnipotence of God. While not a theologian, Hutchinson was extremely learned and able to hold her own with prominent ministers in Massachusetts.

Debates of the sort that engaged Cotton and Hutchinson were not uncommon in Massachusetts Bay. Religious squabbles often arose over biblical interpretation, the theological correctness of ministers, and the behavior of fellow colonists. To a limited extent, Puritan leaders accepted these discussions because they seemed to demonstrate that religion was a vital part of colonists' lives. However, there were very strict limits to what kinds of religious disputes were acceptable. It was one thing for members of a church to contend over a particular Bible passage or discuss how Christians should live in community. But dissent from Puritan tenets and social disruptions that threatened the mission of building their "city upon a hill" simply could not be tolerated.

Contemporary Americans like to believe that the Puritans came to the New World to build a colony (and nation) dedicated to freedom of religion. Puritans did want to be free from Anglican interference to practice their faith as they saw fit. But they most assuredly *did not* believe in freedom of religion. Seeing themselves as the new Israelites, Puritans believed that God had entered into a special covenant with them. As John Winthrop explained, "Thus stands the cause between God and us: we are entered into covenant with Him. . . . The God of Israel is among us." To Puritans, this covenant meant that the entire community had to follow God's laws as interpreted by Puritan leaders. If they did, God would reward them; if they did not, the whole community would be grievously punished. Therefore, community solidarity was essential, and individual desires and thoughts always were subjugated to the needs of the larger society. "We must be knit together in this work as one man," Winthrop insisted. Discord would lead to the breakdown of community cohesion, violation of the covenant, and God's wrath. Therefore, individuals following

other Christian faiths—Baptists and Quakers, for example—were fined, imprisoned, "warned out" (expelled from the colony), and even executed if they refused to repent.[3] Drawing on Old Testament laws, Puritan leaders made adultery, blasphemy, and witchcraft capital offenses, deserving of the same punishment as treason and murder. God's law was strictly enforced in Puritan New England. Violating a Biblical commandment, for example, was not only a spiritual failing but also a civil crime.

The need for Puritans to be "knit together in this work" meant that every part of an individual's life was subject to community oversight, starting with his or her religious faith. New England Puritans placed a tremendous emphasis on having a publicly-validated conversion experience. Only a confirmed conversion would admit a person into full church membership. Men who were not full members of a church could not vote in elections or hold public office. To become a confirmed "saint"—a person whose conversion was validated by the community—one had to be examined by a church committee and demonstrate that he or she had experienced the presence of God and the Holy Spirit. There was no universal agreement among ministers about the exact nature of this revelation. For most it

3. Quakers began arriving in Massachusetts Bay in 1656, hoping to practice their religion and evangelize among the Puritans. Many were jailed, whipped, and banished. Between 1659 and 1661, four were executed for refusing to leave the colony. To learn more, see Carla Gardina Pestana, "The Quaker Executions as Myth and History," *Journal of American History* 80 (September 1993): 441–469.

was closely connected with studying the Bible; God communicated with believers not in direct, immediate revelations, but rather through His word. A few ministers described hearing the voice of God; however, this was quite controversial. And, as you will see in Anne Hutchinson's trial, a layperson claiming so direct a revelation—to say nothing of a woman's doing so—was shocking.

Family life was another essential part of the community order Puritan leaders demanded. Anne Hutchinson's testimony cannot be fully understood without some knowledge of how families were organized in the seventeenth century and how men and women were supposed to interact. Husbands were supposed to head their families just as Christ was head of the church. Wives and children were to defer to that patriarchal authority. While women could become confirmed saints in their churches, as Anne Hutchinson did, they had no separate economic or political identity. According to the legal doctrine of coverture, women were subsumed under the law first by their fathers and then by their husbands. Women rarely owned property, they certainly could not vote, and they were forbidden from speaking at public gatherings that men attended. They did not even have a right to custody of their children should a divorce occur.[4] Signifying the importance of family duty and submission in their lives,

4. Puritans did not consider marriage a sacrament but rather a civil, secular relationship. Divorce was legal for several reasons, including adultery, abandonment, and impotence.

Puritan wives were often referred to not by their own names but as "Goodwife" Smith or "Goody" Jones.

The same kind of hierarchy that prevailed in family life underlay both the colony's churches and its government. Within this hierarchy, ministers played a crucial role. Expected to be highly educated and articulate, the minister of each Puritan church was to be the teacher and leader of his congregation. Of course, the civil officials of Massachusetts Bay, such as the governor and his council, were good Puritans and full members of their churches. The political leaders' job was to ensure that the laws and practices of the colonial government accorded with the requirements of living in a godly community. Civil authorities, then, were expected to support religious authorities, and vice versa. Good Puritans honored both. It is in this light that you should consider Reverend Hugh Peter's charge that Anne Hutchinson had "stepped out of place" and that she "had rather been a husband than a wife; and a preacher than a hearer; and a magistrate than a subject."

By the summer of 1636, Massachusetts Bay was embroiled in a controversy that threatened all these values: the covenant with God, the city upon a hill that would redeem England, the community ethic on which that mission was built, and the souls of true believers. Some Puritans, including Anne's brother-in-law John Wheelwright, had begun to espouse an extreme version of the covenant of grace: they believed that, having been assured of salvation, an individual was virtually freed from the man-made laws of both church and state, taking commands only from God, who communicated his wishes to the saints. Called Antinomians (from *anti,* "against," and *nomos,* "law"), these Puritan extremists attacked what one of them called the "deadness" of church services and charged that several ministers had started preaching a covenant of works. This accusation was extremely offensive to Puritan ministers, who flatly rejected the idea that they were promoting the idea that salvation could be earned through good behavior. Rather, they said they tried to teach their congregants to prepare themselves for the possibility of God's grace by honoring Massachusetts and Biblical values. The Antinomians countered that "sanctification"— living a good life—was no evidence of "justification"—numbering among the elect. In other words, what one did in this world had absolutely nothing to do with his or her fate in the next.

Carried to its logical extension, Antinomianism threatened to overthrow the authority of the ministers and even the colonial government. Growing in number and intensity, the Antinomians in 1636 were able to vote in one of their own, Francis Vane, to replace Winthrop as colonial governor. Vane lodged with Reverend Cotton and attended Anne Hutchinson's meetings. Although Winthrop managed to return to office the next year, he and many of the leading men of Massachusetts Bay understood perfectly the threat this Antinomian crisis posed to everything they were trying to build.

The meetings Anne Hutchinson led at her home thus became the source of increasing distress to Governor Winthrop. Initially, she used those sessions to discuss the previous Sunday's sermon. Then she began to expound on her own religious ideas. At first she drew only a few women. But then scores came, and soon they were joined by men, including some wealthy merchants and political elites like Francis Vane. So many people attended that by 1636 Anne began offering two sessions each week. Governor Winthrop saw it all, for he lived across the road from the Hutchinson family in Boston.

In November 1637, Anne's brother-in-law, Reverend Wheelwright, was banished from the colony because of his radical sermons. Then the General Court sent for Anne. With Governor Winthrop presiding, the court met to decide her fate. Privately, Winthrop called Hutchinson "a woman of ready wit and bold spirit," which was *not* a compliment in seventeenth-century Massachusetts. The governor was determined to be rid of her.

Why were Winthrop and other orthodox Puritans so opposed to Hutchinson? Some of Wheelwright's followers had been punished for having signed a petition supporting him, but Hutchinson had not signed it. Many other Puritans had held religious discussions in their homes, and more than a few had opposed the views of their ministers, but they were not singled out by the General Court. Technically, in fact, Hutchinson had broken no law. Why, then, was she considered such a threat that she was brought to trial and ultimately banished from the colony?

♦

The Method

For two days, Anne Hutchinson stood before the General Court, presided over by Governor John Winthrop. Forty magistrates filled the meeting-house, along with six ministers who offered testimony against Anne. Nearly a dozen judges interrogated the forty-six-year-old mother of twelve living children.

Fortunately, a fairly complete transcript of the civil proceedings has been preserved.[5] That transcript holds the clues that you, as the historian-detective, will need to piece together to understand Hutchinson's expulsion from Massachusetts Bay. Although spelling and punctuation have been modernized in most cases, the portions of the transcript you are about to read are reproduced verbatim. At first some of the seventeenth-century phraseology might seem a bit strange. As are most spoken languages, English is constantly changing (think of how much English has changed since Chaucer's day, or even since Franklin D. Roosevelt spoke on the radio). Yet if you read slowly and carefully, the document should give you no problem.

Before you begin studying the transcript, keep in mind two additional instructions:

1. Be careful not to lose sight of the central question: Why was Anne Hutchinson such a threat to the Massachusetts Bay Colony? There is no single answer, but many, which explains why the threat was so grave as to require her permanent expulsion. The trial record raises several other issues, some of them so interesting that they might pull you off the main track. As you read through the transcript, make a list of the various ways you think Hutchinson might have threatened Massachusetts Bay.

2. Be willing to read between the lines. As you read the primary source, try to deduce what is actually meant by what is being said and done in the context of the early 1600s. Start with the individuals present: what would it feel like to be the only woman publicly confronted by so many powerful men? Sometimes people say exactly what they mean, but often they do not. They might intentionally or unintentionally disguise the real meaning of what they are saying, but the real meaning can usually be found. In face-to-face conversation with a person, voice inflection, body

5. Anne Hutchinson also faced a church trial in March 1638. She was judged guilty there, too, and excommunicated from her church. In 1771, Ezra Stiles, a congregational minister, educator, and later president of Yale University, made a copy of the original church trial manuscript. Alas, the manuscript he used has been lost. But his work survives, housed in the Ezra Stiles Papers at the Beinecke Library at Yale University. In 1888, Franklin Bowditch Dexter, an administrator and librarian at Yale, shared Stiles' transcription with the Massachusetts Historical Society, which published it for the first time in *Proceedings of the Massachusetts Historical Society* 2nd series, volume 4 (1888): 161–191. Many university libraries have digital access to that source.

language, and other visual clues often provide the real meaning to what is being said. In this case, where personal observation is impossible, you must use both logic and imagination to read between the lines. For example, what inferences can you draw about Hutchinson's perception of Winthrop—and vice versa—when she asked him, since "you think it is not lawful for me to teach women," then "why do you call me to teach the court?" And you must always keep the context—the nature of Puritan society and the seventeenth-century worldview—in mind. Consider, for instance, the audacity of and likely unspoken reaction to the first words Anne Hutchinson spoke in court: "I am called here to answer before you but I hear no things laid to my charge."

✦

The Evidence

Source 1: Excerpts from "The Examination of Mrs. Anne Hutchinson at the court at Newtown," November 1637, in Thomas Hutchinson, *The History of Massachusetts, from the Settlement thereof in 1628, until the year 1750* 2 volumes, 3rd edition (Boston: Manning and Loring, 1795), Appendix II, 423–447.[6]

1. The 1637 Examination of Anne Hutchinson in Newton, Massachusetts.[7]

CHARACTERS

Mrs. Anne Hutchinson, the accused

General Court, consisting of the governor, deputy governor, assistants, and deputies

Governor, John Winthrop, chair of the court

Deputy Governor, Thomas Dudley

Assistants, Mr. Bradstreet, Mr. Nowel, Mr. Endicott, Mr. Harlakenden, Mr. Stoughton

Deputies, Mr. Coggeshall, Mr. Bartholomew, Mr. Jennison, Mr. Coddington, Mr. Colborn

---

6. Thomas Hutchinson was a descendent of Anne Hutchinson. In the 1770s, he also was one of the most prominent and hated Loyalists in British America. He rose to the position of Lt. Governor (and acting Governor) in Boston during the revolutionary crisis and became a prime target of the Patriots' contempt.

7. Normally the trial would have been held in Boston, but Anne Hutchinson had numerous supporters in that city, so the proceedings were moved to the small town of Newton, where she had few allies. The manuscript heading spells the town name Newtown, but the name is Newton.

Clergymen and Ruling Elders:

Mr. Peters, minister in Salem

Mr. Leveret, a ruling elder in a Boston church

Mr. Cotton, minister in Boston

Mr. Wilson, minister in Boston, who supposedly made notes of a previous
   meeting between Anne Hutchinson, Cotton, and the other ministers

Mr. Sims, minister in Charlestown

MR. WINTHROP, GOVERNOR. Mrs. Hutchinson, you are called here as one of those
   that have troubled the peace of the commonwealth and the churches
   here; you are known to be a woman that hath had a great share in the
   promoting and divulging of those opinions that are causes of this trouble,
   and to be nearly joined not only in affinity and affection with some of
   those the court had taken notice of and passed censure upon, but you have
   spoken divers things as we have been informed very prejudicial to the
   honour of the churches and ministers thereof, and you have maintained
   a meeting and an assembly in your house that hath been condemned by
   the general assembly as a thing not tolerable nor comely in the sight of
   God nor fitting for your sex, and notwithstanding that was cried down
   you have continued the same. Therefore we have thought good to send for
   you to understand how things are, that if you be in an erroneous way we
   may reduce you so that you may become a profitable member here among
   us. Otherwise if you be obstinate in your course that then the court may
   take such course that you may trouble us no further. Therefore I would
   intreat you to express whether you do assent and hold in practice to those
   opinions and factions that have been handled in court already, that is to
   say, whether you do not justify Mr. Wheelwright's sermon and the petition.

MRS. HUTCHINSON. I am called here to answer before you but I hear no things
   laid to my charge.

GOV. I have told you some already and more I can tell you.

MRS. H. Name one, Sir.

GOV. Have I not named some already?

MRS. H. What have I said or done?

*[Here, in a portion of the transcript not reproduced, Winthrop accused Hutchinson of
harboring and giving comfort to a faction that was dangerous to the colony.]*

MRS. H. Must not I then entertain the saints because I must keep my conscience?

GOV. Say that one brother should commit felony or treason and come to his
   brother's house. If he knows him guilty and conceals him he is guilty
   of the same. It is his conscience to entertain him, but if his conscience

comes into act in giving countenance and entertainment to him that hath broken the law he is guilty too. So if you do countenance those that are transgressors of the law you are in the same fact.

MRS. H. What law do they transgress?

GOV. The law of God and of the state.

MRS. H. In what particular?

GOV. Why in this among the rest, whereas the Lord doth say honour thy father and thy mother.[8]

MRS. H. Ey, Sir, in the Lord.

GOV. This honour you have broke in giving countenance to them.

MRS. H. In entertaining those did I entertain them against any act (for there is the thing) or what God hath appointed?

GOV. You knew that Mr. Wheelwright did preach this sermon and those that countenance him in this do break a law?

MRS. H. What law have I broken?

GOV. Why the fifth commandment.[9]

MRS. H. I deny that for he [Wheelwright] saith in the Lord.

GOV. You have joined with them in the faction.

MRS. H. In what faction have I joined with them?

GOV. In presenting the petition.

MRS. H. Suppose I had set my hand to the petition. What then?

GOV. You saw that case tried before.

MRS. H. But I had not my hand to the petition.

GOV. You have councelled them.

MRS. H. Wherein?

GOV. Why in entertaining them.

MRS. H. What breach of law is that, Sir?

GOV. Why dishonouring of parents.

MRS. H. But put the case, Sir, that I do fear the Lord and my parents. May not I entertain them that fear the Lord because my parents will not give me leave?

GOV. If they be the fathers of the commonwealth, and they of another religion, if you entertain them then you dishonour your parents and are justly punishable.

MRS. H. If I entertain them, as they have dishonoured their parents I do.

GOV. No but you by countenancing them above others put honour upon them.

8. Exodus 20:12. Anne Hutchinson's natural father was in England and her natural mother was dead. To what, then, was Winthrop referring?
9. "Honour thy father and thy mother: that thy days may be long upon the land which the Lord thy God giveth thee." Exodus 20:12.

MRS. H. I may put honour upon them as the children of God and as they do honour the Lord.

GOV. We do not mean to discourse with those of your sex but only this: you do adhere unto them and do endeavour to set forward this faction and so you do dishonour us.

MRS. H. I do acknowledge no such thing. Neither do I think that I ever put any dishonour upon you.

GOV. Why do you keep such a meeting at your house as you do every week upon a set day?…

MRS. H. It is lawful for me so to do, as it is all your practices, and can you find a warrant for yourself and condemn me for the same thing? The ground of my taking it up was, when I first came to this land because I did not go to such meetings as those were, it was presently reported that I did not allow of such meetings but held them unlawful and therefore in that regard they said I was proud and did despise all ordinances. Upon that a friend came unto me and told me of it and I to prevent such aspersions took it up, but it was in practice before I came. Therefore I was not the first.

GOV. For this, that you appeal to our practice you need no confutation. If your meeting had answered to the former it had not been offensive, but I will say that there was no meeting of women alone, but your meeting is of another sort for there are sometimes men among you.

MRS. H. There was never any man with us.

GOV. Well, admit there was no man at your meeting and that you was sorry for it, there is no warrant for your doings, and by what warrant do you continue such a course?

MRS. H. I conceive there lies a clear rule in Titus[10] that the elder women should instruct the younger and then I must have a time wherein I must do it.

GOV. All this I grant you, I grant you a time for it, but what is this to the purpose that you Mrs. Hutchinson must call a company together from their callings to come to be taught of you?

MRS. H. Will it please you to answer me this and to give me a rule for then I will willingly submit to any truth. If any come to my house to be instructed in the ways of God what rule have I to put them away?

10. Here Hutchinson is referencing Titus 2:3–5, which in the New International Version reads, "Likewise, teach the older women to be reverent in the way they live, not to be slanderers or addicted to much wine, but to teach what is good. Then they can train the younger women to love their husbands and children, to be self-controlled and pure, to be busy at home, to be kind, and to be subject to their husbands, so that no one will malign the word of God." The text in the Geneva Bible, which was popular among seventeenth-century Puritans, reads: "The elder women likewise, that they be in such behauiour as becommeth holinesse, not false accusers, not subject to much wine, but teachers of honest things, That they may instruct the yong women to be sober minded, that they loue their husbands, that they loue their children, That they be temperate, chaste, keeping at home, good & subject unto their husbands, that the word of God be not euill spoken of."

GOV. But suppose that a hundred men come unto you to be instructed. Will you forbear to instruct them?

MRS. H. As far as I conceive I cross a rule in it.

GOV. Very well and do you not so here?

MRS. H. No, Sir, for my ground is they are men.

GOV. Men and women all is one for that, but suppose that a man should come and say, "Mrs. Hutchinson, I hear that you are a woman that God hath given his grace unto and you have knowledge in the word of God. I pray instruct me a little." Ought you not to instruct this man?

MRS. H. I think I may. Do you think it is not lawful for me to teach women and why do you call me to teach the court?

GOV. We do not call you to teach the court but to lay open yourself.

[In this portion of the transcript not reproduced, Hutchinson and Winthrop continued to wrangle over specifically what law she had broken.]

GOV. Your course is not to be suffered for. Besides that we find such a course as this to be greatly prejudicial to the state. Besides the occasion that it is to seduce many honest persons that are called to those meetings and your opinions being known to be different from the word of God may seduce many simple souls that resort unto you. Besides that the occasion which hath come of late hath come from none but such as have frequented your meetings, so that now they are flown off from magistrates and ministers and since they have come to you. And besides that it will not well stand with the commonwealth that families should be neglected for so many neighbours and dames and so much time spent. We see no rule of God for this. We see not that any should have authority to set up any other exercises besides what authority hath already set up and so what hurt comes of this you will be guilty of and we for suffering you.

MRS. H. Sir, I do not believe that to be so.

GOV. Well, we see how it is. We must therefore put it away from you or restrain you from maintaining this course.

MRS. H. If you have a rule for it from God's word you may.

GOV. We are your judges, and not you ours and we must compel you to it.

[Here followed a discussion of whether men as well as women attended Hutchinson's meetings. In response to one question, Hutchinson denied that women ever taught at men's meetings.]

DEPUTY GOVERNOR. I would go a little higher with Mrs. Hutchinson. About three years ago we were all in peace. Mrs. Hutchinson from that time she came hath made a disturbance, and some that came over with her in the ship did inform me what she was as soon as she was landed. I being then in place dealt with the pastor and teacher of Boston and desired them to enquire of her, and then I was satisfied that she held nothing different from us. But within half a year after, she had vented divers of her strange opinions and had made parties in the country, and at length it comes that Mr. Cotton and Mr. Vane[11] were of her judgment, but Mr. Cotton had cleared himself that he was not of that mind. But now it appears by this woman's meeting that Mrs. Hutchinson hath so forestalled the minds of many by their resort to her meeting that now she hath a potent party in the country. Now if all these things have endangered us as from that foundation and if she in particular hath disparaged all our ministers in the land that they have preached a covenant of works, and only Mr. Cotton a covenant of grace, why this is not to be suffered, and therefore being driven to the foundation and it being found that Mrs. Hutchinson is she that hath depraved all the ministers and hath been the cause of what is falled out, why we must take away the foundation and the building will fall.

MRS. H. I pray, Sir, prove it that I said they preached nothing but a covenant of works.

DEP. GOV. Nothing but a covenant of works. Why a Jesuit[12] may preach truth sometimes.

MRS. H. Did I ever say they preached a covenant of works then?

DEP. GOV. If they do not preach a covenant of grace clearly, then they preach a covenant of works.

MRS. H. No, Sir. One may preach a covenant of grace more clearly than another, so I said.

DEP. GOV. We are not upon that now but upon position.

MRS. H. Prove this then Sir that you say I said.

DEP. GOV. When they do preach a covenant of works do they preach truth?

MRS. H. Yes, Sir. But when they preach a covenant of works for salvation, that is not truth.

DEP. GOV. I do but ask you this: when the ministers do preach a covenant of works do they preach a way of salvation?

MRS. H. I did not come hither to answer to questions of that sort.

11. Henry Vane, supported by the Antinomians and merchant allies, was elected governor of Massachusetts Bay colony in 1636 and lost that office to Winthrop in 1637.
12. The Society of Jesus (Jesuits) is a Roman Catholic order that places special emphasis on missionary work. The Jesuits were particularly detested by the Puritans for their evangelical efforts in the New World. Jesuits played a prominent role in founding New France, which was just to the north of Massachusetts Bay, and in spreading Catholicism among the Native American nations there. That Catholic, French colony represented both a secular and a sacred rival to the New Englanders.

DEP. GOV. Because you will deny the thing.

MRS. H. Ey, but that is to be proved first.

DEP. GOV. I will make it plain that you did say that the ministers did preach a covenant of works.

MRS. H. I deny that.

DEP. GOV. And that you said they were not able ministers of the New Testament, but Mr. Cotton only.

MRS. H. If ever I spake that I proved it by God's word.

COURT. Very well, very well.

MRS. H. If one shall come unto me in private, and desire me seriously to tell then what I thought of such an one, I must either speak false or true in my answer.

[In this lengthy section, Hutchinson was accused of having gone to a meeting of ministers and accusing them all—except John Cotton—of preaching a covenant of works rather than a covenant of grace. The accusation, if proved, would have been an extremely serious one. Several of the ministers testified that Hutchinson had made this accusation.]

DEP. GOV. I called these witnesses and you deny them. You see they have proved this and you deny this, but it is clear. You said they preached a covenant of works and that they were not able ministers of the New Testament; now there are two other things that you did affirm which were that the scriptures in the letter of them held forth nothing but a covenant of works and likewise that those that were under a covenant of works cannot be saved.

MRS. H. Prove that I said so.

GOV. Did you say so?

MRS. H. No, Sir. It is your conclusion.

DEP. GOV. What do I do charging of you if you deny what is so fully proved?

GOV. Here are six undeniable ministers who say it is true and yet you deny that you did say that they did preach a covenant of works and that they were not able ministers of the gospel, and it appears plainly that you have spoken it, and whereas you say that it was drawn from you in a way of friendship, you did profess then that it was out of conscience that you spake and said, "The fear of man is a snare. Wherefore shall I be afraid, I will speak plainly and freely."

MRS. H. That I absolutely deny, for the first question was thus answered by me to them: They thought that I did conceive there was a difference between them and Mr. Cotton. At the first I was somewhat reserved. Then said Mr. Peters, "I pray answer the question directly as fully and as plainly as you desire we should tell you our minds. Mrs. Hutchinson we come for plain dealing and telling you our hearts." Then I said I would deal as plainly as I could, and whereas they say I said they were under a covenant of works and in the state of the apostles why these two speeches cross one another. I might say they might preach a covenant of works as did the apostles, but to preach a covenant of works and to be under a covenant of works is another business.

DEP. GOV. There have been six witnesses to prove this and yet you deny it.

MRS. H. I deny that these were the first words that were spoken.

GOV. You make the case worse, for you clearly shew that the ground of your opening your mind was not to satisfy them but to satisfy your own conscience.

[There was a brief argument here about what Hutchinson actually said at the gathering of ministers, after which the court adjourned for the day.]

[The next morning.]

GOV. We proceeded the last night as far as we could in hearing of this cause of Mrs. Hutchinson. There were divers things laid to her charge: her ordinary meetings about religious exercises, her speeches in derogation of the ministers among us, and the weakening of the hands and hearts of the people towards them. Here was sufficient proof made of that which she was accused of in that point concerning the ministers and their ministry, as that they did preach a covenant of works when others did preach a covenant of grace, and that they were not able ministers of the New Testament, and that they had not the seal of the spirit, and this was spoken not as was pretended out of private conference, but out of conscience and warrant from scripture alleged the fear of man is a snare and seeing God had given her a calling to it she would freely speak. Some other speeches she used, as that the letter of the scripture held forth a covenant of works, and this is offered to be proved by probable grounds. If there be any thing else that the court hath to say they may speak.

[At this point, a lengthy argument erupted when Hutchinson demanded that the ministers who testified against her be recalled as witnesses, put under oath, and repeat their accusations. One member of the court said that "the ministers are so well known unto us, that we need not take an oath of them."]

GOV. I see no necessity of an oath in this thing seeing it is true and the substance of the matter confirmed by divers. Yet that all may be satisfied, if the elders will take an oath they shall have it given them. . . .

MRS. H. I will prove by what Mr. Wilson hath written[13] that they [the ministers] never heard me say such a thing.

MR. SIMS. We desire to have the paper and have it read.

13. Wilson had taken notes at the meeting between Hutchinson and the ministers. Hutchinson claimed that these notes would exonerate her. They were never produced and are now lost.

MR. HARLAKENDEN. I am persuaded that is the truth that the elders do say and therefore I do not see it necessary now to call them to oath.

GOV. We cannot charge any thing of untruth upon them.

MR. HARLAKENDEN. Besides, Mrs. Hutchinson doth say that they are not able ministers of the New Testament.

MRS. H. They need not swear to that.

DEP. GOV. Will you confess it then?

MRS. H. I will not deny it or say it.

DEP. GOV. You must do one.

[More on the oath followed.]

DEP. GOV. Let her witnesses be called.

GOV. Who be they?

MRS. H. Mr. Leveret and our teacher and Mr. Coggeshall.

GOV. Mr. Coggeshall was not present.

MR. COGGESHALL. Yes, but I was. Only I desired to be silent till I should be called.

GOV. Will you, Mr. Coggeshall, say that she did not say so?

MR. COGGESHALL. Yes, I dare say that she did not say all that which they lay against her.

MR. PETERS. How dare you look into the court to say such a word?

MR. COGGESHALL. Mr. Peters takes upon him to forbid me. I shall be silent.

MR. STOUGHTON. Ey, but she intended this that they say.

GOV. Well, Mr. Leveret, what were the words? I pray, speak.

MR. LEVERET. To my best remembrance when the elders did send for her, Mr. Peters did with much vehemency and intreaty urge her to tell what difference there was between Mr. Cotton and them, and upon his urging of her she said, "The fear of man is a snare, but they that trust upon the Lord shall be safe." And being asked wherein the difference was, she answered that they did not preach a covenant of grace so clearly as Mr. Cotton did, and she gave this reason of it: because that as the apostles were for a time without the spirit so until they had received the witness of the spirit they could not preach a covenant of grace so clearly.

[Here Hutchinson admitted that she might have said privately that the ministers were not able preachers of the New Testament.]

GOV. Mr. Cotton, the court desires that you declare what you do remember of the conference which was at the time and is now in question.

MR. COTTON. I did not think I should be called to bear witness in this cause and therefore did not labour to call to remembrance what was done; but the greatest passage that took impression upon me was to this purpose. The

[43]

elders spake that they had heard that she had spoken some condemning words of their ministry, and among other things they did first pray her to answer wherein she thought their ministry did differ from mine. How the comparison sprang I am ignorant, but sorry I was that any comparison should be between me and my brethren and uncomfortable it was. She told them to this purpose that they did not hold forth a covenant of grace as I did. . . . I told her I was very sorry that she put comparisons between my ministry and theirs, for she had said more than I could myself, and rather I had that she had put us in fellowship with them and not have made the discrepancy. She said she found the difference. . . . And I must say that I did not find her saying they were under a covenant of works, not that she said they did preach a covenant of works.

[Here John Cotton tried to defend Hutchinson, mostly by saying he did not remember much about the events in question.]

MRS. H. If you please to give me leave I shall give you the ground of what I know to be true. Being much troubled to see the falseness of the constitution of the Church of England, I had like to have turned Separatist. Whereupon I kept a day of solemn humiliation and pondering of the thing, the scripture was brought unto me—he that denies Jesus Christ to be come in the flesh is antichrist. This I considered of and in considering found that the papists[14] did not deny him to come in the flesh, nor we did not deny him. Who then was antichrist? Was the Turk antichrist only? The Lord knows that I could not open scripture; he must by his prophetical office open it unto me. So after that being unsatisfied in the thing, the Lord was pleased to bring this scripture out of the Hebrews. He that denies the testament denies the testator, and in this did open unto me and give me to see that those which did not teach the new covenant had the spirit of antichrist, and upon this he did discover the ministry unto me, and ever since, I bless the Lord. He hath let me see which was the clear ministry and which the wrong. Since that time I confess I have been more choice and he hath left me to distinguish between the voice of my beloved and the voice of Moses, the voice of John Baptist and the voice of antichrist, for all those voices are spoken of in scripture. Now if you do condemn me for speaking what in my conscience I know to be truth I must commit myself unto the Lord.

MR. NOWEL. How do you know that that was the spirit?

MRS. H. How did Abraham know that it was God that bid him offer his son, being a breach of the sixth commandment?[15]

DEP. GOV. By an immediate voice.

14. *Papists* is a derisive Protestant term for Roman Catholics, referring to the papacy.
15. The sixth commandment prohibited murder.

MRS. H. So to me by an immediate revelation.

DEP. GOV. How! an immediate revelation.

MRS. H. By the voice of his spirit to my soul. . . .

*[In spite of the general shock that greeted her claim that she had experienced
an immediate revelation from God, Hutchinson went on to state that God had
compelled her to take the course she had taken and that God had said to her, as He
had to Daniel of the Old Testament, that "though I should meet with affliction, yet I
am the same God that delivered Daniel out of the lion's den, I will also deliver thee."]*

MRS. H. You have power over my body but the Lord Jesus hath power over
my body and soul, and assure yourselves thus much: you go on in this
course you begin you will bring a curse upon you and your posterity, and
the mouth of the Lord hath spoken it.[16]

DEP. GOV. What is the scripture she brings?

MR. STOUGHTON. Behold I turn away from you.

MRS. H. But now having seen him which is invisible I fear not what man can
do unto me.

GOV. Daniel was delivered by miracle. Do you think to be deliver'd so too?

MRS. H. I do here speak it before the court. I took that the Lord should deliver
me by his providence.

MR. HARLAKENDEN. I may read scripture and the most glorious hypocrite may
read them and yet go down to hell.

MRS. H. It may be so.

[Hutchinson's "revelations" were discussed among the stunned court.]

MR. BARTHOLOMEW. I speak as a member of the court. I fear that her revelations
will deceive.

[More on Hutchinson's revelations followed.]

DEP. GOV. I desire Mr. Cotton to tell us whether you do approve of Mrs.
Hutchinson's revelations as she hath laid them down.

MR. COTTON. I know not whether I do understand her, but this I say: If she
doth expect a deliverance in a way of providence, then I cannot deny it.

DEP. GOV. No, sir. We did not speak of that.

MR. COTTON. If it be by way of miracle then I would suspect it.

DEP. GOV Do you believe that her revelations are true?

MR. COTTON. That she may have some special providence of God to help her is
a thing that I cannot bear witness against.

DEP. GOV. Good Sir, I do ask whether this revelation be of God or no?

16. The Bible contains several references to punishing subsequent generations, including
Exodus 20:5, Numbers 14:18, and Deuteronomy 5:9.

MR. COTTON. I should desire to know whether the sentence of the court will bring her to any calamity, and then I would know of her whether she expects to be delivered from that calamity by a miracle or a providence of God.

MRS. H. By a providence of God I say I expect to be delivered from some calamity that shall come to me.

[Hutchinson's revelations were further discussed.]

DEP. GOV. These disturbances that have come among the Germans[17] have been all grounded upon revelations, and so they that have vented them have stirred up their hearers to take up arms against their prince and to cut the throats of one another, and these have been the fruits of them, and whether the devil may inspire the same into their hearts here I know not, for I am fully persuaded that Mrs. Hutchinson is deluded by the devil, because the spirit of God speaks truth in all his servants.

GOV. I am persuaded that the revelation she brings forth is delusion.

[All the court but some two or three ministers cried out, "We all believe—we all believe it." Hutchinson was found guilty. Coddington made a lame attempt to defend Hutchinson but was silenced by Governor Winthrop.]

GOV. The court hath already declared themselves satisfied concerning the things you hear, and concerning the troublesomeness of her spirit and the danger of her course amongst us, which is not to be suffered. Therefore if it be the mind of the court that Mrs. Hutchinson for these things that appear before us is unfit for our society, and if it be the mind of the court that she shall be banished out of our liberties and imprisoned till she be sent away, let them hold up their hands.

[All but three did so.]

GOV. Those that are contrary minded hold up yours.

[Only Mr. Coddington and Mr. Colborn did so.]

MR. JENNISON. I cannot hold up my hand one way or the other, and I shall give my reason if the court require it.

GOV. Mrs. Hutchinson, the sentence of the court you hear is that you are banished from out of our jurisdiction as being a woman not fit for our society, and are to be imprisoned till the court shall send you away.

MRS. H. I desire to know wherefore I am banished?

GOV. Say no more. The court knows wherefore and is satisfied.

17. This reference is to the bloody and violent fighting that took place between orthodox Protestants and the followers of the radical Anabaptist John of Leiden in 1534 and 1535.

Questions to Consider

Now that you have examined the evidence, at least one point is clear: the General Court of Massachusetts Bay was determined to get rid of Anne Hutchinson, whether or not she actually had broken any law. They tried to bait her, force admissions of guilt from her, confuse her, browbeat her. Essentially, they had already decided on the verdict before the trial began. So we know that Anne Hutchinson was a threat—and a serious one—to the colony.

And yet the colony had dealt quite differently with Roger Williams, a Puritan minister banished in 1635, also because of his controversial religious beliefs. Williams was given every chance to mend his ways, Governor Winthrop remained his friend throughout Williams' appearances before the General Court, and it was only with great reluctance that the Court finally decided to exile him.

Anne's brother-in-law, Reverend Wheelwright, was banished before her, but his actions were far different than hers. At the close of an afternoon lecture by Reverend Cotton, Wheelwright rose before the crowd to give his own sermon against men who thought living a virtuous life was somehow evidence of their salvation. "The more holy they are," he proclaimed, "the greater enemies they are to Christ." Then he called on the "true" Christians, the ones who still acknowledged the omnipotence of God, to rise up against these "enemies of Christ"—which, he implied, included most of the ministers in Massachusetts and most of the civil authorities: "We must lay loade upon them, we must

kille them with the worde of the Lorde." He was consequently convicted of sedition. Even then the General Court, under Governor Winthrop's leadership, delayed sentencing and sought reconciliation with Wheelwright for months before banishing him.

Why, then, was Anne Hutchinson's case so threatening and her punishment so swift and severe? Obviously, she did pose a religious threat. As you look back through the evidence, try to clarify the exact points of religious disagreement between Hutchinson and the ministers. What specific challenges did she present to Puritan orthodoxy? What was the basis of the argument over covenants of grace and works? What was Hutchinson supposed to have said? Under what circumstances had she allegedly said this? To whom? What was the role of her minister, John Cotton, in the trial?

Remember that Hutchinson's trial took place in the midst of the Antinomian crisis. What social and political threat did Antinomianism pose to the stability of Massachusetts Bay? What threat did it pose to the mission of building a "city upon a hill"? Did Hutchinson say anything in her testimony that would indicate she was an Antinomian? How would you prove whether or not she was?

A pivotal moment in the trial came when Hutchinson announced that she had received an immediate revelation from the voice of God. Why? And why was Anne's likening of herself to Daniel and Abraham so upsetting to

[47]

the Court? What theological beliefs and what social values did she violate with these statements?

Hutchinson's role in the community also came into question during the trial. What do the questions about the meetings she held in her home reveal? Look beyond what the governor and members of the court actually said. Try to imagine what they might have been thinking. How did Hutchinson's meetings pose a threat to the larger community?

Finally, the transcript provides many clues, some subtle and some overt, about the roles of and relationships between men and women in colonial Massachusetts. How did Anne's gender factor into her examination? What

did it mean when Governor Winthrop said: "We do not mean to discourse with those of your sex"? Would the same thing have happened during the proceedings were Anne a man? Or did the fact that Anne was a woman play a crucial role in her treatment before the General Court? What Puritan assumptions about how women should behave and how they should relate to men was Hutchinson accused of violating? Why was this dangerous enough to require her expulsion?

In conclusion, try to put together all you know from the evidence to answer the central question: Why was Anne Hutchinson too dangerous to remain in the Massachusetts Bay Colony?

◆

Epilogue

After her civil case concluded, Anne Hutchinson was kept in Roxbury, under house arrest, during the winter of 1637–1638, awaiting a church court trial. She had been deemed a heretic in the civil trial, so ministers and elders from churches throughout Massachusetts needed to either cleanse her of her sins or, failing that, excommunicate her from the community of saints. The latter is exactly what happened in March 1638. Expelling a congregant was a public affair, just like confirming a saint. The meetinghouse at Boston was packed when Hutchinson was excommunicated. "I not only pronounce you worthy to be cast out, but I do cast you out," proclaimed one of the ministers who participated in the trial, "And in the name of Jesus Christ, I do deliver you up to Satan."

After the civil trial, John Cotton distanced himself from Anne Hutchinson. As to their two-decade-long friendship, he now claimed, "Mistress Hutchinson seldom resorted to me and when she did come to me, it was seldom or never . . . that she tarried long. I rather think she was loathe to resort much to me . . . lest she might seem to learn somewhat from me." He joined the ministers and elders who sat in judgment of her during the church trial. Cotton conceded that when she first came to Massachusetts Hutchinson had "been an instrument for doing some good." But forced to choose between allying with his fellow ministers and defending his protégée, Cotton succumbed to the pressure. "I do admonish you and charge you," he proclaimed, "in the name of

Jesus Christ, in whose place I stand, that you would sadly consider the just hand of God against you, the great hurt you have done to the churches, the great dishonour you have brought to Jesus Christ, and the evil that you have done to many a poor soul."

Most of Anne's supporters had fled Massachusetts or been exiled or silenced in the months following her civil trial. A handful of friends stood with her at the church proceedings; many of them joined her in the new settlement in Rhode Island. She and William were reunited, after living six months apart, in mid-April.

John Winthrop kept himself well informed of his vanquished rival's new life in Rhode Island. When a mild earthquake struck the settlement a few weeks after Anne's arrival, he pronounced the tremor proof of "God's continued disquietude against the existence of Anne Hutchinson." And when the forty-six-year-old suffered a miscarriage, Winthrop—along with Reverend Cotton—publicly proclaimed the "monster" birth proof of Hutchinson's religious heresy. Winthrop counted the number of fetal deformities—thirty—as exactly matching the number of "misshapen opinions" Hutchinson voiced while in Massachusetts Bay. "See how the wisdom of God fitted this judgment to her sin every way," he exclaimed.

In 1642, William Hutchinson died, and Anne moved with her six youngest children to the Dutch colony of New Netherland in what is now the Bronx borough of New York City. The next year, she and all but one of her children were killed in an Indian raid. The leading men of Boston rejoiced at her murder. They saw "God's hand" in her death. "The Lord heard our groans in Heaven," concluded one minister, "and freed us from this great and sore affliction."

Six years after Hutchinson died, in March 1649, John Winthrop passed away, having spent nearly twenty years at the center of political power in Massachusetts Bay. Winthrop believed to the end of his life that he had had no choice but to expel Hutchinson. However, even one of Winthrop's most sympathetic biographers, historian Edmund S. Morgan, described the Hutchinson trial and its aftermath as "the least attractive episode" in Winthrop's long public career.

John Winthrop triumphed over Anne Hutchinson, but he was unable to leave to the Massachusetts Bay Colony a permanent legacy of religious uniformity. The second and third generations of colonists did not always share their parents' zeal for building a model Christian community. New migrants came, bringing different ideas and building new towns. As the colony's size increased and its population diversified, religious conformity became more and more difficult to enforce. Growth and prosperity seemed to foster an increased interest in individual wealth and a corresponding decline in religious fervor. In the mid-seventeenth century, reports of sleeping during sermons, blasphemous language, and growing attention to physical pleasures were numerous, as were election disputes, declining conversions among young people, and intrachurch squabbling.

For more than a century after the founding of the Massachusetts Bay Colony, New Englanders struggled with tensions over drifting toward Arminianism versus reasserting Calvinism. Jeremiads—sermons predicting disasters because of declining religious zeal that were especially popular in the 1660s—offered one example of this pattern. The witchcraft trials that consumed Salem in 1692 provided another.[18] Although the Puritans' congregational church remained the established religion of Massachusetts until 1833—two centuries after the Great Migration—New Englanders had long since abandoned John Winthrop's practical plans for being "knit together in this work" and creating a "city upon a hill." His conviction that America held a special, preordained destiny lingered, though, and lingers still.

18. There are many outstanding books on the Salem witchcraft ordeal. Classics include Carol F. Karlsen, *The Devil in the Shape of a Woman: Witchcraft in Colonial New England* (New York: W.W. Norton, 1987); and Paul Boyer and Stephen Nissenbaum, *Salem Possessed: The Social Origins of Witchcraft* (Cambridge: Harvard University Press, 1974).

CHAPTER

3

From English Servants to African Slaves: Creating Racial Slavery in Colonial Virginia

◆

The Problem

In 1649, in Northampton County, Virginia, an unmarried woman and man, named Mary and William, were found guilty of fornication. As punishment, the couple was sentenced to stand in the Elizabeth River Church and be shamed by parishioners.[1] This was not a rare or even particularly scandalous occurrence. Extramarital sex, though forbidden, was fairly common in early Virginia. In fact, county courts and churchwardens designed specific punishments for the offenses of fornication and adultery (when a married person had sex with someone other than his or her legal spouse). So, Mary and William paid for their wrongdoing in the usual way.

William was a free man and Mary an indentured servant—also very

typical in the colony. The first generation of Virginia settlers faced an almost unspeakable ordeal: relentless deprivation, vicious infighting, and even starvation so bad it led to cannibalism during the terrible winter of 1609–1610. Had the Powhatan Indians actually thought the colonists a threat, they could surely have routed them, ending England's dreams of establishing in Virginia a challenge to Spain's vast New World empire.[2] There was but one glimmer of hope: tobacco. In 1617, Virginia farmers shipped to England their first cargo of tobacco. Though not of a quality to rival Spanish tobacco, Virginia tobacco

1. Edmund S. Morgan, *American Slavery, American Freedom: The Ordeal of Colonial Virginia* (New York: W.W. Norton, 1975), 155.

2. A century before the founding of Jamestown, Spain established its imperial power in Central and South America and the Caribbean. For Virginia's earliest and dreadful origins, see James Horn, *A Land as God Made It: Jamestown and the Birth of America* (New York: Basic Books, 2005).

[51]

◆ CHAPTER 3

From English
Servants to
African Slaves:
Creating Racial
Slavery in Colonial
Virginia

still sold well. Tobacco was fashionable in seventeenth-century Europe, and it addicted the consumer. More than anything else, tobacco allowed the Virginia colony to survive. Over the course of the seventeenth century, the promises of profits and landownership, tied to the growing tobacco market, attracted more and more migrants to Virginia. By the time of Mary and William's prosecution, the colony, which started in 1609 with only 104 settlers, was home to over 15,000 residents. The great majority of this population increase came from immigration from England.

Some colonists came as free men and women, owning their own property, running artisan shops, and trading with Native Americans. Many others migrated as indentured servants: contractually bound to work a certain number of years (usually 5 to 7) for the person who owned their indenture, in exchange for food and shelter. If a servant was lucky enough to survive the period of indenture and to be bound to a master who honored the legal contract, that servant could become free. Often, however, masters invented reasons to extend indentures. If a servant broke a tool, for example, the master charged time for the cost. A female servant getting pregnant was very distressing, because it cut into the time the woman could work and added household expenses. For that reason, the punishment inflicted on a man for fornicating with a servant woman was often greater than if he had extramarital sex with a free woman. This did not, however, appear to be the case with Mary and William.

The Northampton clerk explained their status but records don't designate any extra punishment inflicted on William. (Mary probably had another year added to her indenture, as additional punishment and a hoped-for deterrent.)

The clerk also noted that Mary was black and William was white, but their race had nothing to do with their punishment, either. In the middle of the seventeenth century, Virginia's labor system was dependent on indentured servitude. Some servants, like Mary, were African, but most were English. Some slaves, all of African descent, lived in Virginia, too, but probably not more than a few hundred. They worked alongside white and black servants. Some men of African descent owned their own land and even held indentured servants. Virginia's racial order was fluid in those years. Black and white Virginians worked together and lived together, and couples (like Mary and William) had sex and married across color lines.

But within a generation, Virginia changed profoundly. African slaves replaced English servants as the dominant labor force, and laws and customs hardened the lines between black and white Virginians. Whites were free and blacks became enslaved. By the early decades of the eighteenth century, Virginia was a slave-based society. Slavery was no longer just one form of labor among many; it was the dominant model for labor and for organizing society along racial lines. Slavery permeated every part of Virginia: culture, economy, government, law, family, and religion.

As reflected in the 1649 case against Mary and William, the surviving sources from early Virginia are spotty at best. We don't know Mary's age or her last name or whether William was an artisan or farmer. Indeed, no firsthand sources exist from African Americans who lived in seventeenth-century Virginia, and there are very few materials from English colonists in that era. But if you look closely enough at the surviving evidence you can begin to understand a crucial issue in American history: **How and why did racial slavery develop in colonial Virginia?**

✦

Background

In 1696, English entrepreneurs secured from King James a charter for the Virginia Company of London. Through this company, they hoped to challenge Spanish domination in the New World and to get rich in the process. This was not Englishmen's first attempt at a North American colony. Roanoke had failed utterly a few decades before; the men and women who founded that colony disappeared without a trace in the 1580s.[3] The men the Virginia Company investors convinced to go to America shared many of their dreams of easy wealth and glory. In particular, the first colonists to Virginia—104 settlers arrived in the early summer of 1607— hoped to find gold, like the Spanish had in Central America, and/or a passage to the Far East, and so get access to coveted Asian markets.

There was, alas, no gold in Virginia and no quick route to the Pacific Ocean. Instead, the colonists were met by a powerful Confederation of some

3. The best book on Roanoke is James Horn, *A Kingdom Strange: The Brief and Tragic History of the Lost Colony of Roanoke* (New York: Basic Books, 2010).

20,000 Powhatan Indians. Unprepared and downright unwilling to work for a living, unfamiliar with the dangerous physical environment of the coastal Chesapeake, quick to antagonize the Powhatans, and ill-supplied by the London company, the colonists found themselves in a near deathtrap. As one colonial leader put it, "a world of miseries ensued." By the second winter, Virginia colonists were at the point of starvation. They ate snakes and rats and boiled their shirt collars and shoes before some turned to cannibalism, eating their deceased neighbors. One man killed and salted his own wife, for which he was summarily executed.

In the short term, the colony was saved when a supply ship, bound for Virginia in 1609, wrecked off the coast of the uninhabited island of Bermuda. That happy accident gave the Virginia Company its second colony, and this one thrived while Virginia floundered. The redemption of the Bermuda castaways—no one died despite the shipwreck and being marooned on the small island for ten months—was interpreted in England as providential

◆ CHAPTER 3

From English
Servants to
African Slaves:
Creating Racial
Slavery in Colonial
Virginia

design. God, they concluded, wanted the Protestant English to succeed in the New World (and oppose the Catholic Spanish).[4] So, while nearly every circumstance argued for abandoning Virginia, company leaders resolved to stay the course.

In the long term, tobacco saved Virginia. Tobacco, shipped from Virginia starting in 1617, became the first profitable staple crop in English America. In 1624, the Virginia Company collapsed, and the colony came under royal authority. But that political change did not alter tobacco's importance. Tobacco dominated Virginia's commerce for the entire colonial period. People even paid their taxes in tobacco!

Raising tobacco was both grueling and profitable. Labor demands and profit margins fueled immigration into Virginia. Tobacco farmers needed laborers to produce their tobacco crops— mostly unskilled workers rather than artisans. But unskilled workers did not have the money or wherewithal to get to Virginia. So, tobacco planters sought out middling rank and poor English men and women as indentured servants. In exchange for a passage to America and food and shelter, servants contractually bound themselves to work for a number of years for tobacco planters. (Source 1 is a typical indenture contract.)

Prospective servants knew the work in Virginia would be hard, but they saw moving to the colony as a good opportunity for a fresh start. A poor

person in England had virtually no chance of acquiring land. In fact, they risked being jailed if they fell into debt. In the early modern world, land was the most important marker of status and financial security. So, the idea of someday actually owning land, even if the path seemed long and difficult, was too attractive for many English to pass up. Virginia seemed a place where through hard work and resolve a person could start from nothing and become something. The hopes of servants were stoked by wildly misleading propaganda. As early as the 1610s, when Virginia was basically a death-trap, colonial insiders and promoters circulated pamphlets and stories depicting the colony as a new Eden, a land of milk and honey, where prosperity awaited anyone daring enough to make the passage. The propaganda conveniently failed to mention the Powhatan Indians, the pervasive disease and violence, and the winter of starvation.

By the 1650s, indentured servants were flooding into Virginia. Several thousand migrated every year. Most had signed their indentures in England, so they arrived in the colony legally bound to work for no pay. But not everyone made that choice. Some servants were forced to migrate to Virginia: debtors and criminals shipped abroad to work off their punishments. Corrupt traffickers, called "spirits," also haunted the port cities of England, manipulating and even kidnapping men and women they sold as servants to Virginia planters.

Even for the relatively well-informed, the reality of a servant's

4. For the story of Bermuda, see Lorri Glover and Daniel Blake Smith, *The Shipwreck That Saved Jamestown: The Sea Venture Castaways and the Fate of America* (New York: Henry Holt, 2008).

life in Virginia seldom matched the promises made in England. The tobacco market was volatile, and production of the crop depended on brutality and the ruthless commodifying of human labor and life. Masters were often domineering and violent, the work relentless and exhausting. Many servants in the first half of the seventeenth century did not live long enough in the harsh Virginia environment even to reach the end of their period of indenture. (This, some historians speculate, factored into the decision to pay short-term lower costs for servants rather than make a longer-term, higher investment in slaves.)

In the middle decades of the seventeenth century, servants who survived their lawful period of indenture sometimes found their masters added on time as punishment or even refused to give them the land promised in the contract. Other bondholders behaved honorably, and their former servants were able to prosper as landowning farmers and artisans. But oftentimes, the land granted to former servants turned out to be inferior if not outright unsuitable for a family farm or even located in Indian Country. By the 1640s, the Powhatan Confederation had been pushed westward, away from English settlements. They and other Indian nations continued to resent and resist white encroachment on their territory. So, it could be dangerous, even untenable for poorly supplied former servants to try and defend a specious land claim in the interior regions of Virginia. Faced with such difficulties, many former servants found themselves in debt to and forced to work at low wages for their former masters.

On the other end of the social spectrum was an emerging gentry class: men who owned the best land and profited most from the tobacco trade by systematically exploiting their laborers. These self-styled gentlemen typically held poor people in contempt. They saw servants as dangerous and dishonest and unworthy of joining their rank. To give part of their estate to such individuals, even if contractually required to do so, cut into their own profits and power. Members of the gentry class did not want to supply potential rivals with land, and many tried everything in their power to thwart servants' ambitions. This became increasingly difficult as mortality rates stabilized. In the middle decades of the seventeenth century, more and more servants survived their period of indenture. Planters had to either honor the terms of indenture contracts or risk retribution from their former servants. And they had to always be recruiting new servants while dealing with nearly constant contractual claims for land and money.

The result of former servants' frustrations and former masters' exploitation was a great deal of tumult. In the 1650s and 1660s, Virginia saw a series of uprisings, conspiracies between bondsmen and freeholders (men who owned small farms) to challenge gentry power and even to overthrow the colonial government. William Berkeley, the royally appointed Governor of Virginia from 1642–1652 and 1660–1677, knew exactly where to lay blame. It was all but impossible, he complained, to control "a People wher six parts of seaven at least are Poore Endebted Discontented and Armed."

✦ CHAPTER 3

From English
Servants to
African Slaves:
Creating Racial
Slavery in Colonial
Virginia

This class tension reached a breaking point in 1676. A backcountry farmer named Nathaniel Bacon led the uprising that bore his name. Bacon's Rebellion started as a series of skirmishes with Indian nations in the west. Non-elite colonists envied and routinely violated Indian land rights in the western regions of Virginia. Eastern elites had no desire to spend tax money policing the backcountry, where Bacon and his lower class allies lived, and they did not like such men making trouble with Indians. Bacon, emboldened by an enthusiastic alliance of white and black freemen, servants, and slaves, demanded a military appointment to wage war against Indians in the west. Governor Berkeley knew that backcountry violence would be costly and disruptive to the tobacco trade and was not in the interest of eastern elites. He made a series of political maneuvers, none of which placated Bacon and his followers. Before long, Bacon's band turned their wrath from western Indians to the government in Jamestown. Claiming to speak for "the people," Bacon condemned Governor Berkeley and his elite inner circle as traitors and demanded their arrest (Source 16). Shortly after issuing that declaration, Bacon led a successful coup, forcing Governor Berkeley to flee Jamestown and burning down much of the capital in September 1676. Bacon's sudden death in October from "bloody flux" (dysentery) essentially ended the rebellion. But fear of social instability and another class-based revolution weighed heavy on the minds of Virginia elites.

Some of the men joining Bacon's insurrection were freeholders and bound laborers of African descent. Africans had lived in Virginia since August 1619, but they did not comprise a significant percentage of the population until late in the seventeenth century. During the early decades of the seventeenth century, most men and women of African descent came to Virginia from the Caribbean, where England also developed colonies. They understood English ways and language. Africans were not systematically enslaved in Virginia in this era. The material circumstances and legal status of black freeholders and servants before the 1660s did not appear to differ much from that of their white counterparts. Their lives were often difficult and their labor arduous, and members of the planter class apparently viewed them with disdain— as they did poor whites. In the early and mid-seventeenth century, black and white Virginia laborers seemed to identify with one another as exploited by the gentry class; they ran away and even plotted rebellions together. Only over time, as you will see in Sources 2–10, did that change according to colonial laws.

Although slow to develop in Virginia, slavery was a very familiar labor system. It had a long history in Europe, dating back to the ancient Romans. Slavery also existed in African nations and in indigenous communities in the Americas before the arrival of European colonizers. Both in Africa and the Americas, slavery was very different, however, from what emerged after colonization. Slaves were not held in perpetuity, and slavery was neither inheritable nor racially defined. Many slaves were taken prisoner during wars and eventually integrated into the communities of their captors.

Among sixteenth and seventeenth-century European colonizers, the Dutch took a leading role in human trafficking from African nations. The first Africans arriving in Virginia actually came on a Dutch ship. The Dutch remained key players in the Atlantic slave trade for many decades thereafter.

English colonists in the Caribbean bought into the Atlantic slave trade rather quickly, but that was not the case in Virginia, for a variety of reasons. Tobacco planters in Virginia feared slave rebellions. It was sometimes difficult to acquire slaves from Dutch traders. And it appears that some Virginians calculated the brief life expectancy of early seventeenth-century immigrants when they weighed the short-term costs of hiring a servant against the long-term investment in buying a slave. On the other hand, when mortality rates stabilized and life expectancy rose after the middle of the century, it made more financial sense to invest in slaves. And, unlike frustrated servants, slaves had no expectations than an owner was contractually bound to consider.

Most historians who have studied colonial Virginia agree that slavery grew slowly and fitfully until the last third of the seventeenth century and then surged into the early eighteenth century. Demographic factors of the sort you will consider in Sources 11–15 shaped that transformation in labor.

But why was the labor transformation racialized? Why not enslave the English servants already in Virginia? Or, why not begin to enslave the Irish? The English had conquered Ireland before they set their sights on North America, and they considered the Irish a separate, inferior race of people. Instead, in the last decades of the seventeenth century, Virginia increasingly participated in the African slave trade and gradually instituted a distinctive system of racial slavery. Your challenge is to sort out how and why.

As you consider the evidence in this chapter and try to reach a conclusion about **how and why racial slavery developed in colonial Virginia**, there are a few more things you will want to keep in mind, specifically relating to English imperial policies. In 1660, Parliament passed a Navigation Act that curtailed colonial trade with the Dutch (still the main source of slaves). That same year, England created a company, eventually known as the Royal African Company, and granted it a monopoly over trade in Africa, including slaves. Until 1698, the Royal Africa Company trafficked every person lawfully sold into slavery in an English colony. (English Americans were notorious smugglers, and they routinely bought goods and slaves though illegal networks.) When that monopoly ended, North America saw a significant diversification and growth of slave trafficking: African men and women were now available from many different sources. Finally, in 1682, King Charles II issued a decree regarding indentures in response to the "spirits" duping English men and women. Indenture contracts were no longer valid unless signed in the presence of a magistrate in England. This decreased the number of servants going to Virginia. And, the servants who went after 1682 tended to be better informed, more often skilled at a craft, and less poor and desperate than servants migrating in earlier decades.

◆ CHAPTER 3

From English
Servants to
African Slaves:
Creating Racial
Slavery in Colonial
Virginia

◆

The Method

The evidence in this chapter allows you to explore change over time: in this particular case, the gradual development of racial slavery in colonial Virginia. The surviving evidence regarding the Africans who arrived in Virginia in 1619 does not indicate whether they were free, indentured servants, or sold into slavery. Within a decade or two, clear evidence does reveal Africans being enslaved in Virginia. But even then, the colony was home to free blacks and indentured servants of African descent, and the great majority of unfree laborers continued to be indentured servants coming from Europe. Gradually, between the middle of the seventeenth century and the early decades of the eighteenth century, Virginia moved from being a society with slaves (as well as indentured servants, apprentices, criminals working off their sentences, debtors, and other varied unfree laborers) to a slave society (where slavery was the dominant labor system and society was ordered around slavery).[5]

The slavery system that Virginia settlers created was based wholly on race: only people of African descent were enslaved in the colony. Race is a socially constructed idea, not a fixed reality. Race has no basis in human biology; the only meaning of race is what members of a society assign to

it. So, in colonial Virginia both slavery and race had to be created, in practice and in law. The evidence in this chapter will, if carefully considered, allow you to witness the long process of making racial slavery in the most important colony in North America.

Historians have been deeply curious about slavery in Virginia for a long time and for many reasons. Virginia was the first permanent English colony in the New World and so marked the beginning of the English empire as well as the colonies that eventually broke from England to create the United States. By the early eighteenth century, Virginia was the largest and most populous of all the mainland English settlements. Racial slavery allowed Virginia to prosper, as it did all the English colonies—and, for that matter, Spanish and French colonies, too. By the time of the American Revolution, over 500,000 African American slaves lived in mainland English America, the greatest number in Virginia.

A cohort of Virginia slaveholders played a leading role in the American Revolution. The commander of the Continental Army, George Washington, was a rich slaveholder from Fairfax County. His neighbor George Mason, who owned scores of slaves, wrote the first state constitution and the Virginia Declaration of Rights— the model for other states as well as for the U.S. Bill of Rights. Thomas Jefferson, who owned several hundred slaves over the course of his life, was the architect of the Declaration of

5. Historian Ira Berlin explained this transformation in *Many Thousands Gone: The First Two Centuries of Slavery in North America* (Cambridge: Harvard University Press, 1998).

Independence, and his friend James Madison, another wealthy enslaver, designed the U.S. Constitution. In short, the ideas that framed the American Republic emerged in the great houses of Virginia's slaveholders. Historians, understandably, want to explore and explain how the foundations of the American Republic—human equality, self-government, and individual liberty—could have been designed by men presiding over a brutal system of racial enslavement.

Early American historians almost never have all the evidence they would like, and they often do not have sufficient primary sources to definitely answer their questions. This is definitively true when it comes to understanding colonial Virginia. Unlike their contemporaries in New England, who carefully preserved many essays, speeches, sermons, court proceedings, and personal letters and diaries, Virginia colonists were sporadic at best with their record keeping. In New England, ministers and lay leaders carefully tended to their church records, too, preserving detailed sources of births, baptisms, deaths, and church trials. But Virginians were not nearly as religious as New Englanders; Churches were less numerous and ministers less likely to keep the more modest records generated by their congregations. High mortality rates, widespread disease, and frequent migration also undermined Virginians' ability to preserve family and civic records. Military campaigns during the Revolutionary War and Civil War inadvertently destroyed many historical sources. When residences and county courthouses burned, precious documents were lost forever.

The list of sources we do not have from colonial Virginia can seem daunting. There are no first-person accounts from African American men or women, enslaved or free. There are no written records by Native Americans; everything we know about early contact between Indians and settlers comes from the pens and minds of English colonists. First-hand accounts from white indentured servants are exceedingly rare. Indeed, very few of the English men and women who migrated to Virginia left any personal records at all. The letters, journals, account books, sermons, and essays that survive come from a tiny fraction of the overall population—overwhelmingly from the gentry class.

Rather than discouraged by these evidentiary limitations, historians have been very imaginative in their investigations of colonial Virginia. Legal records and statistics offer two important ways to illuminate the experiences and values of early Virginia colonists and to see how they created slavery and race. Historians have mined surviving tax and probate records, ship manifests, slave auction and plantation account books, and property deeds to piece together statistical summaries of life in colonial Virginia. By charting change over time in wealth, mortality, and population, they can reconstruct important trends in Virginia's history. In this chapter, you will study five such charts, which reveal important demographic patterns that will enable you to begin to understand how and why racial slavery developed in colonial Virginia.[6]

6. Demography is the statistical study of a human population.

[59]

♦ CHAPTER 3

From English
Servants to
African Slaves:
Creating Racial
Slavery in Colonial
Virginia

Legal records, read alongside these statistics, can further add to your understanding. The first legal document you will read is a typical indenture contract from the early seventeenth century. It lays out the legal obligations of the two parties: the person who is becoming a servant and the individuals who hold the indenture. Begin by thinking about how different this contractual relationship is from the lawful ownership of another human being, which happened with slavery. The rest of the legal materials are acts passed by the Virginia government. Such laws reveal both society's values and individuals' behavior—and that the two sometimes collided. You will see in the legal changes over time the intentional and gradual process of differentiating black from white, slave from free. You will also see, in both the statistics and the laws, how Virginia was becoming a slave society.

The last document in this chapter comes from the hand of Nathaniel Bacon, who led the uprising in 1676. It provides a snapshot of Virginia in this critical transitional period, when white Virginians were weighing the costs and benefits of African slavery compared to English servitude.

Balancing these varied sources, reading documents written in early modern English language and spelling, and making sense of the charts may seem difficult at the outset. It might be helpful to form a small study group with a few of your classmates. You can work through the challenging materials together. Each member will likely see and contribute something that the others in your group might miss, thereby broadening everyone's understanding. Remember as you investigate the evidence, either individually or in a group, to keep in mind you are trying to explain change over time and understand how and why Virginia colonists adopted racial slavery as their dominant labor system.

♦

The Evidence

Source 1 from Susan Myra Kingsbury, editor, *Records of the Virginia Company, 1606–1626*, Volume III: Miscellaneous Records, 210–211. Accessed through Library of Congress: http://hdl.loc.gov/loc.mss/mtj.mtjbib026605

1. A 1619 Indenture Contract

September 7, 1619

This Indenture made the seventh day of September. 1619. In the xviith year of the raigne of our soveraigne lord kinge James of England &c. Between Sr. Willm Throkmorton knight and baronet Richard Berkley Esq, George

Thorpe Esq, and John Smith gent on the one [part] And Robert Coopy of Northnibly in the county of Glouc Husbandman on th' other [part]. Witnesseth That the said Robert doth hereby covenant faithfully to serve the said Sr Willm, Richard George and John for three years from date of his landing in the land of Virginia, there to be imployed in the lawfull and reasonable workes and labors of them the said Sr Willm Richard George and John and their assignes, and to be obedient to such governors his and their assistants and counsell as they the said Sr Willm Richard George and John shall from time to time appoint and set over him. In consideracon whereof, the said Sr Willm Richard George and John doe covenant with the said Robert to transport him (with gods assistance) with all convenient speed into the said land of Virginia at their cost and charges in all things, and there to maintain him with convenient diet and apparell meet for such a servant, And in the end of the said term to make him a free man of the said Country theirby to enjoy all the liberties freedomes and priviledges of a freeman there, And to grant to the said Robert thirty acres of land within their Territory or hundred of Barkley in the said land for the term of his life and of two others then by him to be named (if he be then living) under the yearly rent of twelve pence for each acre, and such other reasonable condicons and services as at or before the sealinge thereof shall be agreed between the said [parties]. And to pay each quarter of a year ten shillings to the wife of the said Robert at her house in Northnibly aforesaid towards her maintenance during the said term if he so long live, Wherof is already payd thirty shillings. Given Enterchangeably under their hands and seales the day and year first above written.

Ric: Berkeley (Seal)

Geo: Thorpe (Seal)

John Smyth (Seal)

Sources 2–10 from William Waller Hening, ed., *The Statutes at Large, Being a Collection of All the Laws of Virginia* (Richmond, 1819), volumes 1–3.

2. Virginia Law, Act XXII, March 1660[7]

ACT XXII. *English running away with negroes.*

BEE itt enacted That in case any English servant shall run away in company with any negroes who are incapable of makeing satisfaction by addition of

7. Hening, ed., *The Statutes at Large* 2: 26.

◆ CHAPTER 3

From English
Servants to
African Slaves:
Creating Racial
Slavery in Colonial
Virginia

time,[8] *Bee itt enacted* that the English so running away in company with them shall serve for the time of the said negroes absence as they are to do for their owne by a former act.

3. Virginia Law, Act XII, December 1662[9]

ACT XII. *Negro womens children to serve according to the condition of the mother. (a)*

WHEREAS some doubts have arrisen whether children got by any English-man upon a negro woman should be slave or free, *Be it therefore enacted and declared by this present grand assembly,* that all children borne in this country shall be held bond or free only according to the condition of the mother, *And* that if any christian shall committ fornication with a negro man or woman, he or she so offending shall pay double the fines imposed by the former act.

4. Virginia Law, Act XVIII, September, 1663[10]

ACT XVIII. *An act prohibiting servants to goe abroad without a lycence.*

FOR better suppressing the unlawful meetings of servants, *It is thought fitt and enacted by this present grand assembly and the authority thereof* that all masters of families be enjoyned and take especiall care that their servants doe not depart from their houses on Sundays or any other days without perticuler lycence from them, and that the severall respective counties (as they find cause) to take especiall care to make such by laws within themselves, as by the act dated the third of December 1662, they are impowred as may cause a further restraint of all unlawfull meetings of servants and punish the offenders.

5. Virginia Law, Act III, September 1667[11]

ACT III. *An act declaring that baptisme of slaves doth not exempt them from bondage.*

WHEREAS some doubts have risen whether children that are slaves by birth, and by the charity and piety of their owners made pertakers of the blessed sacrament of baptisme, should by vertue of their baptisme be made free; *It is enacted and declared by this grand assembly, and the authority thereof,* that the conferring of baptisme doth not alter the condition of the

8. This refers to individuals held in lifelong bondage. Servants could have their period of inden-ture extended. Slaves, however, worked until they died with no chance of freedom—and so there was no way to extend their period of enslavement.
9. Hening, ed., *The Statutes at Large* 2: 170.
10. Hening, ed., *The Statutes at Large* 2: 195.
11. Hening, ed., *The Statutes at Large* 2: 260.

person as to his bondage or freedome; that diverse masters, freed from this doubt, may more carefully endeavour the propagation of christianity by permitting children, though slaves, or those of greater growth if capable to be admitted to that sacrament.

6. Virginia Law, Act I, October 1669[12]

ACT I. *An act about the casuall killing of slaves.*

WHEREAS the only law in force for the punishment of refractory servants *(a)* resisting their master, mistris or overseer cannot be inflicted upon negroes,[13] nor the obstinacy of many of them by other then violent means supprest, *Be it enacted and declared by this grand assembly,* if any slave resist his master (or other by his masters order correcting him) and by the extremity of the correction should chance to die, that his death shall not be accounted felony, but the master (or that other person appointed by the master to punish him) be acquit from molestation, since it cannot be presumed that prepensed malice (which alone makes murther felony) should induce any man to destroy his own estate.

7. Virginia Law, Act VIII, September 1672[14]

ACT VIII. *An act for the apprehension and suppression of runawayes, negroes and slaves.*

FOR AS MUCH as it hath been manifested to this grand assembly that many negroes have lately been, and now are out in rebellion in sundry parts of this country, and that no meanes have yet been found for the apprehension and suppression of them from whome many mischeifes of very dangerous consequence may arise to the country if either other negroes, Indians or servants should happen to fly forth and joyne with them; for the prevention of which, *Be it enacted by the governour, councell and burgesses of this grand assembly, and by the authority thereof,* that if any negroe, molatto, Indian slave, or servant for life, runaway and shall be persued by warrant or hue and cry[15], it shall and may be lawfull for any person who shall endeavour to take them, upon the resistance of such negroe, molatto, Indian slave, or servant for life, to kill or wound him or them so resisting. . . . And if it happen that such negroe, molatto, Indian slave, or

12. Hening, ed., *The Statutes at Large* 2: 270.
13. This refers to the extension of a servant's period of indenture.
14. Hening, ed., *The Statutes at Large* 2: 299–300.
15. A warrant authorized a sheriff or other legal official to arrest an accused criminal. A "hue and cry" could be raised by the residents of a community and empowered civilians to participate in apprehending an accused criminal.

◆ CHAPTER 3

From English
Servants to
African Slaves:
Creating Racial
Slavery in Colonial
Virginia

servant for life doe dye of any wound in such their resistance received the master or owner of such shall receive satisfaction from the publique for his negroe, molatto, Indian slave, or servant for life, so killed or dyeing of such wounds; and the person who shall kill or wound by virtue of any such hue and cry any such so resisting in manner as aforesaid shall not be questioned for the same, he forthwith giving notice thereof and returning the hue and cry or warrant to the master or owner of him or them so killed or wounded or to the next justice of peace. *And it is further enacted* by the authority aforesaid that all such negroes and slaves shall be valued at four thousand five hundred pounds of tobacco and caske a piece, and Indians at three thousand pounds of tobacco and caske a piece, And further if it shall happen that any negroe, molatto, Indian slave, or servant for life, in such their resistance to receive any wound whereof they may not happen to dye, but shall lye any considerable time sick and disabled, then also the master or owner of the same so sick or disabled shall receive from the publique a reasonable satisfaction for such damages . . .

8. Virginia Law, Act X, June 1680[16]

ACT X. *An act for preventing Negroes Insurrections.*

WHEREAS the frequent meeting of considerable numbers of negroe slaves under pretence of feasts and buriall is judged of dangerous consequence; for prevention whereof for the future, *Bee it enacted by the kings most excellent majestie by and with the consent of the generall assembly, and it is hereby enacted by the authority aforesaid,* that from and after the publication of this law, it shall not be lawfull for any negroe or other slave to carry or arme himselfe with any club, staffe, gunn, sword or any other weapon of defence or offence, nor to go or depart from of his masters ground without a certificate from his master, mistris or overseer, and such permission not to be granted but upon particular and necessary occasions[17]; and every negroe or slave so offending not haveing a certificate as aforesaid shall be sent to the next constable, who is hereby enjoyned and required to give the said negroe twenty lashes on his bare back well layd on, and so sent home to his said master, mistris or overseer. *And it is further enacted by the authority aforesaid* that if any negroe or other slave shall presume to lift up his hand in opposition against any christian, shall for every such offence, upon due proofe made thereof by the oath of the

16. Hening, ed., *The Statutes at Large* 2: 481–482.
17. Note that Virginia law is now restricting the leniency of enslavers.

party before a magistrate, have and receive thirty lashes on his bare back well laid on. *And it is hereby further enacted by the authority aforesaid* that if any negroe or other slave shall absent himself from his masters service and lye hid and lurking in obscure places, committing injuries to the inhabitants, and shall resist any person or persons that shall by any lawfull authority be imployed to apprehend and take the said negroe, that then in case of such resistance, it shall be lawfull for such person or persons to kill the said negroe or slave so lying out and resisting, and that this law be once every six months published at the respective county courts and parish churches within this colony.

9. Virginia Law, Act III, November 1682[18]

ACT III. *An additionall act for the better preventing insurrections by Negroes.*

WHEREAS a certaine act of assembly held at James City the 8th day of June, in the year of our Lord 1680, intituled, [entitled] an act preventing negroes insurrections hath not had its intended effect for want of due notice thereof being taken; *It is enacted by the governour, councell and burgesses of this generall assembly, and by the authority thereof,* that for the better putting the said act in due execution, the church wardens of each parish in this country at the charge of the parish by the first day of January next provide true copies of this present and the aforesaid act, and make or cause entry thereof to be made in the register book of the said parish, and that the minister or recorder of each parish shall twice every year vizt. some one Sunday or Lords day in each of the months of September and March in each parish church or chappell of ease in each parish in the time of divine service, after the reading of the second lesson, read and publish both this present and the aforecited act under paine such churchwarden minister or reader makeing default, to forfeite each of them six hundred pounds of tobacco, one halfe to the informer and the other halfe to the use of the poore of the said parish. And for the further better preventing such insurrections by negroes or slaves, *Bee it likewise enacted by the authority aforesaid,* that no master or overseer knowingly permitt or suffer, without the leave or licence of his or their master or overseer, any negroe or slave not properly belonging to him or them, to remaine or be upon his or their plantation above the space of four hours at any one time, contrary to the intent of the aforerecited act upon paine to forfeite, being thereof lawfully convicted, before some one justice of peace within the county where the fact shall be comitted, by the

18. Hening, ed., *The Statutes at Large* 2: 492–493.

◆ CHAPTER 3

From English
Servants to
African Slaves:
Creating Racial
Slavery in Colonial
Virginia

oath of two witnesses at the least, the summe of two hundred pounds of tobacco in cask for each time so offending to him or them that will sue for the same, for which the said justice is hereby impowered to award judgment and execution.

10. Virginia Law, Act XVI, April 1691[19]

ACT XVI. *An act for suppressing outlying Slaves.*

WHEREAS many times negroes, mulattoes, and other slaves unlawfully absent themselves from their masters and mistresses service, and lie hid and lurk in obscure places killing hoggs and committing other injuries to the inhabitants of this dominion, for remedy whereof for the future, *Be it enacted by their majesties lieutenant governour, councell and burgesses of this present generall assembly, and the authoritie thereof, and it is hereby enacted,* that in all such cases upon intelligence of any such negroes, mulattoes, or other slaves lying out, two of their majesties justices of the peace of that county . . . where such negroes, mulattoes or other slave shall be . . . are hereby impowered and commanded to issue out their warrants directed to the sherrife of the same county to apprehend such negroes, mulattoes, and other slaves, which said sherriffe is hereby likewise required upon all such occasions to raise such and so many forces from time to time as he shall think convenient and necessary for the effectual apprehending such negroes, mulattoes and other slaves, and in case any negroes, mulattoes or other slave or slaves lying out as aforesaid shall resist, runaway, or refuse to deliver and surrender him or themselves to any person or persons that shall be by lawfull authority employed to apprehend and take such negroes, mulattoes or other slaves that in such cases it shall and may be lawfull for such person and persons to kill and destroy such negroes, mulattoes, and other slave or slaves by gunn or any otherwise whatsoever.

Provided that where any negroe or mulattoe slave or slaves shall be killed in pursuance of this act, the owner or owners of such negro or mulatto slave shall be paid for such negro or mulatto slave four thousand pounds of tobacco by the publique. And for prevention of that abominable mixture and spurious issue which hereafter may encrease in this dominion, as well by

19. Hening, ed., *The Statutes at Large* 3: 86–88.

negroes, mulattoes, and Indians intermarrying with English, or other white women, as by their unlawfull accompanying with one another, *Be it enacted by the authoritie aforesaid, and it is hereby enacted,* that for the time to come, whatsoever English or other white man or woman being free shall intermarry with a negroe, mulatto, or Indian man or woman bond or free shall within three months after such marriage be banished and removed from this dominion forever, and that the justices of each respective county within this dominion make it their perticular care, that this act be put in effectuall execution. *And be it further enacted by the authoritie aforesaid, and it is hereby enacted,* That if any English woman being free shall have a bastard child by any negroe or mulatto, she pay the sum of fifteen pounds sterling, within one month after such bastard child shall be born, to the Church wardens and disposed of for five years, and the said fine of fifteen pounds, or whatever the woman shall be disposed of for, shall be paid, one third part to their majesties for and towards the support of the government and the contingent charges thereof, and one other third part to the use of the parish where the offence is committed, and the other third part to the informer, and that such bastard child be bound out as a servant by the said Church wardens untill he or she shall attaine the age of thirty years, and in case such English woman that shall have such bastard child be a servant, she shall be sold by the said church wardens, (after her time is expired that she ought by law to serve her master) for five years, and the money she shall be sold for divided as is before appointed, and the child to serve as aforesaid.

And forasmuch as great inconveniences may happen to this country by the setting of negroes and mulattoes free, by their either entertaining negro slaves from their masters service, or receiving stolen goods, or being grown old bringing a charge upon the country; for prevention thereof, *Be it enacted by the authority aforesaid, and it is hereby enacted,* That no negro or mulatto be after the end of this present session of assembly set free by any person or persons whatsoever, unless such person or persons, their heirs, executors or administrators pay for the transportation of such negro or negroes out of the country within six months after such setting them free, upon penalty of paying of ten pounds sterling to the Church wardens of the parish where such person shall dwell with, which money, or so much thereof as shall be necessary, the said Church wardens are to cause the said negro or mulatto to be transported out of the country, and the remainder of the said money to imploy to the use of the poor of the parish.

✦ CHAPTER 3

From English
Servants to
African Slaves:
Creating Racial
Slavery in Colonial
Virginia

Source 11 from U.S. Bureau of the Census, *Historical Statistics of the United States* (Washington, DC: U.S. Government Printing Office, 1975), pt. 2, p. 1168; Jim Potter, "Demographic Development and Family Structure," in Jack P. Greene and J.R. Pole, eds., Colonial British America: Essays in the New History of the Early Modern Era (Baltimore: The Johns Hopkins University Press, 1984), p. 138.

11. Population Growth in Virginia, 1640–1770

Year	Whites	Increase (%)	Blacks	Increase (%)	Blacks as % of Total Pop.
1640	10,292	—	150	—	1
1650	18,326	78	405	170	—
1660	26,070	42	950	135	—
1670	33,309	28	2,000	111	6
1680	40,596	22	3,000	50	—
1690	43,701	8	9,345	212	—
1700	42,170	−4	16,390	75	28
1710	55,163	31	23,118	41	—
1720	61,198	11	26,559	15	—
1730	84,000	37	30,000	13	26
1740	120,440	43	60,000	100	—
1750	129,581	8	101,452	69	—
1760	199,156	35	140,570	39	41
1770	259,411	30	187,605	33	42

Source 12 from U.S. Bureau of the Census, Historical Statistics of the United States (Washington, DC: U.S. Government Printing Office, 1975), 1168.

12. Population Growth in Middlesex County, Virginia

	Middlesex County, Virginia: Annual Growth by Race, 1668–1704				
Year	Population		Annual Percentage Change Since Previous Census		
	White	Nonwhite	White	Nonwhite	Both
1650	1	1	—	—	—
1668	825	63	37.3	23.0	37.7
1687	1,337	117	2.5	3.3	2.6
1699	1,374	397	.2	10.2	1.6
1704	1,436	553	.9	6.6	2.3

Source 13 from John C. Coombs, "The Phases of Conversion: A New Chronology of the Rise of Slavery in Early Virginia," *William and Mary Quarterly* 3rd series, volume 68 (July 2011), 355.

13. Slave Ownership Trends, 1651–1700

Slave Ownership Trends in Virginia Officeholder Inventories, 1651–1700			
	No. officeholder inventories with labor	Percent of officeholders with slaves	Percent of officeholders' bound laborers enslaved
1651–60	17	47.1	32.0
1661–70	26	53.8	48.8
1671–80	38	89.5	54.3
1681–90	23	69.6	76.2
1691–1700	45	91.1	90.9

Source 14 from Philip Morgan, *Slave Counterpoint: Black Culture in the Eighteenth-Century Chesapeake and Lowcountry* (Chapel Hill: University of North Carolina Press, 1998), 61.

14. Africans in Virginia Slave Populations, 1700–1800

Africans in the Virginia Slave Populations, 1700–1800			
Year	Total Slaves	Africans	Percentage
1700	13,000	6,500	50
1710	19,500	10,161	52
1720	27,000	12,209	45
1730	40,000	17,530	44
1740	65,000	22,288	34
1750	105,000	22,544	21
1760	140,500	19,236	14
1770	180,500	15,973	9
1780	224,000	10,916	5
1790	293,000	4,740	2
1800	346,000	678	*

*Less than .5%.

◆ CHAPTER 3

From English
Servants to
African Slaves:
Creating Racial
Slavery in Colonial
Virginia

Source 15 from U.S., Bureau of the Census, *Historical Statistics of the United States, Colonial Times to 1970* (Washington, DC, 1975), II, 1189–1191.

15. Tobacco Production and Income, 1705–1775

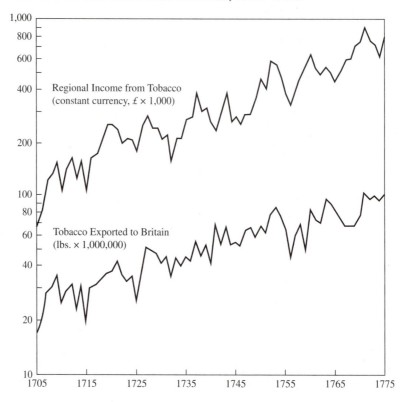

Source 16 from *Virginia Magazine of History and Biography* volume 1 (July 1893), 59–61.

16. Nathaniel Bacon's "Declaration of the People," 1676

THE DECLARATION OF THE PEOPLE.

For having upon specious pretences of Publick works raised unjust Taxes upon the Commonalty for the advancement of private Favourits and other sinnister ends but noe visible effects in any measure adequate.

For not having dureing the long time of his Government in any measure advanced this hopefull Colony either by Fortification, Townes or Trade.

For having abused and rendered Contemptible the Majesty of Justice, of advancing to places of judicature scandalous and Ignorant favourits.

For having wronged his Majesty's Prerogative and Interest by assuming the monopoley of the Beaver Trade.

By having in that unjust gaine Bartered and sould his Majesty's Country and the lives of his Loyal Subjects to the Barbarous Heathen.

For having protected favoured and Imboldened the Indians against his Majesty's most Loyall subjects never contriveing requiring or appointing any due or proper meanes of satisfaction for their many Invasions Murthers and Robberies Committed upon us.

For having when the Army of the English was Just upon the Track of the Indians, which now in all places Burne Spoyle and Murder, and when we might with ease have destroyed them who then were in open Hostility for having expresly Countermanded and sent back our Army by passing his word for the peaceable demeanour of the said Indians, who imediately prosecuted their evill Intentions Committing horrid Murders and Robberies in all places being protected by the said Engagement and word pass'd of him the said Sr William Berkley having ruined and made desolate a great part of his Majesty's Country, have now drawne themselves into such obscure and remote places and are by their successes so imboldened and confirmed and by their Confederacy so strengthened that the cryes of Blood are in all places and the Terrour and consternation of the People so great, that they are now become not only a difficult, but a very formidable Enemy who might with Ease have been destroyed. When upon the Loud Outcries of Blood the Assembly had with all care raised and framed an Army for the prevention of future Mischiefs and safeguard of his Majesty's Colony.

For having with only the privacy of some few favourits without acquainting the People, only by the Alteration of a Figure forged a Commission by we know not what hand, not only without but against the Consent of the People, for raising and effecting of Civil Wars and distractions, which being happily and without Bloodshed prevented.

For having the second time attempted the same thereby, calling downe our Forces from the defence of the Frontiers, and most weak Exposed Places, for the prevention of civil Mischief and Ruine amongst ourselves, whilst the barbarous Enemy in all places did Invade murder and spoyle us his Mats most faithful subjects.

Of these the aforesaid Articles we accuse Sr William Berkely, as guilty of each and every one of the same, and as one, who hath Traiterously attempted, violated and Injured his Majesty's Interest here, by the loss of a great Part of his Colony, and many of his Faithful and Loyal subjects by him betrayed, and in a barbarous and shamefull manner exposed to the Incursions and murthers of the Heathen.

◆ CHAPTER 3

From English
Servants to
African Slaves:
Creating Racial
Slavery in Colonial
Virginia

And we further declare these the Ensueing Persons in this List, to have been his wicked, and pernitious Councellors, Aiders and Assisters against the Commonalty in these our Cruell Commotions

Sr Henry Chicherly, Knt.

Col. Charles Wormley

Phil. Dalowell

Robert Beverly

Robert Lee

Thos. Ballard

William Cole

Richard Whitacre

Nicholas Spencer

Jos. Bridger

William Clabourne

Thos. Hawkins, Juni'r

William Sherwood

Jos. Page, Clerk

Jo. Cliffe, Clerk

Hubberd Farrell

John West

Thos. Reade

Mathew Kemp

And we do further demand, That the said Sr William Berkley, with all the Persons in this List, be forth with delivered up, or surrender themselves, within four days, after the notice hereof, or otherwise we declare, as followed. That in whatsoever house, place, or ship, any of the said Persons shall reside, be hide, or protected, We do declare, that the Owners, masters, or Inhabitants of the said places, to be Confederates, and Traitors to the People, and the Estates of them, as also of all the aforesaid Persons to be Confiscated, This we the Commons of Virginia do declare desiring a prime Union among ourselves, that we may Joyntly, and with one Accord defend ourselves against the Common Enemy. And Let not the Faults of the guilty, be the Reproach of the Innocent, or the Faults or Crimes of ye Oppressors divide and separate us, who have suffered by their oppressions.

These are therefore in his Majesty's name, to Command you forthwith to seize, the Persons above mentioned, as Traytors to ye King and Country, and them to bring to Middle Plantation, and there to secure them, till further Order, and in Case of opposition, if you want any other Assistance, you are forthwith to demand it in the Name of the People of all the Counties of Virginia

[Signed],

NATHANIEL BACON, Gen'l.

By the Consent of ye People.

Questions to Consider

In this chapter, you will practice reading meaning into statistical data. You will also interpret context and consequences using legal sources. Finally, you will read the declaration written by Nathaniel Bacon to better understand the kinds of social turmoil that Virginians experienced in the seventeenth century, as the colony moved from being a society with slaves to a slave society. All of these sources together will help you understand how and why Virginia colonists gradually moved from English servitude to African slavery as their dominant labor system. Understanding that transition will require you to weigh and prioritize multiple factors that shaped change over time.

As you and your classmates work through the evidence to try and develop thoughtful interpretations of this important issue, not everyone will agree. This is perfectly reasonable. Professional historians disagree too, because the available evidence is limited and points in sometimes contradictory directions.[20] In particular, historians of early Virginia have long disagreed over which came first: slavery or racism. Did white Virginians enslave people of African descent because of long-held, deep-seated racial prejudices? Or, did participating in the existing system of African slavery and witnessing the debasement of slaves foster racial biases? Historians also disagree about how to interpret legal changes in colonial Virginia. Should laws be seen as efforts of the most politically powerful people to change the behavior of non-elite black and white Virginians? Or, do the statutes reflect a broad-based consensus about how race relations should operate? Are laws proactive or reactive?

Such disagreements often occur when we seek to understand complex issues; by definition they defy simple answers. History can teach you the invaluable skill of developing reasonable interpretations while respecting differing perspectives.

As you seek to understand the transition from servitude to slavery, you will want to keep in mind some key information about Virginia's main cash crop, tobacco. Tobacco is an extremely labor intensive crop, requiring nearly continuous hoeing and worming as well as topping the plants (to prevent flowering and stimulate growth) and suckering (removing new growth to force the plant's energy into existing leaves). Harvesting tobacco required physically exhausting cutting, hanging, stripping, and packing into large barrels, called hogsheads, for shipping to international

20. Several outstanding digital humanities projects are available for students curious to learn more about seventeenth-century Virginia and the emergence of racial slavery. Virtual Jamestown (www.virtualjamestown.org) offers the most complete collection of accurately transcribed print sources from the period. The Geography of Slavery website (www2.vcdh.virginia.edu/gos), includes a wealth of material, including Virginia laws passed about slavery, newspaper advertisements for slave sales, and records from the House of Burgesses. The Trans-Atlantic Slave Trade Database (www.slavevoyages.org) provides information on 35,000 slave voyages and nearly 100,000 individuals trafficked from Africa to the Americas.

✦ CHAPTER 3

From English
Servants to
African Slaves:
Creating Racial
Slavery in Colonial
Virginia

markets. It took nearly a year to bring a tobacco crop to market, and it was quite a complicated process, requiring specialized knowledge and vigilance. Tobacco plants depleted nutrients in the soil very quickly, so planters were often moving to new land, pushing into dangerous regions of Virginia and requiring the burdensome task of clearing fields. And Virginia's tobacco fields were dangerous. Insect-born diseases such as malaria, brackish water, and epidemics of smallpox and dysentery made life difficult and short for most seventeenth-century Virginians.

Start with the statistical tables. When analyzing statistics, look at each table individually and ask the following questions:

1. What exactly does the set of statistics measure?
2. How did the data change over time?
3. Why might this change have taken place?

The answer to this last question may be found in another table or it might require greater speculation on your part.

The first table attempts to recreate the population of Virginia between the middle of the seventeenth century and the eve of the American Revolution. We know that population growth varied significantly by region, so the second table looks at a shorter period of time and only at Middlesex County, which was north of Williamsburg bordering the Rappahannock River. What can these two charts reveal about population growth in Virginia? How did the racial composition of the colony and this single county change over time?

When did the most important population changes take place?

The next table shows slave ownership trends among men who held public office in the second half of the seventeenth century. What is the difference between the two statistical sets: percentage of officeholders with slaves versus percentage of officeholders' bound laborers who were enslaved? What does this table reveal to you about the connection between political power and slave ownership? What does it reveal about the transition from servitude to slavery? When do the most important changes take place?

Next, you encounter a chart revealing the percentage of Africans in the Virginia slave population in the eighteenth century. Philip Morgan, the historian who created this table, studied slave importation patterns in Virginia to see what percentage of the slave community was captured in Africa and transported to America and what percentage was born in Virginia. This chart, then, reveals patterns of natural increase—that is, when slave mothers bore enough children to offset deaths, thus curtailing the need for human trafficking across the Atlantic. What can you infer about slavery in Virginia from this data? What might this information reveal about wealth and social stability, from the point of view of enslavers? What might it reveal about African American families and communities, from the point of view of the enslaved?

The last chart shows tobacco exports and income, in roughly the same time period. How important was tobacco to eighteenth-century Virginians? What was the relationship between tobacco and slavery and the success of the colony of Virginia?

Considering all the statistical evidence together, what general interpretations can you make? How did populations change over time? How did tobacco culture factor into other changes? When and why did slavery likely supplant servitude? Remember, answering some of these questions will require a good deal of speculation.

Now, turn to the legal sources. How exactly did servitude differ from slavery? What specific legal changes did Virginia legislators adopt to make slaves' status different from that of white servants? What legal methods did white Virginians use to create racial differences? When did those changes occur? Why do the laws get more complicated over time? How were non-slaveholders, ministers, and magistrates drawn into policing slavery?

Weigh the statistical and legal sources together. Do the laws confirm or contradict the opinions you formed when looking just at the tables? What are the comparable advantages of statistics versus law? Is one kind of evidence more meaningful or compelling than the other?

Now consider Bacon's Rebellion and his "Declaration of the People." What was changing in Virginia demographics on the eve of Bacon's Rebellion? What was changing in Virginia's labor and slave laws in that era? How did demographics and laws change after 1676? How important do you think Bacon's Rebellion was in the transition to racial slavery?

Finally, weigh all the evidence in this chapter to reach some conclusions about how and why racial slavery developed. From the point of view of enslavers, what advantages did they see to a perpetual, racialized labor system? Why did two things that were fluid and varied—labor status and race—become so rigid? When do you think racial slavery was firmly established? How, exactly, were white Virginians able to create such a system? Was the switch more about economics, labor control, or racism?

◆

Epilogue

By the middle of the eighteenth century, Virginia was thriving as a slave society. Elite men presided over vast plantations, turning profits from slave-produced agricultural commodities, most importantly, tobacco. To expand their lucrative slave-based commercial agriculture, they claimed more and more land from Indian nations, which were weakened by decades of epidemics, warfare, and trade and diplomatic manipulation. The estates acquired by some families were staggering. When Robert "King" Carter died in 1732, he owned nearly 300,000 acres of land in Virginia, and perhaps as many as 1000 slaves. The Fairfax family claimed an incredible five million acres, running

◆ CHAPTER 3

From English
Servants to
African Slaves:
Creating Racial
Slavery in Colonial
Virginia

from the Northern Neck of Virginia into the Shenandoah Valley. The Carter and Fairfax families were exceptional, to be sure. George Washington was more typical of Virginia's large planters. He eventually owned 50,000 acres of land—a small figure when compared with the Fairfax family but still an impressive estate that made him very wealthy.

Self-styled gentlemen built lavish houses on their plantation estates, choosing to set their mansions on high places with majestic vistas—Thomas Jefferson's Monticello offers a perfect example. Rich families decorated their houses with imported furniture and commissioned works of art. For instance, when George Washington married Martha Custis in 1759, they ran through tens of thousands of dollars furnishing their home, Mount Vernon, and their gentry lifestyle. They imported exotic foods from around the world, including anchovies, capers, almonds, and mangoes, and bought expensive furniture, curtains, glassware, and specially designed dishes. The couple wore corduroy from India, linen from Ireland, lace from Brussels.[21]

Mostly, though, Virginians bought goods they thought symbolized their English identity—this was of paramount importance to colonial Americans in the early and mid-eighteenth century. Far from imagining themselves separating from the mother country, colonial Americans took tremendous pride in their English

identity and worried about not being "English" enough to impress their friends and business partners in the imperial center. Virginians understood that no matter how much money they made through tobacco and land speculation, they could never really rival the landed aristocracy of England. But they could wear English clothes, read English literature, and drink English tea, performing for themselves and their neighbors that they were respectable English men and women.[22]

In addition to replicating English gentility, planter estates dotting the mid-eighteenth-century Virginia landscape were designed to be self-sufficient, containing everything necessary to run the owners' commercial and farming operations and to provide for scores of residents: white relatives and black slaves. Plantations typically contained stables, vegetable gardens, blacksmith shops, tanneries, orchards, carpentry shops, and even distilleries—all worked by enslaved African Americans. Gentry families used their plantations and the slaves laboring on them to project an image of independence, mastery, and self-sufficiency.

Elite men carried those values into local government, where they held positions of power based on family wealth and reputation (which, in turn, derived from slave ownership). Slaveholding planters controlled the local church vestries, county courts, and colony-wide offices. In particular, they

21. George and Martha Washington kept copies of the orders they placed and the bills they received. You can read their shopping lists and expenditures in the George Washington Papers at www.founders.archives.gov.

22. The centrality of English identity to colonial Americans was convincingly explored in T.H. Breen, "An Empire of Goods: The Anglicization of Colonial America, 1690–1776," *The Journal of British Studies* 26 (October 1986): 467–499.

dominated the Virginia House of Burgesses, the locally-elected legislative branch of the colonial government. The Burgesses were supposed to work with the royally appointed Council and the Royal Governor of Virginia, in a mixed form of government akin to the English system of King, House of Lords, and House of Commons. But over the course of the early eighteenth century, the Burgesses assumed more and more authority, such as the power to pay royally-appointed officials, including the governor. And collectively, Virginia's planters imagined themselves fully in charge of the colony's future, as they were individually on their own estates.

Slavery underlay all of this: the economy, culture, and political structure of eighteenth-century colonial Virginia. Everything elite Virginians had and did came though slave labor. Their core values derived from their enslavement of others, too.

Despite profiting from the brutal exploitation of African Americans, by the 1740s and 1750s many Virginia planters found themselves indebted to English merchants. They usually bought their imported china and fashionable clothes on credit, based on projected profits from the next year's tobacco crop. But tobacco was a difficult crop to raise, susceptible to unpredictable fluctuations in weather. If it rained too much or too little, the yield could be off—sometimes very far off. The international tobacco market was unpredictable, too. The result: Virginia planters led lifestyles they really couldn't afford, financed through credit extended by English merchants.

Beginning in 1763, leaders in the imperial center needed to regularize commercial policy in their North American colonies and tried to bring the provinces, including Virginia, under greater imperial authority. In response, over the next decade North Americans periodically erupted in episodes of civil unrest and sometimes violent resistance against their government's policy innovations. They pronounced the new laws unacceptable violations of their rights as English subjects. (You will learn more about this period of American history and explore a specific incident in the next chapter.) Slaveholding Virginians numbered among the ringleaders of these revolts. "How is it," the English write Samuel Johnson wondered, "that we hear the loudest yelps for liberty from the drivers of Negroes?"

Virginia slaveholders routinely condemned the new imperial policies, especially taxes, as part of a conspiracy to "enslave" English Americans. For example, in his "Liberty or Death" speech in March 1775, in reaction to Parliament closing the port of Boston and shutting down the Massachusetts legislature, Patrick Henry—who owned dozens of slaves—asked: "Is life so dear, or peace so sweet, as to be purchased at the price of chains and slavery?" "Our chains are forged," he warned, without even a hint of irony. "Their clanking may be heard on the plains of Boston!"

Slaveholding Virginians led the North Americans in creating the first independent state government, in writing the first bill of rights to protect individual liberty, in prosecuting the War for Independence, and in designing the Declaration of Independence and the

♦ CHAPTER 3

From English
Servants to
African Slaves:
Creating Racial
Slavery in Colonial
Virginia

U.S. Constitution. How could that be? How could the very men pledging their lives, fortunes, and sacred honor to the radical idea of human equality hold hundreds of men and women in perpetual bondage? How could a brutal, exploitative labor system exist alongside high-minded principles of freedom and independence?

One of America's most respected historians, the late Edmund S. Morgan, argued that the explanation could be found in late seventeenth-century Virginia with the transition to racial slavery. Laws and customs created in that period fostered deep convictions of black inferiority and white solidarity. Race replaced class as the basic divide in colonial Virginia. Men of Thomas Jefferson and James Madison's generation could imagine that all white men were free and equal because, no matter how poor and powerless, they would never be black and enslaved. That some white men owned 500,000 acres of land and some owned nothing at all did not matter nearly so much as that all white men were free; there was a cultural and ideological equality in whiteness that overwhelmed any material and economic reality. Even the poorest white person, just by virtue of skin tone, held a self-evident advantage over every African American. The underclass in Virginia was permanently enslaved, debased and distanced by race. Men like Jefferson, Madison, and Washington also saw the denial of freedom every day in their own homes. They only had to look around their houses or walk out their front doors to see the cruelty and violations of enslavement, which made them extraordinarily vigilant about protecting their own rights. During the Revolutionary era, Virginians saw the world as enslaved or free, as black or white. They read that worldview into the patriot movement in the 1760s and 1770s and, eventually, into the design of the American Republic. At the close of his field-defining book, *American Slavery, American Freedom,* Professor Morgan raised powerful questions about the long-term legacy of Virginia that are still worth asking: "Was the vision of a nation of equals flawed at the source by contempt for both the poor and the black? Is America still colonial Virginia writ large?"[23]

23. Morgan, *American Slavery, American Freedom*, 387.

CHAPTER

4

What Really Happened in the Boston Massacre? The Trial of Captain Thomas Preston

✦

The Problem

On the chilly evening of March 5, 1770, a small group of boys taunted a British sentry (called a *centinel* or *sentinel*) in front of the Boston Custom House. Pushed to the breaking point by this goading, the soldier struck one of his tormentors with his musket. Soon a crowd of fifty or sixty Bostonians gathered around the frightened soldier, prompting him to call for help. The officer of the day, Captain Thomas Preston, and seven British soldiers hurried to the Custom House to protect the sentry.

Upon arriving at the Custom House, Captain Preston must have sensed the precariousness of his position. The crowd had swelled past one hundred, some spoiling for a fight, others simply curiosity seekers, and still others called from their homes by the town's church bells, a traditional signal that a fire had broken out—a dreadful sound

for Boston's narrow streets lined with wooden homes and businesses. Efforts by Preston and others to calm the crowd proved useless. In fact, Preston and his men found themselves surrounded, too, so that retreat was nearly impossible.

What happened next was and remains a subject of considerable controversy. Direct participants gave contradictory reports of what transpired and who was to blame. A few facts are clear. One of the British soldiers fired his musket into the crowd, and others followed suit. The colonists scattered, leaving four dead, a fifth mortally wounded, and others injured, some of whom were probably innocent bystanders.[1] Preston and his men

1. Those killed were Crispus Attucks (a seaman in his forties, of African and Native

[79]

◆ CHAPTER 4

What Really
Happened in the
Boston Massacre?
The Trial of
Captain Thomas
Preston

quickly returned to their barracks, where they were placed under house arrest. They were later taken to jail and charged with murder.

Preston's trial did not begin until October 24, 1770, delayed by Massachusetts authorities in an attempt to cool the emotions of the townspeople. The anger of most Bostonians, however, did not abate. The day after what some people immediately began calling "the massacre," an enormous town meeting insisted that the British troops be removed, a demand that Lieutenant Governor (and acting Governor since his royally appointed superior was in London) Thomas Hutchinson rejected. That same day, witnesses began to appear before the town's justices of the peace to give sworn depositions of their versions of what had taken place, depositions that leaked out in a pamphlet undoubtedly published by anti-British radicals.[2] Then, on March 8, a massive funeral procession of 10,000 to 12,000 mourners—over half of all Boston residents—accompanied the four caskets

to the burial ground.[3] From the pulpits of Massachusetts churches, ministers excoriated Preston and his men while grieving the "victims to the murderous rage of Wicked men." By the end of March, Paul Revere's inflammatory engraving (Source 4 in the Evidence section of this chapter) appeared in the *Boston Gazette*. When Preston's trial finally began seven months after these events, emotions were still running high.

Massachusetts attorneys John Adams, Josiah Quincy, and Robert Auchmuty agreed to defend Preston, even though the first two were staunch Patriots.[4] They believed that the captain was entitled to a fair trial and did their best to defend him. After a difficult jury selection, the trial began, witnesses for the prosecution and the defense being called mostly from those who had given depositions. They told very different stories about that fateful night. The trial lasted four days, an unusually long trial for the times. The case went to the jury at 5:00 P.M. on October 29. Although it took the jury only three hours to reach a verdict, the decision was not announced until the following day. Captain Preston's case was decided, but questions about that March night lingered long after the verdict.

In this chapter, you will be using firsthand accounts, evidence given at the murder trial of Captain Thomas

---

American descent, who also went by the name of Michael Johnson), James Caldwell (a sailor), Patrick Carr (an Irish immigrant who worked as a leather-breeches maker), Samuel Gray (a rope maker), and Samuel Maverick (a seventeen-year-old apprentice). For the best overview of these events and the trials and aftermath, see Hiller B. Zobel, *The Boston Massacre* (New York: W.W. Norton, 1996 reprint).
2. For the ninety-six depositions, see *A Short Narrative of the Horrid Massacre in Boston* (Boston: Edes and Gill, 1770). Thirty-one depositions were taken by those favorable to Preston, delivered to London, and published as *A Fair Account of the Late Unhappy Disturbance at Boston* (London: B. White, 1770).

3. Patrick Carr lived until March 14.
4. Adams, Quincy, and Auchmuty also were engaged to defend the soldiers, a practice that would not be allowed today because of the conflict of interest (defending more than one person charged with the same crime).

Preston, and visual images to answer the question: **What actually happened on that March evening in Boston, Massachusetts?** Was Preston guilty of commanding his men to fire into the crowd, as some witnesses said? Or was he an innocent victim of mob violence and rumor-mongering, as others maintained? How could eyewitnesses see the events of that night so differently? Only by reconstructing the event that we call the Boston Massacre will you be able to answer these questions.

Background

Angry conflict between residents of the town of Boston and British officials was nothing new in the spring of 1770.[5] Tensions had been building since the early 1760s, when the Massachusetts colony became a hotbed of opposition to imperial policy innovations.

Throughout the eighteenth century, colonists in British North America profited from and took great pride in their inclusion in the British Empire. Today, Americans often remember the colonial period as just a lead-in to the Revolution, forgetting the strong identification of white colonists with all things English. Far from seeking separation from Great Britain, colonial leaders in the early eighteenth century worked toward building closer connections to the mother country. Military protection, trade goods, and colonists' identity depended on England. The imperial center and the American colonies shared a relationship no one in North America seriously questioned before the 1760s.

After the Seven Years War (which actually ran from 1754 to 1763 and is sometimes called the French and Indian War), both colonial and English attitudes shifted dramatically. England, though victorious in the war, emerged deeply in debt and stunned at the truculence of colonists who refused to follow English command during battle. Both economic necessity—the interest alone on the war debt was nearly bankrupting England—and the desire for imperial order led Parliament to pass new laws concerning North America. Colonists, imbued with a new sense of accomplishment because of their participation in the military victory, bristled at the fiscal policies passed by Parliament. The first conflict between England and its North American colonies came in 1763, when Parliament closed western lands to colonists. New taxes on sugar led to more anger the following year. Then, in 1765, Parliament

---

5. Although Boston was one of the largest urban centers in the colonies, the town was not incorporated as a city. Several attempts were made, but residents opposed them, fearing they would lose the institution of the town meeting.

[81]

✦ CHAPTER 4

What Really
Happened in the
Boston Massacre?
The Trial of
Captain Thomas
Preston

passed the Stamp Act, levying a tax on all commercial and legal paper used in North America. American radicals responded through their colonial legislatures as well as with civic unrest. More turmoil emerged when new taxes, called the Town-shend Duties, were levied in 1767. During these tumultuous years, Americans invented the boycott, us-ing cooperative economic behavior to undermine laws they found unfair. Merchants signed non-importation agreements, refusing even to trade with England in certain goods—an audacious move given the fact that trade was the main reason for a na-tion to have colonies. Representatives from across North America began to gather together in inter-colonial meetings, seeing for the first time their shared interests in thwarting the policies of their government. Citi-zens paraded, protested, formed vigi-lante groups like the Sons of Liberty, attacked the homes and businesses of English officials and burned them in effigy, and threatened—and occasion-ally followed through with—tarring and feathering men who supported the new English laws. Leaders in Par-liament read this all as further evi-dence of the lawlessness of American colonists and their disloyalty to their mother country. Radicals in North America believed the economic policy innovations threatened their rights as English citizens and that they had a duty, as good English subjects, to stand against the injustice. In the face of such tyranny, they believed, "submission is a crime."

Nowhere was outrage over perceived violations greater nor opposition organization stronger than in Boston, Massachusetts. In the 1760s, men like Samuel Adams succeeded in encour-aging fellow Bostonians to get ever bolder in their protests: both legally through the Massachusetts legisla-ture and extra-legally in the streets of Boston. In response, in 1768, the British government ordered two regiments of soldiers to Boston to restore order and enforce the laws of Parliament. Some 4000 troops began to occupy a town of around 20,000 residents. Know-ing the colonists better than did the British government, three years ear-lier Benjamin Franklin had quipped, "They will not *find* a rebellion; they may indeed *make* one."[6]

Instead of bringing calm to Boston, the presence of soldiers, as Franklin had predicted, only increased ten-sions. Clashes between Bostonians and British soldiers were common on the streets, in taverns, and at the places of employment of soldiers who sought part-time jobs to supplement their meager salaries. Known British sympathizers and informers were harassed and Crown officials—most notably, Thomas Hutchinson—were openly insulted. Indeed, the town of Boston seemed to be a powder keg just waiting for a spark to set off an explosion.

6. For Franklin's statement, see "Testimony to the House of Commons, February 13, 1766," quoted in Walter Isaacson, *Benjamin Franklin, An American Life* (New York: Simon and Schuster, 2003), 230.

On February 22, 1770, British sympathizer and informer Ebenezer Richardson tried to tear down an anti-British sign. He was followed to his house by an angry crowd that proceeded to taunt him and break his windows with stones. One of the stones struck Richardson's wife. Enraged, he grabbed a musket and fired almost blindly into the crowd. Eleven-year-old Christopher Seider fell to the ground with eleven pellets of shot in his chest.[7] The boy died eight hours later. The crowd, by now numbering about one thousand, dragged Richardson from his house and through the streets, finally delivering him to the Boston jail. Four days later, the town conducted a huge funeral for Christopher Seider, probably arranged and organized by Samuel Adams. Seider's casket was carried through the streets by children, and approximately two thousand mourners took part. All through the next week gangs of men and boys roamed the streets at night looking for British soldiers foolish enough to venture out alone. Similarly, off-duty soldiers prowled the same streets looking for someone to challenge them. A fight broke out at a ropewalk between some soldiers who worked there part time and some unemployed colonists. Tempers grew even uglier, and only two days before the violent clash, British Lieutenant Colonel Maurice Carr complained to the Lieutenant Governor "of the

frequent abuses offered to his men, and of very insolent, provoking language given to some of them."[8]

Colonial American towns were rarely placid; demonstrations and riots were almost regular features of the colonists' lives. Destruction of property and burning of effigies were common in these disturbances. In August 1765, for example, Boston crowds protesting against the Stamp Act burned an effigy of Andrew Oliver, the stamp tax collector, and spent several hours dismantling the home of Lieutenant Governor Thomas Hutchinson.[9] Physical assaults on people, however, were quite rare. The restrained, ritualized, often theatrical violence of the radicals proved a brilliant move. Their carefully calibrated conduct mocked and belittled royal officials, setting them apart from other citizens, but no one got seriously hurt, which would have turned public opinion against their cause. Most of the Boston community either actively supported or at least countenanced demonstrations and riots as long as they were confined to parades, loud gatherings, and limited destruction of property. The result

7. Christopher Seider is sometimes referred to as Christopher Snider.

8. Thomas Hutchinson, *The History of the Colony and Province of Massachusetts-Bay,* ed. Lawrence Shaw Mayo, three volumes (Cambridge: Harvard University Press, 1936), 3: 195. For accounts of the fight at the ropewalk, see *A Short Narrative,* 17–20.

9. Hutchinson, *The History of the Colony and Province of Massachusetts-Bay*, 3: 88–91. See also Edmund S. Morgan and Helen M. Morgan, *The Stamp Act Crisis: Prologue to Revolution* (Chapel Hill: University of North Carolina Press, 1953), 123–127.

◆ CHAPTER 4

What Really
Happened in the
Boston Massacre?
The Trial of
Captain Thomas
Preston

was that in almost no cases were there any deaths, and authorities almost never fired into the crowds, no matter how loud and demonstrative they became. Yet on March 5, 1770, both the crowd and the soldiers acted uncharacteristically. The result was the tragedy that colonists dubbed the "Boston Massacre." Why did the crowd and the soldiers behave as they did?

To repeat, your task is to reconstruct the so-called Boston Massacre so as to understand what really happened on that fateful evening. Spelling and punctuation in the evidence have been modernized only to clarify the meaning.

◆

The Method

Many students (and some historians) like to think that facts speak for themselves. This is particularly tempting if analyzing a single incident like the Boston Massacre, when so many people testified at the trial. However, discovering what really happened, even when there are eyewitnesses, is never quite that easy. Witnesses may be confused at the time; they may see only part of the incident; they may subconsciously "see" only what they expect to happen; or their memories might unintentionally change after talking with other people.[10] Obviously, witnesses also may have reasons to lie. Thus the testimony of witnesses must be carefully scrutinized. Therefore, historians approach such testimony with considerable skepticism and are concerned not only with the testimony itself but also with the possible motives of the witnesses.

Of the 81 people who gave depositions to the justices of the peace, only 15 were called by the crown as witnesses. Many of those not called maintained that the soldiers had planned the March 5 incident and, after the shootings, "seemed bent on a further massacre of the inhabitants." On the other side, several pro-Preston deponents asserted that the colonists had planned the incident and intended to attack the main barracks. None of these depositions could be admitted as evidence in the trial because these individuals were not formally called as witnesses, but the publication of their accounts in pamphlets meant that the jurors almost surely knew about them.[11]

10. For analysis of these issues, see Peter B. Ainsworth, *Psychology, Law, and Eyewitness Testimony* (Hoboken: John Wiley and Sons, 1998).

11. For examples of unreliable depositions, see *A Short Narrative,* 14–29.

As for Preston himself, neither he nor the soldiers were allowed to testify at his trial. English legal custom prohibited defendants in criminal cases from testifying on their own behalf, the expectation being that they would perjure themselves. But his voice is not silent in the sources. In late April, an account by Preston, probably written the week after the event, appeared in a London newspaper. In June, copies of that newspaper arrived in Boston, where a local newspaper quickly reprinted the article, titled "Case of Capt. Thomas Preston." It sparked new outrage in the town. Preston's narrative was not introduced at trial, but since it was published in newspapers, the jury very likely knew what he said about the night of March 5. For that reason, we have reproduced a portion of Preston's account. How does it agree or disagree with other eyewitness accounts?[12]

Three months before his trial was scheduled to begin, Preston complained to his commanding general that witnesses favorable to him "are being spirited away or intimidated into silence." While intimidation of potential witnesses would not have been unlikely, especially since their depositions had been published, there is no corroborating evidence to support Preston's charge.[13]

No transcript of Preston's trial survives, if indeed one was ever made. Trial testimony comes from an anonymous person's summary of what each person said; the notes of Robert Treat Paine, one of the lawyers for the prosecution; and Richard Palmes, a witness who reconstructed his testimony and cross-examination. Although historians would prefer to use the original trial transcript and would do so if one were available, the anonymous summary, Paine's notes, and Palmes's recollections are acceptable substitutes because probably all three people were present in the courtroom (Paine and Palmes certainly were) and the accounts tend to corroborate one another.

Almost all the witnesses were at the scene, yet not all their testimony is of equal merit. In an effort to sort all this out, first try to reconstruct the scene itself: the actual order in which the events occurred and where the various participants were standing. Whenever possible, look for corroborating testimony—that of two or more reliable witnesses who heard or saw the same things. Be careful to consider all the evidence. You should be able to develop some reasonable explanation for the conflicting testimony and those

12. Preston's statement appeared in London's *Public Advertiser* on April 28, 1770, and by the *Boston News-Letter,* as *The Massachusetts Gazette Extraordinary,* on June 21, 1770. It also ran in the *Boston Gazette* on June 25, 1770.

13. For Preston's charge, see Preston to Thomas Gage, August 6, 1770, in Randolph G. Adams, "New Light on the Boston Massacre," American Antiquarian Society *Proceedings,* New Series, volume 47 (Oct. 1937): 321–322.

✦ CHAPTER 4

What Really
Happened in the
Boston Massacre?
The Trial of
Captain Thomas
Preston

things that do not fit very well into your reconstruction.

Almost immediately you will discover that some important pieces of evidence are missing. For example, it would be useful to know the individual backgrounds and political views of the witnesses. Unfortunately, we know very little about the witnesses themselves, and we can reconstruct the political ideas of only about one-third of them. Therefore, you will have to rely on the testimonies given, deducing which witnesses were telling the truth, which were lying, and which were simply mistaken.

The fact that significant portions of the evidence are missing is not disastrous. Historians seldom have all the evidence they need—and certainly not all they want—when they attempt to tackle a historical problem. Instead, they must learn to do the best they can with the evidence that is available, using it as thoughtfully and imaginatively as possible. They do so by critically evaluating the available evidence. Which witnesses seem more likely to be telling the truth? Which witnesses were probably lying? When dealing with eyewitness testimony, be sure to determine what is factual and what is an opinion. A diagram of the scene has been provided. How can it help you?

Also included in the evidence is Paul Revere's famous engraving of the incident. It is unlikely that Revere witnessed the Boston Massacre,

yet his engraving gained widespread distribution and credibility. Most people tend to recall that engraving when they think of the Boston Massacre. It ranks among the most effective examples of political propaganda in all of American history. Revere presented an unqualified, inflammatory argument about who was responsible for the trouble in Boston, and it carried tremendous weight in revolutionary America and still does today. His work exemplifies that saying: a picture is worth a thousand words. Do not examine the engraving until you have read the trial accounts closely. Can Revere's engraving help you find out what really happened that night? How does the engraving fit the eyewitnesses' accounts? How do the engraving and the accounts differ? Why is Revere's image so powerful in public memory? What was the consequence of his influence?

Keep the central question in mind: What really happened in the Boston Massacre? Throughout this exercise, you will be trying to determine whether an order to fire was actually given. If so, by whom? If not, how can you explain why shots were fired? As commanding officer, Thomas Preston was held responsible and charged with murder. You might want to consider the evidence available to you from the point of view of either a prosecution or defense attorney. Which side had the stronger case?

The Evidence

Source 1: Diagram of the site of the Boston Massacre.

1. Site of the Boston Massacre, Town House Area, 1770.

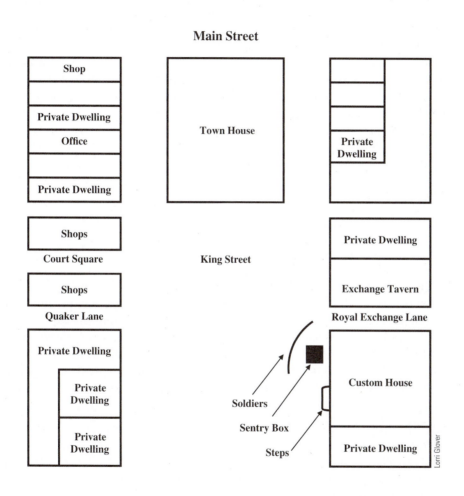

Main Street

Shop

Private Dwelling

Office

Private Dwelling

Town House

Private Dwelling

Shops

Court Square

King Street

Private Dwelling

Exchange Tavern

Shops

Quaker Lane

Royal Exchange Lane

Private Dwelling

Private Dwelling

Private Dwelling

Soldiers

Sentry Box

Steps

Custom House

Private Dwelling

Lorri Glover

◆ CHAPTER 4

What Really
Happened in the
Boston Massacre?
The Trial of
Captain Thomas
Preston

Source 2 from "Case of Capt. Thomas Preston, of the 19th Regiment," *Boston News-Letter, published as The Massachusetts Gazette Extraordinary*, June 21, 1770.

2. Captain Thomas Preston's Account, June 21, 1770.

. . . The Mob still increased, and were more outrageous, striking their Clubs or Bludgeons one against another, and calling out, 'come on you Rascals, you bloody Backs, you Lobster Scoundrels; fire if you dare, G-d damn you, fire and be damn'd; we know you dare not;' and much more such Language was used. At this Time I was between the Soldiers and the Mob, parleying with and endeavouring all in my Power to persuade them to retire peaceably; but to no Purpose. They advanced to the Points of the Bayonets, struck some of them, and even the Muzzles of the Pieces, and seemed to be endeavouring to close with the Soldiers. On which some well-behaved Persons asked me if the Guns were charged: I replied, yes. They then asked me if I intended to order the Men to fire; I answered no, by no Means; observing to them, that I was advanced before the Muzzles of the Men's Pieces, and must fall a Sacrifice if they fired; that the Soldiers were upon the Half-cock[14] and charged Bayonets, and my giving the Word fire, under those Circumstances, would prove me no Officer. While I was thus speaking, one of the Soldiers, having received a severe Blow with a Stick, stept a little on one Side, and instantly fired, on which turning to and asking him why he fired without Orders, I was struck with a Club on my Arm, which for sometime deprived me of the Use of it; which Blow, had it been placed on my Head, most probably would have destroyed me. On this a general Attack was made on the Men by a great Number of heavy Clubs, and Snow-Balls being thrown at them, by which all our Lives were in imminent Danger; some Persons at the same Time from behind me calling out, 'Damn your Bloods, why don't you fire?' Instantly three or four of the Soldiers fired, one after another, and directly after three more in the same Confusion and Hurry.

The Mob then ran away, except three unhappy Men who instantly expired, in which Number was Mr. Gray, at whose Rope-Walk the prior Quarrel took place; one more is since dead, three others are dangerously, and four slightly wounded. The Whole of this melancholy Affair was transacted in almost 20 minutes. On my asking the Soldiers why they fired without Orders, they said they heard the Word "Fire," and supposed it came from me. This might be the Case, as many of the Mob called out "Fire, fire," but I assured the Men that I gave no such Order, that my Words were, "Don't fire, stop your Firing. . . ."[15]

14. The cock of a musket had to be fully drawn back (cocked) for the musket to fire. In half cock, the cock was drawn only halfway back so that priming powder could be placed in the pan. The musket, however, would not fire at half cock. This is the origin of "Don't go off half cocked." 15. Depositions also were taken from the soldiers, three of whom claimed, "We did our Captain's orders and if we don't obey his commands should have been confined and shot."

Source 3 from "Anonymous Summary of Crown Evidence, 24-25 October 1770"; "Anonymous Summary of Defense Evidence, 25–27 October 1770"; and "Anonymous Minutes of Paine's Argument for the Crown, 29 October 1770," all available through Founders Online, National Archives (www.founders.archives.gov). Source: The *Adams Papers*, Legal Papers of John Adams, volume 3 *Cases 63 and 64: The Boston Massacre Trials*, ed., L. Kinvin Worth and Hiller B. Zobel (Cambridge: Harvard University Press, 1965), pp. 50–61, 62–81, 91–93.

3. The Trial of Captain Thomas Preston (*Rex v. Preston*), October 24–29, 1770 (excerpts).[16]

Witnesses for the King (Prosecution)

Edward Gerrish (or Garrick)

I heard a noise about 8 Clock and went down to Royal Exchange lane. Saw some Persons with Sticks coming up Quaker lane. I said [to the sentry] Capt. Goldsmith owed my fellow Prentice. He said he was a Gentleman and would pay every body. I said there was none in the Regiment.[17] He asked for me. I went to him, was not ashamed of my face. He struck me. A Sergeant chased me into Davis's shop and struck into the Shop. The Sentinel left his Post and Struck me. I cried. Me fellow Prentice and a young man came up to the Sentinel and called him Bloody back.[18] He called to the Main Guard. A part came without Guns but with naked Swords and about 1/4 of an hour after Capt. Preston came with his Guard. About 20 or 30 People came up Royal Exchange lane. The first Party chased every body they saw. There was not a dozen people when the Sentinel called the Guard.

William Wyat

I heard the Bell, coming up Cornhill, saw the People running several ways. The largest part went down to the North of the Town house. I went the South side, saw an Officer leading out 8 or 10 Men. Somebody met the officer and said, Capt. Preston for Gods sake mind what you are about and take care of your Men. He went down to the Centinel, drew up his Men, bid them face

16. The National Archives, in partnership with the National Historical Publications and Records Commission and the University of Virginia Press, offers free public online access to transcriptions of the writings of many leading figures of the American Revolution. Anyone can access this remarkable treasure trove of primary sources at www.founders.archives.gov. Treaties, laws, constitutions, diplomatic and legislative records from the era are available through the Avalon Project of Yale Law School at www.avalon.yale.law.edu.
17. To say that there was no gentleman in the regiment was an insult to the sentry's superior officer, Captain Goldsmith.
18. British soldiers' coats were red.

◆ CHAPTER 4

What Really
Happened in the
Boston Massacre?
The Trial of
Captain Thomas
Preston

about, Prime and load. I saw about 100 People in the Street huzzaing, crying fire, damn you fire. In about 10 Minutes I heard the Officer say fire. The Soldiers took no notice. His back was to me. I heard the same voice say fire. The Soldiers did not fire. The Officer then stamped and said Damn your bloods fire be the consequence what it will. Immediately the first Gun was fired. I have no doubt the Officer was the same person the Man spoke to when coming down with the Guard. His back was to me when the last Order was given. I was then about 5 or 6 yards off and within 2 yards at the first. He stood in the rear when the Guns were fired. Just before I heard a Stick, which I took to be upon a Gun. I did not see it. The officer had to the best of my knowledge a cloth coloured Surtout on.[19] After the firing the Captain stepd forward before the Men and struck up their Guns. One was loading again and he dam'd 'em for firing and severely repremanded 'em. I did not mean the Capt. had the Surtout but the Man who spoke to him when coming with the Guard.

John Cox

I saw the officer after the firing and spoke to the Soldiers and told 'em it was a Cowardly action to kill men at the end of their Bayonets. They were pushing at the People who seemd to be trying to come into the Street. The Captain came up and stamped and said Damn their bloods fire again and let 'em take the consequence. I was within four feet of him. He had no Surtout but a red Coat with a Rose on his shoulder.[20] The people were quarrelling at the head of Royal Exchange lane. The Soldiers pushing and striking with their Guns. I saw the People's Arms moving but no Sticks.

Benjamin Burdick

When I came into King Street about 9 o'Clock I saw the Soldiers round the Centinel. I asked one if he was loaded and he said yes. I asked him if he would fire, he said yes by the Eternal God and pushd his Bayonet at me. After the firing the Captain came before the Soldiers and put up their Guns with his arm and said stop firing, dont fire no more or dont fire again. I heard the word fire and took it and am certain that it came from behind the Soldiers. I saw a man passing busily behind who I took to be an Officer. The firing was a little time after. I saw some persons fall. Before the firing I saw a stick thrown at the Soldiers. The word fire I took to be a word of Command.

---

19. A surtout is a type of overcoat.
20. Battalion officers of the 29th Regiment wore a single epaulette, on the right shoulder. For uniform descriptions, see Hugh Edmund E. Everard, *History of Thos Farrington's Regiment, Subsequently Designated the 29th (Worcestershire) Foot 1694 to 1891* (Worcester: Littlebury & Company, 1891), 58–59.

I had in my hand a highland broad Sword which I brought from home. Upon my coming out I was told it was a wrangle[21] between the Soldiers and people, upon that I went back and got my Sword. I never used to go out with a weapon. I had not my Sword drawn till after the Soldier pushed his Bayonet at me. I should have cut his head off if he had stepd out of his Rank to attack me again. At the first firing the People were chiefly in Royal Exchange lane, there being about 50 in the Street. After the firing I went up to the Soldiers and told them I wanted to see some faces that I might swear to them another day. The Centinel in a melancholy tone said perhaps Sir you may.

Daniel Calef

I was present at the firing. I heard one of the Guns rattle. I turned about and lookd and heard the officer who stood on the right in a line with the Soldiers give the word fire twice. I lookd the Officer in the face when he gave the word and saw his mouth. He had on a red Coat, yellow Jacket and Silver laced hat, no trimming on his Coat.[22] The Prisoner is the Officer I mean. I saw his face plain, the moon shone in it. I am sure of the man though I have not seen him since before yesterday when he came into Court with others. I knew him instantly. I ran upon the word fire being given about 30 feet off. The officer had no Surtout on.

Robert Goddard

About 9 oClock heard the Bell ring. Ran into King Street. I saw 8 or 9 men coming down pushing their Bayonets damning. The Soldiers came up to the Centinel and the Officer told them to place themselves and they formd a half moon. The Captain told the Boys to go home least there should be murder done. They were throwing Snow balls. Did not go off but threw more Snow balls. The Capt. was behind the Soldiers. The Captain told them to fire. One Gun went off. A Sailor or Townsman struck the Captain. He thereupon said damn your bloods fire think I'll be treated in this manner. This Man that struck the Captain came from among the People who were seven feet off and were round on one wing. I saw no person speak to him. I was so near I should have seen it. After the Capt. said Damn your bloods fire they all fired one after another about 7 or 8 in all, and then the officer bid Prime and load again. He stood behind all the time. Mr. Lee went up to the officer and called the officer by name Capt. Preston. I saw him coming down from the Guard behind the Party. I went to Gaol [jail] the next day being sworn for the

21. A quarrel.
22. Waistcoats of officers in the 29th Regiment were plain, without embroidery or lace; hats were laced with silver. Everard, *History of the 29th Regiment,* 59.

◆ CHAPTER 4

What Really
Happened in the
Boston Massacre?
The Trial of
Captain Thomas
Preston

Grand Jury to see the Captain. Then said pointing to him [Preston] that's the person who gave the word to fire. He said if you swear that you will ruin me everlastingly. I was so near the officer when he gave the word fire that I could touch him. His face was towards me. He stood in the middle behind the Men. I looked him in the face. He then stood within the circle. When he told 'em to fire he turnd about to me. I lookd him in the face.

Diman Morton

Between 9 and 10 I heard in my house the cry of fire but soon understood there was no fire but the Soldiers were fighting with the Inhabitants. I went to King Street. Saw the Centinel over the Gutter, his Bayonet breast high. He retired to the steps—loaded. The Boys dared him to fire. Soon after a Party came down, drew up. The Captain ordered them to load. I went across the Street. Heard one Gun and soon after the other Guns. The Captain when he ordered them to load stood in the front before the Soldiers so that the Guns reached beyond him. The Captain had a Surtout on. I knew him well. The Surtout was not red. I think cloth colour. I stood on the opposite corner of Exchange lane when I heard the Captain order the Men to load. I came by my knowledge of the Captain partly by seeing him lead the Fortification Guard.

Nathaniel Fosdick

Hearing the Bells ring, for fire I supposed I went out and came down by the Main Guard. Saw some Soldiers fixing their Bayonets on. Passed on. Went down to the Centinel. Perceived something pass me behind. Turned round and saw the Soldiers coming down. They bid me stand out of the way and damnd my blood. I told them I should not for any man. The party drew up round the Centinel, faced about and charged their Bayonets. I saw an Officer and said if there was any disturbance between the Soldiers and the People there was the Officer present who could settle it soon. I heard no Orders given to load, but in about two minutes after the Captain step'd across the Gutter. Spoke to two Men—I don't know who—then went back behind his men. Between the 4th. and 5th. men on the right. I then heard the word fire and the first Gun went off. In about 2 minutes the second and then several others. The Captain had a Sword in his hand. Was dressd in his Regimentals. Had no Surtout on. I saw nothing thrown nor any blows given at all. The first man on the right who fired after attempting to push the People slipped down and drop'd his Gun out of his hand. The Person who stepd in between the 4th and 5th Men I look upon it gave the orders to fire. His back was to me. I shall always think it was him. The Officer had a Wig on. I was in such a situation that I am as well satisfied there were no blows given as that the word fire was spoken.

[92]

Isaac Pierce

The Lieut. Governor asked Capt. Preston didn't you know you had no power to fire upon the Inhabitants or any number of People collected together unless you had a Civil Officer to give order. The Captain replied I was obliged to, to save my Centry. You must know it Sir said the Lieut. Governor.

Joseph Belknap

The Lieut. Governor said to Preston Don't you know you can do nothing without a Magistrate. He answered I did it to save my Men.

Witnesses for the Prisoner (Preston)

Benjamin Davis

I came into King Street. Saw people about in knots. Some at the bottom of the Town House, some at Jackson's corner. Heard a noise down the Street and saw about 20 or 30 people round the Centinel who stood on the Custom House steps, they crying fire, damn you fire. I saw the Centinels Gun sometimes level and sometimes up. When his Gun was up they closed in, when down retreated. When I was up by the Guard two young men Inhabitants came up. One said you must send a party to the Centinel for I heard some of the People say they would kill him. In about 1/2 a minute somebody within said, out Guard and about seven came out and marched down Street and posted themselves round the Centry Box. There were then about 100 People near the Custom house about the Party. I stood about 6 minutes after this, hearing great noise and huzzaing but could distinguish no words, being up at Price's Office. When I was near the Barracks a young Gentleman came to me and asked me to go help be at the Soldiers. I stood at Price's office during all the firing. I never saw the Captain till all was over. There was about six seconds between the first and second firing. I saw about 9 Soldiers running up Silsbys Alley into the Street. I went into the Street but did not see them there.

Richard Palmes

Being at the Coffee House after 9 heard the Bells. Went up King Street. Saw the Centinel walking quietly. Went up by the Town House. People told me the Soldiers at Murrays barracks were abusing the People. I went there saw a number of Officers at the Gate with Guns and People before them about 20 or 30. I ask'd the Officer why they suffered the Men to be out after

♦ CHAPTER 4

What Really
Happened in the
Boston Massacre?
The Trial of
Captain Thomas
Preston

eight oClock. Do you mean to teach me my duty. No but to remind of it. One of the Officers said the Soldiers are gone into the Barracks, let the People go home. Mr. Lamb said home, home. They went off. I came through the alley with Mr. Hickling. I saw Mr. Pool Spear. I walked with him to the Pump. Somebody there said there was a Rumpus in King Street. I went down. When I had got there I saw Capt. Preston at the head of 7 or 8 Soldiers at the Custom house drawn up, their Guns breast high and Bayonets fixed. Found Theodore Bliss talking with the Captain. I heard him say why don't you fire or words to that effect. The Captain answered I know not what and Bliss said God damn you why don't you fire. I was close behind Bliss. They were both in the front. Then I step'd immediately between them and put my left hand in a familiar manner on the Captains right shoulder to speak to him. Mr. John Hickling then looking over my shoulder I said to Preston are your Soldiers Guns loaded. He answered with powder and ball. Sir I hope you dont intend the Soldiers shall fire on the Inhabitants. He said by no means. The instant he spoke I saw something resembling Snow or Ice strike the Grenadier on the Captains right hand being the only one then at his right.[23] He instantly stepd one foot back and fired the first Gun. I had then my hand on the Captains shoulder. After the Gun went off I heard the word fire. The Captain and I stood in front about half between the breech and muzzle of the Guns. I dont know who gave the word fire. I was then looking on the Soldier who fired. The word was given loud. The Captain might have given the word and I not distinguish it. After the word fire in about 6 or 7 seconds the Grenadier on the Captains left fired and then the others one after another. The Captain stood still till the second Gun was fired. After that I turned and saw the Grenadier who fired first attempting to prick me by the side of the Captain with his Bayonet. I had a large Stick in my hand. I struck over hand and hit him in his left arm. Knocked his hand from his Gun. The Bayonet struck the Snow and jarr'd the breech out of his hand. I had not before struck at any body. Upon that I turnd, thinking the other would do the same and struck at any body at first and hit Preston. In striking him my foot slip'd and my blow fell short and hit him, as he afterwards told me, on the arm. When I heard the word fire the Captains back was to the Soldiers and face to me. Before I recovered the Soldier who fired the first Gun was attempting again to push me through. I tossed my Stick in his face. He fell back and I jump'd towards the lane. He push'd at me there and fell down. I turn'd to catch his Gun. Another Soldier push'd at me and I ran off. Returnd soon and saw the dead carrying off and the party was gone. The Gun which went

23. A grenadier was a soldier in the British Grenadier Guards.

off first had scorched the nap of my Surtout at the elbow. I did not hear the Captain speak after he answered me. Was there but about 3/4 of a minute in the whole. There was time enough between the first and second Gun for the Captain to have spoke to his Men. He stood leaning on the dagger in the scabbard. At the time of the firing there was between 50 and 80 People at some distance not crowding upon the Soldiers and thin before them.

Matthew Murray

Heard the Bells and ran out and heard what was in King street. I went in and got the handle of a Broom. Went to King Street. Saw no Soldiers. Went to Murrays Barracks. The Soldiers were gone. They bid me go home. Went into King Street, heard the Barbers boy say this is the man struck me with the breech of his Gun. The Centinel went to the steps and loaded. They dared him to fire. The Guard came down. I saw 'em load. Somebody spoke to the Captain and told him he had best withdraw none of the People would interrupt him. I stood next to the Grenadier. Saw a stick or piece of Ice strike him upon his right side. On which he instantly fired and I went off. I heard no order given. I stood within two yards of the Captain. He was in the front talking with a Person, I dont know who. I was looking at the Captain when the Gun was fired. The Soldier stood on the Captains right. I saw two or three Snow balls thrown at the Soldiers before the Gun was fired, but none after for I went off immediately. The Captain had a Sword in his hand. I know not whether he had a Surtout on but believe he had. I know Capt. Preston by sight. The Prisoner is the Man. A Woman crowded by and spoke to the second Soldier on the right. I think if the Captain had given orders anything loud I should have heard.

Andrew, a Negro servant[24]

. . . I jump'd back and heard a voise cry fire and immediately the first Gun fired. It seemd to come from the left wing from the second or third man on the left. The Officer was standing before me with his face towards the People. I am certain the voice came from beyond him. The Officer stood before the Soldiers at a sort of a corner. I turned round and saw a Grenadier who stood on the Captain's right swing his Gun and fire. I took it to be Killeroy. I look'd a little to the right and saw a Man drop. The Molatto was killed by the first Gun by the Grenadier on the Captains Right. I was so frightened, after, I did not know where I was. . . .

24. Andrew was Oliver Wendell's slave. Oliver appeared in court to testify as to Andrew's veracity.

◆ CHAPTER 4

What Really
Happened in the
Boston Massacre?
The Trial of
Captain Thomas
Preston

Daniel Cornwall

Hearing the Bells ring I ran to King street. Saw a lad who told me a damnd Rascal of a Soldier had struck a Man with a Cutlass. I said where is the damnd villain gone. They gave three Cheers and went to Murrays Barracks. They were not there. Some the People had sticks. I went into a number round the Custom house. Some of them flinging Snow balls and Oyster Shells at the Centinel. Some were for killing him. Some for taking the Sentry Box and burning it. Some for throwing over board. Standing in the middle of the Street saw the Soldiers by the Sentry box. Capt. Preston before 'em. Saw a young man talking with him. I went within two yards of him. He seemed much concerned, but I could not hear any thing. Presently heard a stick come against a Gun—immediately—about 1/4 of a minute a Gun went off. I know not who fired it. Capt. Preston was within 2 yards of me—before the Men—nearest to the right—facing the Street. I was looking at him. Did not hear any order. He faced me. I think I should have heard him. I directly heard a voice say Damn you why do you fire. Dont fire. I thought it was the Captains then. I now believe it but don't know. I then ran away.

Jane Whitehouse

. . . A Man came behind the Soldiers walkd backwards and forwards, encouraging them to fire. The Captain stood on the left about three yards. The man touched one of the Soldiers upon the back and said fire, by God I'll stand by you. He was dressed in dark coloured Cloaths. I don't remember he had a Surtout or any lace about him. He did not look like an Officer. The man fired directly on the word and clap on the Shoulder. I am positive the man was not the Captain. My attention was fixed on him, for the people said there's the Officer damn him lets kill him. I am sure he gave no orders. I saw the People throw at them. I saw one man take a chunk of wood from under his Coat, throw at a Soldier and knocked him. He fell on his face. His firelock out of his hand.[25] Near the little run of water by the Sentry box. He was the right hand Soldier. This was before any firing. The man recovered himself and took up his firelock. The chunk was thrown a few minutes before the man clap'd the Soldier on the back. The second gun went off about a minute after the first. I didn't hear any body say fire before the first and second Gun.

---

25. A firelock was a musket.

Newton Prince, a Negro, a member of the South Church

Heard the Bell ring. Ran out. Came to the Chapple. Was told there was no fire but something better, there was going to be a fight. Some had buckets and bags and some Clubs. I went to the west end of the Town House where were a number of people. I saw some Soldiers coming out of the Guard house with their Guns and running down one after another to the Custom house. Some of the people said let's attack the Main guard, or the Centinel who is gone to King street. Some said for Gods sake don't lets touch the main Guard. I went down. Saw the Soldiers planted by the Custom house two deep. The People were calling them Lobsters, daring 'em to fire saying damn you why don't you fire. I saw Capt. Preston out from behind the Soldiers. In the front at the right. He spoke to some people. The Capt. stood between the Soldiers and the Gutter about two yards from the Gutter. I saw two or three strike with sticks on the Guns. I was going off to the west of the Soldiers and heard the Guns fire and saw the dead carried off. Soon after the Guard Drums beat to arms.[26] The People whilst striking on the Guns cried fire, damn you fire. I heard no Orders given to fire, only the people in general cried fire.

James Woodall

... I saw one Soldier knock'd down. His Gun fell from him. I saw a great many sticks and pieces of sticks and Ice thrown at the Soldiers. The Soldier who was knock'd down took up his Gun and fired directly. Soon after the first Gun I saw a Gentleman behind the Soldiers in velvet or blue or black plush trimd with gold. He put his hand towards their backs. Whether he touched them I know not and said by God I'll stand by you whilst I have a drop of blood and then said fire and two went off and then the rest to 7 or 8. I stood between Capt. Preston and the Lane. The Captain, after, seemed shocked and looked upon the Soldiers. I am very certain he did not give the word fire. ...

Thomas Handaside Peck[27]

I was at home when the Guns were fired. I heard 'em distinct. I went up to the main guard and addressed myself to the Captain and said to him What have you done? He said, Sir it was none of my doings, the Soldiers

26. A special drumbeat used as a signal to soldiers to arm themselves.
27. Peck was the leading exporter of furs in Massachusetts and belonged to a very important merchant family in the colony. Samuel Eliot Morison, *The Maritime History of Massachusetts, 1783–1860* (Boston: Houghton Mifflin, 1921), 49.

◆ CHAPTER 4

What Really
Happened in the
Boston Massacre?
The Trial of
Captain Thomas
Preston

fired of their own accord, I was in the Street and might have been shot. His character is good as a Gentleman and Soldier. I think it exceeds any of the Corps.

Lieutenant Governor Thomas Hutchinson

I suppose I need not mention any thing which preceded my coming into King Street. I was pressed by the people almost upon the Bayonets. The People cried the Governor. I called for the Officer. He came from between the Ranks. I did not know him by Moon light. I had heard no circumstances. I inquired with some emotion, How came you to fire without Orders from a Civil Magistrate? I am not certain of every word. I cannot recollect his answer. It now appears to me that it was imperfect. As if he had more to say. I remember by what he said or his actions I thought he was offended at being questioned. Before I could have his full answer the people cried to the Town house, to the Town house. A Gentleman by me (Mr. Belknap) was extremely civil. I thought he press'd my going into the Town house from a concern for my safety. I was carried by the crowd into the Council Chamber. After some hours Capt. Preston was brought there to be examined. I heard him deny giving Orders. I am very sure it did not occur to me that he had said anything in answer to my question in the Street which would not consist with this denial. My intention in going up was to enquire into the affair. I have no particular intimacy with Capt. Preston. His general character is extremely good. Had I wanted an Officer to guard against a precipitate action I should have pitched upon him as soon as any in the Regiment.

Closing Arguments

For the Defense

[No transcript of John Adams' closing statement exists. From his notes, however, we can reconstruct his principal arguments. Adams began by citing cases that held that when there was doubt as to a defendant's guilt it was always prudent to lean toward acquittal rather than conviction, especially in murder trials. It was better for twenty guilty people to escape death than "that one innocent person should die." Adams also argued that there was ample provocation and that Preston was merely defending himself and his men. Far from malicious, he acted in self-defense. Adams then reviewed the evidence, stating that there was no real proof that Preston had ordered his men to fire into the crowd. Adams also questioned the testimony and the character of prosecution witnesses, saying that Robert Goddard "is not capable of

making observations," that other witnesses were in error, and that William Wyat was "diabolically malicious." [28]]

Conclusion of Prosecution's Summary to the Jury

. . . Now Gentlemen the fact being once proved, it is the prisoner's part to justify or excuse it, for all killing is, *prima facie*, Murder. They have attempted to prove, that the People were not only the aggressors, but attacked the Soldiers with so much Violence, that an immediate Danger of their own Lives, obliged them to fire upon the *Assailants*, as they are pleased to call them. Now this *violent Attack* turns out to be nothing more, than a few Snow-balls, thrown by a parcel of Boys; the most of them at a considerable distance, and as likely to hit the Inhabitants as the Soldiers (which is a common Case in the Streets of Boston at that Season of the Year, when a Number of People are collected in a Body), and one Stick, that struck Grenadier, but was not thrown with sufficient force to wound, or even sally him, whence then this Outrage, fury and abuse so much talk'd of? The Inhabitants collected, Many of them from the best of Motives, to make peace; and some out of mere Curiosity, and what was the Situation of Affairs when the Soldiers begun the fire? In addition to the Testimony of many others, you may collect it from the Conduct of Mr. Palmes, a Witness on whom they principally build their Defence. Wou'd he place himself before a party of Soldiers, and risque his Life at the Muzzels of their Guns, when he thought them under a Necessity of firing to defend their Life? 'Tis absurd to suppose it; and it is impossible you should ever seriously believe, that their Situation could either justify or excuse their Conduct. I would contend, as much as any Man, for the tenderness and Benignity[29] of the Law; but, if upon such trifling and imaginary provocation. Men may o'er leap the Barriers of Society, and carry havock and Desolation among their defenseless Fellow Subjects; we had better resign an unmeaning title to protection in Society and range the Mountains uncontrol'd. Upon the whole Gentlemen the facts are with you, and I doubt not, you will find such a Verdict as the Laws of God, of Nature and your own Conscience will ever approve.

---

28. For specifics, see "Adams' Notes for Authorities for His Argument for the Defense: October 1770" and "Paine's Minutes of Adams' Arguments: 27 October 1770," www.founders.archives.gov.
29. A kindly act.

◆ CHAPTER 4

What Really
Happened in the
Boston Massacre?
The Trial of
Captain Thomas
Preston

Source 4: Paul Revere, "The Bloody Massacre perpetrated in King-Street Boston on March 5th 1770 by a party of the 29th Reg." Library of Congress.

4. Paul Revere's Engraving of the Boston Massacre.
[Notice how he dubbed the Custom House "Butcher's Hall."]

Library of Congress Photos and Photographs Division [LC-DIG-ppmsca-19159]

◆

Questions to Consider

In reconstructing the event, begin by imagining the positions of the soldiers and witnesses. Where were the soldiers standing? Where was Captain Preston standing? Which witnesses were closest to Preston (that is, in the best positions to see and hear what happened)? Where were the other witnesses? Remember that the event took place around 9:00 P.M., when Boston was totally dark.

Next, read closely Preston's account of events and the trial testimony. What major points did Preston make in his own defense? Do you find those points credible? More important, do the witnesses who were closest to Preston agree or disagree with his recounting, or with each other's? On what points? Be as specific as possible.

Now consider the other witnesses, those who were not so near. What did they hear? What did they see? To what degree do their testimonies agree or disagree, both with each other and with Preston and those closest to him?

Lawyers for both sides spent considerable time trying to ascertain what Captain Preston was wearing on that evening. Why did they consider this important? Based on the evidence, what do you think Preston was wearing on the evening of March 5, 1770? What conclusions could you draw from that?

The attorneys were also particularly interested in the crowd's behavior prior to the firing of the first musket. Why did they consider that important? How would you characterize the crowd's behavior? Are you suspicious of testimony that is at direct odds with your conclusion about this point?

Several witnesses (especially Jane Whitehouse) tell a quite different story. To what extent is her recounting of the event credible? Is it corroborated by other witnesses?

We included Paul Revere's engraving, even though he probably was not an eyewitness, because by the time of Preston's trial, surely all the witnesses would have seen it and, more important, because later generations of Americans have obtained their most lasting visual image of the event from that work. How does the engraving conform to what actually happened? How does it conflict with your determination of what took place? If there are major discrepancies, why do you think this is so? (Revere certainly knew a few of the eyewitnesses and could have ascertained the truth from them.) Why did the story he told with his engraving resonate with so many people at the time and for so long in Americans' historical memory?

After you have answered these questions and carefully weighed the eyewitnesses' evidence, can you explain why people saw so many different things that night? Are you able to say definitely who was responsible for the loss of life on March 5, 1770? Finally, how would you answer the central question: What really happened in the Boston Massacre?

◆

Epilogue

In his closing arguments in defense of Captain Preston, John Adams noted that the crowd not only had been harassing the soldiers but also had actually threatened to attack them. Despite that provocation and danger, Adams insisted, no reliable evidence proved that Preston ordered his men to fire into the crowd. In such doubtful cases, he concluded, the jury must vote for an acquittal. In contrast, the prosecution's closing summary portrayed

✦ CHAPTER 4

What Really
Happened in the
Boston Massacre?
The Trial of
Captain Thomas
Preston

Preston as a murderer. The crowd's actions, the prosecution maintained, consisted of "a few Snow-balls, thrown by a parcel of Boys." According to the prosecution, the rest of the people who gathered in the square were peaceful and simply curious about what was happening.

The jury in the Thomas Preston trial took only three hours to reach a verdict of "not guilty." Some of the jurors were sympathetic to the British and thus were determined to find Preston innocent no matter what evidence was presented. Also, the leaking of the depositions ultimately helped the captain's defense because his attorneys knew in advance what the most damaging witnesses would likely say in court. Once the trial began, defense attorney John Adams tried to create so much confusion in the minds of the jurors that they could not be certain what actually had taken place. This tactic proved extremely effective. Finally, it was generally believed that, even if he were found guilty, Preston would be pardoned. As it turned out, the captain had the advantage from the very beginning.[30]

As for Thomas Preston himself, the British officer was quickly packed off to England, arriving in London in February 1771. He retired from military service and received a pension of £200 per year from the king "to compensate him for his suffering." Afterward, he continued to maintain his innocence and insist that he never gave an order to fire. Preston never expressed any gratitude to John Adams for his vigorous, successful defense. In the 1780s, Adams and Preston saw one another on the streets of London, but they passed without speaking.[31] Of the eight soldiers, six were acquitted and two were convicted of manslaughter and punished by being branded on the thumb. From there they disappeared into the mists and crevices of history.

Although they loudly asserted that the verdicts were gross miscarriages of justice, Patriot leaders Sam Adams, Joseph Warren, Josiah Quincy, and others probably were secretly delighted by Preston's and the majority of the redcoats' acquittals. Those verdicts outraged many colonists and allowed Patriot propagandists to whip up even more sentiment against British "tyranny." "It does not require a majority to prevail," Sam Adams understood, "but rather an irate, tireless minority, keen on setting brushfires of freedom in the minds of men."

The so-called Boston Massacre not only was an important event that led to the American Revolution, but it also helped shape Americans' attitudes as to what their revolution was all about. Samuel Adams and others organized annual remembrances of the event. At the 1775 ceremony, held only a month before the battles of Lexington

---

30. Of the twelve jurors, five of them left Massachusetts in 1775 and became loyalist exiles. Of the rumors that Preston would be pardoned if convicted, see Worth and Zobel, eds., *Legal Papers of John* Adams 3: 13.

31. On Preston's maintaining his innocence, see Frederick Kidder, *History of the Boston Massacre, March 5, 1770, Consisting of the Narrative of the Town, the Trial of the Soldiers, and a Historical Introduction* (Albany: Joel Munsell, 1870), 288. On the meeting of Adams, see Worth and Zobel, eds., *Legal Papers of John Adams* 3: 34.

and Concord, Joseph Warren brought his audience to a near frenzy when he thundered, "Take heed, ye infant babes, lest, whilst your streaming eyes are fixed on the ghastly corpse, your feet slide on the stones bespattered with your father's brains."[32]

More than one hundred years after the event, the Massachusetts legislature authorized a memorial honoring the martyrs to be placed on the site of the episode. In the late nineteenth century, many Bostonians remained convinced that the American Revolution had been caused by Britain's corruption and oppression, and those convictions were bolstered by Irish immigrants whose ancestors had known British "tyranny" firsthand. But at the annual meeting of the members of the Massachusetts Historical Society that elite group opposed the monument. One member described the five men killed as "vulgar ruffians" and another disparaged the dead as "victims of their own folly!" The General Court ignored the society and the monument was erected in 1889.[33]

Then, in 1917, the year that the United States entered the Great War against Germany as an ally of Britain, distinguished American historian Albert Bushnell Hart's textbook *New American History* was published. Hart devoted only thirty-three words to the events of March 5, 1770, and avowed that the "unsuitable name of 'Boston Massacre' was applied to the unfortunate affair." As American alliances changed, so also did its history.[34]

Today the site of the Boston Massacre is on a traffic island beside the Old State House (formerly called the Town House and seen in the background of Paul Revere's famous engraving) in the midst of Boston's financial district. With the exception of the Old State House, which is now a museum, the site is ringed by skyscrapers that house, among other institutions, the Bank of America. Thousands of Bostonians and tourists stand on the Boston Massacre site every day, waiting for the traffic to abate.[35]

For his part, John Adams believed that the episode "had been intentionally wrought up by designing Men, who knew what they were aiming at." "Certain busy characters," he said, had worked for months "to excite Quarrells" and "inkindle an immortal hatred" between Boston residents and British soldiers.[36] Even so, Adams

32. Philip Davidson, *Propaganda and the American Revolution* (Chapel Hill: University of North Carolina Press, 1941), 9.
33. Adams, "New Light on the Boston Massacre," 261–262.

34. Albert Bushnell Hart, *New American History* (New York: American Book Col, 1917), 131. For a fine example of American efforts to "sanitize" their own revolution, see Alfred F. Young, *The Shoemaker and the Tea Party: Memory and the American Revolution* (Boston: Beacon Press, 1999). The subject of the first part of Young's book, George Robert Twelves Hewes, was a participant in the Boston Massacre.
35. The Freedom Trail Foundation offers visitors to Boston entry into the city's rich revolutionary era history. The trail is one of the most popular historic destinations in the U.S., attracting over 4,000,000 visitors a year. You can explore at www.thefreedomtrail.org.
36. *The Adams Papers*, Diary and Autobiography of John Adams, volume 3, *Diary, 1782–1804; Autobiography, Part One to October 1776*, ed. L. H. Butterfield (Cambridge: Harvard University Press, 1961), 292.

◆ CHAPTER 4

What Really
Happened in the
Boston Massacre?
The Trial of
Captain Thomas
Preston

later claimed that the move toward American independence was sparked on the evening of March 5, 1770. Although he may have overstated the case, clearly many Americans living today have come to see the event as a crucial one in the buildup to the revolution against Great Britain.

Now that you have examined the evidence, do you think the Boston Massacre was a justifiable reason for rebellion against the mother country?

Could the crowd action on that evening secretly have been directed by the Patriot elite, or was it a spontaneous demonstration of anti-British fury? Why was Paul Revere's engraving at such variance with what actually took place?

Few Americans have stopped to ponder what actually happened on that fateful evening. Like the American Revolution itself, the answer to that question is more complex than we think.

5

The Evolution of American Citizenship: The Louisiana Purchase, 1803–1812

◆

The Problem

As the War for Independence drew to a close, several Americans turned their attention to the new nation's future. Few gave as much time and energy to this subject as did Thomas Jefferson, the architect of the United States' justification for taking up arms against the mother country. Whether he was in Philadelphia, Paris, or his unfinished home Monticello in Virginia, such thoughts were never far from his mind.

By the end of the war, it became clear that none of the European powers had much taste for building empires in America. Spain was weakened by economic distress and corruption, France was on the eve of its own revolution that would soon erupt, and both Britain and Holland appeared to be more interested in commerce than in colonies. For Jefferson, this situation, which could well be only temporary, presented a matchless opportunity for the new nation to expand, to fulfill its destiny of being what Jefferson often

referred to as an "empire of liberty." As one of Jefferson's biographers put it, "The great western country was a vivid reality in his mind . . . and when he started talking he could not hold himself within the boundaries of Virginia."[1]

Jefferson was particularly concerned about the astounding population growth in the United States. From 1750 to 1770, the white population of the thirteen colonies increased by 55 percent, an increase that the Virginian feared would lead to a growing number of landless families that might endanger the stability of the new republic. The obvious answer to this growing problem was more land, land in the West. In one of his most-quoted opinions, Jefferson wrote:

1. On Jefferson's thinking about the West, see Dumas Malone, *Jefferson the Virginian,* vol. 1 of *Jefferson and His Time* (Boston: Little, Brown, 1948), p. 378.

◆ CHAPTER 5

The Evolution
of American
Citizenship:
The Louisiana
Purchase,
1803–1812

Those who labor in the earth are the chosen people of God, if ever he had a chosen people, whose breasts he has made his peculiar deposit for substantial and genuine virtue. . . . It is the manners and spirit of a people which preserve a republican vigor.

Years later Jefferson wrote to Albert Gallatin, "How much better to have every 160 acres settled by an able-bodied militia man, than by purchasers with their hordes of Negroes, to add weakness instead of strength." By that time Jefferson surely was familiar with Thomas Malthus's *An Essay on the Principles of Population* (1798), which predicted that the American population would double every 25 years.[2]

And yet, while he welcomed immigrants, Jefferson was not in favor of Virginia's law which stated that a "foreigner of any nation . . . becomes naturalized by removing to the state to reside, and taking an oath of fidelity; and, thereupon, acquires every right of a native citizen. . . ." In his *Notes on the State of Virginia,* Jefferson explained that the United States

is a composition of the finest principles of the English Constitution, with others derived from natural rights and nat-

ural reason. To these nothing can be more opposed than the maxims of absolute monarchies. Yet, from such, we are to expect the greatest number of emigrants. They will bring with them the principles of the governments they leave, imbibed in their early youth.

In 1788, Jefferson referred to the French in a letter to James Madison: "The misfortune is that they are not yet ripe for receiving the blessings to which they are entitled." It was a belief that he never fully abandoned.[3]

Thus Jefferson faced a serious dilemma when in his first term as President he learned that Napoleon Bonaparte, the First Consul of the French Republic, in 1803 told the two American ministers that he was willing to sell all of the Louisiana Territory to the United States. In Secretary of State James Madison's instructions to the American negotiators, he suggested the following wording of the treaty:

To incorporate the inhabitants of the hereby ceded territory with the citizens of the United States on an equal footing, being a provision, which cannot now be made, from the character and policy of the United States, that

2. For population growth see *The Statistical History of the United States from Colonial Times to the Present* (Stanford, CT: Fairfield Publishers, 1965), p. 756. For Jefferson's quote see *Notes on the State of Virginia,* ed. David Waldstreicher (Boston: Bedford/St. Martin's, 2002), p. 197. For Jefferson's letter to Gallatin see Roger G. Kennedy, *Mr. Jefferson's Lost Cause: Land, Farmers, Slavery, and the Louisiana Purchase* (New York: Oxford Univ. Press, 2003), frontpiece.

3. For Virginia's law see *Notes on the State of Virginia,* p. 172. For Jefferson's opinion see *ibid.,* p. 139 and Jefferson to Madison, November 18, 1788 in Julian Boyd, ed., *The Papers of Thomas Jefferson* (Princeton, NJ: Princeton Univ. Press, 1958), vol. 14, p. 188. In 1803, the majority of Louisiana's population were of French extraction, either Acadians shipped by the British from Canada to Louisiana, French Caribbeans who fled Saint Dominique during the slave rebellion, or emigrants from France who left during the revolution.

such incorporation will take place-without unnecessary delay. . . .

In France, however, minister extraordinary James Monroe, perhaps seeking to avoid Napoleon's anger that the French residents of Louisiana would not immediately become full United States citizens, altered the article so as to read:

> The inhabitants of the ceded territory shall be incorporated in the Union of the United States and admitted as soon as possible according to the principles of the federal Constitution to the enjoyment of all these rights, advantages and immunities of citizens of the United States. . . .

The central issue here was whether the residents of Louisiana, and especially of New Orleans, would become full citizens as soon as both nations approved and signed the treaty. For his part, President Jefferson had not budged regarding his original feelings about full citizenship, as his December 1803 letter to DeWitt Clinton clearly shows: ". . . it is acknowledged that our new fellow citizens are as yet incapable of self-government as children. . . ."[4]

People who lived in one of the former thirteen colonies and who supported the Patriot cause automatically became citizens, as did Loyalists who took an oath of allegiance. Immigrants who arrived in the United States after the war went through a citizenship process, which Congress approved in 1790 and changed in 1795, 1798, and 1802 for political reasons. But this was the first time that the United States had to deal with a large number of people who expected to become American citizens immediately.

Your task in this chapter is to read and analyze the material in the Evidence section of the chapter to answer the following central questions:

1. What criteria did the United States Congress and the President require to be met by the citizens of the Louisiana Territory?

2. How did the residents of the Louisiana Territory respond to those requirements?

3. How was the issue ultimately resolved?

4. Finally, **how did the Louisiana Purchase affect the United States' ideas and policies regarding citizenship?**

4. For the original article and Monroe's altered one, see Peter J. Kastor, ed., *The Louisiana Purchase: Emergence of an American Nation* (Washington, DC: CQ Press, 2002), pp. 177 (original) and 143–144 (Monroe's alteration). For Jefferson's December 3, 1803, letter to Clinton see Paul Leicester Ford, ed., *The Writings of Thomas Jefferson* (New York: G.P. Putnam's Sons, 1897), vol. 8, p. 283.

♦ CHAPTER 5

The Evolution
of American
Citizenship:
The Louisiana
Purchase,
1803–1812

♦

Background

Five months before Thomas Jefferson's inauguration as the third president of the United States, a secret treaty between France and Spain was to set in motion a series of critically important events that would change the character of the new republic and its elected leader. On October 1, 1800, the Treaty of San Ildefonso was signed ceding to France all of the province of Louisiana. Rumors of such an agreement had been circulating for some time, but the new President did not learn of the treaty until May 1801.[5]

The treaty was part of France's First Consul Napoleon Bonaparte's dream to rebuild the French empire in America. The western part of the island of Hispaniola (present-day Haiti) was the French colony of Saint Domingue, where a slave rebellion had overthrown the French colonial government and declared the area an independent nation. Napoleon ordered a French army of 25,000 troops under Gen. Charles Victor Leclerc (Napoleon's brother-in-law) to crush the rebellion and re-enslave the black population. Then, in late 1802 a French army was being assembled in Holland that would sail to new Orleans and take control of that area and move northward, perhaps to Canada.[6]

Jefferson did not know of these two expeditions, but he quickly ordered Minister to France Robert R. Livingston (through a written communication by Secretary of State James Madison) to find out if the retrocession had taken place and, if it had, to attempt to convince the French government to sell to the United States the city of New Orleans and the Floridas. At the same time, in private correspondences Jefferson sought to offer some not-so-subtle threats. To Livingston he wrote,

> The day that France takes possession of N. Orleans fixes the sentence which is to restrain her forever within her low water mark. It seals the union of two nations who in conjunction can maintain exclusive possession of the ocean. From that moment we must marry ourselves to the British fleet and nation.

Such a statement was almost surely a bluff by the President.[7]

Meanwhile in Paris, Livingston was having difficulties working with the French government, in part because, although he could read French, he was nearly deaf and could not hear the language well enough. Therefore, on January 11, 1803, Jefferson nominated

5. France had ceded Louisiana to Spain in 1761, so the 1800 treaty actually was a *retrocession*.
6. Saint Domingue was crucial to Napoleon's plans in that the colony accounted for roughly 40 percent of France's external trade.

7. Madison to Livingston, September 28, 1801, in Mary A. Hackett, et al., eds., *The Papers of James Madison: Secretary of State Series* (Charlottesville: Univ. Press of Virginia, 1993), vol. 2, pp. 144–145. For Jefferson's bluff, see Jefferson to Livingston, April 18, 1802, in Paul L. Ford, ed., *The Writings of Thomas Jefferson* (New York: G.P. Putnam's Sons, 1897), vol. 8, p. 144.

James Monroe as minister extraordinary to move negotiations along. But Monroe was not able to sail for France until March and he did not arrive in Paris until April 12, 1803.[8]

Monroe's delay turned out to be a stroke of good fortune for the United States, for by that time Napoleon had come to realize that his grand scheme for a French empire in America was doomed. To begin with, the French army in Saint Domingue fell victim to brutal fighters and to yellow fever, which killed most of the soldiers as well as Gen. Leclerc. Also, the force being put together in Holland was frozen in the port and could not sail for New Orleans until it was too late. Finally, the mercurial Napoleon needed money for a campaign in Egypt. The day before Monroe arrived in Paris, Bonaparte instructed one of his ministers, "I renounce Louisiana . . . the whole thing, without reserve. . . . I direct you to negotiate the affair. Have an interview this very day with Mr. Livingston." A few hours later, French foreign minister Charles M. Talleyrand offered Livingston the opportunity to buy all of Louisiana. In his report to Madison, Livingston said, "I told him no; that our wishes extended only to New Orleans and the Floridas." The next day Monroe arrived and quickly mended the error. A treaty was signed in Paris on April 30, 1803.[9]

In August 1803, Jefferson called Congress into special session to debate and vote on the treaty selling Louisiana to the United States. As Congress was assembling, Jefferson concentrated on what he believed was the most important issue: was the United States *constitutionally permitted* to acquire territories of any size? The Constitution actually contains no specific grant of such authority. As a person well-known as a strict constructionist of the Constitution, to the President the only thing to do was to draft, pass and ratify a constitutional amendment. Just about everyone close to Jefferson advised him that no such amendment was necessary: Madison, Secretary of the Treasury Albert Gallatin, the rest of the cabinet, and Jefferson's friend Thomas Paine. But Jefferson replied to Gallatin that a constitutional amendment "will be safer" and went about drafting several such amendments. In the end, the issue (which Jefferson considered to be the most difficult having to do with Louisiana) was not nearly so troubling at all, especially after Livingston warned that Napoleon was beginning to have second thoughts and might consider pulling out entirely. On October 28, the House of Representatives approved the treaty, the Senate having done so earlier. A few grumbled about the unconstitutionality of the purchase, but not many.[10]

---

8. Monroe had studied law in Jefferson's office from 1780 to 1783, was considered a protégé of Jefferson, and was trusted by the third President to negotiate as Jefferson would have. Actually, Monroe fell ill and Livingston carried on most of the talks.
9. For Napoleon's April 11 outburst, see Henry Adams, *History of the United States During the First Administration of Thomas*

Jefferson (New York: Charles Scribner's Sons, 1891), vol. 2, p. 27. For Livingston's mistake, see *ibid*. Monroe's correction of Livingston's error meant that the American negotiators had exceeded their instructions. Also, technically the Treaty of San Ildefonso forbid France from ceding Louisiana to any third party.
10. For Jefferson's qualms about the constitutionality of the acquisition, see Jefferson

◆ CHAPTER 5

The Evolution
of American
Citizenship:
The Louisiana
Purchase,
1803–1812

There were, however, three other issues that could become major problems. The first of these was the fact that the treaty that ceded Louisiana to the United States made no mention of any actual borders of that territory. The United States assumed, incorrectly as it turned out, that the cession included West Florida, which it did not. Nor was there any mention of the western boundaries. When Livingston first asked Talleyrand about this, the French minister simply denied knowing anything. When Livingston pressed the issue, Talleyrand simply replied, "I can give you no direction . . . you have made a noble bargain for yourselves, and I suppose you will make the most of it." That statement seems to have been acceptable to both parties.[11]

The second potential problem had to do with the price the United States was expected to pay. Interestingly, negotiations went surprisingly rapidly and in less than two weeks both sides had agreed to a total price of 80 million francs, or $15 million. That price amounted to roughly twenty dollars for each American, but once again the price was agreed to by Congress. Secretary of the Treasury Albert Gallatin was convinced he could pay for this by cutting federal expenses, Gallatin's usual answer when confronted with a large expenditure.[12]

As it turned out, the constitutional issue, the borders of the purchased territory, and the price were dealt with quickly and easily. The fourth issue, however, was an exceedingly difficult one that it took years ultimately to resolve and was brought to a conclusion in a most unusual way. That issue was the issue of *citizenship*. As noted earlier, in order to avoid any difficulty with Napoleon regarding the immediate citizenship of the Louisiana population, Monroe actually exceeded his instructions and amended the article in the treaty having to do with citizenship. The French had signed the treaty with Monroe's alteration, and Congress probably felt some pressure to do likewise. Instead of that, Congress approved the altered treaty *and* (a very important "and") established additional criteria that the residents of Louisiana would have to meet. Thus, it was confusing as to who was a citizen and who was not, an issue that is usually settled at the nation's initial formation. What were those criteria?

to Breckinridge, August 12, 1803, quoted in Peter J. Kastor, ed., *The Louisiana Purchase: Emergence of an American Nation* (Washington, DC: CQ Press, 2012), pp. 192–193; to Gallatin in January 1803 in Henry Adams, ed., *The Writings of Albert Gallatin* (Philadelphia: J. B. Lippincott, 1879), vol. 1, p. 115. For Jefferson's five drafts of a constitutional amendment, see Jon Kukla, *A Wilderness So Immense: The Louisiana Purchase and the Destiny of America* (New York: Knopf, 2003), pp. 359–361.

11. No one would know the actual size of the territory, 828,000 square miles, for years. As for West Florida, the United States purchased the territory from Spain in the Adams-Onis Treaty of 1819, the same agreement that set the western boundary of the territory. For Talleyrand's denials, see Henry Adams, *History of the United States During the First Administration of Thomas Jefferson* (New York: Charles Scribner's Sons, 1896), vol. 2, pp. 43–44.

12. Of the total 80 million francs, 60 million went to the French government and 20 million paid French debts to American citizens arising from the United States' Quasi-War with France, 1798–1800. Jefferson believed correctly that the sale was quite a bargain, since he was prepared to offer $10 million for New Orleans and West Florida alone.

How did the residents of the Orleans Territory react to those criteria? How was that issue ultimately resolved? Finally, how did the Louisiana Purchase affect the United States' ideas and policies regarding citizenship?

❖

The Method

The evidence you will be using to answer this chapter's central question begins with an excerpt from Secretary of State Madison's instructions to Livingston and Monroe regarding citizenship (Source 1) and concludes with the 1811 Enabling Act granting Louisianans the power to draw up a state constitution for their admission to statehood (Source 17). As you will see, the central issue in the dialogue between United States leaders and Louisianans was the criteria Louisianans would have to meet before being granted citizenship. Also, you will quickly recognize that the criteria were not static but instead changed over time. How did they change? Why did they change? What role, if any, did Louisianans play in effecting those changes? What other factors influenced American Leaders?

The debate proved to be exceedingly confusing. For one thing, the author of the Declaration of Independence who wrote that "governments are instituted among men, deriving their just powers from the consent of the governed" as president was willing to ignore both his own words and the 1803 Louisiana Purchase treaty. Too, Federalist leaders who in the 1790s had embraced a broad interpretation of the Constitution in 1803–1804 attacked Jefferson for his excessive use of executive authority. Finally, in 1787, the Articles of Confederation government had approved the Northwest Ordinance that established a clear process of a region moving from territorial status to statehood. Yet at first, few even considered using that standard in Louisiana. Why not? Why did American leaders change their minds? As you examine and analyze each piece of evidence, consider the above questions. They will help you answer the central question.

Take notes as you go along, remembering that the debate over the nature of American citizenship was not static but instead changed over the years.

✦ CHAPTER 5

The Evolution
of American
Citizenship:
The Louisiana
Purchase,
1803–1812

✦

The Evidence

Source 1 from Madison to Livingston & Monroe, March 3, 1803 in Mary A. Hackett, et. al, The Papers of James Madison: *Secretary of State Series* (Charlottesville: Univ. Press of Virginia, 1998, vol. 4, p. 371.

1. Article VII from Madison's treaty draft and instructions, March 2, 1803.

To incorporate the inhabitants of the hereby ceded territory with the citizens of the United States on an equal footing, being a provision, which cannot now be made, it is expected, from the character and policy of the United States, that such incorporation will take place without unnecessary delay. In the meantime, they shall be secure in their persons and property, and in the free enjoyment of their religion.

Source 2 from Perley Poore, comp., *The Federal and State Constitutions, Colonial Charters, and Other Organic Laws of the United States,* 2nd ed. (Washington, DC: Government Printing Office, 1878).

2. Article 3 of Treaty ceding Louisiana, October 30, 1803 (Monroe's alteration).

ART. 3. The inhabitants of the ceded territory shall be incorporated in the Union of the United States, and admitted as soon as possible, according to the principles of the Federal Constitution, to the enjoyment of all the rights, advantages, and immunities, of citizens of the United States; and, in the mean time, they shall be maintained and protected in the free enjoyment of their liberty, property, and the religion which they profess.

Source 3 is excerpts from letters of Louisiana governor W.C.C. Claiborne[13] to Secretary of State James Madison, January 2, 10, 1804, in Dunbar Rowland, ed. *Official Letter Books of W. C. C. Claiborne,* 1801–1816 (Jackson, MS: State Department of Archives and History, 1917).

3. Claiborne to Madison, January 2, 1804.

[B]y far the greater part of the people are deplorably uninformed. The wretched Policy of the late Government having discouraged the Education of youth. . . . Frivolous diversions seem to be among their primary pleasures. . . .

Republicanism has many profound admirers here. There is something in the plain principle of equal rights which comes within the Scope of the meanest Capacity, and is sure to be agreeable because it is flattering to . . . every individual. But I fear that Republicanism among all her Friends here will find but a few who have cultivated an acquaintance with her principles. . . .

Permit me before I conclude to repeat my Solicitude for the early establishment of some permanent Government for this province . . . for the sake of the country. When the charms of novelty have faded, and the people have leisure to reflect, they will I fear become very impatient in their present situation. I could wish that the constitution to be given to this District may be as republican as the people can be safely intrusted with. But the principles of a popular Government are utterly beyond their comprehension. The Representative system is an enigma that at present bewilders them. . . . Not one in fifty of the old inhabitants appear to me to understand the English Language. Trials by Jury at first will only embarrass the administration of Justice. . . .

Claiborne to Madison, January 10, 1804.

The more I become acquainted with the inhabitants of this Province, the more I am convinced of their unfitness for a representative Government. The Credulity of the People is indeed great, and a virtuous Magistrate resting entirely for Support on the Suffrages and good will of his fellow Citizens in this quarter, would often be exposed to immediate ruin by the Machinations of a few base individuals who with some exertion and address, might make many of the people think against their will, and act against their interests. . . .

13. William C.C. Claiborne (1775–1817) was a Tennessee congressman whom Jefferson appointed Governor of the Mississippi Territory from 1801–1803 and Governor of the Louisiana Territory from 1804-1816.

✦ CHAPTER 5

The Evolution
of American
Citizenship:
The Louisiana
Purchase,
1803–1812

Until therefore the progress of information shall in some degree remove that mental darkness which at present so unhappily prevails, and a general knowledge of the American Language, laws and customs be understood, I do fear that a representative Government in Louisiana, would be a dangerous experiment.

God forbid that I should recommend for this people Political provisions under which oppression of any kind could be practised [sic] with impunity, by persons in power, but I do think that their own happiness renders it advisable that they remain for some years under the immediate Guardianship of Congress, and that for the present a local and temporary government for Louisiana upon principles somewhat similar to our Territorial government in their first grade, be established. . . . I have learned in some circles a Sentiment is cherished, that at the close of the War between England and France, the great Bonaparte will again raise his standard in this country. For my part, I attach no importance to this little Political Speculation;–It is directed more by the wishes of those who busy themselves on the subject, than by any reasonable ground of expectation. . . .

Source 4 from *Debates and Proceedings in the Congress of the United States,* 8th Congress, 1st Session (Washington, DC: Gales and Seaton, 1852).

4. Excerpt from Speech by Congressman Roger Griswold (Conn.), October 25, 1803.

The third article of the treaty is thus expressed.

"The inhabitants of the ceded territory shall be incorporated in the union of the United States, and admitted as soon as possible, according to the principles of the Federal Constitution, to the enjoyment of all the rights, advantages and immunities of citizens of the United States; and in the mean time they shall be maintained and protected in the free enjoyment of their liberty, property, and the religion which they profess."

It is, in my opinion, scarcely possible for any gentlemen on this floor to advance an opinion that the President and Senate may add to the members of the Union by treaty whenever they please, or, in the words of this treaty, may "incorporate in the union of the United States" a foreign nation who, from interest or ambition, may wish to become a member of our Government. Such a power would be directly repugnant to the original compact between the States, and a violation of the principles on which that compact was formed. It has been already well observed that the union of the States was formed on the principle of a copartnership, and it would be absurd to suppose that the agents of the parties who have been appointed to execute the business of the compact, in behalf of the principals, could admit a new partner, without the consent of the parties themselves. And yet, if the first construction is assumed, such must be the case under this constitution, and the President and Senate may admit at will any foreign nation into this copartnership without the consent of the States.

[Griswold said that the "incorporation of a foreign nation into the Union, so far from tending to preserve the Union, is a direct inroad upon it; it destroys the perfect union contemplated between the original parties by interposing an alien and a stranger to share the powers of Government with them."]

The Government of the United States was not formed for the purpose of distributing its principles and advantages to foreign nations. It was formed with the sole view of securing those blessings to ourselves and our posterity. . . .

Excerpt from Speech by Congressman Samuel Latham Mitchill (NY), October 25, 1803.

But the gentleman from Connecticut, Mr. Chairman, (Mr. Griswold) contends that even if we had a right to purchase soil, we have no business with the inhabitants. His words, however, are very select; for he said and often repeated it that the treaty-making power did not extend to the admission of foreign nations into this confederacy. To this it may be replied that the President and Senate have not attempted to admit foreign nations into our confederacy. They have bought a tract of land, out of their regard to the good of our people and their welfare. And this land, Congress are called upon to pay for. . . .

In the case of Louisiana no injury is done either to the nation or to any State belonging to that great body politic. There was nothing compulsory upon the inhabitants of Louisiana to make them stay and submit to our Government. But if they chose to remain, it had been most kindly and wisely provided, that until they should be admitted to the rights, advantages, and immunities of citizens of the United States, they shall be maintained and protected in the enjoyment of their liberty, property, and the religion which they profess. What would the gentleman propose that we shall do with them? Send them away to the Spanish provinces, or turn them loose in the wilderness? No, sir, it is our purpose to pursue a much more dignified system of measures. It is intended, first, to extend to this newly acquired people the blessings of law and social order. To protect them from rapacity, violence, and anarchy. To make them secure in their lives, limbs, and property, reputation, and civil

♦ CHAPTER 5

The Evolution
of American
Citizenship:
The Louisiana
Purchase,
1803–1812

privileges. To make them safe in the rights of conscience. In this way they are to be trained up in a knowledge of our own laws and institutions. They are thus to serve an apprenticeship to liberty; they are to be taught the lessons of freedom; and by degrees they are to be raised to the enjoyment and practice of independence. All this is to be done as soon as possible; that is, as soon as the nature of the case will permit; and according to the principles of the Federal Constitution. Strange! that proceedings declared on the face of them to be constitutional, should be inveighed against as violations of the Constitution! Secondly, after they shall have been a sufficient length of time in this probationary condition, they shall, as soon as the principles of the Constitution permit, and conformably thereto, be declared citizens of the United States. Congress will judge of the time, manner, and expediency of this. The act we are now about to perform will not confer on them this elevated character. They will thereby gain no admission into this House, nor into the House of Congress. There will be no alien influence thereby introduced into our councils. By degrees, however, they will pass on from the childhood of republicanism, through the improving period of youth and arrive at the mature experience of manhood. And then, they may be admitted to the full privileges which their merit and station will entitle them to. At that time a general law of naturalization may be passed. For I do not venture to affirm that, by the mere act of cession, the inhabitants of a ceded country become, of course, citizens of the country to which they are annexed. It seems not to be the case, unless specially provided for. By the third article it is stipulated, that the inhabitants of Louisiana shall hereafter be made citizens; *ergo* they are not made citizens of the United States by mere operation of treaty.

Source 5 from *The Writings of Thomas Jefferson* (New York: G. P. Putnam's Sons, 1897).

5. Jefferson to John Breckinridge.[14]

[The President sends to Breckinridge some ideas (suggestions?) of the new constitution. He hopes that Breckinridge will "know that I have pen to paper on the subject. . . . I . . . know what bloody teeth & fangs the federalists will attack any sentiment or principle known to come from me."]

14. John Breckinridge (1760–1806) was a Senator from Kentucky and a political ally and confidante of Jefferson. In 1798 he introduced the Kentucky Resolutions (secretly authored by Jefferson) in the Kentucky legislature and in 1804 did the same with the Louisiana Governance bill. He was grandfather of John C. Breckinridge, who ran for president in 1860 as the candidate of the southern wing of the fractured Democratic Party.

Source 6 from Public Statutes at Large of the United States of America (Boston: Little & Brown, 1845).

6. Excerpts from the Louisiana Governance Bill, introduced into the Senate on December 30, 1803, and supposedly authored by Sen. John Breckinridge, but more probably written by Jefferson. See Source 5.

SEC. 2. The executive power shall be vested in a governor, who shall reside in the said Territory, and hold his office during the term of three years, unless sooner removed by the President of the United States. He shall be commander-in-chief of the militia of the said Territory, shall have power to grant pardons for offences against the said Territory, and reprieves for those against the United States, until the decision of the President of the United States thereon shall be made know; and to appoint and commission all officers, civil and of the militia, whose appointments are not herein otherwise provided for, and which shall be established by law. He shall take care that the laws be faithfully executed. . . .

SEC. 4. The legislative powers shall be vested in the governor, and in thirteen of the most fit and discreet persons of the Territory, to be called the legislative council, who shall be appointed annually by the President of the United States from among those holding real estate therein, and who shall have resided one year at least in the said Territory, and hold no office of profit under the Territory or the United States. The governor, by and with advice and consent of the said legislative council, or of a majority of them, shall have power to alter, modify, or repeal the laws which may be in force at the commencement of this act. Their legislative powers shall also extend to all the rightful subjects of legislation; but no law shall be valid which is inconsistent with the Constitution and laws of the United States, or which shall lay any person under restraint, burden, or disability, on account of his religious opinions, professions, or worship; in all which he shall be free to maintain his own, and not burdened for those of another. The governor shall publish throughout the said Territory all the laws which shall be made, and shall from time to time report the same to the President of the United States to be laid before Congress; which, if disapproved of by Congress, shall thenceforth be of no force. The governor or legislative council shall have no power over the primary disposal of the soil, nor to tax the lands of the United States, nor to interfere with the claims to land within the said Territory. The governor shall convene and prorogue the legislative council whenever he may deem it expedient. It shall be his duty to obtain all the information in his power in relation to the customs, habits, and dispositions

◆ CHAPTER 5

The Evolution
of American
Citizenship:
The Louisiana
Purchase,
1803–1812

of the inhabitants of the said Territory, and communicate the same from time to time to the President of the United States.

SEC. 5. The judicial power shall be vested in a superior court, and in such inferior courts, and justices of the peace, as the legislature of the Territory may from time to time establish. The judges of the superior court and the justices of the peace shall hold their offices for the term of four years. . . .

SEC. 6. The governor, secretary, judges, district attorney, marshal, and all general officers of the militia, shall be appointed by the President of the United States in the recess of the Senate; but shall be nominated at their next meeting for their advice and consent. The governor, secretary, judges, members of the legislative council, justices of the peace, and all other officers, civil and of the militia, before they enter upon the duties of their respective offices, shall take an oath or affirmation to support the Constitution of the United States, and for the faithful discharge of the duties of their office. . . .

SEC. 10. It shall not be lawful for any person or persons to import or bring into the said Territory, from any port or place without the limits of the United States, or cause or procure to be so imported or brought, or knowingly to aid or assist in importing or bring any slave or slaves [who had been brought to the United States after May 1, 1798].

[In the debate over the Louisiana Governance Bill in the U.S. Senate from January 24 to February 18, 1804, the two main issues were whether or not the people of Louisiana were capable of electing a legislature or "enjoying the blessings of a free government," and whether slaves should be admitted into the territory. Senator Jonathan Dayton of New Jersey argued that slavery "must be tolerated, it must be established in that country, or it can never be inhabited. White people cannot cultivate it—your men cannot bear the burning sun & the damp dews of that country—I have traversed a large portion of it. If you permit slaves to go there only from your States, you will soon find there the very worst species of slaves— The slave holders in the United States will collect and send into that country their slaves of the worst description." On the other side of the issue Sen. James Hillhouse of Connecticut argued that increasing the number of slaves would invite a rebellion.]

[The bill was passed by Congress on March 26, 1804.]

Source 7 from "Remonstrance of the People of Louisiana Against the Political System Adopted by Congress for Them, May 1804," in Peter J. Kastor, ed., *The Louisiana Purchase: Emergence of an American Nation*, Washington, D.C.: CQ Press, 2002, pp. 212–213.

7. Remonstrance of the People of Louisiana, May 1804.

We the subscribers, planters, merchants and other inhabitants of Louisiana, respectfully approach the Legislature of the United States with a memorial of our rights, a remonstrance against certain laws which contravene them, and a petition for that redress to which the laws of nature, sanctioned by positive stipulation, have entitled us.

Without any agency in the events which have annexed our country to the United States, we yet considered them as fortunate, and thought our liberties secured even before we knew the terms of the cession. Persuaded that a free people would acquire territory only to extend the blessings of freedom; that an enlightened nation would never destroy those principles on which its government was founded, and that their Representatives would disdain to become the instruments of oppression, we calculated with certainty that their first act of sovereignty would be a communication of all the blessings they enjoyed. . . . It was early understood that we were to be American citizens: this satisfied our wishes, it implied every thing we could desire, and filled us with that happiness which arises from the anticipated enjoyment of a right long withheld. We knew that it was impossible to be citizens of the United States without enjoying personal freedom, protection for property, and above all the privileges of free representative government, and did not therefore imagine that we could be deprived of these rights even if there should have existed no promise to impart them; yet it was with some satisfaction we found these objects secured to use by the stipulations of treaty, and the faith of Congress pledged for their uninterrupted enjoyment. We expected them from your magnanimity, but were not displeased to see them guaranteed by solemn engagements. . . .

With a firm persuasion that these engagements would be soon fulfilled, we passed under your jurisdiction with a joy bordering on enthusiasm, submitted to the inconveniences of an intermediate dominion without a murmur, and saw the last tie that attached us to our mother country severed with less regret. . . . We could not bring ourselves to believe that we had so far mistaken the stipulations in our favor, or that Congress could so little regard us, and we waited the result with anxiety which distance only prevented our expressing before the passing of the bill. After a suspense which continued to the last moment of the session, after debates which only tended to show how little our true situation was known, after the rejection of every amendment declaratory

◆ CHAPTER 5

The Evolution
of American
Citizenship:
The Louisiana
Purchase,
1803–1812

of our rights, it at length became a law, and, before this petition can be present, will take effect in our country. . . .

. . .Uninformed as we are supposed to be of our acquired rights, is it necessary for us to demonstrate that this act does not "incorporate us in the Union," that it vests us with none of the "rights," gives us no advances and deprives us of all the "immunities" of American citizens. . . .

Source 8 from Dunbar Rowland, ed. Official Letter Books of W. C. C. Claiborne, 1801–1816 (Jackson, MS: StateDepartment of Archives and History, 1917).

8. Excerpts of Letters from Gov. Claiborne to Secretary of State Madison, May 3, 29, October 22, November 5, 1804.

May 3, 1804

The Law for the Government of Louisiana will not be Satisfactory to all the Citizens. Many of the old inhabitants had expected immediate admission into the Union, and the Law does not hold out the means of gratifying the Ambition of Some of the late adventurers from the United States. Complaints therefore upon this subject will be made. For myself however I do firmly believe that the constitution temporarily prescribed is well adapted to the present Situation of Louisiana.

May 29, 1804

I am Sorry to inform you that the Citizens here continue dissatisfied on the Subject of the Slave trade, and I find that many natives of the United States who have emigrated hither and some of the old Settlers are by no means pleased with the Government which Congress has prescribed for them. . . .

The Louisianans or rather the Natives of Louisiana are a pacific amiable people much attached to this Country, and to peace and good order: but many adventurers who are daily coming into the Territory from every quarter, possess revolutionary principles and restless, turbulent dispositions:–these Men will for some years give trouble more or less to the local Government, and will unquestionably excite some partial discontents, for although the Louisianans are by nature as amiable a people as I ever lived among, yet for the want of general information they are uncommonly credulous, and a few designing intriguing men may easily excite some inquietude in the public mind. . . .

November 5, 1804

[The Louisiana Governance Act established a council of thirteen men appointed by Jefferson to serve as a territorial legislature. But a majority of his nominees refused to serve, led by Evan Jones, a merchant who opposed Claiborne, and Etienne Bore, the mayor of New Orleans.]

I had no Idea that any Citizen here named a Councillor would decline, from party motives, until after I had received the nominations of the President, and I early communicated to you, my fears, that the Sentiments conveyed by Mr. Jones in his letter to me would be embraced by others, and that it was doubtful, whether a Council would be formed.—. . .

Source 9 from *Interim Appointment: W. C. C. Claiborne Letter Book, 1804–1805* (Baton Rouge, LA: Louisiana State University Press, 2002).

9. Gov. Claiborne's Speech to the First Legislative Council of the Territory of Orleans, December 5, 1804.

To you Gentlemen is first committed the important trust of giving such Laws to this flourishing District, as local wants Shall Suggest, and the Interest of the Citizens may require. I trust important and arduous, but one of which Patriotism and Talents will insure a faithful and able discharge. I confidently look to you Gentlemen for these qualifications, and I doubt not but your Labors will be brought to a fortunate close. The obstacles however we have to Surmount, ought not to be concealed. To miscalculate them in any way might prove injurious. To esteem our duties too light to require extraordinary execution, would be to err in one extreme, to be dismayed by an apprehension of their gigantic weight would be equally unfortunate on the other. To know that they are within the compass of our powers and not much below them, is the happy mean which encourages exertion and insures Success. For my part I am deeply Sensible of the delicacy and importance of the Situation in which my present office places me. I enter upon it with a degree of Diffidence produced by existing circumstances, and the expectations of the Districts—My only Sources of confidence are in your wisdom and experience, and in an honest intention on my part to assist your Councils in every measure that may tend to promote the public good. . . .

[Gov. Claiborne said that the first object of the Council's attention should be fashioning a system of jurisprudence and of criminal jurisprudence.]

◆ CHAPTER 5

The Evolution
of American
Citizenship:
The Louisiana
Purchase,
1803–1812

In adverting to your primary duties, I have yet to Suggest one, than which none can be more important or interesting; I mean Some general provision for the education of youth. If we revere Science for her own Sake, or for the innumerable benefits She confers on Society;—if we love our children and cherish the laudable ambition of being respected by our posterity, let not this great duty be overlooked. Permit me to hope then that under your Patronage, Seminaries of Learning will prosper, and the means of acquiring information, be placed within the reach of each growing family. Under a free Government, every Citizen has a Country, because he partakes of the Sovereignty and may fill the highest offices. Free America will always present flattering prospects for talents and merit. Let exertions then be made to rear up our Children in the Paths of Science and virtue, and to impress upon their tender hearts a love of civil and religious liberty. Among the Several States of the union an ingenuous emulation happily prevails, in encouraging Literature, and literary institutions, and Some of these are making rapid Strides towards rivaling the proudest establishments of Europe. In this Sentiment So favorable to the general good, you Gentlemen, I am certain will not hesitate to Join. I deem it unnecessary to trouble you with any detail of arrangements—I am however persuaded that parsimonious plans will Seldom Succeed. My advice therefore is that your System be extensive and liberally Supported. . . .

Before I conclude Gentlemen I should be wanting in duty did I not Solicit your attention to the Militia of the Territory—In the age in which we live, as well as in almost every one that has preceded it, we find that neither moderation nor wisdom nor Justice can protect a people against the encroachments of tyrannical power. The abundance of agriculture, the advantages of Legislation, the usefulness of the arts, in a word anything dear to a *free people* may be considered as insecure unless they are prepared to resist aggression—Hence we find that the Congress of the United States, and the Legislatures of the Several States, are particularly Solicitous to keep the Citizens armed and disciplined, and I persuade myself that a Policy So favorable to the general Safety will be pursued by this assembly. . . .

Source 10 from *William Plumer's Memorandum of Proceedings in the United States Senate, 1803–1807* (New York: Macmillan, 1923).

10. Recollections of a Dinner Held on December 15, 1804, with New Hampshire Senator William Plumer, Massachusetts Senator Timothy Pickering, and Three Louisianans.[15]

They complain in decent but firm language of the government that Congress established over them at the last session. They say nothing will satisfy that people but an elective government.

That Claiborne, their present governor, is unable to speak a word of French, the language that is most generally used in that country. That the proceedings in the courts of law are in a language that most of the people do not understand—That they have in many instances been convicted of breaches of laws the existence of which they were ignorant. That Claiborne is incompetent to discharge the duties of Governor.

That the President had selected some very respectable men whom he has appointed members of the legislative Council. That out of these all except three have positively declined the appointment. That no man who wishes to enjoy the friendship and esteem of the people of that country can accept of an office under the existing system of government.

They say that they have visited Mr. Jefferson—that he has not made any enquires of them relative either to their government, or the civil or natural history of their country–That he studiously avoided conversing with them upon every subject that had relation to their mission here. . . .[16]

Source 11 from Dunbar Rowland, ed. Official Letter Books of W. C. C. Claiborne, 1801–1816 (Jackson, MS: StateDepartment of Archives and History, 1917).

11. Claiborne to Madison, December 31, 1804.

A great anxiety exists here to learn the fate of the Memorial to Congress. The importation of Negroes continues to be a favorite object with the Louisianans, and I believe the privilege of Electing one Branch of the Legislature would give very general satisfaction. Immediate admission into the Union is not expected by the reflecting part of society, nor do I think there are many who would wish it. I find in some anonymous publications to the Northward, I have been represented

15. Plumer and Pickering were Federalists, political opponents of President Jefferson and the acquisition of Louisiana.
16. The three Louisianans at the dinner party had come to Washington to present the remonstrance and petition to Jefferson and to the House of Representatives.

◆ CHAPTER 5

The Evolution
of American
Citizenship:
The Louisiana
Purchase,
1803–1812

as opposing the assemblage of the people to sign in Memorial, and that on one occasion the Troops were called out in order to intimidate the Citizens.

These statements are incorrect. I never did oppose the meeting of the People; but it is true, that in the then unsettled State of the Government, I saw with regret any manifestation of public discontent, and the more so, since suspected there were many designing men among us, whose attachments were foreign, that might labor to give an improper direction to the public deliberations.

I remember to have been strongly urged, to suppress by force the first meeting which took place in March last, and by some of those who are now great advocates of the Memorial. But I answered that "the people had a right peaceably to assemble together to remonstrate against grievances" and would not be prevented by me. In consequence several subsequent public meetings took place in this City, without experiencing interruption by me. . . .

The Troops were under Arms on the first day of July, and on that day there was a meeting of a part of the Memorialists;—But the Parade was altogether accidental. . . .

Source 12 from *American State Papers. Documents, Legislative and Executive, of the Congress of the United States, Miscellaneous* (Washington, DC: Gales and Seaton, 1834).

12. Remonstrance and Petition to the House of Representatives by the Freemen of Louisiana, January 4, 1805.[17]

[The Memorial began by stating how happy the petitioners were to learn that Louisiana had been ceded to the United States. That delight, however, turned to disappointment when they read the Louisiana Governance Act that Congress had approved on March 26, 1804.]

May we not be long doomed, like the prisoners of Venice, to read the word LIBERTY on the walls of prisons! We trust to your wisdom and goodness; you are the guardians of our constitutional rights, and we repose our hopes in you as in the sanctuary of honor.

The right of the people peaceably to assemble and petition the Government for a redress of grievances is declared and warranted by the first amendment

17. Although his name appears nowhere in the Memorial, its author undoubtedly was Edward Livingston (1764–1836), younger brother of Minister to France R. R. Livingston and former New York congressman and mayor of the city of New York. The unfortunate victim of a financial scandal in city government, Livingston moved to New Orleans where he hoped to rebuild his financial and political fortunes. He cast his lot with the political opposition to Gov. Claiborne.

to the constitution. To this constitution we appeal; we learned from you to resist, by lawful means every attempt to encroach on our *rights and liberties*; the day we became Americans we were told that we were associated to a free people. We cannot suppose that the language of men jealous of their freedom can possibly be unwelcome to your ears.

By the third article of the treaty between the United States and the French republic, it is agreed "that the inhabitants of the ceded territory shall be incorporated in the Union of the United States, and admitted as soon as possible, according to the principles of the federal constitution, to the enjoyment of all the rights, advantages, and immunities of citizens of the United States, and in the mean time they shall be maintained and protected in the free enjoyment of their liberty, property, and the religion they profess."

Your petitioners beg leave to represent to your honorable Houses, that according to the principles contained in the third article of the treaty above quoted, they conceive that had not Congress thought proper to divide Louisiana into two Territories, they should now be entitled by their population to be incorporated in the Union as an independent State. . . .

[The Louisiana Governance Act divided Louisiana into two territories: the Territory of Orleans (approximately modern-day Louisiana) and the District of Louisiana, to be governed by the government of the Territory of Indiana. The petitioners referred to the statehood process stated in the 1787 Northwest Ordinance and then compared the governments of the Territory of Indiana and the Territory of Mississippi to their own.]

Your petitioners have thus gone through the painful, yet they conceive indispensable task of remonstrating against grievances, in compliance with the duty they owed to their country, to themselves, and to posterity. Your petitioners are sensible that in the discussion of interests of such magnitude, involving their dearest rights, they may perhaps appear to have deviated a little, either in some of their conclusions or expressions, from the respect they never intended to refuse to the highest authority of their country: but let your honorable Houses remember that your petitioners feel themselves injured, deeply injured. Could they tamely submit, could they even represent with more moderation in such a case, you yourselves would not consider them worthy to be admitted into a portion of the inheritance of the heroes who fought and bled for the independence of America.

Your petitioners ask, 1st, For the repeal of the act erecting Louisiana into two Territories, and providing for the temporary government thereof.

◆ CHAPTER 5

The Evolution
of American
Citizenship:
The Louisiana
Purchase,
1803–1812

2dly. That legal steps should be immediately taken for the permanent division of Louisiana.

3dly. That a Governor, secretary, and judges, should be appointed by the President, who shall reside in the district Louisiana, and hold property therein to the same amount as is prescribed by the ordinance respecting the Territory northwest of the river Ohio.

4thly. That the Governor, secretary, and judges, to be thus appointed, for the district of Louisiana, should, in preference, be chosen from among those who speak both the English and the French languages.

5thly. That the records of each county, and the proceedings of the courts of justice in the district of Louisiana should be kept, and had in both the English and French languages, as it is the case in a neighboring country, under a monarchical Government, and acquired by conquest.

6thly. That supposing the district of Louisiana to be divided into five counties, ten members, two from each county, shall be elected by the people having a right to vote in each county, according to the rules prescribed by the ordinance respecting the Northwestern Territory every two years, or such another number as Congress may appoint, which said members shall, jointly with the Governor, form the legislative council of said district of Louisiana.

7thly. That Congress would acknowledge the principle of our being entitled, in virtue of the treaty, to the free possession of our slaves, and to the right of importing slaves into the district of Louisiana, under such restrictions as to Congress in their wisdom will appear necessary. . . .

And now your petitioners trust their remonstrances and petition to the justice of your honorable Houses, and they do not entertain the least doubt but that a nation, who, in their declaration of independence, has proclaimed that the governors were intended for the governed, and not the governed for the governors; a nation who complained so loudly of their right of representation, a right inestimable to them, and formidable to tyrants, only being violated; a nation who presented it to the world, as one of their reasons of separation from England, that the King of England had endeavored to prevent the population of their States; a nation who waged war against her mother country for imposing taxes on them without their consent; a nation who styles the Indians "the merciless Indian savages whose known rule of warfare is an undistinguished destruction of all ages, sexes, and conditions," will not be deaf to their just complaints; and, by redressing their grievances, will deserve forever the most unbounded affection of the inhabitants of this district of Louisiana. . . .

Source 13 from *Public Statutes at Large of the United States of America,* 8th Congress, 2nd Session (Boston: Little & Brown, 1845).

13. Second Louisiana Governance Act, March 2, 1805.

Be it enacted by the Senate and House of Representatives of the United States of America in Congress assembled, That the President of the United States be, and he is hereby authorized to establish within the Territory of Orleans a government in all respects similar (except as is herein otherwise provided) to that now exercised in the Mississippi Territory; and shall, in the recess of the Senate, but to be nominated at their next meeting, for their advice and consent, appoint all the officers necessary therein, in conformity with the ordinance of Congress, made on the thirteenth day of July, one thousand seven hundred and eighty-seven; and that from and after the establishment of the said government, the inhabitants of the Territory of Orleans shall be entitled to and enjoy all the rights, privileges, and advantages secured by the said ordinance, and now enjoyed by the people of the Mississippi Territory.

SEC. 2. *And be it further enacted,* That so much of the said ordinance of Congress as relates to the organization of a general assembly, and prescribes the powers thereof, shall, from and after the fourth day of July next, be in force in the said Territory of Orleans; and in order to carry the same into operation, the governor of the said Territory shall cause to be elected twenty-five representatives, for which purpose he shall lay off the said Territory into convenient election-districts, on or before the first Monday of October next, and give due notice thereof throughout the same; and shall appoint the most convenient time and place within each of the said districts, for holding the elections; and shall nominate a proper officer or officers to preside at and conduct the same, and to return him the names of the persons who may have been duly elected. All subsequent elections shall be regulated by the legislature; and the number of representatives shall be determined, and the apportionment made, in the manner prescribed by the said ordinance.

SEC. 3. *And be it further enacted,* That the representatives to be chosen as aforesaid shall be convened by the governor, in the city of Orleans, on the first Monday in November next; and the first general assembly shall be convened by the governor as soon as may be convenient, at the city of Orleans, after the members of the legislative council shall be appointed and commissioned; and the general assembly shall meet, at least once in every year, and such meeting shall be on the first Monday in December, annually, unless they shall, by law, appoint a different day. Neither house,

◆ CHAPTER 5

The Evolution
of American
Citizenship:
The Louisiana
Purchase,
1803–1812

during the session, shall, without the consent of the other, adjourn for more than three days, nor to any other place than that in which the two branches are sitting. . .

SEC. 7. *And be it further enacted,* That whenever it shall be ascertained by an actual census or enumeration of the inhabitants of the Territory of Orleans, taken by proper authority, that the number of free inhabitants included therein shall amount to sixty thousand, they shall thereupon be authorized to form for themselves a constitution and State government, and be admitted into the Union upon the footing of the original States, in all respects whatever, conformably to the provisions of the third article of the treaty concluded at Paris on the thirteenth of April, one thousand eight hundred and three, between the United States and the French Republic: *Provided,* That the constitution so to be established shall be republican, and not inconsistent with the Constitution of the United States, nor inconsistent with the ordinance of the late Congress, passed the thirteenth day of July one thousand seven hundred and eighty-seven, so far as the same is made applicable to the territorial government hereby authorized to be established: *Provided, however,* That Congress shall be at liberty, at any time prior to the admission of the inhabitants of the said Territory to the right of a separate State, to alter the boundaries thereof as they may judge proper: *Except only,* That no alteration shall be made which shall procrastinate the period for the admission of the inhabitants thereof to the rights of a State government according to the provision of this act.

SEC. 8. *And be it further enacted,* That so much of an act entitled "An act erecting Louisiana into two Territories, and providing for the temporary government thereof," as is repugnant with this act, shall, from and after the first Monday of November next, be repealed.

Sources 14–16 from Dunbar Rowland, ed. *Official Letter Books of W. C. C. Claiborne,* 1801–1816 (Jackson, MS: State Department of Archives and History, 1917).

14. Claiborne to Judge J. White, October 11, 1808.

The Code[18] will probably be greatly censured by many native Citizens of the United States who reside in the Territory. From principle and habit,

18. "The Code" was the new code of civil laws adopted by the territorial legislature. Although Jefferson, Claiborne, and Congress had strongly urged the discarding of the French legal system, over the years it became clear that the vast majority of native Louisianans preferred keeping it. The 1808 code, therefore, was an amalgam of the two systems.

they are attached to that system of Jurisprudence, prevailing in the several States under which themselves and their Fathers were reared: For myself I am free to declare the pleasure it would give me to see the Laws of Orleans assimilated to those of the states generally, not only from a conviction, that such Laws are for the most part wise and just, but the opinion I entertain, that in a Country, where a unity of Government and Interests exists, it is highly desirable to introduce thro'out the same Laws and Customs. We ought to recollect however, the peculiar circumstances in which Louisiana is placed, nor ought we to be unmindful of the respect due the sentiments and wishes of the Ancient Louisianans who compose so great a proportion of the population. Educated in a belief of the excellencies of the Civil Law, the Louisianans have hitherto been unwilling to part with them. . . .

15. Claiborne's address to both Houses of the Territorial Legislature, January 14, 1809.

I do not learn Gentlemen that the "act to provide for the means of establishing public schools in the Parishes of the Territory" is likely to produce the desired effect. . . .

The instruction of our children in the various branches of science, should be accompanied with every effort to instill into their minds principles of morality; to cherish their virtuous propensities; to inspire them with an ardent patriotism, & with that spirit of laudable emulation, which "seeks the esteem of posterity for good and virtuous actions." Youths thus reared into life, become the pride of their parents, the ornaments of society & the pillars of their country's glory. You cannot, Gentlemen, but be sensible of the importance of this subject; it embraces the best interest of the community & mingles with the warmest affections of the heart. . . .

16. Claiborne to Robert Smith, November 18, 1809.

[Claiborne reported to Smith that there were seven newspapers published in the city of New Orleans—four in French and English, two in French only, and one in English only.]

The *Moniteur* has a limited circulation, and being published only in French is not taken by the Citizens whose native language is English; so also the *Louisiana Gazette* being published only in English does not circulate among Citizens whose native Language is French.—*The Louisiana Courrier—Orleans Gazette—*and *Telegraph* are subscribed for by both descriptions of citizens.—The *first* is understood to have the most extensive circulation.

♦ CHAPTER 5

The Evolution
of American
Citizenship:
The Louisiana
Purchase,
1803–1812

As regards European politicks the *Louisiana Courrier* and *Telegraph* appear to take great Interest in the successes of Bonaparte, the *Orleans Gazette,* and the *Louisiana Gazette,* manifest a Bias in favour of England and her allies.

Source 17 from *Public Statutes at Large of the United States of America,* 11th Congress, 3rd Session, February 20, 1811 (Boston: Little & Brown, 1845).

17. An Act to Enable the People of the Territory of Louisiana to Form a Constitution and a State Government, and For the Admission of such State into the Union, on an Equal Footing with the Original States, February 20, 1811.

Be it enacted by the Senate and House of Representatives of the United States of America in Congress assembled, That the inhabitants of all that part of the territory or country ceded under the name of Louisiana, by the treaty made at Paris on the thirtieth of April, one thousand eight hundred and three, between the United States and France. . . . are hereby, authorized to form for themselves a constitution and State government, and to assume such name as they may deem proper, under the provisions and upon the conditions hereinafter mentioned.

SEC. 2. *And be it further enacted,* That all free white male citizens of the United States, who shall have arrived at the age of twenty-one years, and resided within the said Territory at least one year previous to the day of election, and shall have paid a territorial, county, or district, or parish tax, and all persons having in other respects the legal qualifications to vote for representatives in the general assembly of the said Territory, be, and they are hereby, authorized to choose representatives to form a convention, who shall be apportioned amongst the several counties, districts, and parishes in the said Territory of Orleans in such manner as the legislature of the said Territory shall by law direct. The number of representatives shall not exceed sixty, and the elections for the representatives aforesaid shall take place on the third Monday in September next, and shall be conducted in the same manner as is now provided by the laws of the said Territory for electing members for the house of representatives.

SEC. 3. *And be it further enacted,* That the members of the convention, when duly elected, be, and they are hereby, authorized to meet at the city of New Orleans, on the first Monday of November next, which convention, when met, shall first determine, by a majority of the whole number elected, whether it be expected or not, at that time, to form a constitution and State government for the people within the said Territory, and if it be determined to be expedient, then the convention shall in like manner declare, in behalf of the people of the said Territory, that it adopts the Constitution of the United States; whereupon the said convention shall be, and hereby is, authorized to form a constitution and State government for the people of the said Territory: *Provided,* The constitution to be formed, in virtue of the authority herein given, shall be republican, and consistent with the Constitution of the United States; that it shall contain the fundamental principles of civil and religious liberty; that it shall secure to the citizen the trial by jury in all criminal cases, and the privilege of the writ of *habeas corpus*, conformable to the provisions of the Constitution of the United States.

Questions to Consider

The evolution of the concept of American citizenship was a process that was sometimes cooperative and often contentious.[19] As you already have seen, United States leaders were by no means in agreement regarding either the definition or the process of citizenship. Nor were the Louisianans themselves of one mind.

To begin with, Louisianans who insisted that Article 3 of the treaty of cession (Source 2) granted them full citizenship and immediate statehood obviously were naïve. And yet, the Northwest Ordinance of 1787 clearly set forth a process whereby the nation's western lands would become states, and three territories (Ohio, Indiana, and Mississippi) already were at some point in that process.[20] Why didn't President Jefferson or Congress choose to apply that process to Louisiana?

Both Jefferson and Congressman Samuel L. Mitchill referred to Louisianans as "children." What did they mean by that? Louisianans doubtless were different in several ways from people living in Ohio, Indiana, Mississippi, and other western lands. But *precisely what was different about them* that caused American leaders to deny them the process laid out in the Northwest Ordinance? See Governor Claiborne's opinions in his letters in Source 3.

Federalists in Congress were genuinely concerned about the constitutionality of what was taking place, the erosion of the political power of New England, and the expansion of slavery. But many of them also used the issue as a way to embarrass President Jefferson. How do the remarks of Roger Griswold (Source 4) and the Federalists in Source 15 reveal these points?

19. **contentious:** quarrelsome, belligerent.
20. For the process set at by the 1787 Northwest Ordinance, consult your text or your instructor. Ohio became a state in 1803, Indiana in 1816, and Mississippi in 1817.

✦ CHAPTER 5

The Evolution
of American
Citizenship:
The Louisiana
Purchase,
1803–1812

The Louisiana Governance Bill (secretly authored by Jefferson and introduced by Sen. Breckinridge) touched off a fiery debate in the Senate. What were the principal provisions of the bill (Source 6)? What were the major points of contention (Sources 6 and 7)? Did the bill contain any provisions for eventual statehood?

Claiborne reported the general dissatisfaction with the Louisiana Governance Act among Louisianans (Sources 8 and 11). What were the objections? Note especially Claiborne's inability to put together a Legislative Council (letter of November 5, 1804).

A key piece of evidence is Source 9, Governor Claiborne's first address to the Legislative Council. What did Claiborne tell Louisianans they must do in order to impress Congress and achieve statehood? See also his earlier letters to Secretary of State Madison in Source 3.

In Source 10, Senator William Plumer recalled objections that certain Louisianans had regarding the Louisiana Governance Act and Governor Claiborne. What do you think was the purpose of the dinner? What do those points tell you? Add to those the objections you find in the formal Remonstrance and Petition (that had been approved by 150 New Orleans residents and then distributed to adjoining parishes for an additional 2,000 signatures). To what group did the Louisianans compare themselves?

The Second Louisiana Governance Act (Source 13) established a process for being granted statehood and made basic changes in the Louisianan government. Based on the Evidence in this chapter, how had Louisianans conformed to the wishes of Congress and Claiborne *before the Second Governance Act?* In your view, why did Congress make those critical alterations? How do you think the concept of citizenship was changing . . . if indeed it was?

Sources 14–16 demonstrate clearly how, in Claiborne's opinion, the majority of Louisianans had *not* changed. Even so, in 1811, Congress authorized Louisiana to begin the process of moving toward statehood, a process that was finally approved by Congress on April 8, 1812. According to the 1787 Northwest Ordinance, a territory had to reach a white population of 60,000 before being admitted to statehood. Yet the 1810 census reported that the Territory of Orleans had only 34,311 free whites, and all of Louisiana contained only 51,538 whites. In your view, why was the state of Louisiana (the former Territory of Orleans) admitted to the Union with less than the mandated population?[21]

Finally, return to the central questions. After examining and analyzing all the evidence *and* reading between the lines when necessary, answer the following questions:

1. What criteria did the U.S. Congress and the President require to be met by the citizens of the Louisiana Territory?

21. For 1810 census returns, see Kastor, ed., *The Louisiana Purchase,* p. 273. On December 17, 1810, Julien Poydras (1746-1824), the nonvoting delegate from the territory to the House of Representatives, reported that the 60,000 population had been reached, although it may not have been. *Debates and Proceedings of Congress.* 11th Congress, 3rd. Session, p. 481.

2. How did the residents of the Louisiana Territory react and respond to those requirements?

3. How was the issue ultimately resolved?

4. How did the Louisiana Purchase affect the United States' ideas and policies regarding citizenship?

Epilogue

It is virtually impossible to overestimate the significance of the Louisiana Purchase to the United States. Not only was the size of the young nation virtually doubled (all or part of fourteen states were carved from it), but a literal treasure of natural resources was found within it. As Napoleon Bonaparte himself put it, "This accession of territory strengthens for ever the power of the United States; and I have just given to England a maritime rival, that will sooner or later humble her pride."[22]

Nor were Americans themselves unaware of the purchase's importance. Perhaps it was an overstatement uttered by historian Thomas McIntyre Cooley, who said in 1887 that "nearly all leading events of later American history were either traceable to or in some measure shaped or determined by it." Uncharacteristically more restrained was Theodore Roosevelt, who wrote, in 1900, "The Purchase therefore provided the impetus for Americans to fulfill their national destiny."[23]

Virtually ignored, however, is the effect the debates after the Louisiana Purchase had on reshaping the concept of American citizenship. For the first time, a sizable body of non-British people with a different language, legal and political systems, customs, and religion had become a part of the United States. Due to these differences, they were not included in the citizenship and statehood process enacted by the Northwest Ordinance. Rather than alter their ways, most Louisianans defied efforts to change them. Without making any attempts to become absorbed into the larger American culture, native Louisianans for the most part stubbornly but peacefully resisted. Thus, even though some congressmen were not convinced that Louisianans had undergone the proper "Americanization" process, they ultimately gave in, hoping that citizenship and statehood would *make* them Americans.

If Louisianans had not been fully accepted as American citizens, the Battle of

---

22. Quoted in Alexander DeConde, *This Affair of Louisiana* (New York: Charles Scribner's, 1976), p. 173.
23. Thomas McIntyre Cooley, "The Acquisition of Louisiana," in *Indiana Historical Society Publications,* vol. 2 (1887), p. 65; Theodore Roosevelt, *The Winning of the West* (New York: P.F. Collier and Sons, 1896), vol. 4, p. 297.

✦ CHAPTER 5

The Evolution
of American
Citizenship:
The Louisiana
Purchase,
1803–1812

New Orleans (January 8, 1815) convinced many Americans of the Louisianans' loyalty, if not their desire for cultural homogeneity. Kentucky congressman Solomon Sharp asked whether "there be an American, whose bosom does not beat high with joy to call Louisiana a legitimate daughter of the Union, and hail her citizens as brothers?"[24.]

If Americans had been willing to accept Louisianans of a different culture than their own to citizenship, this did not set a permanent precedent for later generations. During the late nineteenth and all of the twentieth century, furious debates took place over groups of immigrants who chose to retain their own languages, customs, religions, and the like, and whether they should be granted full citizenship. Ironically, some Americans who insisted the loudest that these groups should adopt the core American culture were the same ones who had to struggle the hardest for citizenship and acceptance themselves. Thus the definition of American citizenship remains ever-changing, as is the nation itself.[25.]

Often ignored, however, is the impact the Louisiana Purchase had on Native Americans east of the Mississippi River. The acquisition of such a vast territory gave white Americans the opportunity to entice, influence, or force Native Americans to cede their lands to ever encroaching whites and move to what many whites saw as the "empty" frontier. In 1803 President Thomas Jefferson wrote to Indian agent Benjamin Hawkins advocating removal. The President wrote that "I feel it consistent with pure morality to lead them towards it. . . ." As Louisianans ultimately became citizens, it was decades before that status and those rights were offered to the original settlers.[26.]

To Our Readers

As noted earlier, the criteria that an individual was required to meet in order to become a citizen has changed over time. Today, applicants for citizenship must pass a "citizenship test" of 100 multiple choice questions, some having to do with the organization of the state and federal governments, others regarding American history, and still others dealing with American geography etc. Several sets of test questions can be found in Google.com.

Other nations have different requirements for citizenship, some of them considerably more demanding than those of the United States. They can be found on the Internet.

24. *Debates and Proceedings in Congress.* 11th Congress, 3rd. Session, pp. 321, 494–505, 542, 574–576.
25. Finally, in 1828 the U.S. Supreme Court upheld the constitutionality of the acquisition of territory in *American Insurance Company v. Canter* (1 Peters 511).

26. Jefferson to Hawkins, February 18, 1803, in Paul Leicester Ford, ed., *The Works of Thomas Jefferson* (New York: G.P. Putnam's Sons, 1905), vol. 9, p. 448. See also one of Jefferson's draft constitutional amendments in Kastor, *The Louisiana Purchase*, pp. 193–194.

CHAPTER

6

Church, State, and Democracy: The Sunday Mail Controversy, 1827–1831

◆

The Problem

On July 4, 1827, most of those who attended the Independence Day service at Philadelphia's Seventh Presbyterian Church probably expected to enjoy a traditional patriotic homily honoring Revolutionary War veterans (some of whom were still alive), General Washington, and the other Founders. Little did they suspect that the religious message they were about to hear would become one of the most important sermons delivered in the still-young republic, one that was widely published and distributed throughout much of the United States.

Instead of paying tribute to heroes of the past, guest pastor Ezra Stiles Ely (1786–1861) issued a ringing call for all Christians of all denominations to unite to elect fellow Christians to office who would enact laws reflecting their own beliefs and social principles:

> I propose, fellow-citizens, a new sort of union, or, if you please, a *Christian party in politics*, which I am exceedingly desirous all good men in our country should join: not by . . . the formation of a new society, . . . but by adopting, avowing, and determining to act upon truly religious principles in all civil matters.[1]

And although Ely denied that he was advocating a political party similar to the emerging political coalitions of the early nineteenth century, his call for organization, platforms, and voter drives certainly bore striking similarities to the political parties that were forming in the United States in the 1820s and 1830s.

In one sense, Ely's stirring remarks marked the climax of the religious excitement known collectively as the

---

1. Ezra Stiles Ely, *The Duty of Christian Freemen to Elect Christian Rulers: A Discourse Delivered on the Fourth of July, 1827, In the Seventh Presbyterian Church, in Philadelphia* (Philadelphia: William F. Geddes, 1828), p. 8.

✦ CHAPTER 6
Church, State,
and Democracy:
The Sunday Mail
Controversy,
1827–1831

Second Great Awakening. During the period from the late 1790s to the mid-1830s, thousands of Americans attended religious revivals and camp meetings, joined existing denominations or formed new ones, and founded or supported ecumenical "improvement associations" such as the American Bible Society, the American Tract Society, the American Sunday School Union, and countless others. Why, Ely and others reasoned, couldn't this increased interest in religion be channeled in part toward drafting and enacting legislation that would bring secular society more in conformity with Christian moral beliefs and commandments? As Baptist leader John Mason Peck prophesied, "Jesus Christ is about to possess the whole land."[2]

The first test of whether Christians would be able to act together to change federal laws was the effort to pressure Congress to close all post offices on Sundays and prohibit the carrying of mail on the Christian Sabbath. An earlier attempt to do so in the 1810s had collapsed, but supporters reasoned that better organization and leadership would succeed this time where earlier efforts had failed. Such a success, many believed, would be but the first step in an ambitious campaign to legislate Christian principles. In its first annual report, the recently established General Union for Promoting the Observance of the Christian Sabbath explained that the success or failure of the Sunday

mail campaign would "in the main determine all the rest [of the Society's efforts]."[3]

Although the men who drafted and ratified the federal Constitution had given a great deal of thought to the proper relationship between the federal government and religious institutions, the vast majority of Americans had paid almost no attention to church-state relations and had never debated the issues arising from them. The efforts to close the post offices on the Christian Sabbath gave them the first opportunity to do so.

Your task in this chapter is to examine arguments for and against the closing of post offices on Sunday. **What did the advocates and opponents of closing the post offices and prohibiting the carrying of mail on Sunday see as the *significance* or *importance* of the conflict? How did their views of that significance or importance *go beyond* the Sunday mail controversy?**

The U.S. Constitution was less than a half-century old when the conflict erupted. **How did each side interpret the Constitution?**

A historian who is analyzing a particular debate attempts to be fair to all sides. In this chapter, you should do likewise. Remember that those who considered themselves devout Christians were on both sides of the issue, as were those who could not be described as religious.

---

2. For a partial list of associations, see John R. Bodo, *The Protestant Clergy and Public Issues, 1812–1848* (Princeton: Princeton University Press, 1954), p. 20. For Peck's remark see *ibid*, p. 22.

3. *First Annual Report of the General Union for Promoting the Observance of the Christian Sabbath: Adopted May 12, 1829* (New York: J. Collard, 1829), p. 13.

Background

One of the most perceptive visitors to the United States during the nation's first century was the Frenchman Alexis de Tocqueville (1805–1859), who spent nine months in 1831–1832 traveling and observing the government, people, and institutions of the young republic. In his book *Democracy in America*, published in French in 1835 and in English in 1836, Tocqueville offered many comparisons between the United States and his native land, one of the most startling to him being the widespread popularity of religious beliefs and institutions. "In France," Tocqueville claimed, ". . . the spirit of religion and the spirit of liberty almost always pulled in opposite directions. In the United States, I found them intimately intertwined: together they ruled the same territory."[4]

And yet, if Tocqueville had come to America with his fellow countryman the Marquis de Lafayette a half century earlier, he would have found a very different environment. In spite of the fact that almost every one of the thirteen original states had a government-supported established church as well as a multitude of state and local ordinances having to do with the Sabbath and many aspects of moral—or immoral—behavior, most Americans were not church members (only about 17 percent in 1789) and

regularly ignored laws governing behavior on the Sabbath. Even so, the vast majority of free Americans would have identified themselves as Christians (overwhelmingly Protestant) and do not seem to have wanted to strike down these state and local ordinances so long as they were able to ignore them.[5]

When those who were later called the Founders met in 1787 to draft a new federal constitution, however, they were extremely aware of the dangers inherent in an alliance of the national government and any religion. Indeed, since most of the Founders had come from an English background, their own history made them all too aware that any unification of church and state was potentially disastrous. Ever since English King Henry VIII had broken with the Roman Catholic Church in 1534, England had witnessed wholesale religious persecutions and executions, two civil wars, the beheading of one king (Charles I, in 1647), and the overthrow of another (James II, in 1688). To most of the Founders, therefore, any artificial or forced religious conformity could lead, as it had in England, to tyranny and enormous bloodshed. Therefore, they wrote a constitution that purposely made almost no mention of religion. The document was to be, as they saw it, a framework on how the new central government would be organized and

4. Alexis de Tocqueville, Democracy in America, trans. Arthur Goldhammer (New York: Library of America, 2004 ed.), p. 341. Tocqueville and his traveling companion Gustave de Beaumont (1802–1865) carried letters of introduction from Lafayette.

5. For colonial and early state Sabbath ordinances see William Addison Blakely, comp., *American State Papers Bearing on Sunday Legislation* (Washington, DC: Religious Liberty Association, 1911), pp. 34–57.

✦ CHAPTER 6

Church, State,
and Democracy:
The Sunday Mail
Controversy,
1827–1831

would operate. As such, they believed, perhaps naively, that there was no real need for any statement on religion, since that was in a totally different sphere.

Not unexpectedly, there were complaints. In a June 15, 1789 letter to John Adams, Dr. Benjamin Rush spoke for many when he wrote, "Many pious people wish the name of the Supreme Being had been introduced somewhere in the new Constitution. Perhaps an acknowledgement may be made of his goodness or of his providence in the proposed amendments." As a suggestion to the new Vice President, Rush added, "In all enterprises and parties I believe the *praying* are better allies than the *fighting* part of communities."[6] Ignoring Rush's suggestion, the Constitution's First Amendment contained only 16 words concerning religion:

> Congress shall make no law respecting an establishment of religion, or prohibiting the free exercise thereof.

Clearly the intention of that part of the First Amendment was to protect the state from a religious denomination *and* all religious denominations from the state, creating what President Thomas Jefferson in 1802 described as a "wall of separation." In spite of considerable grumbling, the "wall of separation" held fast.[7]

This did not mean, however, that the Founders intended that there should be an absence of religion in Americans' private and public lives. Indeed, they *hoped* for it. An overwhelming majority of Americans would have agreed with John Adams when he opined, "Religion I hold to be essential to morals. I have never read of an irreligious character in Greek or Roman history, or in any other history, nor have I known one in life who was not a rascal. Name one if you can, living or dead." Even Benjamin Franklin, whose ideas about religion were, to say the least, unconventional, wrote:

> I have lived, sir, a long time; and the longer I live, the more convincing proofs I see of this truth: that God governs the affairs of men! And if a sparrow cannot fall to the ground without his notice, is it probable that an empire can rise without his aid?[8]

Thus almost no one objected when President Washington took the presidential oath of office with his hand on a Bible, a practice that has been repeated by every subsequent president except one (Franklin Pierce, in 1853). And while more than a few chafed at state or local ordinances having to do with religion, there appears to have been no general movement to have them repealed. As they joined the Union, most of the new states followed suit. To the Founders and most of their contemporaries, the goal was *not to separate religion from politics*, as Americans hoped that their

6. Rush to Adams, June 15, 1789, in L. H. Butterfield, ed., *Letters of Benjamin Rush* (Princeton: Princeton University Press, for the American Philosophical Society, 1951), vol. I, p. 517.
7. See Jefferson to the Danbury (CT) Baptist Association, January 1, 1802, cited in Dumas Malone, *Jefferson the President: First Term, 1801–1805* (Boston: Little, Brown, 1970) pp. 108–109.

8. Jon Meacham, *American Gospel: God, the Founding Fathers, and the Making of a Nation* (New York: Random House, 2006), pp. 28, 89.

religious-based moral senses would inform their political decisions. Rather, the goal was to *separate the church from the state,* so that neither institution could infect or dominate the other. To many twenty-first century Americans, these two goals appear to be the same, but to the generation of the Founders they were distinctly different. To that generation, most very likely would have agreed with James Madison when he wrote, "If men were angels, no government would be necessary."[9]

Beginning in the early 1800s, however, a major shift began to take place in American religion. In the new western states, evangelical preachers (mostly Methodist circuit riders, independent Baptist clergymen, and Presbyterian missionaries) began to reach the new communities that were sprouting up west of the original thirteen states. Many of these men and women had never attended a religious service and were initially drawn to the excitement of the huge revivals and camp meetings (week-long revivals in which people came and "camped" on the ground). In August 1801, for example, in Cane Ridge, Kentucky, Presbyterian, Methodist, and Baptist evangelists preached for about a week to approximately 20,000 people. According to one of the clergymen, many exhibited their religious spirit by shouting, rolling on the ground, and other physical manifestations of their "salvation." At the same time, in many northeastern cities, many people who had grown fearful of

rapid changes in urban growth, technology, the market economy, embraced religious institutions as rocks in the swiftly flowing stream. Church membership, once an anemic 17 percent in 1789, had burgeoned to 34 percent by 1850. According to Presbyterian cleric Lyman Beecher (1775–1863), around 100,000 Americans joined churches in 1831 alone. Many were attracted to new religious denominations that had grown up or had broken off from older churches. Cumberland Presbyterians, United Brethren, Republican Methodists, Disciples of Christ, New School Presbyterians, Latter-Day Saints (Mormons), Millerites (Seventh-Day Adventists), Unitarians, and several varieties of Baptists all sprung from this Second Great Awakening.[10]

At the same time that thousands of American men and women were swept up in this religious excitement, a series of national organizations emerged to marshal these new converts to spread the Gospel even further and demonstrate their own personal salvations through good works. Indeed, many evangelical preachers had predicted that good works to improve society would hasten the second coming of Jesus Christ. Often financed by wealthy business figures, such as silk merchant Lewis Tappan and flour merchant Josiah Bissell, these national organizations established state and local chapters to distribute

9. James Madison, "Federalist #51," in Clinton Rossiter, ed., *The Federalist Papers* (New York: New American Library, 1961), p. 290.

10. For two descriptions of revival meetings, see Frances Trollope, *Domestic Manners of the Americans,* ed. Donald Smalley (New York: Alfred A. Knopf, 1949), pp. 167–175; Anne Royal "A Tennessee Revival" [1830] in *The Annals of America* (Chicago: Encyclopedia Britannica, 1968), vol. 5, pp. 383–385.

✦ CHAPTER 6
Church, State,
and Democracy:
The Sunday Mail
Controversy,
1827–1831

tracts and Bibles, fund missionaries at home and abroad, organize Sunday Schools, and support reform movements such as temperance which, in terms of numbers, was the largest reform movement in the United States prior to the Civil War. Leadership of these organizations often overlapped. For example, New Jersey U.S. Senator Theodore Frelinghuysen (1787–1862) was at approximately the same time the president of the American Tract Society and the American Bible Society, vice president of the Sunday School Union, the American Education Society, and the Home Mission Society, and an active officer of the Temperance Union and Peace Society. Several other leading clerics were either officers or participants in numerous "improvement" societies. Not only did all these organizations publish and mass distribute reports and pamphlets (the General Union for Promoting the Observance of the Christian Sabbath, for example, distributed 100,000 copies of its constitution), but each denomination established numerous sectarian newspapers to reach their new members.[11]

The first major effort to bring all these people, denominations, and national societies together was the Sunday mail issue. Since most town and village businesses were closed on Sundays, the post office was a "conspicuous exception" to the general Sabbath observance in small-town America, and

as such was a good test of the potential power of American Protestants in the political arena.[12]

From independence to around 1830, a United States Postal System employee was often the only federal officer that a vast majority of Americans ever met. With only sixty-nine employees in 1788, the postal system had grown to 8,450 officers by 1830 and was delivering 13.8 million letters and 16.0 million newspapers per year. The mileage of post roads by 1828 had increased approximately 452 percent and by 1831, 76.3 percent of the federal government's civilian work force were postmasters. To religious leaders, therefore, the postal service was the most visible and, they reasoned, the most vulnerable. Stagecoaches carrying the mail on the Sabbath were noisy reminders that the federal government was not observing the Sabbath. Moreover, most postmasters also were storekeepers who sold alcoholic beverages on Sundays while the post offices were open.[13]

In 1810, Congress passed a law requiring post offices to be open on Sundays for a minimum of one hour. Religious leaders responded with a poorly organized petition effort and from 1814 to 1817, no less than seven bills to overturn the 1810 statute

11. For Frelinghuysen, see Clifford S. Griffin, *Their Brothers' Keepers: Moral Stewardship in the United States, 1800–1865* (New Brunswick: Rutgers University Press, 1960), p. 56. For other leaders, see Bodo, *Protestant Clergy*, pp. 20–22.

12. Daniel Walker Howe, *What Hath God Wrought: The Transformation of America, 1815–1848* (New York: Oxford University Press, 2007), p. 229.
13. Richard R. John, *Spreading the News: The American Postal System from Franklin to Morse* (Cambridge: Harvard University Press, 1995), pp. 3, 4, 25, 51; Wayne E. Fuller, *Morality and the Mail in Nineteenth Century America* (Urbana: University of Illinois Press, 2003), pp. 2, 22. For Sunday liquor sales see Howe, *What Hath God Wrought*, pp. 229.

were introduced in Congress, with none ever getting to a vote. But when an 1825 law strengthened the 1810 statute, leaders of an invigorated religious movement were prepared to test their organization and their strength. If even the most excited Christians were becoming lethargic, surely, they believed, this issue would rouse them to do battle.[14]

Your task in this chapter is to examine and analyze arguments for and against the closing of post offices on Sunday. What did the advocates and opponents see as the *significance* or *importance* of the conflict? How did their views of that significance or importance *go beyond* the Sunday mail controversy? Finally, how did each side interpret the United States Constitution?

♦

The Method

Once having gathered all the available evidence, the first thing historians must do is to arrange the evidence. In this chapter, we have arranged the ten pieces of evidence in roughly chronological order, based on when each piece was either written, published or spoken. To answer the central questions, however, you will want to rearrange the evidence by dividing it into two general groups: those pieces of evidence that support the effort to close post offices on Sundays and those that oppose that effort. When you do that, you will see that there are four pieces of evidence supporting closings, five that oppose it, and one (Source 8) that appears to be on the fence.

Before examining and analyzing the evidence in further detail, however, it would be enormously helpful to know something about the authors of the evidence. Learning about the authors will not only help you to understand their general opinions but will also make your reading of their pieces

14. Blakely, *American State Papers*, pp. 176–185.

easier. All but one of the pieces of evidence (Source 3) had individuals who revealed their authorship, and almost all of them can be found in the multivolume *Dictionary of American Biography* (in print or online), on Google .com, or in other sources.

Now that you have rearranged the evidence and learned something about the authors, you are ready to examine and analyze the evidence in detail. Here it would be very helpful to make a chart listing on one side all the arguments in favor of closing the post offices on Sunday and on the other side all the points against it. Also list what each side understood to be the *principal issues* involved in the controversy. As you find and write down each point, make sure to use numbers to help you remember which piece (or pieces) of evidence made that point. Also be aware that almost all the pieces of evidence contain more than one point. Finally, some pieces of evidence (especially Sources 7 and 10) do not address the issue directly. You will have to infer how they stood on the issue.

◆ CHAPTER 6

Church, State,
and Democracy:
The Sunday Mail
Controversy,
1827–1831

Once you have analyzed the evidence *and* answered the three central questions, adopt the role of a historian and explain what *you* believe was the *historical significance* of the controversy *today*, over 185 years since the conflict. This will take a good deal of thought as well as historical imagination. The Epilogue section at the end of the chapter may be of some help.

◆

The Evidence

Source 1 from *The Duty of Christian Freemen to Elect Christian Rulers: A Discourse Delivered on the Fourth of July, 1827* (Philadelphia: William F. Geddes, 1828).

1. Ely, Duty of Christian Freemen, 1827.

We have assembled, fellow citizens, on the anniversary of our Nation's birth day, in a rational and religious manner, to celebrate our independence of all foreign domination, and the goodness of God in making us a free and happy people. On what subject can I, on the present occasion, insist with more propriety, than on the duty of all the rulers and citizens of these United States in the exercise and enjoyment of all their political rights, to honour the Lord Jesus Christ.

Let it then be distinctly stated and fearlessly maintained IN THE FIRST PLACE, that every member of this Christian nation, from the highest to the lowest, ought to serve the Lord with fear, and yield his sincere homage to the Son of God. Every ruler *should be* an avowed and a sincere friend of Christianity. He should know and believe the doctrines of our holy religion, and act in conformity with its precepts. This *he ought* to do; because as a man he is required to serve the Lord. . . .

I would guard, however, against misunderstanding and misrepresentation, when I state, that all our rulers ought in their official stations to serve the Lord Jesus Christ. I do not wish any religious test to be prescribed by constitution, and proposed to a man on his acceptance of any public trust. Neither can any intelligent friend of his country and of true religion desire the establishment of any one religious sect by civil law. Let the religion of the Bible rest on that everlasting rock, and on those spiritual laws, on which Jehovah has founded his kingdom: let Christianity by the spirit of Christ in her members support herself: let Church and State be for ever distinct: but, still, let the doctrines and precepts of Christ govern all men, in all their relations and employments. If a ruler is not a Christian he ought to be one, in this land of evangelical light, without delay; and he ought, being a follower of Jesus, to honour him even as he honours the Father. . . .

SECONDLY, Since it is the duty of all our rulers to serve the Lord and kiss the Son of God, it must be most manifestly the duty of all our Christian fellow-citizens to honour the Lord Jesus Christ and promote Christianity by electing and supporting as public officers the friends of our blessed Saviour. . . .

[Here Ely explained that if Christians do not unite to elect fellow Christians to office, then elections will be "controlled by others."]

I propose, fellow-citizens, a new sort of union, or, if you please, a *Christian party in politics,* which I am exceedingly desirous all good men in our country should join: not by *subscribing a constitution* and the formation of a new society, to be added to the scores which now exist; but by adopting, avowing, and determining to act upon, truly religious principles in all civil matters. I am aware, that the true Christians of our country are divided into many different denominations; who have, alas! too many points of jealousy and collision; still, a union to a very great extent, and for the most valuable purposes is not impracticable. . . .

[Here Ely maintained that members of all Christian denominations could agree on what was bad moral character. In addition, he argued that good men "who profess no experimental acquaintance with Christianity, might unite and co-operate with our Christian party."]

All who profess to be Christians of any denomination ought to agree that they will support no man as a candidate for any office, who is not professedly friendly to Christianity, and a believer in divine Revelation. We do not say that true or even pretended Christianity shall be made a constitutional test of admission to office; but we do affirm that Christians may in their elections lawfully prefer the avowed friends of the Christian religion to Turks, Jews, and Infidels.

[Ely then explained that a new Christian party would be able to draw Presbyterians, Baptists, Methodists, Congregationalists, German Christians, Reformed Dutch churchmen, and even "members of the Protestant Episcopal church in our country."]

It deprives no man of his right for me to prefer a Christian to an Infidel. If Infidels were the most numerous electors, they would doubtless elect men of their own sentiments; and unhappily such men not unfrequently get into power in this country, in which ninety-nine hundredths of the people

◆ CHAPTER 6

Church, State,
and Democracy:
The Sunday Mail
Controversy,
1827–1831

are believers in the divine origin and authority of the Christian religion. If hundreds of thousands of our fellow citizens should agree with us in an effort to elect men to public office who read the Bible, profess to believe it, reverence the Sabbath, attend public worship, and sustain a good moral character, who could complain? Have we not as much liberty to be the supporters of the Christian cause by our votes, as others have to support anti-Christian men and measures?

Let us awake, then, fellow Christians, to our duty to our Divine Master; and let us have no rulers, without consent and co-operation, who are not known to be avowedly Christians. . . .

If they are of no religious denomination, they belong to the party of infidels. . . .

We are a Christian nation: we have a right to demand that all our rulers in their conduct shall conform to Christian morality; and if they do not, it is the duty and privilege of Christian freemen to make a new and a better election.

May the Lord Jesus Christ for ever reign in and over these United States, and call them peculiarly his own.

Amen.

Source 2 from *Report of Senate Committee on Post Offices and Postal Roads, January 19, 1829.* 20th Congress, 2nd session, Senate Report #74.

2. Report of Senate Committee on Post Offices and Postal Roads, January 19, 1829. Sen. Richard M. Johnson, Chairman.[15]

[The Report began by listing several American citizens (Jews, Seventh-Day Adventists, etc.) who celebrated the Sabbath on Saturday, and Christians who kept their Sabbath on Sunday but who refused to force it upon others.]

With these different religious views, the committee are of opinion that Congress cannot interfere. It is not the legitimate province of the legislature to determine what religion is true, or what false. Our government is a civil, and not a religious institution. Our constitution recognises in every person, the right to choose his own religion, and to enjoy it freely, without molestation. Whatever may be the religious sentiments of citizens, and however variant,

15. There was considerable doubt at the time, and later, over whether Johnson actually wrote the report. Some attribute the authorship to O. B. Brown, a Baptist minister and federal employee who shared a boardinghouse with Johnson. Others claim that the true author was Alexander Campbell (see Source 9), a Kentucky clergyman who was a friend of Johnson.

they are alike entitled to protection from the government, so long as they do not invade the rights of others.

The transportation of the mail on the first day of the week, it is believed, does not interfere with the rights of conscience. The petitioners for its discontinuance appear to be actuated from a religious zeal, which may be commendable if confined to its proper sphere; but they assume a position better suited to an ecclesiastical than to a civil institution. They appear, in many instances, to lay it down as an axiom, that the practice is a violation of the law of God. Should Congress, in their legislative capacity, adopt the sentiment, it would establish the principle, that the Legislature is a proper tribunal to determine what are the laws of God. It would involve a legislative decision in a religious controversy; and on a point in which good citizens may honestly differ in opinion, without disturbing the peace of society, or endangering its liberties. If this principle is once introduced, it will be impossible to define its bounds. Among all the religious persecutions with which almost every page of modern history is stained, no victim ever suffered, but for the violation of what government denominated the law of God. To prevent a similar train of evils in this country, the Constitution has wisely withheld from our government the power of defining the Divine Law. It is a right reserved to each citizen; and while he respects the equal rights of others, he cannot be held amenable to any human tribunal for his conclusions.

Extensive religious combinations, to effect a political object, are, in the opinion of the committee, always dangerous. This first effort of the kind, calls for the establishment of a principle, which, in the opinion of the committee, would lay the foundation for dangerous innovations upon the spirit of the Constitution, and upon the religious rights of the citizens. If admitted, it may be justly apprehended, that the future measures of government will be strongly marked, if not eventually controlled, by the same influence. All religious despotism commences by combination and influence; and when that influence begins to operate upon the political institutions of a country, the civil power soon bends under it; and the catastrophe of other nations furnishes an awful warning of the consequence. . . .

[Here the Report explained that postal employees were fully aware of their workloads when they took employment and were not required to work any hours if that conflicted with their consciences. The Report also stated that the closing of post offices on Sunday would set a precedent for other federal employees (army, navy, etc.) and could lead to "the erection of edifices for the worship of the Creator." Finally, delay of the mails would be a burden to private businesses and other government agencies.]

◆ CHAPTER 6
Church, State,
and Democracy:
The Sunday Mail
Controversy,
1827–1831

Our constitution recognizes no other power than that of persuasion, for enforcing religious observances. Let the professors of Christianity recommend their religion by deeds of benevolence—by Christian meekness—by lives of temperance and holiness. Let them combine their efforts to instruct the ignorant—to relieve the widow and the orphan—to promulgate to the world the gospel of their Saviour, recommending its precepts by their habitual example: government will find its legitimate object in protecting them. It cannot oppose them, and they will not need its aid. Their moral influence will then do infinitely more to advance the true interests of religion, than any measures which they may call on Congress to enact.

The petitioners do not complain of any infringement upon their own rights. They enjoy all that Christians ought to ask at the hand of any government— protection from all molestation in the exercise of their religious sentiments.

Resolved, That the Committee be discharged from the further consideration of the subject.

Source 3 from *An Account of Memorials Presented to Congress During the Last session . . . Praying that the Mails May not be Transported, Nor Post-Offices kept Open, on the Sabbath* (New York: T. R. Marvin, May 1829).

3. Account of Memorials, May 1829.

Ever since the mail was first transported in the United States on the Sabbath, this violation of the day of rest has been a source of grief and pain to many individuals, who are justly ranked among the most intelligent, useful, and virtuous of our citizens. To the certain knowledge of the compiler of these pages, much regret has been expressed, by persons residing in many parts of the Union, that a practice so pernicious in its tendency and consequences, should have been sanctioned by any department of our national government.

Post-offices, in our large towns, were gradually opened, one after another, for a *part of the Sabbath*; and in 1810, a section was inserted, in the law regulating the post-office, by which post-masters were obliged to deliver letters at all reasonable hours, *on every day of the week*. This law attracted very little attention at the time; and it is supposed, that the section alluded to was scarcely considered at all, except by the Committee that introduced it. A member of Congress recently declared it to be very strange, that such a provision should have crept into the law; for it was clearly a repeal of the *Fourth Commandment.* . . .

[146]

The keeping open of post-offices, on the day of sacred rest, has been to many hearts a still greater grief and burden, than the transportation of the mail on that day. In many towns, both large and small, the post-office is so located, as to attract crowds of idlers, who do not pretend to any plea of necessity. The young, if they have not pious parents or guardians, are led, by this public and authorized show of business to disregard the Sabbath, and to withdraw themselves from public worship. All these consequences were foreseen at once, by those who are accustomed to regard moral causes and their effects. . . .

From that time to the present, the multiplied evils of Sabbath-breaking have become more and more apparent; and the apprehension has between extensively felt, that an irresistible flood of business and pleasure will roll over the sacred institutions of religion, and leave our beloved land a moral desolation. Hence it has been a subject of conversation for years, in many a circle of reflecting and patriotic men, and in many states of the Union, if not in every state, that the friends of the Sabbath should come forward, and plead its claims before the national legislature. . . .

[The Account then rejoiced that the committee's invitation to "friends of religion" to draft petitions requesting the closing of post offices and the ceasing of carrying mail on Sunday to be sent to Congress was extremely successful. In one month alone, 441 petitions were received by the House of Representatives and 26 by the Senate. The Account then listed all the towns from which petitions were sent and the names of those who either drafted or signed these petitions.]

CONCLUDING OBSERVATIONS

From what has appeared in the preceding pages, it must be manifest to every candid mind, that the petitions to Congress, in relation to the transportation and opening of the mail on the Sabbath, did not originate in any transient feeling, nor in any narrow, or local, or personal views; but that they were the result of much reflection, and a solemn conviction of duty, in regard to a subject, which is deemed by the petitioners to be vitally important to their country and to individuals—to the present generation and to posterity. It is plain, therefore, that the purpose of the petitioners cannot be relinquished, and that no suitable means of attaining it should be neglected.

The reasons, which they assign, are of the gravest character, resting on a sense of obligation to obey an express command of God—a full persuasion that a disregard of this command will bring down upon our land the displeasure of Heaven—a deliberate opinion, that the Sabbath is one of the most glorious proofs of the divine beneficence—that it is eminently calculated to make communities, wherever it is properly observed, virtuous,

◆ CHAPTER 6

Church, State,
and Democracy:
The Sunday Mail
Controversy,
1827–1831

prosperous and happy; that the loss of this institution would be a calamity so awful, as that any well-grounded apprehension of it might reasonably excite the most gloomy forebodings; that the present regulations of the post-office tend strongly toward the abolition of the Sabbath; that they are, therefore, in the highest sense, adverse to the public good; that, as the preservation of moral integrity; or a sense of responsibility of God, extensively among the people, is confessedly essential to the continuance of a republican government—every enlightened patriot, as well as every true Christian, must cherish the institutions of religion, as the great means of perpetuating our free government; that the laws of the several States are disregarded, and the religious privileges of the people invaded, by the present regulations of the post-office; and the inconvenience of having the mails at rest and the post-offices closed on the Sabbath, is very small, compared with great and alarming evils of a contrary course.

[The account then addressed the question of whether the nondelivery of mail on Sundays would be damaging to commerce. The account said that this would be an extremely rare occurrence that easily could be dealt with.]

In conclusion, the people of the United States have it in their power to secure their religious freedom, their civil institutions and their national prosperity, to themselves and to future ages, if they will satisfy the Sabbath, and thus enjoy all its benign, restraining, and enlightening influences; but if they unwisely disregard the voice of experience and the voice of God, it may be said of them, by the SUPREME LAWGIVER, as it was said of the Jewish commonwealth: *But if ye will not hearken unto me to hallow* THE SABBATH DAY, *and not to bear burden, even entering in at the gates of Jerusalem on the Sabbath day; then I will kindle a fire in the gates thereof, and it shall devour the palaces of Jerusalem, and it shall not be quenched.*

Source 4 from *The Logic and Law of Col. Johnson's Report to the Senate, on Sabbath Mails* (Utica, NY: G. S. Wilson, 1829).

4. Logic and Law of Col. Johnson's Report, 1829.

This report appears to have been drawn up by Col. Johnson, and is of course a draught of opinions for which he has committed himself to the public; and in speaking of the Report we shall briefly refer to the author. We greatly respect Col J. as a man—have the greatest confidence in his patriotism—believe him possessed naturally of a strong mind—but knowing as we do his history, he will not, we presume, set up for his opinions, however honest, the claim of infallibility. The whole Report, is courteous, plausible,--but as we deem, fundamentally erroneous in its principles, and singularly illogical in its deductions. It deserves respectful treatment from the character of the author, but every citizen owes it a thorough examination, since it avowedly intends to "settle a principle;"—a principle too fundamental to the character of the Government and nation, and designed to be a pole star in all its future policy. The patriot ought to search it well, as it involves one of the most momentous points in the whole affair of government. Col. J. indeed, claims that the point is already settled by the "Constitution," and that his Report is only a necessary application of this decision; neither of which, we trust, will be found correct. The Constitution is from the people; let the people judge of the interpretation. . . .

[*The author asserts that similar petitions had failed before, but the question has reappeared "more formidable than ever" due to the "growth of moral principle and intelligence in our country." The pamphlet then asserts the people's constitutional right to petition, especially when they see actions and opinions (Johnson's) "endangering directly or indirectly the moral character of the community." Any notions contrary to that would be opined by "an irreligious DESPOTISM."*

Then, countering Sen. Johnson's description of religious combinations as "dangerous," the author states that no denomination ever has advocated a measure in conflict with the Constitution. "Till Col. J. can prove the contrary, we cannot but view his insinuations as unkind and libelous."]

We come now to a review of the fundamental principle of Col. Johnson's Report, that *for Congress* to grant the plea of the petitioners against the transportation of the mails and the obligation to open the Post Offices on Sunday, would be a *violation of the Constitution.* In the language of the Colonel, the petitioners "call for the establishment of a principle which would lay the foundation for dangerous innovations upon the spirit of the Constitution;" and, therefore, "the observance of a holy day cannot be incorporated in our institution." "The spirit of the Constitution regards the General Government in no other light than that of a civil institution."

The inference from all this is manifest, though not drawn out. It was enough for the present, to settle the principle, that the good citizens of the states might henceforth abstain from "religious combination." Colonel J. will please to enlighten us, if this be not the idea he intended the petitioners should receive— that the General Government is ATHEISTICAL: That when government binds a citizen to official duties in the Post Office or any other department, on Sunday, this is not a fit subject for complaint, petition, "religious combination,"—is a political object—the General Government knows no religion. . . .

◆ CHAPTER 6
Church, State,
and Democracy:
The Sunday Mail
Controversy,
1827–1831

We knew, that at the formation of the Constitution, some, because it contained neither creed, nor religious establishment, nor religious test, espoused the idea that the constitution was *atheistical*. We also knew, that the policy of some of our statesmen was *atheistical*, and their measures tending to introduce the principle. But we confess our skill in "discerning spirits" is not great; and we cannot to this day, see any thing in the "spirit of the Constitution," atheistical, or that constitutionally binds the General Government to run over the religious feelings of the nation, or forbids Congress to authorize the Postmaster General to delay a little on any day of the week, till the moral feelings of the nation are removed out of his way.

[The Report then argued that all the citizens of the United States were also citizens of the several states, nearly all of which contained articles in their own constitutions relating to religion, the Sabbath, religious qualifications for holding office, etc. Would the sons of the Pilgrims, the Report argued, "have consented to union in any government which claimed the prerogatives of Atheism? Finally, even before the Constitution, the Continental Congress "observed the Sabbath" and granted "a Sabbath cessation from official business." At last, it noted that "are we to infer, as the spirit of the Constitution, because it says nothing on the subject of religion, it says something against it?]

Another principle on which Col. J. proceeds, in reasoning down the petitioners, is, that restoring the Sabbath to its ancient quiet, does not comport with the spirit of the government, since *the Government knows no religion*. This too is "news" to the good citizens of the States, which no doubt will make 3,000 copies of the Report exceedingly appropriate. Having lived so long under the Government, and loved it too as we imagined, and carefully noticed its character, we had very charitably, but it seems erroneously, taken up a different fancy. Henceforth we must away with all such vain imaginations. Know all men by these presents (3,000 copies) that this Government is no longer to be baptized *"Christian"*— " The Government knows no religion." Query: are the oaths and treaties of our Government good in law? What guarantee of their veracity have "we the people?". . . .

[Having claimed that the notion of the federal government "knowing no religion" is a novel idea, the tract then goes into an extended (10 pages) treatise showing the numerous times that colonial and state governments and the federal government referred to God, Nature's God, Divine Providence, and so forth. Especially noted were the openings of legislatures with prayers, special days of fasting and prayer, Benjamin Franklin's (the first Postmaster General) belief "in the Providence of God as governing the world; that the Constitution was influenced, guided, and governed

by that omnipotent, omnipresent, and beneficent Ruler," President Washington's remark that "Of all the dispositions and habits which lead to political prosperity, religion and morality are indispensable supports," and the countless use of chaplains, religious-based oaths, and prayers before battles, conventions, legislative sessions, and the like. Especially interesting was Franklin's writing to those who were contemplating immigrating to America.]

Contemplating the preceding facts, we put the question to Col. J. as an honorable man—Supposing the petitioners to possess the spirit of '76—the standard of pure and enlightened patriotism, might they not, as *patriots*, feel concerned at the introduction of a mercantile or a political system, which "woke up" the very day so generally devoted to cherishing the principles and sentiments of religion, which our Government has assured us was the *"only solid* foundation of public liberty?" Would it have been *charitable* in the petitioners, to have supposed that the religious and moral sentiments of '76 were no longer possessed by the Government? That, enjoying the fruits of former patriotism and piety, "Jeshurun [in the Hebrew Bible, a poetic name for Israel] waxed fat and kicked?" Was it rational to suppose that the Government and nation, in '76, were *not Christian*, and knew no religion?— when "the United States, in Congress assembled," (though there were *then* Jews and possibly a few Deists), yet officially promoted the circulation of the Old and New Testaments; bound themselves by the sanctity of an oath on that Holy Volume; rejoiced "above all," in the possession of the gospel of peace; attributed all national blessings to Almighty God; and implored, and recommended the people to implore, his directions in their councils and his forgiveness of their sins, through the merits of the Divine Redeemer; and measured our national existence by "the year of our Lord:" when they urged the States to cherish "pure and undefiled religion," which the states never understood other than the Christian; when they carefully provided and paid Christian chaplains of various denominations, that their armies and hospitals might be supplied with Christian instruction and consolation; when they reverently waived national business on the Sabbath, when a Christian nation is engaged in worshipping the Father of Mercies—and even tenderly accommodated those denominations that would celebrate the crucifixion of the Redeemer. We have seen that the spirit of '76 on these subjects was still possessed in the administration of Washington. If, therefore, our Government is no longer Christian, but Jewish, Mahomedan, Pagan, or Atheistical, it is incumbent on Col. J. to point out *when* and *how* the change was introduced! The 3,000 do not suffice. Till then, please to allow the petitioners to abide by the spirit of '76. It is, and they glory in it, their only spirit, as it was once the spirit of Congress and the nation; though now to be baptized "religious combination!"

◆ CHAPTER 6

Church, State,
and Democracy:
The Sunday Mail
Controversy,
1827–1831

Source 5 from *First Annual Report of the General Union for Promoting the Observance of the Christian Sabbath: adopted May 12, 1829* (New York: J. Collard, 1829).

5. Address by the Rev. Matthias Bruen, Corresponding Secretary of the General Union.

This General Union grew out of the conscious want, on the part of the Christian community, of that equal respect unto all God's commandments which is essential to temporal and spiritual prosperity. It was believed that the public conscience in every branch of Christ's nation might appear, as the Scriptures present it, exceeding sinful. On solemn consideration it was believed that the safety and honor of the Church loudly called for some plan, in which Christians of every name might co-operate to excite a livelier sense of the divine authority and paramount importance of the Christian Sabbath.

It was further considered, that the exact observance of the Lord's day, according to the commandment, is not only the chief support and defense of the church of Christ on earth, but is also a wall of safety to the civil community. It was believed that if new energy could be given to the public conscience on this vital subject, that the sum of national happiness would be proportionately increased. The concurrence of all was therefore earnestly asked, and your executive committee were made the organ of expressing this desire.

In conformity with the purpose for which they were appointed, they published, soon after the convention which formed the constitution of this Union, an address to the people of the United States, of which upwards of one hundred thousand copies in pamphlet or newspaper form were circulated. In this age of philanthropy perhaps no single document bearing upon the morals of the land has been more timely and effective.

[Bruen was overjoyed by the response to the 100,000 pamphlets. Local chapters of the Union were established and the word went out from "the pulpit and the press, the two great organs for influencing public sentiment." As Bruen put it, the land has been agitated.]

We believe self submission to God's law to be the good old gospel way, and that in this land of freedom, no just offense can be taken with any measures, associated or individual, based upon a conscientious regard to every one of the ten commandments. We have had the pleasure of seeing many, doubtful at first of the utility of this Union, become its warm advocates; and feel assured that nothing but misapprehension or bigotry, the spirit that would lord it over our free institutions, and over liberty of conscience, can object to any association of individuals refusing to trample upon what they believe to be a law of the Highest. Here all profess to respect the rights of conscience. For conscience's sake, more than for this world's wealth, our ancestors converted the forest waste into our fruitful fields; and your committee congratulate[s] this Union upon its operation, because it has drawn forth this voice of conscience from our countrymen, and confirmed that oral sense which alone elevates the character and secures the prosperity of our beloved republic. Republican institutions can never be disservered from virtue: virtue is but another name for the sense of moral responsibility to God; and this moral sense never lived but in sabbath time.

The churches in this land, however divided on some other subjects, for the most part feel alike in this sabbath question; and with the churches are connected large congregations, embodying the moral strength of our nation. . . .

Yet this comparatively happy republic is overflooded with sabbath profanation. Every canal carries it, every river wafts it down, every bay embosoms it; our great cities are the emporiums of the crime, at once the volcanoes which receive the fuel and disperse the flame;—here the public gardens, the common tippling shops, the capacious steam boats, are filled with those deeply tainted with this sin; and while there is not a command in the decalogue more precise in its prohibitory clause, there is no rest upon God's holy day. The animals subjected to our dominion for six days, and relieved by the divine law from the rigour of unintermitted toil, share the burden—the whole creation groaneth and travaileth together. In many parts, the stalls of the butchers, the baskets of the bakers, the fruits of the market, the pages of the newspaper, the documents of the lawyer, the accounts of the merchant, have more or less of the odour of this sin, The poor are under slavery to the rich; their children, and orphans hindered from the sabbath school, and the community at large subjected to a training most expensive in its results in pauperism and prison, ignorance and unhappiness, coupled with the loss of all the benefits of Christianity for the life that is to come. . . .

While renewing their invitation to all to aid in this work, your committee are encouraged by the effects of the question brought before the Congress of the United States at its late session, of discontinuing the public mails upon the sabbath. As the object of this Union is not to affect the government directly, but the government through the people; as we appeal from the few to the many, and would make radical reform among those who have the keys of power, that is, the great body of our fellow citizens, and who, if they will reform themselves, will find the work completed, your committee have not regarded in their duty to act in their associate capacity in that important matter. But we have watched its whole movement with great interest, sensible that the result must in the main determine all the rest; and that so

◆ CHAPTER 6

Church, State,
and Democracy:
The Sunday Mail
Controversy,
1827–1831

long as one steam boat, or one stage, can plead an United States' contract and legislative injunction for sabbath breaking, and thus run over State rights, the rights of conscience, and the rights of God, we are parties to a flagrant violation of the divine law, and to a wide source of temporal and spiritual calamity. . . .

Christianity can only exist where the sabbath is reverenced, and Christianity has here introduced free government and general happiness. Its heavenly spirit alone ever civilized and beautified any region of the globe, and it has done its wonders in soils most uncongenial. It has given the sceptre of this world's opinions to the descendant of the Goth, and of the dwellers in northern wilds, and seems to have entrusted itself for safety, and for universal propagation, to our native language. No state of this Union has grown out of heathenism. Christianity founded all our glorious institutions; and with no other compulsory sway than that of light and love, as the sun reigns over the world, will pour its temporal and eternal riches upon our canals and our rivers, our plains and our mountains. . . .

Source 6 from *Report of the House Committee on Post Offices and Postal Roads, March 4–5, 1830.* 21st Congress, 1st session, House Report #271.

6. Report of House Committee on Post Offices and Postal Roads, March 4, 1830. Rep. Richard M. Johnson, Chairman, and Minority Report by Rep. William McCreery.

[The 1830 report was somewhat different from and considerably longer than the Senate ommittee's 1829 report. This report began by stating that the committee could find no constitutional power permitting Congress to determine whether any time "has been set apart by the Almighty for religious exercises," and that Congress was not empowered to pass any law respecting the establishment of religion. Moreover, elected officials are chosen to represent voters' political and not their religious views. The committee went on to suggest that the closing of post offices on Sunday would open the door to a plethora of religious laws that eventually would impinge the rights of all.]

With the exception of the United States, the whole human race, consisting, it is supposed, of eight hundred millions of rational beings, is in religious bondage; and, in reviewing the scenes of persecution which history every where presents, unless the committee could believe that the cries of the burning victim, and the flames by which he is consumed, bear to Heaven grateful incense, the conclusion is inevitable, that the line cannot be too strongly drawn between Church and State. If a solemn act of legislation shall, in *one* point, define the law of God, or point out to the citizen one religious duty, it may, with equal propriety, proceed to define every part of divine revelation; and enforce *every* religious obligation, even to the forms and ceremonies of worship; the endowment of the church, and the support of the clergy.

It was with a kiss that Judas betrayed his Divine Master, and we should all be admonished—no matter what our faith may be—that the rights of conscience cannot be so successfully assailed as under the pretext of holiness. The Christian religion made its way into the world in opposition to all human Governments. Banishment, tortures, and death, were inflicted in vain to stop its progress. But many of its professors, as soon as clothed with political power, lost the meek spirit which their creed inculcated, and began to inflict on other religions, and on dissenting sects of their own religion, persecutions more aggravated than those which their own apostles had endured. The ten persecutions of Pagan Emperors, were exceeded in atrocity by the massacres and murders perpetrated by Christian hands; and in vain shall we examine the records of Imperial tyranny for an engine of cruelty equal to the *Holy Inquisition*. Every religious sect, however meek in its origin, commenced the work of persecution as soon as it acquired political power. The framers of the constitution recognised the eternal principle, that man's relation with his God is above human legislation, and his rights of conscience inalienable. Reasoning was not necessary to establish this truth: we are conscious of it in our bosoms. It is this consciousness which, in defiance of human laws, has sustained so many martyrs in tortures and in flames. They *fell* that their duty to God was superior to human enactments, and that man could exercise no authority over their consciences: it is an inborn principle which nothing can eradicate.

The bigot, in the pride of his authority, may lose light of it—but strip him of his power; prescribe a faith to him which his conscience rejects; threaten him in turn with the dungeon and the faggot; and the spirit which God has implanted in him, rises up in rebellion and defies you. Did the primitive Christians ask that Government should recognize and observe their religious institutions? All they asked was *toleration;* all they complained of, was persecution. What did the Protestants of Germany, or the Hugenots [sic] of France, ask of their Catholic superiors? *Toleration.* What do the persecuted Catholics of Ireland ask of their oppressors? *Toleration.*

Do not all men in this country enjoy every religious right which martyrs and saints ever asked? Whence, then the voice of complaint? Who is it, that, in the full enjoyment of every principle which human laws can secure, wishes to arrest a portion of these principles from his neighbor? Do the petitioners allege that they cannot conscientiously participate in the profits of the mail

◆ CHAPTER 6

Church, State,
and Democracy:
The Sunday Mail
Controversy,
1827–1831

contracts and post offices, because the mail is carried on Sunday? If this be their motive, then it is worldly gain which stimulates to action, and not virtue or religion. Do they complain that men, less conscientious in relation to the Sabbath, obtain advantages over them, by receiving their letters and attending to their contents?

Still their motive is worldly and selfish. But if their motive be to induce Congress to sanction, by law, their *religious opinions* and *observances,* then their efforts are to be resisted, as in their tendency fatal, both to religious and political freedom. Why have the petitioners confined their prayer to the mails? Why have they not requested that the Government be required to suspend *all* its executive functions on that day? why do they not require us to enact that our ships shall not sail? that our armies shall not march? that officers of justice shall not seize the suspected, or guard the convicted? They seem to forget that government is as necessary on Sunday as on any other day of the week. The spirit of evil does not rest on that day. It is the Government, ever active in its functions, which enables us all, even the petitioners, to worship in our churches in peace. Our Government furnishes very few blessings like our mails. They bear from the centre of our Republic to its distant extremes, the acts of our legislative bodies, the decisions of the judiciary, and the orders of the Executive. Their speed is often essential to the defense of the country, the suppression of crime, and the dearest interest of the people. Were they suppressed one day of the week, their absence must be often supplied by public expresses; and, besides, while the mail bags might rest, the mail coaches would pursue their journey with the passengers. The mail bears, from one extreme of the Union to the other, letters of relatives and friends, preserving a communion of heart between those far separated, and increasing the most pure and refined pleasures of our existence: also, the letters of commercial men convey the state of the markets, prevent ruinous speculations, and promote general, as well as individual interest: they bear innumerable religious letters, newspapers, magazines and tracts, which reach almost every house throughout this wide Republic. Is the conveyance of these a violation of the Sabbath? The advance of the human race in intelligence, in virtue, and religion itself, depends in part upon the speed with which a knowledge of the past is discriminated. Without an interchange between one country and another, and between different sections of the same country, every improvement in moral or political science, and the arts of life, would be confined to the neighborhood where it originated. The more rapid and the more frequent this interchange, the more rapid will be the march of intellect, and the progress of improvement. The mail is the chief means by which intellectual light irradiates to the extremes of the Republic. Stop it one day in seven, and you retard one seventh the advancement of our country. So far from stopping the mail on Sunday, the committee would recommend the use of all reasonable means to give it a greater expedition and a greater extension. What should be the elevation of our country, if every new conception could be made to strike every mind in the Union at the same time? It is not the distance of a Province or State from the seat of Government, which endangers its separation; but it is the difficulty and unfrequency of intercourse between them. Our mails reach Missouri and Arkansas in less time than they reached Kentucky and Ohio in the infancy of their settlement; and now, when there are three millions of people extending a thousand miles West of the Alleghany, we hear less of discontent, than when there were a few thousands scattered along their Western base. . . .

Our fathers did not wait to be oppressed, when the mother country asserted and exercised an unconstitutional power over them. To have acquiesced in the tax of three pence upon a pound of tea, would have led the way to the most cruel exactions; they took a bold stand against the principle, and liberty and independence was the result. The petitioners have not requested Congress to suppress Sunday mails upon the ground of political expediency, but because they violate the sanctity of the first day of the week.

This being the fact, and the petitioners having indignantly disclaimed even the wish to unite politics and religion, may not the committee reasonably cherish the hope, that they will feel reconciled to its decision, in the case; especially, as it is also a fact, that the counter memorials, equally respectable, oppose the interference of Congress, upon the ground that it would be legislating upon a religious subject, and therefore unconstitutional.

Resolved, That the committee be discharged from the further consideration of the subject.

Minority Report by Rep. McCreery, March 5, 1830.

All Christian nations acknowledge the first day of the week, to be the Sabbath. Almost every State in this Union have, by positive legislation, not only recognized this day as sacred, but has forbidden its profanation under penalties imposed by law.

It was never considered, by any of those States, as an encroachment upon the rights of conscience, or as an improper interference with the opinions of the few, to guard the sacredness of that portion of time acknowledged to be holy by the many.

✦ CHAPTER 6

Church, State,
and Democracy:
The Sunday Mail
Controversy,
1827–1831

The petitioners ask not Congress to expound the moral law; they ask not Congress to meddle with theological controversies, much less to interfere with the rights of the Jew or the Sabbatarian, or to treat with the least disrespect the religious feelings of any portion of the inhabitants of the Union; they ask the introduction of no religious coercion into our civil institutions; no blending of religion and civil affairs; but they do ask, that the agents of government, employed in the Post Office Department, may be permitted to enjoy the same opportunities of attending to moral and religious instruction, or intellectual improvement, on that day, which is enjoyed by the rest of their fellow citizens. They approach the Government, not for personal emolument, but as patriots and Christians, to express their high sense of the moral energy and necessity of the Sabbath for the perpetuity of our republican institutions; and respectfully request that Congress will not, by legislative enactments, impair those energies. . . .

[McCreery opined that one day of each week devoted to worship or rest was reasonable and that it was the postal workers who were forced to choose between their faiths and their jobs.]

The arguments which have been urged for the transportation of the mail, &c. on the Sabbath, are mainly derived from commercial convenience, and from alleged derangement of business and intercourse. This doctrine militates against the first principles of good morals. If these are important at all, they are paramount to the claims of expediency; but this plea makes them subservient to the pressure of worldly business, and converts them into mere questions of profit and loss.

Granting the prayer of the petitioners cannot interfere with the religious feelings or consciences of any portion of the citizens; because, they ask no service to be performed; no principle to be professed. It is only asked that certain duties be not required on a certain day. Were it imposing any service, or requiring the profession of any opinions, those whose religious sentiments were different, might justly complain. But he who conscientiously believes that he is bound to observe the seventh day of the week, in a religious manner, can have no just reason to complain: because Government takes nothing from him, in permitting all classes of citizens to observe the first day of the week, as a day of religious rest. The case would be quite different, did the privilege of resting on that day, impose anything on any class of citizens, contrary to their conscience.

Source 7 from Zelotes Fuller, *The Tree of Liberty. An Address in Celebration of the Birth of Washington, Delivered at the Second Universalist Church in Philadelphia, Sunday Morning, February 28, 1830, in The Annals of America* (Chicago: Encyclopedia Brittanica, 1968).

7. Zelotes Fuller, The Tree of Liberty.[16]

Fifty-three years have we been in possession of national independence and political freedom. Our fathers willed themselves free and independent, and behold, liberty followed the sun in his path! *To continue free, we have but to will it*! And will you not do it, O people of America—ye who know the sweets of liberty? To support the liberties of our country, as did your fathers, so have ye pledged your lives, your fortunes, and your sacred honor. And are ye not ready to make good the pledge? Ye who are the friends of American freedom, and of humankind, have but one answer to give, and that answer is yea! Ye will duly honor the cause, that is committed to your keeping. Ye will never prove false to the liberties of your country—nor violate the pledge of your fathers—the pledge of yourselves as Americans.

Remember that the civil and religious liberty which ye enjoy, and which ye hold to be the birth-right of every man, was purchased with toil, and blood, and suffering. Dear was the price which it cost—precious the lives that were sacrificed. Never, O never suffer yourselves to be robbed of such an invaluable heritage, nor quietly submit to any infringement of the rights and privileges which it confers.

I have said, we fear not that the civil and religious rights and privileges, which our excellent constitution guarantees, will be infringed by those abroad, but they may be by a certain class at home, if no precaution be taken to prevent it. Yea, we deem it a truth, too evident to admit of doubt, and too generally conceded to require proof on the present occasion, that it is the intention of a certain religious sect in our country, to bring about, if possible, a union of church and state. To effect this purpose, a deep and artful scheme has been laid, and which may ultimately be consummated, unless it is speedily and vigorously opposed. Yea, the declaration has gone forth, that in ten years, or certainly in twenty, the political power of our country, will be in the hands of those who shall have been educated to believe in and probably *pledged* to support, a certain creed. Merciful god! forbid the fulfillment of the prophecy! Forbid it all ye, who have at heart, the prosperity and happiness of our nation!

16. Zelotes Fuller (1773–1857) was a Universalist minister and editor of the newspaper *Philadelphia Liberalist*, which began publication in 1832.

◆ CHAPTER 6
Church, State,
and Democracy:
The Sunday Mail
Controversy,
1827–1831

People of this free and happy land! we ask, will you give your consent to the political dominancy of any one religious sect, and the establishment of their religious creed by law? Will you in any way encourage certain popular religious measures, got up by a certain popular religious sect, in our humble opinion, for a very *unpopular* object, but which in the view of many, is very popular to approve? Be assured, whatever may be the *ostensive* objects of these measure, if they should be generally adopted, they will tend to infuse the spirit of religious intolerance and persecution into the political institutions of our country, and in the end, completely to annihilate the political and religious liberty of the people. Are you willing that a connection should be formed between politics and religion, or that the equal rights of conscience, should in any degree be mutilated? Are ye prepared to bow your necks to an intolerant and persecuting system of religion; for instance, like that of England? Are ye prepared to submit to such an unrighteous system of tithes, taxations and exactions, for the support of a *national religion*, as the great mass of her people are compelled to submit to? Are ye prepared to debase yourselves, like so many beasts of burden, before a dissipated nobility and an intolerant corrupted priesthood? . . .

Never I beseech of you, encourage a certain *"Christian party in politics,"* which under moral and religious pretences, is officiously and continually interfering with the religious opinions of others, and endeavoring to effect by law and other means, equally exceptionable, a systematic course of measures, evidently calculated, to lead to a union of Church and State. If a union of church and state should be effected, which may God avert, then will the doctrines of the prevailing sect, become the creed of the country, to be enforced by fines, imprisonment, and doubtless death! Then will superstition and bigotry frown into silence, everything which bears the appearance of liberality; the hand of genius will be palsied, and a check to all further improvements in our country, will be the inevitable consequence. If we now permit the glorious light of liberty to be extinguished, it may never more shine to cheer a benighted world with the splendour of its rays. . . .

Even now there are regions where the infuriated demon of persecution unfurls her blood stained banner, and demands that unnumbered victims should bleed at the foot of her unrighteous throne! The past history of the Christian Church, should be a solemn warning to us, never to permit an alliance to be formed, between the priesthood and the civil magistracy— *between Church and State powers.* . . .

Source 8 from *Christian Messenger,* vol. 4 (1830).

8. The Rev. Barton W. Stone on the Sabbath Mail controversy, May 1830.

We are grieved to see . . . a disposition to destroy the idea of a Sabbath under any name. I should rejoice to see that day more religiously observed by all. I have disapproved the attempt to urge Congress to legislate on the subject, and have been disgusted at the zeal of the clergy in their bold attempts to have it effected; yet I have seen the opposite party run into a criminal extreme. . . . These last by their untempered zeal against stopping the mail on the sabbath, have . . . done real injury to their cause. . . . While the clergy are suspected of having designs to establish their religion by law; these are suspected as having designs to overthrow Christianity *in toto.*

Source 9 from *Christian Baptist,* June 7, 1830.

9. The Rev. Alexander Campbell on the Sabbath Mail controversy, June 1830.

HEAR THE PRIESTLY HIERARCHS!

The intolerant zeal with which some of the most aspiring sectaries urge governmental interference in behalf of the cessation of Sunday mails, has convinced me that political designs are at the bottom of the prayers of many of the petitioners. The leaders evince a spirit of resentment against those who do not coincide with their schemes . . . which illly comports with that zeal for holiness which they profess in favor of the Sabbath.

Source 10 from Alexis de Tocqueville, *Democracy in America,* trans. Arthur Goldhammer (New York: Library of America, 2004), pp. 595–599.

10. Alexis de Tocqueville, "On the Use That Americans Make of Association in Civil Life."

Americans of all ages, all conditions, and all minds are constantly joining together in groups. In addition to commercial and industrial associations in which everyone takes part, there are associations of a thousand other kinds: some religious, some moral, some grave, some trivial, some quite

◆ CHAPTER 6

Church, State,
and Democracy:
The Sunday Mail
Controversy,
1827–1831

general and others quite particular, some huge and others tiny. Americans associate to give fêtes, to found seminaries, to build inns, to erect churches, to distribute books, and to send missionaries to the antipodes. This is how they create hospitals, prisons, and schools. If, finally, they wish to publicize a truth or foster a sentiment with the help of a great example, they associate. Wherever there is a new undertaking, at the head of which you would expect to see in France the government and in England some great lord, in the United States you are sure to find an association.

In America I came across types of associations which I confess I had no idea existed, and I frequently admired the boundless skill of Americans in setting large numbers of people a common goal and inducing them to strive toward that goal voluntarily. . . .

In democratic nations associations must take the place of the powerful private individuals who have been eliminated by equality of conditions. . . .

Thus the most democratic country on earth is the one whose people have lately perfected the art of pursuing their common desires in common and applied this new science to the largest number of objects. Is this an accident, or might there actually be a necessary relation between associations and equality? . . .

Nothing, in my view, is more worthy of our attention than America's intellectual and moral associations. The political and industrial associations of the Americans leap to the eye more readily, but these others escape our notice, and if we do recognize them, we misunderstand them because we have almost never seen anything analogous. It is essential, however, to recognize that they are as necessary to the American people as political and industrial associations, and perhaps more so.

In democratic countries, the science of association is the fundamental science. Progress in all the other sciences depends on progress in this one.

Of all the laws that govern human societies, one seems more precise and clear than all the rest. If men are to remain civilized, or to become so, they must develop and perfect the art of associating to the same degree that equality of conditions increases among them. . . .

◆

Questions to Consider

Begin by looking at the evidence in favor of closing the post offices on Sundays. The Rev. Ezra Stiles Ely (Source 1) advocated "a Christian Party in Politics," but denied it would be a political party like the Democrats, National Republicans, or any other organization. What, then, did he mean by a "Christian party"? Does the fact that he tried to recruit Andrew Jackson to seek the presidency as a member of that party clarify Ely's position in your mind? What points do you think Jackson would have made on closing the post offices on Sundays? On Ely, see also Source 4, written anonymously by him. How do the two sources "fit" together?

Joseph L. Blau (1909–1986), a professor of religious studies whose specialties were Jewish history, philosophy, and the history of American liberalism and religious freedom, praised Richard M. Johnson's report (Source 2) as "one of the finest defenses of the principle of religious freedom in the United States."[17] Johnson began the report by stating that there was no general agreement among Americans regarding on what day the Sabbath actually fell, even noting that one denomination of Christians (the Seventh-Day Adventists) actually celebrated the Sabbath on Saturday, as did Jews. Why was this point the central core of Johnson's argument? Why did Johnson maintain that he could not honor the many petitions (considerably more than the 467 claimed in Source 3) in favor of closing the post offices on Sundays?

Johnson claimed that "extensive religious combinations to effect a political object are . . . always dangerous." In his opinion, why was this so? What else did Johnson suggest would happen if Congress did act to close post offices on Sunday?

Now you should be able to answer the central questions of this chapter:

1. What did the advocates and opponents of closing the post offices see as the *significance* or *importance* of the conflict?
2. How did their views of that significance or importance *go beyond* the Sunday mail controversy?
3. How did each side interpret the Constitution?
4. Finally, what do you believe was the historical significance of the controversy today, over 185 years since the debate itself?

Source 3 is a summary of all the petitions sent to Congress in favor of closing post offices on Sundays. According to historian Bertram Wyatt-Brown, this was the first time that the tactic of flooding Congress with petitions had been attempted on a national scale.[18] Why did the *Account* (Source 3) claim that allowing the post offices to remain open was bad? What would be the inevitable results?

The exhaustive pamphlet *The Logic and Law of Col. Johnson's Report to the Senate* (Source 4) basically maintained that the Johnson report discriminated against Christians. How did the anonymous author (almost surely the Rev. Ezra Stiles Ely) support that claim? Ely also argued that, even though many American leaders at the time of the drafting and ratification of the Constitution were "atheistical," the Constitution itself contained no such spirit and, indeed, no power "to run over the religious feelings and usages of the nation." Why did the author consider that point

---

17. Joseph L. Blau, *Cornerstones of Religious Freedom in America* (Boston: Beacon Press, 1950), p. 108.

18. Bertram Wyatt-Brown, "Prelude to Abolitionism: Sabbatarian Politics and the Rise of the Second Party System," *Journal of American History*, vol. 58 (Sept. 1971), p. 329.

◆ CHAPTER 6

Church, State,
and Democracy:
The Sunday Mail
Controversy,
1827–1831

important? According to the Tenth Amendment (1791) what governmental body, if any, could legitimately legislate on religion? Was, therefore, Johnson's position grounded in the 1787 Constitution or some "new" notions? How could that accusation be proven?

The excerpt of the *First Annual Report of the General Union for Promoting the Observance of the Christian Sabbath* (Source 5) was an address by the Union's corresponding secretary the Rev. Matthias Bruen (1793–1829), a Presbyterian clergyman who had been in poor health for years and would die within months of the meeting. In the opinion of Bruen, why was such a national association necessary? At one point in his address, Bruen stated that the goal of the Union "is not to affect the government directly, but the government through the people." What do you think he meant by that?

By 1830, Johnson was no longer in the Senate but was a member of the House of Representatives. In this position, he also wrote the report of the House Committee on Post Offices and Postal Roads. How did the House report

differ from the earlier Senate report of 1829? What additional points did he make? How did Rep. William McCreery counter Johnson's assertions?

Sources 7 through 9 all are writings that opposed the closing of the post offices on Sundays, and yet they all were written by Protestant clergymen. Why did these four clerics take that stand? What was Fuller's main concern? Fuller's *Tree of Liberty* (Source 7) was specifically written to counteract Ely's *Duty of Christian Freemen* (Source 1). Review Ely's sermon, comparing it to Fuller's remarks.

Stone and Campbell both were independent clergymen who, in 1832, merged their followers into a movement called the Restoration. Both opposed the efforts to close the post offices on Sunday, principally because they believed that the commandments contained in the Old Testament (including the Ten Commandments) applied only to the Jewish people and to no one else. But in Sources 8 and 9, the two preachers offered another reason for opposing the petitions. What was it? Compare that point to Sources 1 and 7.

◆

Epilogue

In her travel account *Domestic Manners of the Americans* (1832), British author Frances Trollope commented on the American religious climate: "My residence in the country has shewn me that a religious tyranny may be exerted very effectually without the aid of the government . . . persecution exists to a degree unknown, I believe,

in our well-ordered land since the days of Cromwell."[19] Trollope had arrived in the United States in the midst of the great debate over Sabbath mails and post offices (1827–1831). What

19. Trollope, *Domestic Manners of Americans*, pp. 107, 115. She was referring to the English civil war of the 1640s.

Trollope clearly failed to see, however, was that the majority of Americans thought more of their individual rights and freedoms than they did of their churches' doctrines. In spite of the numerous petitions to Congress that the post offices be closed on Sundays, the signatories were but a fraction of the adult population. Johnson's reports were allowed to stand. When it came to a choice between their individual rights and their religions' commandments, most Americans chose the former.

Petition leaders tried to get President Andrew Jackson, nominally a Presbyterian, to take up their cause, but he wisely refused. The President had been in office less than a year, and was almost overwhelmed with the Eaton Affair and with Cherokee removal. He allowed his allies, principally Johnson, to speak for him. For his part, the politically ambitious Johnson was rewarded by being nominated for vice president as Martin Van Buren's running mate in 1836. But his common-law relationship with one of his slaves and, at her death, two others in succession, along with his 1829 and 1830 reports, probably ended his political career. He failed to receive his party's renomination in 1840 and after that made several unsuccessful attempts to return to national office. Johnson died in 1850.[20]

And yet, the voluntary associations had pioneered tactics that became influential and important later. National organizations (with state, county, and local chapters) and mass petition drives were adopted by many of these same organizations to advocate temperance, defend Cherokees against removal, and ultimately call for the abolition of slavery. Indeed, many of the leaders of these reform movements had learned these tactics from the Sunday mail controversy.

Not everyone, however, embraced the voluntary associations. Clergyman William Ellery Channing (1780–1842) warned Americans of the danger of these associations. "They accumulate power in a few hands, and this takes place just in proportion to the surface over which they spread.... They are perilous instruments [and] ought to be suspected...."[21]

Nor did the effort to legislate Christian beliefs and morality die with the post office debates. In 1864, a petition was presented to President Abraham Lincoln to alter the Preamble to the Constitution to read:

> We, the people of the United States, humbly acknowledging Almighty God as the source of all authority and power in civil government, The Lord Jesus Christ as the Governor among the Nations, and His revealed will as of supreme authority, in order to constitute a Christian government . . . do ordain and establish this Constitution for the United States of America.[22]

---

20. Johnson was the only vice president chosen by the U.S. Senate, because he had not received enough electoral votes.

21. On Channing see "Remarks on Associations," in *Church and State in American History: Key Documents, Decisions, and Commentary from the Past Three Centuries*, eds. John F. Wilson and Donald Drakeman (Boston: Westview Press, 3rd ed. 2003), pp. 108, 109.

22. For the petition see David Goldfield, *America Aflame: How the Civil War Created a Nation* (New York: Bloomsbury Press, 2011), pp. 359–360. See also *Morton Borden, Jews, Turks, and Infidels* (Chapel Hill: Univ. of North Carolina Press, 1984), pp. 68–70.

◆ CHAPTER 6

Church, State,
and Democracy:
The Sunday Mail
Controversy,
1827–1831

Delegates from the National Reform Association were received cordially and tactfully, but the petition went nowhere. In that same year, however, Lincoln did not oppose putting the phrase "In God We Trust" on United States coins.

In 1885, the Sabbath Question resurfaced, with similar results. In 1892, however, in his opinion in *Church of the Holy Trinity v. United States* (143 U.S. 457), Supreme Court Justice David J. Brewer wrote that "America is a Christian nation" and spent almost half of his text demonstrating the United States' Christian identity. Then, in 1954, Congress changed the Pledge of Allegiance by adding the two words "under God."

In the meantime, states had been pretty much free to do as they wished about religion. The Congregational Church was the established denomination in Massachusetts and Connecticut until the 1830s; five states maintained taxes supporting the clergy; twelve continued religious tests for holding office; prayer was sanctioned in public schools; sales of contraceptives were outlawed in a few states; and "blue laws" remained in force.

In 1940, however, in the Supreme Court case *Cantwell v. Connecticut* (310 U.S. 296), the Court ruled that the First and Fourteenth Amendments applied to the states as well as to the federal government. Almost immediately a veritable flood of cases began to come forward, often striking down many of these state laws. At this point, as in 1829–1830, many concerned Christians arose, believing that the federal government was discriminating against them. The debate continues.[23]

Meanwhile, in 1912, Congress finally repealed regulations requiring post offices to be open on Sundays. Instead of religious petitioners (although there were, again, many of them), however, the victory should be credited to the postal workers' union.

23. On *Cantwell v. Connecticut* see John J. Patrick, *The Supreme Court of the United States: A Student Companion* (New York: Oxford Univ. Press, 3rd ed. 2006), pp. 286–287.

7

Land, Growth, and Justice: The Removal of the Cherokees

◆

The Problem

In the spring of 1838, General Winfield Scott and several units of the U.S. Army (including artillery regiments) were deployed to the Southeast to collect Native Americans known as the Cherokees[1] and remove them to lands west of the Mississippi River. Employing bilingual Cherokees to serve as interpreters at $2.50 per day, Scott constructed eleven makeshift stockades and on May 23 began rounding up Native Americans and herding them into these temporary prisons. According to John G. Burnett, a soldier who participated in the removal,

Men working in the fields were arrested and driven to the stockades. Women were dragged from their homes by soldiers whose language they could not understand. Children were often separated from their parents and driven into the stockades with the sky for a blanket and the earth for a pillow. And often the old and infirm were prodded with bayonets to hasten them to the stockades.[2]

Just behind the soldiers came whites, eager to claim homesteads, search for gold, or pick over the belongings that the Cherokees did not have time to carry away.

On August 23, 1838, the first of thirteen parties of Cherokees began their forced march to the West, arriving in what had been designated as Indian Territory (later Oklahoma) on January 17, 1839. With some traveling by boat while others journeyed overland, a total of approximately thirteen thousand Cherokees participated in what became known as the Trail of Tears.

1. The Cherokees referred to themselves as Ani'Yun'wiya ("principal people"). The origin of the term *Cherokee* is unknown, but the name almost certainly was given to them by Native American neighbors. See Russell Thornton, *The Cherokees: A Population History* (Lincoln: Univ. of Nebraska Press, 1990). pp. 7–8.

2. See John G. Burnett, "The Cherokee Removal Through the Eyes of a Private Soldier," *Journal of Cherokee Studies* 3 (1978): 180–185.

(See Map 1.) It has been estimated that over four thousand died in the squalid stockades or along the way.[3] But recent research has determined that the figure may have been higher than that, in part because of shoddy record keeping and in part because numerous Cherokees died in an epidemic almost immediately upon reaching their destination. In addition, conflict broke out between new arrivals and those Cherokees (around six thousand) who had earlier moved. And, once in the West, those who opposed removal took out their vengeance on the leaders of the Cherokee removal faction. Cherokee advocates of removal (including leaders Major Ridge, John Ridge, Elias Boudinot, and Thomas Watie) were murdered.[4]

The forced removal of the Cherokees marked the end of a debate that was older than the United States itself. As white populations mushroomed and settlements moved ever westward, the question of how to deal with Native Americans came up again and again, especially when Native American peoples refused to sell or give their lands to whites by treaty.

In 1829, Andrew Jackson became president. For at least ten years, it was

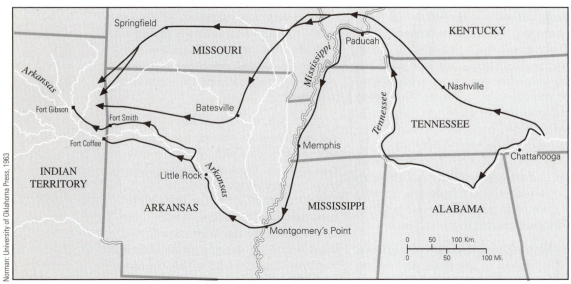

Norman: University of Oklahoma Press, 1963

Map 1. The Trail of Tears, 1838–1839.

Adapted from Grace Steele Woodward, *The Cherokees* (Norman: University of Oklahoma Press, 1963), pp. 206–207. Copyright © 1963 by the University of Oklahoma Press, Norman, Publishing Division of the University of Oklahoma. Reprinted by permission.

3. The official U.S. Army count of those removed to Indian Territory totaled 13,149, of whom 11,504 actually arrived in the West. Based on the tribal census of 1835, at least 2,000 died in the stockades.

4. See Russell Thornton, "The Demography of the Trail of Tears Period: A New Estimate of Cherokee Population Losses," in William L. Anderson, ed., *Cherokee Removal: Before and After* (Athens, Ga: Univ. of Georgia Press, 1991), pp. 75–95.

well known that he believed that Native Americans had no legitimate titles to their lands and should be removed from all of their lands east of the Mississippi River to make way for white settlement. And although he was not known as an accomplished speaker or writer (his spelling was nearly as poor as that of George Washington), in his First Annual Message to Congress (Source 4 in the Evidence section), Jackson almost surely was one of the most articulate voices in favor of removal.[5]

The major difficulty, however, involved the Cherokee lands in the state of Georgia, roughly five million acres. In 1802, the U.S. government and the state of Georgia had reached an agreement whereby the federal government had promised to "extinguish, for the use of Georgia, as early as the same can be peaceably obtained upon reasonable terms . . . the Indian titles to all lands lying within the limits of the state." The state of Georgia was becoming more insistent that the federal government honor its 1802 promise. At the same time, having already ceded portions of their lands in Georgia in treaties of 1785, 1791, 1794, 1798, 1817, and 1819, the Cherokee National Council reached "a decisive and unalterable conclusion not to cede away any more lands."[6]

The hardening of attitudes of both white Georgians and Cherokees presented the federal government with a serious dilemma. Although President Jackson was not the only white person to argue in favor of removal, whites both in and out of the government advocated several alternatives to removal, and these alternatives were debated—sometimes fiercely—both in Congress and among the white population at large.

Of course, the Cherokees themselves were deeply divided as to what response they should make if the federal government ultimately decided to remove them. Here again several possible alternatives were offered and, as with whites, they were debated with considerable ferocity.

In this chapter, you will be analyzing the two debates, the first among whites, who in the end would determine the fate of the Cherokees, and the second, among the Cherokees as to how they would respond to the whites' final decision. **What alternatives did whites consider? What were the strengths and weaknesses of each alternative? Then, what alternatives did the Cherokees consider? What were the strengths and weaknesses of each position?**

For both whites and Cherokees, significant segments of both populations did not view removal as inevitable. Many years later, people look back

5. For Jackson's early opinions, see Joseph McMinn to Secretary of War William Crawford, October 25, 1816, in *American State Papers: Indian Affairs* (Washington, DC: Gales and Seaton, 1834), vol. 2, p. 115.

6. For the 1802 agreement, see *American State Papers: Public Lands* (Washington: Gales and Seaton, 1834), vol. 1, p. 114. For the Cherokee decision, see Joseph McMinn to Secretary of War John C. Calhoun, June 24, 1823, in W. Edwin Hemphill, ed., *The Papers of John C. Calhoun* (Columbia, SC: Univ. of South Carolina Press, 1975), vol. 8. pp. 129–130; Cherokee National Council to Cherokee National Committee, October 25, 1823, in *American State Papers: Indian Affairs,* vol. 2, pp. 470–471; and Cherokee Delegation to the President of the United States, January 19, 1824, in *ibid.*, vol. 2, p. 473.

on a particular decision (to fire on Fort Sumter, for instance, or to support the Civil Rights Movement of the twentieth century) as inevitable. Most contemporaries, however, did not see it that way. As a historian, you should avoid the concept of "inevitability" as well.

✦

Background

Sometime before their regular contact with Europeans, the Cherokees became sedentary. Women performed most of the farm duties, raising corn and beans, whereas men hunted deer and turkey and caught fish to complete their diet. The Cherokees built towns organized around extended families. Society was *matrilineal,* meaning that property and position passed from generation to generation through the mother's side of the family. Each town theoretically was autonomous, and there were no leaders (or chiefs, in European parlance) who ruled over all the towns. Local leaders led by persuasion and example, and all adults, including women, could speak in town councils. Indeed, Cherokee governing practices were considerably more democratic and consensual than the Europeans' hierarchical ways.

Initial contacts with Europeans were devastating. Europeans brought with them measles and smallpox, against which Native Americans were not immune. Also, Cherokees were attracted to European goods, such as fabrics, metal hoes and hatchets, firearms, and (tragically) alcohol. To acquire these goods, Cherokees traded deerskins for them. By the early 1700s, Cherokees were killing an average of fifty thousand deer each year to secure their hides for barter, and estimates are that by 1735 over one million deer had been killed, almost certainly depleting the herds. Gradually, the Cherokees were losing their self-sufficiency and becoming increasingly dependent on European goods.

With European colonization and expansion in North America, the Cherokees became swept up into European peoples' wars. Initially siding with the British against the French, the Cherokees turned against the British when the colonial governor of South Carolina called thirty-two chieftains to a conference and then killed twenty-nine of them. The British retaliated against a Cherokee outburst by destroying the Lower Towns, killing over one hundred Cherokee warriors, and driving the survivors into the mountains. In the American Revolution, the Cherokees, hoping to stem white western expansion, again sided with the British. American Patriots destroyed over fifty Cherokee towns, scalping men and women indiscriminately.

After the American Revolution, the new U.S. government pursued a policy of attempting to "civilize" the Cherokees.

Apic/Hulton Archive/Getty Images

John Ridge (left) and Elias Boudinot (right), two of the Cherokee Nation's leaders, educated in the mission school in Cornwall, Connecticut.

For their part, some Cherokee leaders recognized that less land and fewer deer demanded major changes in their way of life, and they accepted "civilization." As Chief Eskaqua explained to President Washington, "Game is going fast away from us. We must plant corn and raise cattle."[7] Aided by government Indian agent Return J. Meigs (who lived with the Cherokees from 1801 to 1823) and a number of missionaries (sent by the American Board of Commissioners for Foreign Mission), several Cherokees were able to embrace many of the "white man's ways." Many men gave up hunting and took over agriculture from women. Plows, spinning wheels, and looms were introduced, and many Cherokee women took up the making of cloth and clothing. As it did with white settlers, land ownership and agriculture produced a class system. By 1824, the most affluent

Cherokees lived in stately homes and owned 1,277 African American slaves. For some, therefore, the "civilization" process led to a vastly improved standard of living.

Mission boarding schools, supported by white contributions, dotted the landscape. For some of the most promising young boys, the American Board of Commissioners for Foreign Missions founded a school in Cornwall, Connecticut, where two of the Cherokee Nation's most prominent future leaders, John Ridge and Elias Boudinot, were educated.[8] At the same time, a Native American man, Sequoyah, began devising a Cherokee alphabet (he called

7. Chief Eskaqua to Washington, 1792, quoted in William G. McLoughlin, *Cherokee Renascence in the New Republic* (Princeton: Princeton Univ. Press, 1986), p. 3.

8. The American Board of Commissioners for Foreign Missions was chartered in 1812. The purpose of the school was to train Native Americans to become Christian missionaries. Elias Boudinot's Cherokee name was (anglicized) Buck Watie. When traveling to the school in Cornwall, he stayed with Elias Boudinot (1740–1821), a former member of the Continental Congress, Director of the United States Mint (1795–1805), and a sponsor of the Board School for Indians in Cornwall. The young student then took Boudinot's name.

Universal History Archive/Getty Images

Portrait of Sequoyah Displaying His Cherokee Syllabary, c. 1838.

it a syllabary) of eighty-five phonetic symbols that allowed Cherokees to write what previously had been their oral language. In 1828, the first edition of the bilingual newspaper the *Cherokee Phoenix and Indians' Advocate* appeared, edited by Elias Boudinot.

Governmental and political forms were also modeled after Anglo-European institutions. A Native American police force was instituted in 1808, and in the following year a detailed census was taken. In 1827, a formal constitution was adopted, modeled on the United States Constitution, setting up a representative government and courts for the Cherokee Nation. Women, who were more nearly equal to men in traditional Cherokee society, saw their position deteriorate, as they were prohibited from voting or serving as representatives by the new constitution. In many

ways, then, Cherokees remade their economy, society, culture, and government.

Yet, in the eyes of some whites, the Cherokees' progress toward "civilization" was frustratingly slow. Several Cherokees, perhaps a majority, resisted the new ways, refused to adopt Anglo-European gender roles, ignored the mission schools, and opposed efforts to teach them the English language or convert them to Christianity. Moreover, those who interacted with whites realized that no matter how "civilized" they had become, they were still looked down upon, often abused, and generally referred to as "savages." Indeed, the school in Connecticut was forced to close its doors when two of its students (John Ridge and Elias Boudinot) planned to marry two local white girls, as this news very nearly caused a riot. Angered, John Ridge wrote:

> If an Indian is educated in the sciences, has a good knowledge of the classics, astronomy, mathematics, moral and natural philosophy, and his conduct [is] equally modest and polite, yet he is an Indian, and the most stupid and illiterate white man will disdain and triumph over this worthy individual.[9]

For those who had lost confidence in the Cherokees' abilities to embrace "white men's civilization," a powerful alternative was removal. Even Indian agent Return J. Meigs had given up hope and advocated it, even though he remained with the Cherokees for the rest of his life.[10]

The Louisiana Purchase (1803) acquired roughly 500 million acres, some of which theoretically could be used for the relocation of the eastern Native Americans. The emergence of harsher white attitudes about Native Americans undoubtedly increased public opinion in favor of removal. The major question, therefore, was how to induce Cherokees and other Native American peoples to cede their lands and accept relocation. Since the founding of the nation, it was generally agreed that no Native American lands could be acquired except by treaty. (see the 1790 Intercourse Act, Source 1). General Andrew Jackson, however, believed that no such land agreements were necessary and therefore the United States could take these lands by eminent domain, a notion that in 1818 was rejected by the House Committee on Public Lands. But when President James Monroe stated that "there is no obligation on the United States to remove the Indians by force," a showdown had become very nearly unavoidable. In an effort to avoid violence, in 1818, a trickle of Cherokees began to migrate to lands west of the Mississippi River.[11]

The vast majority of Cherokees, however, refused to move. They had built farms, sawmills, tanneries, ferries, stores, and towns. The Treaty of Hopewell (1785) had promised that they would be able to hold onto their lands "forever." In addition, Christian missionaries who lived among the Cherokees strengthened their resolve to resist removal, believing that the Cherokees were making great strides at becoming "civilized" right where they were. Yet one Cherokee chieftain's 1775 statement turned out to be prophetic: "Indian Nations before the Whites are like balls of snow before the sun."[12]

The conclusion of the War of 1812 touched off a tremendous white population boom in the West, thereby

---

9. *Christian Herald*, December 20, 1823, quoted in Thurman Wilkins, *Cherokee Tragedy: The Story of the Ridge Family and of the Decimation of a People* (New York: Macmillan, 1970), p. 145.
10. Meigs to Secretary of War Henry Dearborn, June 11, 1808, quoted in Theda Perdue and Michael D. Green, *The Cherokee Nation and the Trail of Tears* (New York: Viking Books, 2007), p. 38.

11. *Ibid.,* p. 92. for Jackson's opinion, see Jackson to Monroe, March 4, 1817, in *ibid.,* p. 50. For Monroe's view, see Wilkins, *Cherokee Tragedy*, p. 155. The early migrants initially moved to the Arkansas Territory but were forced to relocate to the Indian Territory (Oklahoma) in 1836 when Arkansas became a state. Those who migrated prior to the Trail of Tears became known as the Old Settlers.
12. J.G.M. Ramsey, *Annals of Tennessee* (Charleston, S.C.: Walker and James, 1853), pp. 117–118.

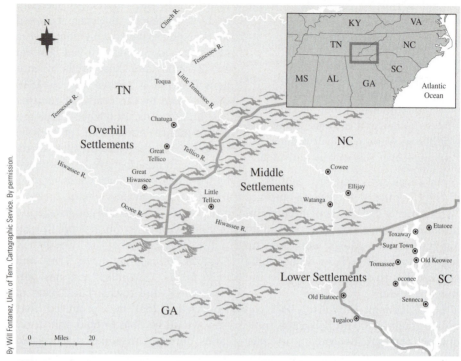

By Will Fontanez, Univ. of Tenn. Cartographic Service. By permission.

Map 2. Principal Cherokee Village Settlements, c. 1830.

increasing the difficulty of Native Americans holding onto their lands. From 1810 to 1830, the white population of the area that comprised the states of Georgia, Tennessee, Mississippi, and Alabama more than tripled, and the white population of Georgia alone more than doubled. Ignoring treaty lines, whites began drifting into Cherokee country. Cherokees retaliated by attacking and burning the buildings and crops of the white settlers, and federal troops had to be dispatched to restore order. In the past, the federal government had been able to restore order by negotiating treaties to obtain lands that whites had overrun. But the decision by Cherokee

leaders not to give up any more lands heightened an already tense situation. For its part, Georgia increased its demands that the federal government honor its 1802 agreement and remove the Cherokees immediately.

The election of Andrew Jackson in 1828 was a signal to Georgians that they now could move with impunity. In December 1828, over three months before Jackson's inauguration, the Georgia legislature passed an act declaring that as of June 1, 1830, all Cherokee territory would be subject to Georgia laws, and Cherokee laws (including their constitution) would be null and void. At roughly the same time, the Georgia legislature also made provisions for a lottery to be used to distribute Cherokee lands to whites. The discovery of gold in Cherokee territory touched off another land rush of around four thousand whites, accompanied by predictable violence.[13]

Against almost insurmountable odds, the Cherokees continued to resist, supported by a number of white missionaries who had built churches and schools throughout the territory. Here again, the American Board of Commissioners for Foreign Missions was at the center of missionary activity as well as efforts to strengthen Cherokee resolve to stand firm against the Georgia state government and white encroachment. As a result, Georgia passed an act requiring all whites living in Cherokee territory to secure licenses, an obvious attempt to expel the missionaries. When the missionaries refused to apply for the required licenses, eleven of them were arrested and sentenced to terms of four years in the Milledgeville state penitentiary. When the Georgia governor offered executive clemency to all those who would leave voluntarily, only two (Samuel Worcester and Elizur Butler) refused. Worcester appealed to the United States Supreme Court and in *Worcester v. Georgia* (6 Peters 515) Chief Justice John Marshall declared that the Cherokee territory was a distinct, independent political community in which Georgia laws did not apply.

President Jackson ignored Marshall's decision, and Worcester served out his term of four years, then moved to the West to establish a mission among the Cherokees. Before his death in 1859, he had translated the Bible into the Cherokee language.[14]

By the time Worcester was released from prison, however, the conflict was almost over. In his First Annual Message to Congress of December 8, 1829 (see Source 4), President Jackson made his case for the "voluntary" removal of all Native Americans east of the Mississippi River. Responding to the president's message in February 1830, the House of Representatives took up the Indian Removal Bill. The bill, however, reignited a furious debate both in Congress and among the general public. Hundreds of petitions were sent to Congress, the majority from religious groups and benevolent societies opposed to removal. Many congressional opponents of the bill were genuinely concerned about the welfare of Native Americans, but at least an equal number were Jackson's political opponents, seeking to embarrass the president. On April 23, 1830, the Senate approved the Indian Removal Bill by a vote of 28–19, the House following

13. Some of those who made a great deal of money from the Georgia gold rush included the South Carolina political leader John C. Calhoun, his son-in-law Thomas G. Clemson (who used some of the profits to found Clemson College in South Carolina), and future governor of New York and Democratic presidential candidate Samuel J. Tilden.

14. Both Worcester and Butler were American Board missionaries. For their difficulties, see Jack Frederick Kilpatrick and Anna Gritts Kilpatrick, *New Echota Letters: Contributions of Samuel A. Worcester to the Cherokee Phoenix* (Dallas: Southern Methodist University Press, 1968), p. 113. Worcester, one of the American Board's original commissioners, corresponded with the Rev. Ezra Stiles Ely, another officer of the American Board. Worcester to Ely, March 10, 1830, in *ibid.*, pp. 74–77. For Ely, see Chapter 6.

suit on May 24 by the close margin of 102–97. Jackson signed the bill on May 28, 1830.[15] The act empowered the president to trade land in the West for lands on which Native Americans east of the Mississippi then resided, to pay Native Americans for improvements they had made to lands they were giving up, to assist and protect Native Americans during their migration, and to superintend and care for them once they had reached their destinations.

The Removal Act, however, only *authorized* removal, and longstanding U.S. policy still required that all land cessions or sales of Native American lands must be completed by treaty. Therefore, while Cherokees debated over how to respond to the Removal Act, the federal government began to search for pliable Cherokee leaders who would approve a removal treaty.

By 1835, the Ridge-Watie-Boudinot extended family provided the core of a small minority of Cherokees that originally had vehemently opposed relocation but had come to see it as the only realistic alternative. President Jackson then named John F. Schermerhorn, a retired Dutch Reformed minister, to negotiate a treaty. The Treaty of New Echota finally was approved, in late 1835, by a "council" of twenty and a committee of eighty-six Cherokees. Neither group, however, had the authority to negotiate such an agreement

and had no legal standing with the Cherokees' National Council.[16]

Meanwhile, the state of Georgia instituted its lottery. In late 1832, surveying had begun and some lottery winners began to move into Cherokee territory to claim their prizes, resulting in more violence. In the same month that the Treaty of New Echota was approved by the "Treaty Party," the Georgia legislature authorized all lottery winners to take possession of their lands by November 1836, an obvious ploy to induce Cherokees to leave the state.

Outraged by the actions of both the "Treaty Party" (as they had been derisively labeled) and the state of Georgia, Principal Chief John Ross and the National Council circulated a petition to the U.S. Congress that was purportedly signed by 15,665 Cherokees. The petition maintained that the Treaty of New Echota was invalid because it never had been approved by the National Council, and begged that Congress would reverse its position on removal and protect the Cherokees from the incursions of white Georgians. At last, on April 9,

15. For the full text of the Removal Act, see Wilcomb E. Washburn, ed., *The American Indian and the United States: A Documentary History* (New York: Random House, 1973), Vol. III, pp. 2169–2171.

16. For biographies of the principal "Treaty Party" leaders, see Edward Everett Dale and Gaston Litton, eds., *Cherokee Cavaliers: Forty Years of Cherokee History As Told in the Correspondence of the Ridge-Watie-Boudinot Family* (Norman: Univ. of Oklahoma Press, 1939). Most of the Treaty Party leaders were well-educated Cherokees, had numerous white ancestors, and in some cases had married white women. For his part, Schermerhorn was nicknamed the "Devil's Horn" by Cherokees because of his reputation as a "notorious womanizer." Perdue and Green, *Cherokee Nation*, p. 111.

1838, the U.S. Senate, which earlier had ratified the Treaty of New Echota by a single vote, voted to table the petition, and General Winfield Scott was given his orders.

About eleven hundred Cherokees remained in North Carolina, principally because these Cherokees convinced a white merchant named William Holland Thomas to use money from the Treaty of New Echota to purchase thousands of acres in western North Carolina on which these Cherokees settled (he kept the land title in his own name). In 1837, the North Carolina General Assembly acknowledged the Cherokees' right to remain in North Carolina. The fact that the land Thomas purchased for the Cherokees was land that virtually no one else wanted probably was a factor in the legislature's decision. In addition to the eleven hundred Cherokees who were allowed to stay in North Carolina, an additional three hundred remained scattered throughout Georgia, Alabama, and Tennessee. Some had hidden themselves from Scott's soldiers; others were related by blood and marriage to their white neighbors.

Eyewitness accounts of the Trail of Tears, by both Native Americans and U.S. Army escorts, make for grim reading. As many as twenty-five hundred or more died in the makeshift stockades prior to the journey. And of the 13,149 (cited by army records) who began the trip, only 11,504 arrived in Indian Territory. In addition, several hundred died soon after their arrival, by either disease or violence between the new arrivals and earlier migrants or between the "accommodationists" and the last-ditch resisters.[17]

What alternatives did whites consider? What were the strengths and weaknesses of each alternative? For the Cherokees, answer the same two questions. Note that some Cherokees actually favored relocation. What were their reasons for doing so?

The Method

As you examine and analyze the principal arguments both in favor of and opposed to Cherokee removal, almost immediately you will see that some of the speakers and writers chose to *rephrase* the question. For example, instead of listing the reasons the Cherokees should be removed, President Jackson preferred to discuss *why the Cherokees could not remain where they were* (Source 4). By carefully reading his answers (there were several) to that question, you will be able to infer

17. Burnett, "The Cherokee Removal Through the Eyes of a Private Soldier," pp. 180–185; Vicki Rozema, ed., *Voices from the Trail of Tears* (Winston-Salem, N.C.: John F. Blair, 2003); and

what his answers would have been to the question of *why the Cherokees ought to be removed.*

The same holds true for speakers and writers opposed to Cherokee removal. In some cases, they offered what they thought were alternatives that would have been superior to that of removal. As with Jackson's message, you will have to infer from what opponents said or wrote what they *would have* said or written regarding why the Cherokees ought *not to have been removed.*

Similarly to Jackson, many other speakers and writers offered more than one answer to the question. Therefore, as you examine and analyze the evidence, be sure to take notes carefully.

The second central question in this chapter regards the strengths and weaknesses of the principal points both in favor of and opposed to Cherokee removal. This is not nearly so easy as it may first appear. For one thing, you may not be able to uncover the real reasons a speaker or writer took a particular position. For example, almost no one in favor of removal said that Cherokees should be removed because whites wanted their lands. Even Georgia Governor Wilson Lumpkin (Source 9), who allowed whites to begin settling on Cherokee lands before any treaty was negotiated and who wanted to speed up the process so that he would still be in office when the issue was finally settled, was not willing to be so obvious. Similarly, no opponent of removal would have been crass enough

Theda Perdue and Michael D. Green, eds., *The Cherokee Removal: A Brief History with Documents* (Boston: Bedford St. Martin's, 2005).

to say that the opponent's true motive was to embarrass President Jackson politically. Without considerably more information than is available here, you will have to take the speaker's or writer's comments at face value. Jackson, for example, always claimed that removal was the most humane policy for the Cherokees themselves. Is there any evidence to the contrary?

Moreover, as you assess the strengths and weaknesses of each speaker's or writer's position, you will almost inevitably be drawn into the interesting but highly dangerous process of evaluating the alternatives to removal. Typically, historians concern themselves with what *actually did* happen rather than what *might have* happened. To be sure, some of the opponents of removal did advocate alternatives to removal, and in some cases you may have to deal with such alternatives as you determine the strengths and weaknesses of a particular position. If you plan to do this, however, use the actual facts at your disposal to assess a particular alternative. Do not *create* facts to fit your hypothesis—perhaps the worst charge that can be made against a historian. Also remember that you are dealing with people from the early 1800s, *not* the twenty-first century. Avoid putting ideas and thought processes contemporary to you into their minds.

The process of removing Cherokees from the East took decades. During that period, several principal figures in this drama actually changed their minds regarding removal. For example, several members of the Treaty Party at first had vehemently opposed relocation but in the end came to embrace it. Is there any clue in the evidence as to why they might have done so? What arguments did they use?

Let us offer a final note of caution. As you examine each piece of evidence, avoid the temptation to "take sides" in the debate or to make the historical individuals into one-dimensional heroes or villains. Analyze the logic of each of the arguments, even when you find the conclusions of a speaker or writer to be reprehensible.

Beneath the surface of all the arguments is the *image* of Native Americans, both in the eyes of European Americans and in those of Native Americans. What underlying assumptions regarding Cherokees can you detect in both the white and Cherokee evidence?

Now proceed to the Evidence section of the chapter. Take notes as you read each selection. Once again, a chart may prove helpful.

◆

The Evidence

WHITE SOURCES

Source 1 from Intercourse Act of July 22, 1790, in Wilcomb Washburn, ed., *The American Indian and the United States: A Documentary History* (New York: Random House, 1973), vol. 4, p. 2152.

1. Section IV of Intercourse Act of 1790.

And be it enacted and declared. That no sale of lands made by any Indians or any nation or tribe of Indians within the United States, shall be valid to any person or persons, or to any state, whether having the right of pre-emption to such lands or not, unless the same shall be made and duly executed at some public treaty, held under the authority of the United States.

Source 2 from Jefferson to Hawkins, Feb. 18, 1803, in Paul Leicester Ford., ed., *The Works of Thomas Jefferson* (New York: G. P. Putnam's Sons, 1905) vol. 9, pp. 446–448.

2. President Jefferson to Benjamin Hawkins,[18] February 18, 1803.

Altho' you will receive, thro' the official channel of the War Office, every communication necessary to develop to you our views respecting the Indians, and to direct your conduct, yet, supposing it will be satisfactory

18. Benjamin Hawkins (1754–1816), negotiated the Treaty of Hopewell with the Cherokees in 1785 and in 1803 was the agent to the Creeks.

to you, and to those with whom you are placed, to understand my personal dispositions and opinions in this particular, I shall avail myself of this private letter to state them generally. I consider the business of hunting as already become insufficient to furnish clothing and subsistence to the Indians. The promotion of agriculture, therefore, and household manufacture, are essential in their preservation, and I am disposed to aid and encourage it liberally. This will enable them to live on much smaller portions of land, and indeed will render their vast forests useless but for the range of cattle; for which purpose, also, as they become better farmers, they will be found useless, and even disadvantageous. While they are learning to do better on less land, our increasing numbers will be calling for more land, and thus a coincidence of interest will be produced between those who have lands to spare, and want other necessaries, and those who have such necessaries to spare, and want lands. This commerce, then, will be for the good of both, and those who are friends to both ought to encourage it. . . . In truth, the ultimate point of rest & happiness for them is to let our settlements and theirs meet and blend together, to intermix, and become one people. Incorporating themselves with us as citizens of the U.S., this is what the natural progress of things will of course bring on, and it will be better to promote than to retard it. Surely it will be better for them to be identified with us, and preserved in the occupation of their lands, than be exposed to the many casualties which may endanger them while a separate people. I have little doubt but that your reflections must have led you to view the various ways in which their history may terminate, and to see that this is the one most for their happiness. . . .

It is possible, perhaps probable, that this idea may be so novel as that it might shock the Indians, were it even hinted to them. Of course, you will keep it for your own reflection; but, convinced of its soundness, I feel it consistent with pure morality to lead them towards it, to familiarize them to the idea that it is for their interest to cede lands at times to the U.S., and for us thus to procure gratifications to our citizens, from time to time, by new acquisitions of land.

Source 3 from Theda Perdue and Michael D. Green, eds., "A Brief View of the Present Relations Between the Government and People of the United States and the Indians Within Our National Limits," from *The Cherokee Removal: A Brief History with Documents* (Boston, MA: Bedford Books, 1995).

3. Excerpt from William Penn (pseudonym for Jeremiah Evarts of the American Board of Commissioners for Foreign Missions), "A Brief View of the Present Relations between the Government and People of the United States and the Indians Within Our National Limits," November 1829.

The positions here recited are deemed to be incontrovertible. It follows, therefore,

That the removal of any nation of Indians from their country by force would be an instance of gross and cruel oppression:

That all attempts to accomplish this removal of the Indians by bribery or fraud, by intimidation and threats, by withholding from them a knowledge of the strength of their cause, by practising upon their ignorance, and their fears, or by vexatious opportunities, interpreted by them to mean nearly the same thing as a command;—all such attempts are acts of oppression, and therefore entirely unjustifiable:

That the United States are firmly bound by treaty to protect the Indians from force and encroachments on the part of a State; and a refusal thus to protect them would be equally an act of bad faith as a refusal to protect them against individuals: and

That the Cherokees have therefore the guaranty of the United States, solemnly and repeatedly given, as a security against encroachments from Georgia and the neighboring States. By virtue of this guaranty the Cherokees may rightfully demand, that the United States shall keep all intruders at a distance, from whatever quarter, or in whatever character, they may come. Thus secured and defended in the possession of their country, the Cherokees have a perfect right to retain that possession as long as they please. Such a retention of their country is no just cause of complaint or offence to any State, or to any individual. It is merely an exercise of natural rights, which rights have been not only acknowledged but repeatedly and solemnly confirmed by the United States.

Although these principles are clear and incontrovertible, yet many persons feel an embarrassment from considering the Cherokees as *living in the State of Georgia*. All this embarrassment may be removed at once by bearing in mind, that the Cherokee country is not in Georgia. . . .

[Here Penn argued that the Cherokees owned their land by treaty with the U.S. government, that in 1825 the state of Georgia made a treaty with the Creek Nation to acquire their land, and hence would have to do so with the Cherokees as well.]

[181]

If the separate existence of the Indian tribes *were* an inconvenience to their neighbours, this would be but a slender reason for breaking down all the barriers of justice and good faith. Many a rich man has thought it very inconvenient, that he could not add the farm of a poor neighbour to his possessions. Many a powerful nation has felt it to be inconvenient to have a weak and dependent state in its neighbourhood, and has therefore forcibly joined the territory of such state to its own extensive domains. But this is done at the expense of honour and character, and is visited by the historian with his severest reprobation.

[Here Penn stated that the Cherokees already have ceded their best lands and what is left is "almost inaccessible" and mostly "utterly worthless." Penn claimed that Georgia already was the second largest state (the largest being Virginia) and had "but six or seven souls to a square mile." Why does Georgia want more?]

There is one remaining topic, on which the minds of many benevolent men are hesitating; and that is, *whether the welfare of the Indians would not be promoted by a removal.* Though they have a right to remain where they are; though the whole power of the United States is pledged to defend them in their possessions; yet it is supposed by some, that they would act wisely, if they would yield to the pressure, quietly surrender their territory to the United States, and accept a new country beyond the Mississippi, with a new guaranty.

In support of this supposition, it is argued, that they can never remain quiet where they are; that they will always be infested by troublesome whites; and that the states, which lay claim to their territory, will persevere in measures to vex and annoy them.

Let us look a moment at this statement. Is it indeed true, that, in the very prime and vigour of our republican government, and with all our boasted reliance upon constitutions and laws, we cannot enforce as plain an act of Congress as is to be found in our national statute-book? Is it true, that while treaties are declared in the constitution to be the supreme law of the land, a whole volume of these supreme laws is to be at once avowedly and utterly disregarded? Is the Senate of the United States, that august body, as our newspapers have called it a thousand times, to march in solemn procession, and burn a volume of treaties? Are the archives of state to be searched, and a hundred and fifty rolls, containing treaties with the Indians, to be brought forth and consigned to the flames on Capitol Hill, in the presence of the representatives of the people, and all the dignitaries of our national government? When ambassadors from foreign nations inquire, *What is the cause of all this burning?* are we to say, "Forty years ago President Washington and the Senate made treaties with the Indians, which have been repeated and confirmed by successive administrations. The treaties are plain, and the terms reasonable. But the Indians are weak, and their white neighbors will be lawless. The way to please these white neighbours is, therefore, to burn the treaties, and then call the Indians our dear children, and deal with them precisely as if no treaties had ever been made?" Is this answer to be given to the honest inquires of intelligent foreigners? Are we to declare to mankind, that in our country law is totally inadequate to answer the great end for which human laws are made, that is, the protection of the weak against the strong? And is this confession to be made without feeling and without shame? It cannot be. The people of the United States will never subject themselves to so foul a reproach.

Source 4 from James D. Richardson, *A Compilation of the Messages and Papers of the Presidents* (New York: Bureau of National Literature, 1897).

4. Excerpt from President Andrew Jackson's First Annual Message to Congress, December 8, 1829.[19]

The condition and ulterior destiny of the Indian Tribes within the limits of some of our States, have become objects of much interest and importance. It has long been the policy of Government to introduce among them the arts of civilization, in the hope of gradually reclaiming them from a wandering life. This policy has, however, been coupled with another, wholly incompatible with its success. Professing a desire to civilize and settle them, we have, at the same time, lost no opportunity to purchase their lands, and thrust them further into the wilderness. By this means they have not only been kept in a wandering state, but been led to look upon us as unjust and indifferent to their fate. Thus, though lavish in its expenditures upon the subject, Government has constantly defeated its own policy; and the Indians, in general, receding further and further to the West, have retained their savage habits. A portion, however, of the Southern tribes, having mingled much with the whites, and made some progress in the arts of civilized life, have lately attempted to erect an independent government, within the limits of Georgia and Alabama. These States, claiming to be the only sovereigns within their territories, extended their laws over the Indians; which induced the latter to call upon the United States for protection. . . .

19. From George Washington to Woodrow Wilson, no president of the United States appeared in person before Congress. All communications between the president and Congress were conducted in writing.

Actuated by this view of the subject, I informed the Indians inhabiting parts of Georgia and Alabama, that their attempt to establish an independent government would not be countenanced by the Executive of the United States; and advised them to emigrate beyond the Mississippi, or submit to the laws of those States.

Our conduct towards these people is deeply interesting to our national character. Their present condition, contrasted with what they once were, makes a most powerful appeal to our sympathies. Our ancestors found them the uncontrolled possessors of these vast regions. By persuasion and force, they have been made to retire from river to river, and from mountain to mountain; until some of the tribes have become extinct, and others have left but remnants, to preserve, for a while, their once terrible names. Surrounded by the whites, with their arts of civilization, which, by destroying the resources of the savage, doom him to weakness and decay; the fate of the Mohegan, the Narragansett, and the Delaware, is fast overtaking the Choctaw, the Cherokee, and the Creek. That this fate surely awaits them, if they remain within the limits of the States, does not admit of a doubt. Humanity and national honor demand that every effort should be made to avert so great a calamity. It is too late to inquire whether it was just in the United States to include them and their territory within the bounds of new States whose limits they could control. That step cannot be retraced. A State cannot be dismembered by Congress, or restricted in the exercise of her constitutional power. But the people of those States, and of every State, actuated by feelings of justice and a regard for our national honor, submit to you the interesting question, whether something cannot be done, consistently with the rights of the States, to preserve this much injured race?

As a means of effecting this end, I suggest, for your consideration, the propriety of setting apart an ample district West of the Mississippi, and without the limits of any State or Territory, now formed, to be guarantied to the Indian tribes, as long as they shall occupy it: each tribe having a distinct control over the portion designated for its use. There they may be secured in the enjoyment of governments of their own choice, subject to no other control from the United States than such as may be necessary to preserve peace on the frontier, and between the several tribes. There the benevolent may endeavor to teach them the arts of civilization; and, by promoting union and harmony among them, to raise up an interesting commonwealth, destined to perpetuate the race, and to attest the humanity and justice of this Government.

This emigration should be voluntary: for it would be as cruel as unjust to compel the aborigines to abandon the graves of their fathers, and seek a home in a distant land.[20] But they should be distinctly informed that, if they remain within the limits of the States, they must be subject to their laws. In return for their obedience, as individuals, they will, without doubt, be protected in the enjoyment of those possessions which they have improved by their industry. But it seems to me visionary to suppose, that, in this state of things, claims can be allowed on tracts of country on which they have neither dwelt nor made improvements, merely because they have seen them from the mountain, or passed them in the chace [sic]. Submitting to the laws of the States, and receiving, like other citizens, protection in their persons and property, they will, ere long, become merged in the mass of our population.

Sources 5, 6, and 7 are from *Speeches on the Passage of the Bill for the Removal of the Indians, Delivered in the Congress of the United States, April and May, 1830* (Boston, MA: Perkins and Marvin, 1830).

5. Excerpt from Speech of Senator Theodore Frelinghuysen.[21]

It is alleged, that the Indians cannot flourish in the neighborhood of a white population—that whole tribes have disappeared under the influence of this propinquity. As an abstract proposition, it implies reproach somewhere. Our virtues certainly have not such deadly and depopulating power. It must, then, be our vices that possess these destructive energies—and shall we commit injustice, and put in, as our plea for it, that our intercourse with the Indians has been so demoralizing that we must drive them from it, to save them? True, Sir, many tribes have melted away—they have sunk lower and lower—and what people could rise from a condition to which policy, selfishness, and cupidity, conspired to depress them?

Sir, had we devoted the same care to elevate their moral condition, that we have to degrade them, the removal of the Indians would not now seek for an apology in the suggestions of humanity. But I ask, as to the matter of fact, how stands the account? Wherever a fair experiment has been made, the Indians have readily yielded to the influences of moral cultivation. Yes, Sir, they flourish under this culture, and rise in the scale of being. They have shown themselves to be highly susceptible of improvement, and the ferocious feelings and habits of the savage are soothed and reformed by the

20. Jackson believed, perhaps naively, that a majority of Cherokees would move to the West voluntarily. See his Third Annual Message to Congress, December 6, 1831, in Richardson, *Messages and Papers of the Presidents,* vol. III, p. 1117.
21. Theodore Frelinghuysen (1787–1862) was president of the American Board of Commissioners for Foreign Missions from 1841 to 1857. For more on Frelinghuysen, see Chapter 6.

mild charities of religion. They can very soon be taught to understand and appreciate the blessings of civilization and regular government.

Prompted and encouraged by our counsels, they have in good earnest resolved to become men, rational, educated, Christian men; and they have succeeded beyond our most sanguine hopes. They have established a regular constitution of civil government, republican in its principles. Wise and beneficent laws are enacted. The people acknowledge their authority, and feel their obligation. A printing press, conducted by one of the nation, circulates a weekly newspaper, printed partly in English, and partly in the Cherokee language. Schools flourish in many of their settlements. Christian temples, to the God of the Bible, are frequented by respectful, devout, and many sincere worshippers. God, as we believe, has many people among them, whom he regards as the "apple of his eye." They have become better neighbors to Georgia. . . .

Let the general government come out, as it should, with decided and temperate firmness, and officially announce to Georgia, and the other States, that if the Indian tribes choose to remain, they will be protected against all interference and encroachment; and such is my confidence in the sense of justice, in the respect for law, prevailing in the great body of this portion of our fellow-citizens, that I believe they would submit to the authority of the nation. I can expect no other issue.

6. Excerpt from 50-Page Speech of Representative Henry R. Storrs of New York.

Mr. Chairman: If I believed that the real object and only effect of the bill were to further the policy of providing a country beyond the Mississippi for such of the Indian tribes as might be inclined, of their own free choice, to remove there, I should have cheerfully given my support to the measure; for I heartily respond to the opinion expressed by the honorable member at the head of the committee on Indian affairs, who spoke yesterday, (Mr. Bell), that no philanthropic man can look at the condition to which these unfortunate people have become reduced by a combination of circumstances, which now press upon them in some quarters with intolerable severity, without fervently wishing that they were already removed far beyond the reach of the oppression, and—I was about to say—the example of the white man. I hope that I am too well aware of the responsibility of the country to the opinion of the world, and too sensible of the duties we owe to these people, to be found resisting any measure here, which may really improve their condition, or encouraging them to reject any propositions of the government, which may be offered to them for their free acceptance or refusal. But, Sir, although the bill now before you presents nothing on its face, which, on a superficial examination, appears to be objectionable, yet we cannot shut our eyes, if we would, to the circumstances which have brought this subject before us at the present session. The papers before the house have convinced me, that it is chiefly intended and expected to come in aid of the measures recently taken by the States along the southern line of the Union, for removing the Indian nations within their limits from the country which they now occupy; and finding a purpose so unjust to these people, and so mischievous to the reputation of the country, lurking under it, I cannot give it my countenance or support.

7. Transcript from Speech of Representative David Crockett of Tennessee.

Mr. Crockett said, that, considering his very humble abilities, it might be expected that he should content himself with a silent vote; but, situated as he was, in relation to his colleagues, he felt it to be a duty to himself to explain the motives which governed him in the vote he should give on this bill. Gentlemen had already discussed the treaty-making power; and had done it much more ably than he could pretend to do. He should not therefore enter on that subject, but would merely make an explanation as to the reasons of his vote. He did not know whether a man within 500 miles of his residence would give a similar vote; but he knew, at the same time, that he should give that vote with a clear conscience. He had his constituents to settle with, he was aware; and should like to please them as well as other gentlemen; but he had also a settlement to make at the bar of his God; and what his conscience dictated to be just and right he would do, be the consequences what they might. He believed that the people who had been kind enough to give him their suffrages, supposed him to be an honest man, or they would not have chosen him. If so, they could not but expect that he should act in the way he thought honest and right. He had always viewed the native Indian tribes of this country as a sovereign people. He believed they had been recognised as such from the very foundation of this government, and the United States were bound by treaty to protect them; it was their duty to do so. And as to giving the money of the American people for the purpose of removing them in the manner proposed, he would not do it. He would do that only for which he could answer to his God. Whether he could answer it before the people was comparatively nothing, though it was a great satisfaction to him to have the approbation of his constituents.

Source 8 from United States Statutes at Large. *Removal Act* of May 28, 1830, ch. 148, Stat. 1.

8. Sections 3 and 6 from the Removal Act of May 28, 1830.

III. That in the making of any such exchange or exchanges, it shall and may be lawful for the President solemnly to assure the tribe or nation . . . that the United States will forever secure and guaranty to them, and their heirs or successors, the country so exchanged. . . .

VI. And be it further enacted. That it shall and may be lawful for the President to cause such tribe or nation to be protected, at their new residence, against all interruption or disturbance from any other tribe or nation of Indians, or from any other person or persons whatever.

Source 9 from Wilson Lumpkin, *The Removal of the Cherokee Indians from Georgia* (New York: Dodd, Mead & Co., 1907).

9. Georgia Governor Wilson Lumpkin to the Georgia Assembly, December 2, 1831.

Executive Department, Georgia, Milledgeville, December 2nd, 1831.

It is believed that a crisis has arrived, in which we cannot permit the course of our policy in relation to the Cherokee part of Georgia to remain in its present perplexed and extraordinary condition without jeopardizing the interest and prosperity, if not the peace and safety, of the State.

Circumstances within the recollection of our whole people emperiously demanded the extension of the laws and jurisdiction of our State over our entire population and territory.

This step has been taken, and cannot be retraced. The State cannot consent to be restricted in the exercise of her constitutional rights.[22] It is now too late for us to theorize on this subject; we are called upon to act; the public functionaries of the State stand pledged to their constituents, and the world, to sustain the ground which they have taken. It is our constitutional

22. In his memoirs, Governor Lumpkin stated that "at the very threshold of my Executive administration it became my duty to resist Federal usurpation [and] . . . Federal encroachments." Lumpkin, *Removal of the Cherokee*, vol. 1, p. 94. What was Lumpkin referring to here?

right, and moral duty, fortwith [*sic*] to interpose and save that part of our State from confusion, anarchy, and perhaps from bloodshed. . . .

[Here Gov. Lumpkin asserted that a "few thousand half civilized men, both indisposed and incompetent," can never live peacefully under a civil government. Therefore, the territory cannot be governed "until we have a settled, freehold, white population" residing there. Otherwise, the Cherokees, he claimed, would be able to maintain a regular government only for a few months. Also, the gold mines would attract "the most abandoned portions of society." And yet, the Cherokees are being swayed by "impertinent intermeddling 'busy-bodies'" who have brought on the present crisis.]

Our true situation and motives on this question are still misunderstood, and often misrepresented, by those at a distance. In order to appreciate our policy, our true situation must be understood. I will not attempt to enumerate the wrongs, embarrassments, and perplexities, which this State has encountered, by what I am constrained to deem the impertinent intermeddling of "busy-bodies." Officious persons of various descriptions have unfortunately succeeded in inducing our Indian people to believe that we are their enemies and oppressors, and in alienating their affections from us. These various intermeddlings hastened the crisis which compelled the State to the course which she has taken; and the day must speedily arrive when all the heart-burnings on this subject must be put to final rest. The combined and combining influences now in operation against the character, interest, peace, and prosperity of the State, cannot be much longer deplored in silent inaction; nor ought we to place any reliance on inefficient measures. Unfounded calumny and prejudice, kept at a distance, may be endured; but domestic and household enemies produce unceasing disquietude and danger.

The unfortunate remnant of Cherokee Indians remaining in Georgia ought now to consider themselves the admitted charge of our peculiar care; and if possible we ought, as their friends and benefactors, to preserve and cherish them. They ought not forcibly to be dispossessed of their homes, or driven from the land of their fathers; they ought to be guarded and protected in the peaceable enjoyment of a sufficient portion of land to sustain them, with their families, in their present abodes, so long as they may choose to remain; and their rights and property should be as well secured from all lawless depredation as those of the white man. It would be as cruel as unjust, to compel the aborigines to abandon the graves of their fathers; but in the present extraordinary state of things it would be visionary to suppose, that the Indian claim can be allowed to this extensive tract of country—to lands on which they have neither dwelt, nor made improvements.[23]

Principles of natural law and abstract justice have often been appealed to, to show that the Indian tribes within the territorial limits of the States ought to be regarded as the absolute owners and proprietors of the soil they occupy.

All civilized nations have acknowledged the validity of the principles appealed to, with such modifications and interpretations of these principles as the truth of history has verified, especially in the settlement of this country.

The foundations of the States which form this confederacy were laid by civilized and Christian nations who considered themselves instructed in the nature of their duties by the precepts and examples contained in the Sacred Volume which they acknowledged as the basis of their religious creed and obligations. To go forth, subdue, and replenish the earth, were considered Divine commands....

The present state of things in the Cherokee country, it is believed, is strengthening the adversaries of Georgia, at home and abroad.

In order to secure and protect the Indians in their abodes, and their property of every kind under our laws, their individual and separate possessions ought to be defined by actual survey; in accomplishing which it will be least expensive and most compatible with the views of the State (as provided by the act of the Legislature at its last session), to survey the entire country.

Until we have a population planted upon the unoccupied portion of this territory, possessed of all the ordinary inducements of other communities to sustain our laws and government, our present laws providing for the government of this part of the State should not only be continued, but ample power should be afforded to enforce obedience to their requirements. to effect this object, the Executive should be vested with full power promptly to control the agents who have been, or may be, selected to maintain the authority of the laws in that portion of the State....

CHEROKEE SOURCES

Source 10 from Treaty of Hopewell, Washburn, *The American Indian and the United States*, vol. 3, pp. 2272–2273.

10. Cherokees to President Washington, May 19, 1789.

... we gave up to our white brothers all the land we could anyhow spare, and have but little left to raise our women and children upon, and we hope you won't let any people take any more from us without our consent.

23. See similarity to Jackson's phrase in Source 4.

Sources 11 and 12 from Theda Perdue and Michael Green, *The Cherokee Removal: A Brief History with Documents* (Boston, MA: Bedford Books, 1995).

11. Petition of Cherokee Women, May 2, 1817.

The Cherokee ladys now being present at the meeting of the chiefs and warriors in council have thought it their duty as mothers to address their beloved chiefs and warriors now assembled.

Our beloved children and head men of the Cherokee Nation, we address you warriors in council. We have raised all of you on the land which we now have, which God gave us to inhabit and raise provisions. We know that our country has once been extensive, but by repeated sales has become circumscribed to a small track [*sic*], and [we] never have thought it our duty to interfere in the disposition of it till now. If a father or mother was to sell all their lands which they had to depend on, which their children had to raise their living on, which would be indeed bad & to be removed to another country. We do not wish to go to an unknown country [to] which we have understood some of our children wish to go over the Mississippi, but this act of our children would be like destroying your mothers.

Your mothers, your sisters ask and beg of you not to part with any more of our land. We say ours. You are our descendants; take pity on our request. But keep it for our growing children, for it was the good will of our creator to place us here, and you know our father, the great president,[24] will not allow his white children to take our country away. Only keep your hands off of paper talks for its our own country. for [if] it was not, they would not ask you to put your hands to paper, for it would be impossible to remove us all. For as soon as one child is raised, we have others in our arms, for such is our situation & will consider our circumstance.

Therefore, children, don't part with any more of our lands but continue on it & enlarge your farms. Cultivate and raise corn & cotton and your mothers and sisters will make clothing for you which our father the president has recommended to us all. We don't charge any body for selling any lands, but we have heard such intentions of our children. But your talks become true at last; it was our desire to forewarn you all not to part with our lands.[25]

24. President James Monroe.
25. Despite the women's petition, Cherokees signed two more treaties, in 1817 and 1819, before deciding to cede no more land. See Cherokee Delegation to the U.S. Senate, April 16, 1824, "Views of the Cherokees in Relation to Further Cessions of Their Lands," *American State Papers: Indian Affairs,* vol. 2, p. 502.

12. John Ridge (a Cherokee leader) to Albert Gallatin,[26] February 27, 1826.

[In this long letter, Ridge began by giving a geographic location of the Cherokee Nation, its population, its successful adoption of agriculture, its government, the status of women, its religious beliefs, and its educational institutions.]

Col. Silas Dinsmore was appointed by Genl. Washington as Agent of the Nation, who from the Indian Testimony itself labored indefatigably in Teaching the Cherokees the art of agriculture by distributing hoes & ploughs & giving to the women Spinning wheels, cards & Looms. It appears when this change of Hunter life to a civilized one was proposed by the Agent to the Chiefs in council, that he was unanimously laughed at by the Council for attempting [to] introduce white peoples' habits among the Indians, who were created to pursue the chase. Not discouraged here, the Agent turned to Individuals & succeeded to gain some to pay their attention to his plan by way of experiment, which succeeded. An anecdote is related of a Chief who was heartily opposed to the Agent's view. He came to Col. Dinsmore & said, "I don't want you to recommend these things to my people. They may suit white people, but will do [nothing] for the Indians. I am now going to hunt & shall be gone six moons & when I return, I shall expect to hear nothing of your talks made in [my] absence to induce my people to take hold of your plan." But in his absence the Agent induced his wife & daughters to spin & weave with so much assiduity as to make more cloth in value, than the Chief's Hunt of six months amounted to. He was astonished & came to the Agent with a smile, accusing him for making his wife & daughters better hunters than he & requested to be furnished a plough & went to work on his farm. In the meantime, the Moravians opened their School for the Indians, cleared a farm, cultivated a garden & planted an orchard. The Venerable Rev. John Gambold & his amiable Lady were a standing monument of Industry, Goodness & friendship. As far as they had means, they converted the "Wilderness to blossom as the Rose." There the boys & girls were taught to read & write, & occasionally labor in the Garden & in the field. There they were first taught to sing & pray to their Creator, & here Gospel Worship was first Established. Never shall I forget father Gambold & mother Mrs. Gambold. By them the clouds of ignorance which surrounded me on all sides were dispersed. My heart received the rays of civilization & my intellect expanded & took a wider range. My superstition vanished & I began to reason correctly. . . .

26. Albert Gallatin (1761–1849) was a congressman, secretary of the treasury, and diplomat. When Ridge wrote to Gallatin, Gallatin had just been nominated as U.S. minister to Great Britain.

Source 13 from Elias Boudinot, in *Cherokee Phoenix*, March 13, 1828, in Theda Perdue, ed., *Cherokee Editor: The Writings of Elias Boudinot* (Knoxville: Univ. of Tennessee Press, 1983), pp. 95–96.

13. Elias Boudinot in *Cherokee Phoenix*, March 13, 1828.

CONGRESS.—Our last Washington papers contain a debate which took place in the house of representatives, on the resolution, recommended by the Committee on Indian Affairs, published in the second Number of our paper. It appears that the advocates of this new system of civilizing the Indians are very strenuous in maintaining the novel opinion, that it is impossible to enlighten the Indians, surrounded as they are by the white population, and that they assuredly will become extinct, unless they are removed. It is a fact which we would not deny, that many tribes have perished away in consequence of white population, but we are yet to be convinced that this will always be the case, in spite of every measure taken to civilize them. We contend that suitable measures to a sufficient extent have never been employed. And how dare these men make an assertion without sufficient evidence? What proof have they that the system which they are now recommending, will succeed[?] Where have we an example in the whole history of man, of a nation or tribe, removing in a body, from a land of civil and religious means, to a perfect wilderness, *in order to be civilized[?]* We are fearful these men are building castles in the air, whose fall will crush those poor Indians who may be so blinded as to make the experiment. We are sorry to see that some of the advocates of this system speak so disrespectfully, if not contemptuously, of the present measure of improvement, now in successful operation among most of the Indians in the United States—the only measures too, which have been crowned with success, and bid fair to meliorate the condition of the Aborigines.

Source 14 from Speckled Snake's "*Response to President Andrew Jackson's First Annual Message to Congress*, December 8, 1829," Wayne Moquin and Charles Van Doren, eds., *Great Documents in American Indian History* (New York: Praeger, 1973), pp. 149–150.

14. Speckled Snake's "Response to President Andrew Jackson's First Annual Message to Congress, December 8, 1829," (1830).

Brothers! We have heard the talk of our great father; it is very kind. He says he loves his red children. *Brothers!* When the white man first came to these shores, the Muscogees gave him land, and kindled him a fire to make him comfortable; and when the pale faces of the south made war on him, their young men drew the tomahawk, and protected his head from the scalping knife. But when the white man had warmed himself before the Indian's fire, and filled himself with the Indian's hominy, he became very large; he stopped not for the mountain tops, and his feet covered the plains and the valleys. His hands grasped the eastern and the western sea. Then he became our great father. He loved his red children; but said, "You must move a little farther, lest I should, by accident, tread on you." With one foot he pushed the red man over the Oconee [River], and with the other he trampled down the graves of his fathers. But our great father still loved his red children, and he soon made them another talk. He said much; but it all meant nothing, but "move a little farther; you are too near me." I heard a great many talks from our great father, and they all begun and ended the same, *Brothers!* When he made us a talk on a former occasion, he said, "Get a little farther; go beyond the Oconee and the Oakmulgee [River]; there is a pleasant country." He also said, "It shall be yours forever." Now he says, "The land you live on is not yours; go beyond the Mississippi; there is game; there you may remain while the grass grows or the water runs." *Brothers!* Will not our great father come there also? He loves his red children, and his tongue is not forked.

Source 15 from Francis Paul Prucha, ed., *Cherokee Removal: The 'William Penn' Essays and Other Writings By Jeremiah Evarts* (Knoxville, TN: University of Tennessee Press, 1981).

15. Address of the Committee and Council of the Cherokee Nation . . . to the People of the United States, July 24, 1830.[27]

We are aware that some persons suppose it will be for our advantage to remove beyond the Mississippi. We think otherwise. Our people universally think otherwise. Thinking that it would be fatal to their interest, they have almost to a man sent their memorial to Congress, deprecating the necessity of a removal. This question was distinctly before their minds when they signed their memorial. Not an adult person can be found, who has not an opinion on the subject; and if the people were to understand distinctly, that they could be protected against the laws of the neighboring States, there is probably not an adult person in the nation, who would think it best to remove; though possible [sic] a few might emigrate individually. There are doubtless

27. Although the address was issued by the General Council of the Cherokee Nation and published in the *Cherokee Phoenix* on July 24, 1830, it actually was written by Jeremiah Evarts (1781–1831), secretary of the American Board of Commissioners for Foreign Missions. See Source 3. The Council added the last paragraph in this excerpt.

many who would flee to an unknown country, however beset with dangers, privations and sufferings, rather than be sentenced to spend six years in a Georgia prison for advising one of their neighbors not to betray his country. And there are others who could not think of living as outlaws in their native land, exposed to numberless vexations, and excluded from being parties or witnesses in a court of justice. It is incredible that Georgia should ever have enacted the oppressive laws to which reference is here made, unless she had supposed that something extremely terrific in its character was necessary, in order to make the Cherokees willing to remove. We are not willing to remove; and if we could be brought to this extremity, it would be, not by argument; not because our judgment was satisfied; not because our condition will be improved—but only because we cannot endure to be deprived of our national and individual rights, and subjected to a process of intolerable oppression.

We wish to remain on the land of our fathers. We have a perfect and original right to claim this, without interruption or molestation. The treaties with us, and laws of the United States made in pursuance of treaties, guaranty our residence, and our privileges, and secure us against intruders. Our only request is, that these treaties may be fulfilled, and these laws executed. . . .

It is under a sense of the most pungent feelings that we make this, perhaps our last appeal to the good people of the United States. It cannot be that the community we are addressing, remarkable for its intelligence and religious sensibilities, and pre-eminent for its devotion to the rights of man, will lay aside this appeal, without considering that we stand in need of its sympathy and commiseration. We know that to the Christian and the philanthropist, the voice of our multiplied sorrows and fiery trials will not appear as an idle tale. In our own land, our own soil, and in our dwellings, which we reared for our wives and for our little ones, when there was peace on our mountains and in our valleys, we are encountering troubles which cannot but try our very souls. But shall we, on account of these troubles, forsake our beloved country? Shall we be compelled by a civilized and Christian people, with whom we have lived in perfect peace for the last forty years, and for whom we have willingly bled in war, to bid a final adieu to our homes, our farms, our streams, and our beautiful forests? No. We are still firm. We intend still to cling, with our wonted affection, to the land which gave us birth, and which, every day of our lives, brings to us new and stronger ties of attachment. We appeal to the Judge of all the earth, who will finally award us justice, and to the good sense of the American people, whether we are intruders upon the land of others. Our consciences bear us witness that we are the invaders of no man's rights—we have robbed no man of his territory—we have usurped no man's authority, nor have we deprived any one of his unalienable privileges.

How then shall we indirectly confess the right of another people to our land by leaving it forever? On the soil which contains the ashes of our beloved men, we wish to live, on this soil we wish to die. . . .

Source 16 from Theda Perdue, ed., *Cherokee Editor: The Writings of Elias Boudinot.* Copyright © 1983 by The University of Tennessee Press. Reproduced by permission, pp. 175–179.

16. Elias Boudinot, "Resolutions," October 2, 1832.

Whereas, a crisis of the utmost importance, in the affairs of the Cherokee people has arrived, requiring from every individual the most serious reflection and the expression of views as to the present condition and future prospects of the Nation; and whereas a portion of the Cherokees have entertained opinions which have been represented as hostile to the true interest and happiness of the people, merely because they have not agreed with the Chiefs and leading men; and as these opinions have not heretofore been properly made known, therefore.

Resolved, That it is our decided opinion, founded upon the melancholy experience of the Cherokees within the last two years, and upon facts which history has furnished us in regard to other Indian nations, that our people cannot exist amidst a white population, subject to laws which they have no hand in making, and which they do not understand; that the suppression of the Cherokee Government, which connected this people in a distinct community, will not only check their progress in improvement and advancement in knowledge, but, by means of numerous influences and temptations which this new state of things has created, will completely destroy every thing like civilization among them, and ultimately reduce them to poverty, misery, and wretchedness.

Resolved, That, considering the progress of the States authorities in this country, the distribution and settlement of the lands, the organization of counties, the erection of county seats and Courthouses, and other indications of a determined course on the part of the surrounding States, and considering, on the other hand, the repeated refusal of the President and Congress of the United States to interfere in our behalf, we have come to the conclusion that this nation cannot be reinstated in its present location, and that the question left to us and to every Cherokee, is, whether it is more desirable to remain here, with all the embarrassments with which we must be surrounded, or to seek a country where we *may* enjoy our own laws, and live under our own vine and fig-tree.

Resolved, That in expressing the opinion that this nation cannot be reinstated, we do it from a thorough conviction of its truth—that we never will encourage our confiding people with hopes that can never be realized, and with expectations that will assuredly be disappointed—that however unwelcome and painful the truth may be to them, and however unkindly it may be received from us, we cannot, as *patriots* and well-wishers of the Indian race, shrink from doing our duty in expressing our decided convictions. That we scorn the charge of selfishness and a want of patriotic feelings alleged against us by some of our countrymen, while we can appeal to our consciences and the searcher of all hearts for the rectitude of our motives and intentions.

Resolved, That, although *we love the land* of our fathers, and should leave the place of our nativity with as much regret as any of our citizens, we consider the lot of the *Exile* immeasurably more to be preferred than a submission to the laws of the States, and thus becoming witnesses of the ruin and degradation of the Cherokee people.

Resolved, That we are firmly of the opinion, that a large majority of the Cherokee people would prefer to remove, if the true state of their condition was properly made known to them.[28]—We believe that if they were told that they had nothing to expect from further efforts to regain their rights as a *distinct community*, and that the only alternatives left to them is either to remain amidst a white population, subject to the white man's laws, or to remove to another country, where they may enjoy peace and happiness, they would unhesitatingly prefer the latter. . . .

Resolved, That we consider the policy pursued by the Red Clay Council,[29] in continuing a useless struggle from year to year, as destructive to the present peace and future happiness of the Cherokees, because it is evident to every observer that while this struggle is going on, their difficulties will be accumulating, until they are ruined in their property and character, and the only remedy that will then be proposed in their case will be, *submission to the laws of the States* by taking reservations.

28. Boudinot accused Principal Chief John Ross and the National Council of not telling the Cherokees "how seemingly hopeless their situation was." Perdue, *Cherokee Editor,* p. 228, n. 29.
29. "Red Clay Council:" the National Council.

Source 17 from Gary E. Moulton, ed., *The Papers of Chief John Ross* (Norman, OK: University of Oklahoma Press, 1985).

17. John Ross[30] et al. to President Andrew Jackson, January 23, 1835.

It is known to your Excellency, that the history of the Cherokee Nation since the year 1829 up to the present, has been on its part, one of repeated, continued unavailing struggle against the cruel policy of Georgia; on the part of that State, it has been one, of unparalleled aggravated acts of oppression upon the Nation. Actuated by an unextinguishable love of country, confiding implicitly in the good faith of the American Govt. and believing that the Govt. priding itself, as it does upon its justice and humanity would, not only not, disregard its own plighted faith, but would eventually interpose to prevent it from being disregarded, and trampled into dust by the State of Georgia. Being fully convinced in their own judgement that they could not prosper as well any where else as upon their native land, the Cherokees have successively appealed to the Executive, Legislative and Judiciary Departments of this Govt. for redress of wrongs committed and security against injuries apprehended, but as yet those appeals have been unavailing; In defiance of Acts of Congress, decisions of the Supreme Court, and of solemn treaties, Georgia has gone on first, to despoil them of their laws & Govt. and impose upon them laws the most obnoxious, then to distribute their lands unbought, to her own citizens by lottery, and lastly she has put forth her hand under the last Act of her Legislature to expel them from their homes & firesides, to drive them out to hunger and perish in the wild forests—to accomplish this last cruel purpose, armed bands of her citizens are now parading thro' their Country. The Undersigned deeply affected with this deplorable, condition of their people would ask you, Dear Sir, to pity and save them. For, upon the exercise of your power alone, they are firmly persuaded the salvation of their people depend. Let the comforts and enjoyments of life which have been so profusely scattered around you, by a bountiful providence remind you, that hundreds of their people, many of whom are women and children, may now be homeless wanderers, suffering with cold & hunger, for no crime, but, because they did not love their Country less.

The crisis of the fate of the Cherokee people, seems to be rapidly approaching—and the time has come, when they must be relieved of their sufferings—They having fully determined against a removal to Arkansas. The undersigned

---

30. John Ross (1790–1866), the Principal Chief from 1828 to 1860, was one-eighth Cherokee, well-educated and became a wealthy landowner and businessman. In 1836, his property was appraised at $23,665 ($446,085 in 2001 dollars).

Delegation would therefore most respectfully and earnestly ask to be informed, upon what terms will the President negotiate for a final termination of those sufferings, that their people may repose in peace and comfort on the land of their nativity, under the enjoyment of such rights and privileges as belongs to freemen. And the Delegation would in conclusion beg leave to assure the President in great sincerity, that after a due deliberation on the terms which he may offer, should they be found to have been dictated in that spirit of liberality and justice, as in their best judgement would afford their people ample relief and satisfaction by adopting them; it may be done. With sentiments of great respect, they remain, yr. Excellency's most Hble. Servts.

Source 18 from Edward Everett Dale and Gaston Litton, eds., *Cherokee Cavaliers: Forty Years of Cherokee History As told in the Correspondence of the Ridge-Watie-Boudinot Family*, (Norman, OK: University of Oklahoma Press, 1939).

18. John Ridge[31] to Major Ridge et al., March 10, 1835.

I have delayed this long in writing to you in the consequence of the hard struggles I had to make against John Ross & his party. At the outset they told Congress that our people had decided that they would choose to be citizens of the U. States [rather] than to remove. We contradicted this & he has failed to get an answer from Congress. From various indications we ascertained that he was going to act falsely to his people & sell the Nation either by getting Reservations of land or taking the whole in money on pretense of going out of the limits of the U. States. We protested against this & we have succeeded to get a treaty made to be sent home for the ratification of the people.[32] It is very liberal in its terms—an equal measure is given to all. The poor Indian enjoys the same rights as the rich—there is no distinction. We are allowed to enjoy our own laws in the west. Subsistence for one year, $25. for each soul for transportation, fair valuation for ferries & Improvements, $150 for each individual, more than forty thousand dollars perpetual annuity in the west, & a large sum of money to pay for the losses of the Cherokees against the white people. In fact—we get four millions & a half in money to meet all expenses & large addition in land to that already possessed by our brethren in the west. John Ross and his party tried hard to treat & get the whole in money & go as they said out of the limits of the U. States, but they have failed.[33]

31. John Ridge (Cherokee name Yellow Bird) was born in 1792, the son of Major Ridge and cousin of Elias Boudinot. He initially opposed Cherokee relocation but changed his mind after President Jackson's refusal to enforce the Supreme Court decision in *Worchester v. Georgia*.
32. The Treaty of New Echota.
33. Ridge's charge that Ross intended to steal the money appropriated for removal was not true.

Jackson said that he would not trust them with the money of the people. The Indians here under his care wish that he would refer the whole to the people. Ross has failed before the Senate, before the Secretary of War, & before the President. He tried hard to cheat you & his people, but he has been prevented. In a day or two he goes home no doubt to tell lies. But we will bring all his papers & the people shall see him as he is. . . .

The Congress has allowed money enough to pay the expenses of our Councils while the people are signing this treaty if they approve it. We are all well. I shall go to the north & see my wife's parents & in great haste will return to you. Stand, stay. All will be right. The U. States will never have any thing more to do with John Ross. Thus it becomes of selfish men. . . .

Source 19 from Protest of the Cherokee Delegation, laid before the Senate and House of Representatives, June 21, 1836, (Washington, DC: s.n., 1836) in Southeastern Native American Documents 1790–1842, accessible through the Georgia Virtual Library, Galileo, www.galileo.usg.edu.

19. "Protest of the Cherokee Delegation," June 21, 1836.

To the honourable Senate and House of Representatives of the United States of North America, in Congress assembled:

The undersigned representatives of the Cherokee nation, east of the river Mississippi, impelled by duty, would respectfully submit, for the consideration of your honourable body, the following statement: An instrument purporting to be a treaty with the Cherokee people, has recently been made public by the President of the United States, that will have such an operation, if carried into effect. This instrument, the delegation aver before the civilized world, and in the presence of Almighty God, is fraudulent, false upon its face, made by unauthorized individuals, without the sanction, and against the wishes, of the great body of the Cherokee people. Upwards of fifteen thousand of those people have protested against it, solemnly declaring they will never acquiesce. the delegation would respectfully call the attention of your honourable body to their memorial and protest, with the accompanying documents, submitted to the Senate of the United States, on the subject of the alleged treaty, which are herewith transmitted. . . .

It is the expressed wish of the Government of the United States to remove the Cherokees to a place west of the Mississippi. That wish is said to be founded in humanity to the Indians. to make their situation more comfortable, and to preserve them as a distinct people. Let facts show how this *benevolent* design has been prosecuted, and how faithfully to the spirit and letter has the promise of the President of the United States to the Cherokees been fulfilled—that *"those who remain may be assured of our patronage; our aid, and good neighbourhood."* The delegation are not deceived by empty professions, and fear that race is to be destroyed by the mercenary policy of the present day, and their lands wrested from them by physical force; as proof, they will refer to the preamble of an act of the General Assembly of Georgia, in reference to the Cherokees, passed the 2d of December, 1835, where it is said, "from a knowledge of the Indian character, and from the present feelings of these Indians, it is confidently believed, that the right of occupancy of the lands in their possession should be withdrawn, *that it would be a strong inducement to them to treat with the General Government, and consent to a removal to the west;* and whereas, the present Legislature openly avow that their primary object in the measures intended to be pursued, *are founded on real humanity to these Indians,* and with a view, in a distant region, to perpetuate them with their old identity of character, *under the paternal care of the Government of the United States;* at the same time frankly disavowing *any selfish or sinister motives towards them in their present legislation."* This is the profession. Let us turn to the practice of *humanity*, to the Cherokees, by the State of Georgia. In violation of the treaties between the United States and the Cherokee nation, that State passed a law requiring all white men, residing in that part of the Cherokee country, in her limits, to take an oath of allegiance to the State of Georgia. For a violation of this law, some of the ministers of Christ, missionaries among the Cherokees, were tried, convicted, and sentenced to hard labor in the penitentiary. Their case may be seen by reference to the records of the Supreme court of the United States.

Valuable gold mines were discovered upon the Cherokee lands, within the chartered limits of Georgia, and the Cherokees commenced working them, and the Legislature of that State interfered by passing an act, making it penal for an Indian to dig for gold within Georgia, no doubt *"frankly disavowing any selfish or sinister motives towards them."* Under this law many Cherokees were arrested, tried, imprisoned, and otherwise abused. Some were even shot in attempting to avoid an arrest; yet the Cherokee people used no violence, but humbly petitioned the Government of the United States for a fulfilment of treaty engagements, to protect them, which was not done, and the answer given that the United States could not interfere. Georgia discovered she was not to be obstructed in carrying out her measures, *"founded on real humanity to these Indians,"* she passed an act directing the Indian country to be surveyed into districts. This excited some alarm, but the Cherokees were quieted with the assurance it would do no harm to survey the country. Another act was shortly after passed, to lay off the country into lots. As yet there was no authority to take possession, but it was not long before a law was made, authorizing a lottery for the lands laid off into lots. In this act the Indians were secured in possession of all the lots touched by their improvements, and the balance of the country allowed to be occupied by white men. This was a direct violation of the 5th article of the treaty of the 27th of February, 1819. The Cherokees made no resistance, still petitioned the United States for protection, and received the same answer that the President could not interpose. After the country was parcelled out by lottery, a horde of speculators made their appearance, and purchased of the "fortunate drawers," lots touched by Indian improvements, at reduced prices, declaring it was uncertain when the Cherokees would surrender their rights, and that the lots were encumbered by their claims. The consequence of this speculation was that, at the next session of the Legislature, an act was passed limiting the Indian right of occupancy to the lot upon which he resided. . . .

[The memorial gives several examples of Cherokees who were cheated out of their lands or who lost them to white speculators or squatters.]

The delegation must repeat, the instrument entered into at New Echota, purporting to be a treaty, is deceptive to the world, and a fraud upon the Cherokee people. If a doubt exist as to the truth of their statement, a committee of investigation can learn the facts, and it may also learn that if the Cherokees are removed under that instrument, it will be by force.

◆

Questions to Consider

One of the most important decisions a historian must make is *how to collect and arrange* the evidence. In this chapter, the evidence is bountiful both for whites and for Cherokees. The *arrangement* of the evidence, however, presents considerable problems. For significant reasons, we have decided to divide the 19 pieces of evidence into two parts: one part comprised the nine pieces of evidence from whites and the other comprising the ten pieces of Cherokee evidence.

Why did we do this? To begin with, we wanted students to learn about and understand the arguments, debates, and alternatives that took place *among* whites, and then, understand the same conflicts that emerged *among* the Cherokees. Neither whites nor

Cherokees were united in their opinions regarding the future of the Native Americans.

Remember that your task in this chapter is a dual one. First, you must analyze the nine sources by whites (including pertinent legislation in sources 1 and 8) concerning how to deal with Native Americans east of the Mississippi River, noting the strengths and weaknesses of each position. Having done that, then you must repeat the process for the ten sources by Cherokees[34] on the best course for the Cherokee nation to pursue. As you read and make lists of first, the white and then the Cherokee sources, determine what both whites and Cherokees saw as their alternatives. The white and Cherokee sources clearly demonstrate that neither whites nor Cherokees were in agreement as to the Cherokees' future. Indeed, both demonstrated serious internal divisions. Make a chart as you go along, to clarify the positions of all the sources.

Beginning with the white sources, it would be extremely helpful to take President Jackson's message out of chronological order and closely examine it first. This is because Jackson's message to Congress contained the four principal reasons why pro-removal whites believed that Cherokees could not remain east of the Mississippi River. What were those points? Jackson strongly maintained that any such emigration "should be voluntary," but, in his view, what would be the fate of the Cherokees if they refused to move? Why couldn't the President of the United States simply intervene to help the Cherokees remain where they were?

Having examined the President's message, you now can analyze the other white sources. What is the importance of Section IV of the 1790 Intercourse Act (Source 1)? What is the significance of that law?

In Source 2, Thomas Jefferson has generally been viewed as a friend of Native Americans. His 1803 letter to Indian agent Benjamin Hawkins, however, may shed new light on that image. Read this letter with extreme care. Could he be viewed as an ally or opponent of Jackson (Jefferson died four years after Jackson's message)?

Sources 4, 5, 6, and 7 all are written or delivered by opponents of Cherokee removal. What points did they make to counter Jackson's arguments? Source 8 was the Removal Act that was much-debated in 1829 and 1830. Are there problems or flaws in this Legislation? What was the *significance* of the close vote?

Finally, Georgia Governor Wilson Lumpkin offered Georgia's justification for the state's behavior regarding Cherokees' remaining or leaving. How does his thinking compare with that of President Jackson's?[35]

Now complete your chart. What was the nature of the removal issue among whites? What were the strengths and

34. On authorship of source 15, see footnote number 27.

35. Lumpkin's opinion of Native Americans coincided with Jackson's. In his Fifth Annual Message to Congress (1833), the President stated that the Cherokees "have neither the intelligence, the industry, the moral habits, nor the desire of improvement . . . in their condition." James D. Richardson, *A Compilation of the Messages and Papers of the Presidents* (New York: Bureau of National Literature, 1897), vol. 3. p. 1252.

weaknesses of the arguments on all sides?

Now repeat the process for the ten Cherokee sources (Sources 10 through 19). They reveal deep divisions over how—or whether—to oppose their removal. What were the arguments in the Cherokees' letter to President Washington (Source 10)? What were the similar arguments in Source 11?

John Ridge appears twice in the evidence, once in 1826 (Source 12) and the other in 1835 (Source 18). What was the major difference in Ridge's position in the two sources? What was his major point in Source 12? How would that relate to his opinion in 1826 regarding removal in Source 18?

Elias Boudinot (Source 13) was the editor of the *Cherokee Phoenix* who argued in 1828 that "our people cannot exist amidst a white population." But he feared that a mass migration would destroy the Cherokee, and, therefore, should be opposed.

It is not clear that Speckled Snake (Source 14) actually was a Cherokee (sometimes he was identified as a Creek). But his forceful reply to Jackson's message rang through the Indian nations. What did he urge? What was his reasoning? How did he oppose Jackson?

According to the Cherokee leaders' address in 1830 (Source 15), why were

some Cherokees abandoning lands in Georgia and moving west? In their opinion, who were the real "intruders" in Georgia? How would you describe their appeal?

As you can see by comparing Sources 13 and 16, editor and Cherokee leader Elias Boudinot had changed his mind dramatically. What influences did the re-election of President Jackson, the Supreme Court's decision in *Worcester v. Georgia* and Jackson's reaction have on Boudinot's thinking? How did he support voluntary removal? Why did he claim that most of his fellow Cherokees still opposed relocation? How did Cherokee leader John Ross (Source 17) attempt to counter Boudinot's arguments? What was Cherokee leader John Ridge's opinion? How did he differ from Boudinot and Ross?

Source 19 was called by Cherokee opponents of removal as their "last appeal." How did their arguments counter those of Jackson and Lumpkin?

Now that you have examined both the white and Cherokee sources, meld them together chronologically to see how the two groups interacted with one another. How did some members of one group successfully change the positions of members of the other group? What were the principal arguments offered by each side?

◆

Epilogue

The war between the older immigrants and the new arrivals to Indian territory went on for seven years, until peace

between the two factions of Cherokees finally was made in 1846. During that period, some Cherokees reversed their trek and returned to North Carolina. When the Civil War broke out in 1861, factionalism once again emerged, with some Cherokees supporting the Confederacy and others backing the Union. Fighting between these factions (a "mini-Civil War") claimed the lives of as much as 25 percent of the Cherokee population.

In 1868, Congress recognized the obvious fact that the Cherokees who remained in the East had become a distinct group, named the Eastern Band of the Cherokees (as opposed to the migrating group, which was called the Cherokee Nation).[36] In 1875, the federal government began to acquire land in North Carolina for a reservation, named the Qualla Boundary, which ultimately contained around 56,000 acres. In 1889, the Eastern Band received a charter from North Carolina granting the Cherokees what amounted to home rule in the Qualla Boundary. Then the federal government began an intensive program to "civilize" the Eastern Cherokees, an effort that was ultimately unsuccessful. Cherokees clung stubbornly to their own language and traditions, and by 1900, less than one-fourth of the population could speak English—approximately half of them young people in white-administered boarding schools. Because they consistently voted Republican, after 1900 the Democratic majority in North Carolina disfranchised both the African Americans and the Cherokees by passing a law requiring literacy tests prior to voting.

Meanwhile the Cherokee Nation (in the West) was experiencing its own difficulties. In spite of the fact that the 1830 Indian Removal Act guaranteed that Native Americans would always hold the land onto which they were placed, land grants to railroad companies and a territorial land rush stripped a good deal of land away from the Cherokees. In 1891, the Cherokee Nation owned 19.5 million acres. By 1971, it owned but 146,498.

In North Carolina, the creation of the Great Smoky Mountains National Park in 1934 offered the Eastern Band a way out of its economic quagmire. In November 1934, the council appropriated $50,000 for tourist facilities, and in 1937, the first Cherokee-owned motel (Newfound Lodge) was opened for business. In 1939, an estimated 169,000 people visited the national park and purchased around $30,000 worth of Cherokee crafts.

The development of tourism undoubtedly helped alleviate a severe economic crisis for the Eastern Band. In 1932, at the low point of the Great Depression, it was estimated that 200 of the 496 Cherokee families in North Carolina needed public assistance. The New Deal did provide some jobs, through the Indian Emergency Conservation Work Program, a separate version of the Civilian Conservation Corps. But tourism also presented the Eastern Band with the problem of whether Cherokees could retain their cultural identity while at the same time catering to the desires of visitors

36. Technically there is a third group of Cherokees, the United Keetoowah Band, composed mostly of "full-blooded" Old Settlers who were strictly traditionalists. They were recognized as a separate group by the Oklahoma Indian Welfare Act of 1936 and by an Act of Congress in 1950.

with money.[37] In the 1990s, the Eastern Band turned to casino gambling to increase their revenues, although income from tourism and gambling is not evenly dispersed and many Cherokees still live extremely modestly.

By then, of course, the principal voices on both sides of the issue had long been stilled. In 1837 (one year before the beginning of the Trail of Tears), Andrew Jackson left the presidency to his hand-picked successor, Martin Van Buren, and retired to his plantation, the Hermitage, near Nashville, Tennessee. He died in 1845, still convinced that his advocacy of Cherokee removal was the most humane alternative for the Native Americans themselves.

For his part, before his death in 1826, Thomas Jefferson had abandoned his dream that whites and Native Americans could live side by side and ultimately become one people. Frustrated over what he considered the slow progress Native Americans were making in adopting "civilization," the principal author of the Declaration of Independence came to believe that removal was, in his words, the "moral" alternative. Some recent historians, however, are convinced that Jefferson always thought that voluntary removal was best for both races.[38]

The removal of most of the Cherokees in 1838–1839 (and in a second forced migration in 1841 to 1844) is an important, if tragic, chapter in the history of the United States that is important to know. It is also helpful to understand that there were many voices on both sides of the removal issue, thus making the subject of Cherokee removal not only a tragic one but an exceedingly complex one as well.

37. Because tourists expected to see Native Americans with ornate feathered headdresses (typical of Plains Indians but never worn by Cherokees), Cherokees accommodatingly wore them.

38. Bernard W. Sheehan, *Seeds of Extinction: Jeffersonian Philanthropy and the American Indian* (Chapel Hill: Univ. of North Carolina Press, 1973); Anthony F.C. Wallace, *Jefferson and the Indians: The Tragic Fate of the First Americans* (Cambridge, MA: Harvard Univ. Press, 1999), esp. pp. 225, 338.

CHAPTER

8

"Women Out of Their Latitude": Gender in the American Republic

◆

The Problem

In early February 1906, Susan B. Anthony, though in declining health, made a difficult midwinter journey from Rochester, New York, to Baltimore, Maryland. The National American Woman Suffrage Association (NAWSA) annual convention coincided with her eighty-sixth birthday, and the organization was eager to celebrate with her. By 1906, Anthony had spent literally a lifetime advocating for women's civic equality. She and her longtime collaborator, Elizabeth Cady Stanton (1815–1902), fought more than fifty years for basic rights for women: to own property, to divorce abusive husbands, to claim custody of minor children, to collect wages, and, most controversially, to vote.

Stanton, Anthony, and a generation of what are now termed "first-wave" feminists introduced the idea of female civil rights in the 1840s. They pursued their cause through the judicial system, in the court of public opinion, and by

lobbying state legislatures and the U.S. government. Those decades of work resulted in some reforms, in divorce law and property rights, for example. But in 1906, the cornerstone of citizenship—the right to vote—remained an exclusively male privilege. Amazingly, the defeats had not dampened Anthony's zeal for her cause nor her optimism about its eventual success.

Anthony's failing health precluded her giving a full address to the convention. But she would not disappoint the crowd and so rose to briefly talk. Anthony spoke eloquently of all the women of her generation who had dedicated their lives to the yet-unrealized goal of female equality. She assured the rapt audience, "with such women consecrating their lives . . . failure is impossible!"[1]

1. Susan B. Anthony, "Speech to the National American Woman Suffrage Association," February 1906, in Ida Husted Harper, *The Life and Work of Susan B. Anthony*, Vol. 3 (Indianapolis: The Hollenbeck Press, 1908), 1409.

These were the last words Susan B. Anthony ever spoke in public. She died within a month of addressing the NAWSA. Despite sacrificing so much for so long, Anthony died having never cast a legitimate ballot. Stanton had passed four years earlier. Not until 1920, seventy-two years after the Seneca Falls Convention, where Stanton drafted a "Declaration of Sentiments" proclaiming women's equality, did white women in the United States secure suffrage rights.

That was 131 years after the ratification of the U.S. Constitution, and even then women often could not serve on juries, were categorically denied loans and other forms of credit, and con-tinued to endure overt—and lawful—employment discrimination.[2] Voting rights turned out to be an important milestone in, but certainly not the fulfillment of, the controversial quest for gender equality.

In this chapter, you will be analyzing evidence from first-wave feminists explaining their justification for women's rights alongside rebuttals from their critics and political cartoons illuminating the fierce debates about women's place in American society. These sources will help you answer the chapter's central question: **Why was the idea of women's civil rights so controversial in the antebellum era?**

◆

Background

Today, it is difficult to imagine the world that Susan B. Anthony lived in and therefore challenging to understand why many Americans in that era found her message so radical. In 2015, women serve as governors, senators and representatives in the U.S. Congress, cabinet secretaries, and in every part of state and national government. Women head Fortune 500 corporations, Hollywood studios, network news bureaus, and leading universities, including Harvard. They work as lawyers, physicians, ministers, and soldiers. Republican President George W. Bush and Democratic Presidents Bill Clinton and Barack Obama all appointed women to head the State Department, to be the global representatives of American policy. Women had a higher voting rate (64 percent of eligible voters) than males (60 percent) in the 2012 presidential election, just as they have in every presidential election since 1980. As 53 percent of all voters, they cast nearly seven million more ballots than men in the 2012 presidential election.

In the America of Susan B. Anthony's youth, women could not vote, though that was hardly the extent of their civic inequality. Women rarely owned property; wives' assets automatically fell under the control of their husbands. White women were discouraged if not outright prohibited from pursuing an extensive education, speaking in public,

2. As late as 1974 it was legal—and commonplace—for banks to refuse to issue women credit cards in their own names.

or traveling alone. Although the colonial mindset that women were morally inferior to men and more sexually aggressive than them had been replaced by the opposite stereotype—that women were virtuous, passive, and ethereal—belief in female intellectual inferiority remained commonplace. Some antebellum physicians even told their female patients that too much intellectual activity would draw blood from their uteruses to their brains and, as a result, make them infertile. During the tumult of the American Revolution, ideas about women's incapacity for civic contribution were briefly challenged. Women took up the patriot cause and joined men in the grassroots activism—though not the formal politics—that challenged and then overthrew imperial authority. A backlash rather quickly closed that window. After the Revolution, girls also sought and received more education than in previous generations, as growing numbers of Americans equated the education of young people with the health of the republic. But most agreed that women's education should never be as extensive as that afforded men, nor should the expanding number of female schools prepare young women to enter careers such as medicine or law or business. Rather, formal education better prepared women to succeed in their feminine, domestic roles.[3]

3. For more about women's roles in the early national era, see Rosemarie Zagarri, *Revolutionary Backlash: Women and Politics in the Early American Republic* (Philadelphia: University of Pennsylvania Press, 2007); Mary Kelley, *Learning to Stand and Speak: Women, Education, and Public Life in America's Republic* (Chapel Hill: University of North Carolina Press, 2006); and the classic work by Carroll Smith-Rosenberg, *Disorderly*

In nineteenth-century white middle class and elite families, women were taught that their proper place was within the household, raising patriotic, pious children and making a peaceful refuge for their husbands. Ideally, wives occupied the domestic realm and left politics and finance to their husbands. Cultural conventions called for public and private, male and female, to remain largely separated in middling and elite families. For those families, the domestic world, or "sphere" of middle and upper class women was subordinate to the public "sphere" of men. So, for women born into households like Susan B. Anthony —educated, religious, middling rank New Englanders—the path in life was highly gendered and quite narrow. In fighting for women's rights, early feminists challenged these deeply held and widespread convictions that underlay so much of antebellum American culture.

These societal values generally did not apply to African American, immigrant, or poorer white women. The economic realities of their lives made adopting these conventions highly unlikely. In the case of black women— the great majority of whom were enslaved—their labor was exploited at the same level as that of enslaved men.

The activism of women such as Anthony was limited by race and class, and, to a lesser degree, by region. The majority of women in America did not identify with the concerns of Anthony's cohort. Some faced far more immediate difficulties: poverty, labor exploitation, enslavement. Others who did belong to the middle and upper classes rejected

Conduct: Visions of Gender in Victorian America (New York: Knopf, 1985).

the critique of women's sphere, fearing the cost of abandoning gender conventions would vastly outweigh any gains made by attaining civic equality with men. Southern whites overwhelmingly privileged preserving their region's racial hierarchy over any other reformist concerns, including women's rights. First-wave feminists persisted, however, believing that expanding citizenship in the American Republic would benefit all women as well as the greater interests of the nation, and that it was a just and proper expression of America's founding principles.

Feminists wanted to claim citizenship in a young nation already undergoing a series of major political and cultural changes in the antebellum era (1820s–1850s). The republican vision of the founding generation, in which learned, civic-minded, elite men reasoned together to determine the best interests of the nation, was giving way to comparatively raucous democratic reforms. Leaders of the Revolution assumed that only men who owned property held a stake in government, and only they could exercise the independent-mindedness required to put the common good above self-interest. As John Jay argued, "those who own the country ought to run it." So in most states in the 1790s only property-owners could vote. The property qualification for serving in government was often even higher.

In the early nineteenth century, these republican values were supplanted by a growing zeal for democracy—open competition over power. Rather than reasoning together to reach consensus, political leaders increasingly believed that the best ideas should triumph at the polls. In the early decades of the

nineteenth century, most states expanded the franchise to include all adult white males. Political parties, once dreaded as dangerous "factions," now competed openly for votes; partisan contests determined national policy. This expansion of the practical implications of the language of the Declaration of Independence—that "all men are created equal"—did not, however, include African American men. And citizenship continued to be strictly gendered.

The rise of evangelical Christianity, shepherded in through a series of religious revivals known as the Second Great Awakening, also profoundly changed the nation.[4] Unlike political innovations, however, the Awakening did cross racial and gender lines. The Awakening legitimized previously fringe groups, such as the Baptists, and embraced a more emotional, individualistic religious experience. Awakening ministers preached the centrality of the conversion experience: God came into the lives of true believers, irrespective of all concerns other than faith. How learned or rich a person was mattered little to salvation; God welcomed all, regardless of race, class, or gender. Conversion typically brought an outpouring of emotions: contrition, lamentation, euphoria, and sometimes physical spasms. Awakening ministers and converts also placed a great deal of emphasis on post-conversion behavior. Transformed men and women should

4. To understand religious transformations in this era, start with Nathan O. Hatch, *The Democratization of American Christianity* (New Haven: Yale University Press, 1989); and Christine Leigh Heyrman, *Southern Cross: The Beginnings of the Bible Belt* (New York: Knopf, 1997).

daily bear the mark of their faith, and they should work to perfect society—to ready themselves and their communities for the return of Christ.

More women than men embraced evangelicalism which, along with the emotionalism displayed in the conversion experience, led to what historians have called the "feminization" of American Christianity. In other words, women became increasingly attracted to and engaged in religious life, and the expressions of evangelical piety seemed decidedly feminine. Church attendance, particularly among women, skyrocketed because of evangelical zeal. Thousands flocked to outdoor revivals to hear charismatic preachers and witness dramatic, impromptu conversions. Upstate New York was the scene of so many fiery revivals that it came to be known as the "burned-over district."[5]

As the movement spread south, it bore the imprint of the region's increasingly peculiar institution of racial slavery. Early on, Great Awakening ministers who journeyed south preached the equality of all believers. They sought to convert slaves to evangelical Christianity and taught the immorality of slavery. As a result, evangelical Christianity became the dominant faith of the nation's free blacks and slaves. This initial level of egalitarianism was unacceptable to the region's planter elites, so Awakening ministers gradually made concessions to the South's gentry culture and racial attitudes. As a consequence, many of the evangelical denominations split along regional lines, with northern

Baptists, for example, continuing to embrace egalitarianism and southern Baptists deciding to defend the morality of slavery. The South, which had been the least religious region in the colonial era, became the "Bible Belt," and evangelical Christianity the dominant religion of white southerners.

While evangelical Christianity helped conserve traditions in the South, in the North it fueled a progressive set of social reforms. Combined with a series of other changes occurring in the nation, including a rise in immigration and the growth of a market-centered economy, Awakening values, particularly the emphasis on post-conversion behavior, inspired Americans to seek to remedy a number of societal problems. Through moral reform, evangelicals decided, the republic could be perfected. And plenty of problems abounded: excessive drinking, inadequate educational institutions, prostitution, and, outside the South, slavery were all targeted as moral crises imperiling the young nation. Women, who peopled the evangelical churches in disproportionate numbers, championed these reform movements. Sometimes they worked in solely female organizations and sometimes they partnered with like-minded men as they sought to correct these moral failings.

The Beecher family of New England reflected the interconnections of reform efforts in their region.[6] Father Lyman Beecher was a theologian and minister who embraced Awakening

5. See Paul E. Johnson, *A Shopkeeper's Millennium: Society and Revivals in Rochester, New York, 1815–1837* (New York: Hill and Wang, 1978).

6. To learn more about this fascinating family, visit the Harriet Beecher Stowe Center at www.harrietbeecherstowecenter.org, or the digital exhibition "An American Family" at http://www.baruch.cuny.edu/library/alumni/online_exhibits/digital/2001/beecher/intro.htm.

ideals and then founded the American Temperance Society in 1826. Temperance quickly became a nationwide movement, with over two thousand local chapters created within just five years. Lyman Beecher's daughter, Catherine, was an educational innovator. She founded the Hartford Female Seminary in Connecticut, one of the nation's first major educational institutions for women. Her brothers, Charles and Henry, followed their father into the ministry. Charles also composed hymns. Many of the siblings committed themselves to abolitionist activism. When Edward Beecher moved to Illinois, he started that state's first anti-slavery society. Sister Isabella attended Catherine's Hartford Academy and then informally educated herself in the law (women were never lawyers in those days). Harriet, the most famous member of the family, was a teacher, abolitionist, and writer. *Uncle Tom's Cabin,* published in 1852, became the bestselling novel in the entire nineteenth century.

Participation in these interconnected reform associations, particularly the immediatist, abolitionist movement that emerged in the North in the 1830s, taught women the practical skills required for successful social activism.[7] Reformism in general and

7. The outset of the abolition movement is usually marked by the publication of William Lloyd Garrison's *Liberator* in 1831. Variously termed "immediatism," "Garrisonianism," or, most often, "abolitionism," this approach to anti-slavery called for the immediate end to racial slavery and the full and equal inclusion of African Americans into American life. Earlier approaches had focused on gradualism— freeing individuals once they reached a certain age or skill level or gradually outlawing slavery in a territory or state over a period of decades.

abolitionism in particular also instilled in women who joined these organizations a commitment to social justice and human equality. And, for some women, it threw into high relief their legalized subordination, including their disfranchisement. While clearly not on a par with the cruelty and debasement that slavery inflicted on African Americans, the denial of civil rights to white women distressed many reformers. The idea of women's civic equality was roundly rejected in the gentry-dominated, slaveholding South. It was also controversial in the Northeast, including even with some reform-minded women. Many people who heartily supported women's right to own property, acquire an education, and divorce, balked at the radical step toward women's enfranchisement. To other northern activists, male and female, the subjugation of women, like the enslavement of blacks, seemed antithetical to American democracy and patently immoral.

It was an anti-slavery conference that roused to action feminists committed to civic equality. A delegation of American activists had gone to London in 1840 to attend the World Anti-Slavery Convention. The group included Lucretia Mott, a veteran of reform organizations, and Elizabeth Cady Stanton, a young bride on her honeymoon. The convention fell into heated debate over the presence of the women, since mixed-gender groups, particularly ones in which women might speak, remained deeply controversial. The organization refused to accept the American women as participants, and finally compromised by allowing them to sit, silently, behind a curtain in the convention hall. Before they left London, Mott and Stanton were determined to launch a women's rights movement in the United States.

Even in their own circle of like-minded reformers, feminists faced major obstacles. Women such as Lucretia Mott, Elizabeth Cady Stanton, Susan B. Anthony, and the Beecher sisters did not agree on the method, the scope, or even the advisability of challenging social conventions. For example, in a popular 1840s tract, Catherine Beecher—a national leader in the effort to expand women's educational opportunities—insisted that women had no place in politics and that their civic interests should always be "entrusted to the other sex, without her taking part in voting, or making and administering laws."[8] For a host of reasons, the majority of white Americans found the idea of gender equality absurd; to others it seemed downright dangerous. Certainly it was a radical break from a very long past. In 1848, when Mott and Stanton's London dream was finally commenced and the Seneca Falls Convention called for women to claim full citizenship, nowhere in the western world did women vote.

What lay behind the intense debates over women's civil rights? What did women's equality mean for the advocates and the critics of "first-wave" feminism?

The Method

While there are biological differences between men and women, what societies read into those differences varies greatly. Manhood and womanhood—the roles and the defining traits ascribed to males and females—are shaped by larger cultural assumptions and societal needs. In short, gender is socially constructed. Certainly not every male or every female upholds his or her community's values. Massachusetts exile Anne Hutchinson offers us one powerful example of a woman rejecting societal expectations—and the high price that could accompany such independent-mindedness. Of course, seventeenth-century Massachusetts residents placed a premium on conformity and order, so their reaction to Hutchinson's violation of established ethics was particularly strident. Other communities at other times have allowed for more latitude. Women and men in the United States today enjoy far more flexibility in pursuing individual interests than their early American ancestors. But in our own time, cultural assumptions that differentiate between women and men still exist. Can you list jobs, personality traits, or familial responsibilities that are gendered? What do those differences tell you about present-day assumptions about men and women? What are our gendered values?

8. The 1841 tract, *Treatise on Domestic Economy*, was widely reprinted and is accessible through Project Gutenberg.

In this chapter, you will apply the same considerations to the past. You will focus not only on what the nineteenth-century men and women who disagreed about women's rights said. You will also be engaging in cultural analysis—exploring the underlying, sometime unexpressed, gender assumptions behind their arguments.

Part of why the first-wave feminists faced such an uphill battle in winning women's civic equality was that their efforts ran counter to a whole set of deeply entrenched beliefs about the proper role of women (at least white, middle class and elite women) in antebellum America. It should be apparent as you investigate the documents and images in this chapter that opinions on women's proper roles and responsibilities varied enormously. Some of the authors support an expansion of women's opportunities and rights. Others renounce and even ridicule such changes. Still others find themselves in the middle, embracing some changes and rejecting others.

Try not to take sides when you consider the sources. It is deceptively easy to criticize individuals in the past. Remember that your purpose is not to determine who was right or wrong, or even to critique the various opinions. You are trying to use the materials to understand the culture in which these debates took shape. What inspired the feminists to take their stand? Why did this reform emerge in the 1840s? And why did it spark such a diversity of passionate opinions? Always keep in mind

the central question posed: **why was women's civil rights so divisive and controversial for nineteenth-century Americans?**

As you review the print documents, make a list of the contested rights. What new opportunities did women seek? A comprehensive list will require you to consider not only the advocacy pieces supporting women's rights but also the opposition writings. Reading all sides of the debate will allow you to catalog the changes the women's rights movement either intentionally pursued or, by implication, would foster. The images of politically engaged women should be equally telling. Note the dates and consider what changed and what did not change over time.

Now, look again at the print and visual sources. What common patterns do you see? What values, what worldview do these authors and artists seem to have in common? One obvious commonality is religion. But press this issue further: what particular religious ethics and beliefs appear to link the authors together? What is the implied connection, for example, between women's sexuality and their morality? What other cultural values do you perceive? What do the creators of these sources seem to idealize? What do they fear? How did the authors of the written texts use language and tone and structure to express their opinions and move their readers? Think about the images in the same way: What reactions do you think the illustrators hoped to provoke?

The Evidence

Source 1 from Thomas R. Drew, "Dissertation on the Characteristic Differences Between the Sexes," *Southern Literary Messenger* 1 (May 1835): 439–512, in Winston E. Langley and Vivian C. Fox. Westport, eds., *Women's Rights in the United States: A Documentary History*. Westport, CT: Greenwood Press, 1994): pp. 62–63.

1. Dissertation on the Characteristic Differences Between the Sexes (1835).

... The relative position of the sexes in the social and political world, may certainly be looked upon as the result of organization. The greater physical strength of man, enables him to occupy the foreground in the picture. He leaves the domestic scenes; he plunges into the turmoil and bustle of an active, selfish world; in his journey through life, he has to encounter innumerable difficulties, hardships and labors which constantly beset him. His mind must be nerved against them. Hence courage and boldness are his attributes. It is his province, undismayed, to stand against the rude shocks of the world; to meet with a lion's heart, the dangers which threaten him. He is the shield of woman, destined by nature to guard and protect her. Her inferior strength and sedentary habits confine her within the domestic circle; she is kept aloof from the bustle and storm of active life; she is not familiarized to the out of door dangers and hardships of a cold and scuffling world: timidity and modesty are her attributes. In the great strife which is constantly going forward around her, there are powers engaged which her inferior physical strength prevents her from encountering. She must rely upon the strength of others; man must be engaged in her cause. How is he to be drawn over to her side? Not by menace—not by force; for weakness cannot, by such means, be expected to triumph over might. No! It must be by conformity to that character which circumstances demand for the sphere in which she moves; by the exhibition of those qualities which delight and fascinate—which are calculated to win over to her side the proud lord of creation, and to make him an humble suppliant at her shrine. Grace, modesty and loveliness are the charms which constitute her power. By these, she creates the magic spell that subdues to her will the more mighty physical powers by which she is surrounded. Her attributes are rather of a passive than active character. Her power is more emblematical of that of divinity: it subdues without an effort, and almost creates by mere volition; whilst man must wind his way through the difficult and intricate mazes of philosophy; with pain and toil, tracing effects to their causes, and unravelling the deep mysteries of nature—storing his mind with useful knowledge, and exercising, training and perfecting his intellectual powers, whilst he cultivates his strength and hardens and matures his courage; all with a view of enabling him to assert his rights, and exercise a greater sway over those around him. . . .

Source 2 from Angelina Grimke, "Letter XII: Human Rights Not Founded on Sex," in Angelina Emily Grimke, *Letters to Catherine Beecher: In Reply to an Essay on Slavery and Abolotionism, Addressed to A. E. Grimke, Revised by the Author* (Boston: Isaac Knapp, 1838), pp. 114–121.

2. Angelina Grimké Letter to Catherine Beecher (1837).

[Angelina Grimké and her sister Sarah came from a wealthy, prominent South Carolina slaveholding family. They rejected their family's long history of racial slavery, however. In 1833, Angelina published a letter in William Lloyd Garrison's Liberator *calling for the immediate liberation of slaves. In 1837, she and Sarah went on a 67-city tour, speaking out against slavery and breaking new ground as females addressing mixed-gender crowds. Catherine Beecher, though a lifelong advocate for women teachers, was an anti-suffragist. She believed that women should exert influence in the home and in schools—but not through direct action as citizens.]*

. . . The investigation of the rights of the slave has led me to a better understanding of my own. I have found the Anti-Slavery cause to be the high school of morals in our land—the school in which *human rights* are more fully investigated, and better understood and taught, than in any other. Here a great fundamental principle is uplifted and illuminated, and from this central light, rays innumerable stream all around. Human beings have *rights*, because they are *moral* beings: the rights of *all* men grow out of their moral nature; and as all men have the same moral nature, they have essentially the same rights. These rights may be wrested from the slave, but they cannot be alienated: his title to himself is as perfect *now*, as is that of Lyman Beecher: it is stamped on his moral being, and is, like it, imperishable. Now if rights are founded in the nature of our moral being, then the *mere circumstance of sex* does not give to man higher rights and responsibilities, than to woman. To suppose that it does, would be to deny the self-evident truth, that the 'physical constitution is the mere instrument of the moral nature.' To suppose that it does, would be to break up utterly the relations, of the two natures, and to reverse their functions, exalting the animal nature into a monarch, and humbling the moral into a slave; making the former a proprietor, and the latter its property. When human beings are regarded as *moral* beings, *sex*, instead of being enthroned upon the summit, administering upon rights and responsibilities, sinks into insignificance and nothingness. . . .

Source 3 from Sarah M. Grimke, *"Letters on the Equality of the Sexes and the Condition of Woman, addressed to Mary S. Parker, President of the Boston Female Anti-Slavery Society,"* in The Original Equality of Woman (Boston: Isaac Knapp, 1838), reprinted in Larry Ceplair, eds., The Public Years of Sarah and Angelina Grimke: Selected Writings 1835–1839 (New York: Columbia University Press, 1989), pp. 204–210.

3. Sarah Grimké Letter to Mary S. Parker, "The Original Equality of Woman" (1837).

[Sarah Grimké was raised in a devout Episcopal family. She attended church faithfully as a young woman and led Bible study among her family's slaves—much to her parents' alarm. As an adult, she converted to the Quaker faith and took an active role in that community, teaching weekly Bible classes. Her confident understanding of scripture and theology is evident in this letter.]

My Dear Friend, — In attempting to comply with thy request to give my views on the Province of Woman, I feel that I am venturing on nearly untrodden ground, and that I shall advance arguments in opposition to a corrupt public opinion, and to the perverted interpretation of Holy Writ, which has so universally obtained. But I am in search of truth; and no obstacle shall prevent my prosecuting that search, because I believe the welfare of the world will be materially advanced by every new discovery we make of the designs of Jehovah in the creation of woman. It is impossible that we can answer the purpose of our being, unless we understand that purpose. It is impossible that we should fulfil our duties, unless we comprehend them; or live up to our privileges, unless we know what they are.

In examining this important subject, I shall depend solely on the Bible to designate the sphere of woman, because I believe almost every thing that has been written on this subject, has been the result of a misconception of the simple truths revealed in the Scriptures, in consequence of the false translation of many passages of Holy Writ. My mind is entirely delivered from the superstitious reverence which is attached to the English version of the Bible. King James's translators certainly were not inspired. I therefore claim the original as my standard, *believing that to have been inspired*, and I also claim to judge for myself what is the meaning of the inspired writers, because I believe it to be the solemn duty of every individual to search the Scriptures for themselves, with the aid of the Holy Spirit, and not be governed by the views of any man, or set of men.

We must first view woman at the period of her creation. "And God said, Let us make man in our own image, after our likeness; and let them have dominion over the fish of the sea, and over the fowl of the air, and over the cattle, and over all the earth, and over every creeping thing that creepeth upon the earth. So

[217]

God created man in his own image, in the image of God created he him, male and female created he them." In all this sublime description of the creation of man, (which is a generic term including man and woman,) there is not one particle of difference intimated as existing between them. They were both made in the image of God; dominion was given to both over every other creature, but not over each other. Created in perfect equality, they were expected to exercise the vicegerence intrusted to them by their Maker, in harmony and love.

Let us pass on now to the recapitulation of the creation of man: — "The Lord God formed man of the dust of the ground, and breathed into his nostrils the breath of life; and man became a living soul. And the Lord God said, it is not good that man should be alone, I will make him an help meet for him."[9] All creation swarmed with animated beings capable of natural affection, as we know they still are; it was not, therefore, merely to give man a creature susceptible of loving, obeying, and looking up to him, for all that the animals could do and did do. It was to give him a companion, *in all respects* his equal; one who was like himself *a free agent*, gifted with intellect and endowed with immortality; not a partaker merely of his animal gratifications, but able to enter into all his feelings as a moral and responsible being. If this had not been the case, how could she have been an help meet for him? I understand this as applying not only to the parties entering into the marriage contract, but to all men and women, because I believe God designed woman to be an help meet for man in every good and perfect work. She was a part of himself, as if Jehovah designed to make the oneness and identity of man and woman perfect and complete; and when the glorious work of their creation was finished, "the morning stars sang together, and all the sons of God shouted for joy."

This blissful condition was not long enjoyed by our first parents. Eve, it would seem from the history, was wandering alone amid the bowers of Paradise, when the serpent met with her. From her reply to Satan, it is evident that the command not to eat "of the tree that is in the midst of the garden," was given to both, although the term man was used when the prohibition was issued by God. "And the woman said unto the serpent, WE may eat of the fruit of the trees of the garden, but of the fruit of the tree which is in the midst of the garden, God hath said, YE shall not eat of it, neither shall YE touch it, lest YE die." Here the woman was exposed to temptation from a being with whom she was unacquainted. She had been accustomed to associate with her beloved partner, and to hold communion with God and with angels; but of satanic intelligence, she was in all probability entirely ignorant. Through the subtlety of the serpent, she was beguiled. And "when she saw that the tree

9. Genesis, chapters 1 and 2. The chapters recount two differing narratives of the creation story. Grimké's critics pointed to the second accounting, of Eve being formed from Adam's rib, to counter her analysis.

was good for food, and that it was pleasant to the eyes, and a tree to be desired to make one wise, she took of the fruit thereof and did eat."

We next find Adam involved in the same sin, not through the instrumentality of a super-natural agent, but through that of his equal, a being whom he must have known was liable to transgress the divine command, because he must have felt that he was himself a free agent, and that he was restrained from disobedience only by the exercise of faith and love towards his Creator. Had Adam tenderly reproved his wife, and endeavored to lead her to repentance instead of sharing in her guilt, I should be much more ready to accord to man that superiority which he claims; but as the facts stand disclosed by the sacred historian, it appears to me that to say the least, there was as much weakness exhibited by Adam as by Eve. They both fell from innocence, and consequently from happiness, *but not from equality*.

Let us next examine the conduct of this fallen pair, when Jehovah interrogated them respecting their fault. They both frankly confessed their guilt. "The man said, the woman whom thou gavest to be with me, she gave me of the tree and I did eat. And the woman said, the serpent beguiled me and I did eat." And the Lord God said unto the woman, "Thou wilt be subject unto thy husband, and he will rule over thee." That this did not allude to the subjection of woman to man is manifest, because the same mode of expression is used in speaking to Cain of Abel. The truth is that the curse, as it is termed, which was pronounced by Jehovah upon woman, is a simple prophecy. The Hebrew, like the French language, uses the same word to express shall and will. Our translators having been accustomed to exercise lordship over their wives, and seeing only through the medium of a perverted judgment, very naturally, though I think not very learnedly or very kindly, translated it *shall* instead of *will,* and thus converted a prediction to Eve into a command to Adam; for observe, it is addressed to the woman and not to the man. The consequence of the fall was an immediate struggle for dominion, and Jehovah foretold which would gain the ascendancy; but as he created them in his image, as that image manifestly was not lost by the fall, because it is urged in Gen. 9:6, as an argument why the life of man should not be taken by his fellow man, there is no reason to suppose that sin produced any distinction between them as moral, intellectual and responsible beings. Man might just as well have endeavored by hard labor to fulfil the prophecy, thorns and thistles will the earth bring forth to thee, as to pretend to accomplish the other, "he will rule over thee," by asserting dominion over his wife.

> Authority usurped from God, not given.
> He gave him only over beast, flesh, fowl,
> Dominion absolute: that right he holds
> By God's donation: but man o'er woman

[219]

He made not Lord, such title to himself
Reserving, human left from human free.

Here then I plant myself. God created us equal; — he created us free agents; — he is our Lawgiver, our King and our Judge, and to him alone is woman bound to be in subjection, and to him alone is she accountable for the use of those talents with which Her Heavenly Father has entrusted her. One is her Master even Christ.

Thine for the oppressed in the bonds of womanhood,

Sarah M. Grimké

Source 4 from "Pastoral Letter." Extract from a Pastoral Letter of 'the General Association of Massachusetts (Orthodox) to the Churches under their care'—1837," in Elizabeth Cady Stanton, Susan B. Anthony, and Matilda Joslyn Gage, eds. *History of Woman Suffrage*, Vol. 1 (1848–1861) (Rochester, NY: Charles Mann, 187), pp. 81–82.

4. Extract from a Pastoral Letter of "The General Association of Massachusetts (Orthodox) to the Churches under Their Care" (1837).

. . . The appropriate duties and influence of woman are clearly stated in the New Testament. Those duties and that influence are unobtrusive and private, but the source of mighty power. When the mild, dependent, softening influence of woman upon the sternness of man's opinions is fully exercised, society feels the effects of it in a thousand forms. The power of woman is her dependence, flowing from the consciousness of that weakness which God has given her for her protection, and which keeps her in those departments of life that form the character of individuals, and of the nation. There are social influences which females use in promoting piety and the great objects of Christian benevolence which we can not too highly commend.

We appreciate the unostentatious prayers and efforts of woman in advancing the cause of religion at home and abroad; in Sabbath-schools; in leading religious inquirers to the pastors for instruction; and in all such associated effort as becomes the modesty of her sex; and earnestly hope that she may abound more and more in these labors of piety and love. But when she assumes the place and tone of man as a public reformer, our care and protection of her seem unnecessary; we put ourselves in self-defence against her; she yields the power which God has given her for her protection, and her character becomes unnatural. If the vine, whose strength and beauty is to lean upon the trellis-work, and half conceal its clusters, thinks to assume the independence and the overshadowing nature of the elm, it will not only cease to bear fruit, but fall in shame and dishonor into the dust. We can not, therefore, but regret the mistaken conduct of those who encourage females to bear an obtrusive and ostentatious part in measures of reform, and countenance any of that sex who so far forget themselves as to itinerate in the character of public lecturers and teachers. . . .

Source 5 from "Declaration of Sentiments," in Elizabeth Cady Stanton, Susan B. Anthony, and Matilda Joslyn Gage, eds. *History of Woman Suffrage*, Vol. 1 (1848–1861), (Rochester, NY: Charles Mann, 1887), pp. 70–73.

[The Declaration of Sentiments, modeled after the Declaration of Independence, emerged out of the Women's Rights Convention, held July 19–20, 1848, in Seneca Falls, New York. With less than a week's notice, the event drew nearly 300 people, including forty men. Elizabeth Cady Stanton was the principal architect of the Declaration. Telling of that age, none of the women present chose to preside; Lucretia Mott's husband, James, led the deliberations.]

5. Seneca Falls Convention, Declaration of Sentiments (1848).

When, in the course of human events, it becomes necessary for one portion of the family of man to assume among the people of the earth a position different from that which they have hitherto occupied, but one to which the laws of nature and of nature's God entitle them, a decent respect to the opinions of mankind requires that they should declare the causes that impel them to such a course.

We hold these truths to be self-evident: that all men and women are created equal; that they are endowed by their Creator with certain inalienable rights; that among these are life, liberty, and the pursuit of happiness; that to secure these rights governments are instituted, deriving their just powers from the consent of the governed. Whenever any form of government becomes destructive of these ends, it is the right of those who suffer from it to refuse allegiance to it, and to insist upon the institution of a new government, laying its foundation on such principles, and organizing its powers in such form, as to them shall seem most likely to effect their safety and happiness. Prudence, indeed, will dictate that governments long established should not be changed for light and transient causes; and accordingly all experience hath shown that mankind are more disposed to suffer, while evils are sufferable, than to right themselves by abolishing the forms to which they were accustomed. But when a long train of abuses and usurpations, pursuing invariably the same object evinces a design to reduce them under absolute despotism, it is their duty to throw off such government, and to provide new guards for their future security. Such has been the patient sufferance of the women under this government, and such is now the necessity which constrains them to demand the equal station to which they are entitled.

The history of mankind is a history of repeated injuries and usurpations on the part of man toward woman, having in direct object the establishment of an absolute tyranny over her. To prove this, let facts be submitted to a candid world.

He has never permitted her to exercise her inalienable right to the elective franchise.

He has compelled her to submit to laws, in the formation of which she had no voice.

He has withheld from her rights which are given to the most ignorant and degraded men—both natives and foreigners.

Having deprived her of this first right of a citizen, the elective franchise, thereby leaving her without representation in the halls of legislation, he has oppressed her on all sides.

He has made her, if married, in the eye of the law, civilly dead.

He has taken from her all right in property, even to the wages she earns.

He has made her, morally, an irresponsible being, as she can commit many crimes with impunity, provided they be done in the presence of her husband. In the covenant of marriage, she is compelled to promise obedience to her husband, he becoming, to all intents and purposes, her master—the law giving him power to deprive her of her liberty, and to administer chastisement.

He has so framed the laws of divorce, as to what shall be the proper causes, and in case of separation, to whom the guardianship of the children shall be given, as to be wholly regardless of the happiness of women—the law, in all cases, going upon a false supposition of the supremacy of man, and giving all power into his hands.

After depriving her of all rights as a married woman, if single, and the owner of property, he has taxed her to support a government which recognizes her only when her property can be made profitable to it.

He has monopolized nearly all the profitable employments, and from those she is permitted to follow, she receives but a scanty remuneration. He closes against her all the avenues to wealth and distinction which he considers most honorable to himself. As a teacher of theology, medicine, or law, she is not known.

He has denied her the facilities for obtaining a thorough education, all colleges being closed against her.

He allows her in Church, as well as State, but a subordinate position, claiming Apostolic authority for her exclusion from the ministry, and, with some exceptions, from any public participation in the affairs of the Church.

He has created a false public sentiment by giving to the world a different code of morals for men and women, by which moral delinquencies which exclude women from society, are not only tolerated, but deemed of little account in man.

He has usurped the prerogative of Jehovah himself, claiming it as his right to assign for her a sphere of action, when that belongs to her conscience and to her God.

He has endeavored, in every way that he could, to destroy her confidence in her own powers, to lessen her self-respect, and to make her willing to lead a dependent and abject life.

Now, in view of this entire disfranchisement of one-half the people of this country, their social and religious degradation—in view of the unjust laws above mentioned, and because women do feel themselves aggrieved, oppressed, and fraudulently deprived of their most sacred rights, we insist that they have immediate admission to all the rights and privileges which belong to them as citizens of the United States.

In entering upon the great work before us, we anticipate no small amount of misconception, misrepresentation, and ridicule; but we shall use every instrumentality within our power to effect our object. We shall employ agents, circulate tracts, petition the State and National legislatures, and endeavor to enlist the pulpit and the press in our behalf. We hope this Convention will be followed by a series of Conventions embracing every part of the country. . . .

. . . Whereas, The great precept of nature is conceded to be, that "man shall pursue his own true and substantial happiness." Blackstone in his Commentaries remarks, that this law of Nature being coeval with mankind, and dictated by God himself, is of course superior in obligation to any other. It is binding over all the globe, in all countries, and at all times; no human laws are of any validity if contrary to this, and such of them as are valid, derive all their force, and all their validity, and all their authority, mediately and immediately, from this original; therefore,

Resolved, That such laws as conflict, in any way, with the true and substantial happiness of woman, are contrary to the great precept of nature and of no validity, for this is "superior in obligation to any other."

Resolved, That all laws which prevent woman from occupying such a station in society as her conscience shall dictate, or which place her in a position inferior to that of man, are contrary to the great precept of nature, and therefore of no force or authority.

Resolved, That woman is man's equal—was intended to be so by the Creator, and the highest good of the race demands that she should be recognized as such.

Resolved, That the women of this country ought to be enlightened in regard to the laws under which they live, that they may no longer publish their degradation by declaring themselves satisfied with their present position, nor their ignorance, by asserting that they have all the rights they want.

Resolved, That inasmuch as man, while claiming for himself intellectual superiority, does accord to woman moral superiority, it is pre-eminently his duty to encourage her to speak and teach, as she has an opportunity, in all religious assemblies.

Resolved, That the same amount of virtue, delicacy, and refinement of behavior that is required of woman in the social state, should also be required of man, and the same transgressions should be visited with equal severity on both man and woman.

Resolved, That the objection of indelicacy and impropriety, which is so often brought against woman when she addresses a public audience, comes with a very ill-grace from those who encourage, by their attendance, her appearance on the stage, in the concert, or in feats of the circus.

Resolved, That woman has too long rested satisfied in the circumscribed limits which corrupt customs and a perverted application of the Scriptures have marked out for her, and that it is time she should move in the enlarged sphere which her great Creator has assigned her.

Resolved, That it is the duty of the women of this country to secure to themselves their sacred right to the elective franchise.[10]

Resolved, That the equality of human rights results necessarily from the fact of the identity of the race in capabilities and responsibilities.

Resolved, therefore, That, being invested by the Creator with the same capabilities, and the same consciousness of responsibility for their exercise, it is demonstrably the right and duty of woman, equally with man, to promote every righteous cause by every righteous means; and especially in regard to the great subjects of morals and religion, it is self-evidently her right to participate with her brother in teaching them, both in private and

10. All the other resolutions passed unanimously. But suffrage was so radical that even Lucretia Mott initially balked at the idea. The renowned abolitionist and eloquent former slave Frederick Douglass persuaded the crowd to endorse women's voting rights.

in public, by writing and by speaking, by any instrumentalities proper to be used, and in any assemblies proper to be held; and this being a self-evident truth growing out of the divinely implanted principles of human nature, any custom or authority adverse to it, whether modern or wearing the hoary sanction of antiquity, is to be regarded as a self-evident falsehood, and at war with mankind.

Source 6 from "Female Department: Women out of their Latitude," *Mechanic's Advocate* (Albany, NY: 1846–1848), 12 August 1848. Vol. 2, Iss. 34, p. 264. Assessed 31 January 2010.

6. "Women Out of Their Latitude" (1848).

We are sorry to see that the women, in several parts of this State, are holding what they call "Woman's Rights Conventions," and setting forth a formidable list of those Rights, in a parody upon the Declaration of American Independence.

The papers of the day contain extended notices of these Conventions. Some of them fall in with their objects, and praise the meetings highly; but the majority either deprecate or ridicule both.

The women who attend these meetings, no doubt at the expense of their more appropriate duties, act as committees, write resolutions and addresses, hold much correspondence, make speeches, etc. etc. They affirm, as among their rights, that of unrestricted franchise, and assert that it is wrong to deprive them of the privilege to become legislators, lawyers, doctors, divines, etc. etc.; and they are holding conventions and making an agitatory movement, with the object in view of revolutionising public opinion and the laws of the land, and changing their relative position in society in such a way as to divide with the male sex the labors and responsibilities of active life, in every branch of arts, science, trades and professions!

Now it requires no argument to prove that this is all wrong. Every true-hearted female will instantly feel that it is unwomanly, and that to be practically carried out, the males must change their position in society to the same extent in an opposite direction, in order to enable them to discharge an equal share of the domestic duties which now appertain to females, and which must be neglected, to a great extent, if women are allowed the exercise of all the "rights" that are claimed by these Convention-holders. Society would have to be radically remodelled, in order to accommodate itself to so great a change in the most vital part of the compact of the social relations of life; and the order of things established at the creation of mankind, and continued *six thousand years*, would be completely broken up. The organic laws of our country, and of each State, would have to be licked into new shapes, in order to admit of the introduction of the vast change that is contemplated. In a thousand other ways that might be mentioned, if we had room to make, and our readers had patience to hear them, would this sweeping reform be attended, by fundamental changes in the public and private, civil and religious, moral and social relations of the sexes, of life, and of government.

But this change is impracticable, uncalled for and unnecessary. *If effected*, it would get the world by the ears, make "confusion worse confounded," demoralise, and degrade from their high sphere and noble destiny, women of all respectable and useful classes and prove a monstrous injury to all mankind. It would be productive of no positive good, that would not be outweighed, ten fold, by positive evil. It would alter the relations of females, without bettering their condition.

Besides all, and above all, it presents no remedy for the *real* evils that the millions of the industrious, hardworking and much-suffering women of our country groan under and seek to redress.

Source 7 from Elizabeth Cady Stanton, *National Reformer* (Rochester, NY), 14 September 1848, in Susan Groag Bell and Karen M. Offen, eds., Women, the Family, and Freedom, Volume 1, 1750–1880 (Stanford, CA: Stanford University Press, 1983), pp. 259–260 and reprinted from Stanton, Elizabeth Cady, Susan B. Anthony, and Matilda Joslyn Gage. *History of Woman Suffrage*, Vol. 1 1848–1861 (Rochester, NY: Charles Mann, 1887), p. 806.[11]

7. Elizabeth Cady Stanton on Women's Rights (1848).

There is no danger of this question dying for want of notice. Every paper you take up has something to say about it, and just in proportion to the refinement and intelligence of the editor, has this movement been favorably noticed. But one might suppose from the articles that you find in some papers, that there were editors so ignorant as to believe that the chief object of these recent Conventions was to seat every lord at the head of a cradle, and to clothe every woman in her lord's attire. Now, neither of these points, however important they be considered by humble minds, were touched upon in the Conventions. . . . For those who do not yet understand the real objects of our recent Conventions at Rochester and Seneca Falls, I would state that

11. The Elizabeth Cady Stanton and Susan B. Anthony Papers Project maintains an outstanding website, with digital access to some of their most famous writings: http://ecssba.rutgers .edu. The PBS/Ken Burns documentary "Not For Ourselves Alone: The Story of Elizabeth Cady Stanton & Susan B. Anthony" offers an excellent introduction to their lives and work.

we did not meet to discuss fashions, customs, or dress, the rights or duties of man, nor the propriety of the sexes changing positions, but simply our own inalienable rights, our duties, our true sphere. If God has assigned a sphere to man and one to woman, we claim the right to judge ourselves of His design in reference to *us*, and we accord to man the same privilege. We think a man has quite enough in this life to find out his own individual calling, without being taxed to decide where every woman belongs; and the fact that so many men fail in the business they undertake, calls loudly for their concentrating more thought on their own faculties, capabilities, and sphere of action. We have all seen a man making a jackass of himself in the pulpit, at the bar, or in our legislative halls, when he might have shone as a general in our Mexican war, captain of a canal boat, or as a tailor on his bench. Now, is it to be wondered at that woman has some doubts about the present position assigned her being the true one, when her every-day experience shows her that man makes such fatal mistakes in regard to himself?

There is no such thing as a sphere for a sex. Every man has a different sphere, and one in which he may shine, and it is the same with every woman; and the same woman may have a different sphere at different times. The distinguished Angelina Grimké was acknowledged by all the anti-slavery host to be in her sphere, when, years ago, she went through the length and breadth of New England, telling the people of her personal experience of the horrors and abominations of the slave system, and by her eloquence and power as a public speaker, producing an effect unsurpassed by any of the highly gifted men of her day. Who dares to say that in thus using her splendid talents in speaking for the dumb, pleading the cause of the poor friendless slave, that she was out of her sphere? Angelina Grimké is now a wife and the mother of several children. We hear of her no more in public. Her sphere and her duties have changed. She deems it her first and her most sacred duty to devote all her time and talents to her household and to the education of her children. We do not say that she is not *now* in her sphere. The highly gifted Quakeress, Lucretia Mott, married early in life, and brought up a large family of children. All who have seen her at home agree that she was a pattern as a wife, mother, and housekeeper. No one ever fulfilled all the duties of that sphere more perfectly than did she. Her children are now settled in their own homes. Her husband and herself, having a comfortable fortune, pass much of their time in going about and doing good. Lucretia Mott has now no domestic cares. She has a talent for public speaking; her mind is of a high order; her moral perceptions remarkably clear; her religious fervor deep and intense; and who shall tell us that this divinely inspired woman is out of her sphere in her public endeavors to rouse this wicked nation to a sense of its awful guilt, to its great sins of war, slavery, injustice to woman and the laboring poor. . . .

Source 8 from "A Society of Patriotic Ladies, at Edenton in North Carolina," London, 1775.

8. 1775 Editorial Cartoon: "A Society of Patriotic Ladies, at Edenton in North Carolina."

Library of Congress Prints and Photographs Division [LC-DIG-ppmsca-19468]

Source 9 from "Women's Emancipation," *Harper's New Monthly Magazine,* August 1851, p. 424.

9. 1851 Editorial Cartoon: "Women's Emancipation."

from "Women's Emancipation," Harper's New Monthly Magazine, August 1851, p. 424

Source 10 from "The Age of Iron, Man as He Expects to Be," Currier & Ives, 1869.

10. 1869 Editorial Cartoon: "The Age of Iron, Man as He Expects to Be."

Source 11 from "The Age of Brass, or the Triumphs of Women's Rights," Currier & Ives, 1869.

11. 1869 Editorial Cartoon: "The Age of Brass, or the Triumphs of Women's Rights."

✦

Questions to Consider

Obviously these writers and artists did not agree about women's rights. They shared their opinions clearly and emphatically. These disputes took place within a particular historical and cultural context. The parameters of the debate—the shared assumptions and points of disagreement—tell us a great deal about mid-nineteenth-century America. In this chapter, you should discover not only the causes of the controversy surrounding women's civic equality but also develop a deeper understanding of antebellum culture, especially gender values.

Once you have listed the specific points of contention, think about why these issues mattered so much to the men and women who created these historical documents. What assumptions—about civic life, the future of the nation, morality, and human nature—appear in these sources? Can you see the influences of the American Revolution? Of evangelical Christianity? The sources should also help you see changes that had already taken place—in women's political engagement, in their formal education, in their religiosity—by the time of the Seneca Falls meeting. While critics of gender equality found the Declaration of Sentiments (Source 5) dangerous, advocates such as Elizabeth Cady Stanton and Lucretia Mott saw women's rights as essential. These disagreements reflected profound changes that divided antebellum Americans. What were those changes?

Consider the essay by Thomas Dew (Source 1). How does he understand social order? In his view, what is the basic nature of women and of men? Why and in what specific ways are men and women different? What are their proper roles in society? Compare his perceptions with the letter written by Angelina Grimké (Source 2). Does she agree with Dew about physical differences determining social roles? How does she understand social order and gender differences? What does she think is the basic nature of women and of men? What about the General Association of Massachusetts (Source 4)? The signers of the Declaration of Sentiments?

Compare the letter written by Sarah Grimké (Source 3) to the one sent to Massachusetts churches. What religious values do they share in common? Where do they part ways? What underlying assumptions about religion and about gender can you see in these two documents? How does the church leaders' understanding of women's proper place in society differ from that of Sarah and her sister Angelina?

Review again each document, thinking of each as a piece of writing that reflects the values of the author as well as the culture of the era. Compare and contrast the tone of each piece. The recipients of the texts varied, but all the authors sought to persuade readers to adopt their views. Think about the different tactics—ridicule, logic, hyperbole, emotionalism, persuasion—employed by the writers. How might audiences respond to these differing approaches? What can you glean about the women's rights debate from the tone and the structure of the writing? For example, what does Elizabeth Cady Stanton's authoring of the Declaration of Sentiments tell us about women's education and civic engagement? What does Stanton's 1848 essay (Source 7) tell us about her perception of her critics?

Now turn to the images (Sources 8–11). How are the visual representations similar to and different from the writings of critics who assailed women's equality? What influence do you think such images would have exerted?

For all the authors and artists you've studied, the stakes of the debate appeared extraordinarily high. Each acts as if the fate of American society depends on widespread adoption of their viewpoint. Why were they so adamant? What deeper cultural assumptions did their advocacy reflect?

According to the advocates of women's rights, what will be the costs to American society if their position is rejected? According to their opponents, what will be the familial and social consequences of embracing gender equality? What do these stakes tell us about antebellum America? To answer these questions, begin with the Declaration of Sentiments. According to that document, in what ways have women been exploited? At what cost? What are the consequences of women continuing to accept those prescribed parameters? What specific changes do they seek? What would this require of women? Of men? In the essay, "Women out of their Latitude," (Source 6) the author maintains that embracing women's rights will cause "monstrous injury to all mankind" and result in society being "radically remodeled." First, does the author accurately report on the Seneca Falls objectives? Second, what does the author mean when he writes that society would be "radically remodelled" with "monstrous injury"? What sort of changes would embracing women's equality force? Weigh this alongside the four editorial cartoons. How do they depict the consequences of women's political engagement? What, for example, would it mean for families? To what degree do predictions of the dangers of women's equal citizenship change between the eighteenth and nineteenth centuries?

In her rebuttal to the critics of women's rights, Elizabeth Cady Stanton roundly rejects the entire idea of women's "sphere." How does she attempt to recast this paradigm? If her argument holds sway, what would this re-imagination of women's proper roles mean for America? By now you should be confident in explaining why women's civil rights were so controversial in nineteenth-century America.

❖

Epilogue

Elizabeth Cady Stanton and like-minded women and men did not secure women's legal equality in the antebellum era. Certainly there were some successes. Several states adopted women's property rights in the 1850s. Changes came in divorce law as well, with more states allowing abused and abandoned wives to formally end their marriages.[12] But a foundational part of nineteenth-century feminists' definition of gender equality—the right to vote—eluded them.

Stanton and Susan B. Anthony became close friends in the 1850s and remained lifelong allies in the fight for women's equality. They made a terrific team: Stanton the compelling, forceful writer, and Anthony the consummate strategist. Over the course of the next half-century, they tried every approach. They waged their fight in newspapers; they founded organizations; they engaged in public displays of civil disobedience and went to jail; they lobbied legislatures; and they filed lawsuits. The movement fractured in the wake of the Civil War, with some feminists endorsing the 14th and 15th amendments (which extended civil equality and voting rights to former enslaved men), while others withheld their support until women, too, could enjoy equal citizenship. In 1890, the two sides reconciled, creating the National American Woman Suffrage Association. Elizabeth Cady Stanton served as the first president, and Susan B. Anthony succeeded her a few years later.

Neither woman lived to see her dream of women's suffrage realized.

It fell to a new generation of feminists to shepherd their vision. Carrie Chapman Catt was president of the NAWSA, and the face of the women's suffrage movement, when the 19th amendment passed Congress in the summer of 1919. It was ratified by the requisite number of states and added to the U.S. Constitution on August 26, 1920.

But the 19th amendment did not ensure women's full citizenship, and the amendment applied principally to white women. In 1920, the majority of African Americans lived in the South, where Reconstruction had collapsed under the weight of white southern intransigence, northern apathy, and racial violence. Segregation reigned there, and black women, like black men, were threatened and intimidated away from the polls. Not until 1965 could the majority of African American women vote in the United States—one hundred years after the defeat of the Confederacy and nearly two hundred years after Thomas Jefferson's eloquent call for equality and self-government launched the American Republic. In the twenty-first century, women vote in larger numbers than men. But egalitarianism at the voting booth has not produced a gender-neutral society. In 2012, American women still earned 81 cents to every dollar paid to their male counterparts.[13]

12. For divorce law, see Hendrik Hartog, *Man and Wife in America: A History* (Cambridge: Harvard University Press, 2000); and Norma Basch, *Framing American Divorce: From the Revolutionary Generation to the Victorians* (Berkeley: University of California Press, 1999).

13. U.S. Department of Labor, Bureau of Labor Statistics, Current Population Survey, 2013. Using a slightly different model, the Pew Research Center calculated women earned 84 cents to every dollar earned by men. Pew Research Center, 11 December 2013.

The "Peculiar Institution": Slaves Tell Their Own Stories

◆

The Problem

In the spring of 1800, in a rural neighborhood in Henrico County, Virginia, just north of Richmond, men began to gather in the woods under cover of darkness, furtively after church services and funerals, and in fields and workshops—whenever whites were distracted or distant. For months they worked out their plans and slowly built a network of committed men, determined to take back their freedom from the enslavers who held them captive. For reasons never disclosed, women were excluded from participating in what organizers planned as a death blow to the institution of slavery, to be launched in the last days of summer, in the capital of the birthplace of American slavery. Virginia's history with racial slavery ran deep into the seventeenth century and had made the fledgling colony successful. By the time of the American Revolution, Virginia was the most populous and powerful state in the Union, home of the greatest heroes of the Revolution and to the largest number of slaves in

North America: 292,627 according to the 1790 census.

The plan was equal parts daring and dangerous. On the night of August 30, a group of fifty African American men would sneak into Richmond and set fire to mostly wooden, closely situated buildings on the south side of the city. White residents would rush to fight the blaze, leaving key sites underprotected, especially warehouses with weapons. A far larger group of men would then swarm those locations, kill the remaining guards, and seize the weapons, turning Richmonders' defenses against them. For the initial attack, the men had fashioned makeshift bayonets and turned the scythes they used in their field labor into swords for their uprising. Despite laws strictly forbidding African Americans from owning firearms, they had even managed to secret away a few guns. If enough men worked together and fast, they could seize the caches of weapons and lay waste to Richmond. Governor James Monroe (later elected president of the United States) figured prominently into the plan: he would be captured and, if necessary to win the battle, killed.

On August 30, a fierce storm pummeled Virginia. Torrential rain and driving winds made gathering that evening impossible. That very day, unbeknownst to the organizers who agreed to wait one more night, two men they had approached to join the fight turned on them. Known in the historical records only as Pharoah and Tom, the two men disclosed the planned rebellion to Mosby Sheppard, their owner. Sheppard told Governor Monroe, who ordered military and civilian patrols to round up all African Americans even suspected of being involved, including a man named Gabriel, a blacksmith enslaved by Thomas Henry Prosser.[1]

With the initial threat quashed, white Virginians put the full weight of the law to punishing any African Americans involved in the aborted rebellion. As the governor explained, the state "made a display of our force and measure of defence with a view to intimidate those people." Virginia "justice" was swift. By mid-September, ten men had been convicted of the capital offenses of conspiracy and insurrection and publicly hanged. Dozens more awaited trial. After the

state of Virginia had hanged the first ten men, Governor Monroe wrote his good friend, soon-to-be President Thomas Jefferson, to ask how many more African Americans needed to be killed to prevent future rebellions and to ease whites' minds. Jefferson quickly wrote back that he thought enough had died already to satisfy those needs. Besides, he continued, "the other states & the world at large will for ever condemn us if we indulge a principle of revenge, or go one step beyond absolute necessity."[2] The pace of mail delivery meant that five more men died before Monroe received this reply. Monroe failed to convince other government leaders to stop the executions anyway. Gabriel—the man whose name came to define the rebellion—was hanged on October 10, one of twenty-six men publicly executed for their involvement in the planned uprising. By that time, the economics of the suppression was getting the attention of legislators. Virginia law required the state to reimburse slaveowners for the value of enslaved African Americans it executed. And bloodlust meant the costs kept mounting. In the fall, then, capital convictions were increasingly met with pardons—and immediate sale, usually to the Deep South. By selling away the convicted conspirators, Virginia could be rid of these dangerous individuals without draining further the public coffers. It was, in the world of enslavers, a win-win situation.

In the course of the trials, the General Assembly set about tightening Virginia's slave codes, rigidly controlling

1. Gabriel is sometimes referred to in history books as Gabriel Prosser, but there is no evidence he went by that name in his lifetime. In the records from the period, he is referred to only as Gabriel. And although the failed uprising is known as Gabriel's Conspiracy, he was likely one of several important leaders. For more on the planned rebellion and aftermath, see Michael L. Nicholls, *Whispers of Rebellion: Narrating Gabriel's Conspiracy* (Charlottesville: University of Virginia Press, 2012).

2. James Monroe to Thomas Jefferson, 15 September 1800, and Thomas Jefferson to James Monroe, 20 September 1800.

slaves' movements and enhancing slave patrols. They even further circumscribed the rights of free blacks, whom legislators generally suspected of supporting Gabriel's Conspiracy. Finally, to reward their actions on August 30, the General Assembly purchased and manumitted Tom and Pharoah.

Oftentimes when we think about African Americans resisting the institution of slavery, events like Gabriel's Conspiracy come to mind: collective, violent uprisings designed to overthrow the institution of slavery. And such events did inevitably occur in reaction to the systematic violence and brutality of racial slavery: in South Carolina in 1739, for example, in Haiti in 1791, and again in Virginia in 1831.[3] We can investigate these sorts of rebellions in traditional historical evidence: newspapers, correspondence, government documents, and trial transcripts—the main types of sources for exploring what happened in Henrico County and Richmond in 1800. As you can see in the story of Gabriel's Conspiracy, such actions were extraordinarily difficult and dangerous to organize, and so they were comparatively rare. Far more common were daily acts of resistance, individually driven, for families and communities, requiring a different kind of courage and sparking different forms of retribution by white enslavers. Uncovering that history requires scholars to draw on sources generated by African Americans, who personally experienced the institution of slavery, and to read those materials very carefully. In this chapter, you will engage several kinds of primary sources—interviews, court depositions, and firsthand writings—to answer a question that is more complicated than you might think at first: **How did enslaved African Americans challenge the institution of slavery in the antebellum South?**

◆

Background

By the time of the American Revolution, what had begun in 1619 as a trickle of Africans intended to supple-

3. For more on these rebellions, see Peter Charles Hoffer, *Cry Liberty: The Great Stono River Slave Rebellion of 1739* (Oxford: Oxford University Press, 2010); Jeremy D. Popkin, *You Are All Free: The Haitian Revolution and the Abolition of Slavery* (Cambridge: Cambridge University Press, 2010); David F. Allmendinger, Jr., *Nat Turner and the Rising in Southampton County* (Baltimore: Johns Hopkins University Press, 2014).

ment the labor of white indentured servants from England had swelled to a population of approximately 500,000 people of African descent held in bondage throughout mainland British America. Slavery existed in every North American colony. Slaves worked in cities and on farms, in homes and businesses, and in the thriving Atlantic maritime trades. For most of the colonial era, few white colonists other than the Quakers ever questioned the efficacy and morality of holding Africans as chattel. Racial slavery, in sum, was foundational to the stability and financial success of American colonies.

While slavery had a long history in colonial America, the nature of the institution changed significantly over time. In the seventeenth century, African men and women often labored alongside white servants and apprentices and small landowners and craftsmen. Slavery was racially based and brutal, but it was one of several forms of exploitative, unfree labor. Historian Ira Berlin has described this pattern, common throughout North America, as "societies with slaves." By the middle of the eighteenth century, the southern provinces had evolved into "slave societies." Slavery was no longer *a* labor system but *the* labor system and a foundational institution in society.[4] By mid-century the economy, culture, and social order of southern colonies, most notably South Carolina and Virginia, depended on racial slavery. The majority of slaves worked on plantations in these two colonies, producing lucrative agricultural commodities, such as rice and tobacco. Slavery became more rigid and pervasive, shaping religion, social relationships, and culture. As you learned in Chapter 3, laws increasingly defined blacks as inferior to whites and attempted to grant owners nearly unchecked power over slaves. At the same time, racial slavery continued to enrich white colonists throughout North America, from

4. Ira Berlin, *Many Thousands Gone: The First Two Centuries of Slavery in North America* (Cambridge: Harvard University Press, 1998).

the traders in Rhode Island to the merchants of New York.

Although it unleashed a flood of debates about slavery, the American Revolution did not reverse those trends. The founding generation clearly understood the contradiction of allowing slavery in a republic. Slaveholders such as Thomas Jefferson, principal author of the Declaration of Independence, and James Madison, architect of the Constitution, engaged in anguished discussions about the problem of perpetuating racial slavery in the new nation they were designing. Jefferson famously confessed, "I tremble for my country when I reflect that God is just; that his justice cannot sleep forever." But he, Madison, and the great majority of their fellow southern planters failed to act on their concerns. (Jefferson freed some of his children with Sally Hemings, but neither he nor Madison undertook any substantive emancipatory plan during their lives or in their wills).

Meanwhile, northern states, where African American slavery was not so directly and deeply rooted, began instituting gradual emancipation programs after the Revolution. These new laws, which often freed men and women upon their reaching a certain age, sometimes took decades to reach fruition. As late as the 1840 census, slaves still resided in New England states. And, in some cases, freedom came with strings: in 1818 and 1822 Connecticut and Rhode Island, respectively, rescinded the voting rights of free black men. When New York revised its state constitution in 1821, it disfranchised African Americans as well. Some New England towns even revived the colonial practice of "warning out"—expelling undesirable residents—in decidedly racialized terms. And northern merchants still profited from the persistence of racial slavery in southern states, trading in and producing for foreign markets goods derived from slave-based commodities. Still, the differences between the increasingly free North and the slave South appeared stark enough to James Madison in 1787 that he declared, "the real difference of interests" at the Constitutional Convention, "lay, not between the large & small but between the N. & Southern States. The institution of slavery & its consequences formed the line of discrimination."[5]

The South's commitment to slavery was deepened by the invention of the cotton gin in the 1790s. The gin enabled seeds to be removed from the easily grown short staple cotton, which, in turn, allowed southern planters to expand into commercial cotton production. The subsequent cotton boom proved transformative for the American South and for African American men and women held in bondage as well as for the United States overall. Indeed, cotton production helped to fuel global capitalism in the early nineteenth century. The exploitation of enslaved African Americans turned profits not only for southern enslavers but also manufacturers in the American North and across Europe.[6] In the United States, cotton also fueled the westward movement of commercial agriculture and racial slavery. In the early nineteenth century, southern planters carried slavery into nearly every area of the South, including Tennessee, Kentucky, Alabama, Mississippi, Missouri, and ultimately Texas. Simultaneously, the slave population burgeoned, roughly doubling every thirty years (from approximately 700,000 in 1790 to 1.5 million in 1820 to more than 3.2 million in 1850). Because importation of slaves from Africa was banned in 1808 (although there was some illegal slave smuggling), slave population growth derived principally from natural increase.

As the institution of slavery changed, so too did the experiences of men and women held in bondage. In colonial America, differences in nationality, language, and customs, owing to the prevalence of slaves imported directly from Africa, had worked against the ability of bondspersons to forge a common, shared culture. Moreover, because slaves engaged in a wide range of occupations in the various colonies, African American cultures tended to be regionally rooted. The lives of slaves in colonial South Carolina differed significantly from those in colonial Virginia; the culture that emerged in urban areas diverged from that forged on plantations. But in the antebellum era (1830s–1850s), slave cultures converged, driven by forced migration into the Deep South, to places like Alabama, Mississippi, and Louisiana. Second and third generation native–born African Americans comprised an increasing majority of slave populations on cotton plantations on the

5. James Madison, *Notes of Debates in the Federal Convention of 1787* (New York: W.W. Norton, 1966), 295.
6. For more on the power of cotton in global capitalism see Edward E. Baptist, *The Half Has Never Been Told: Slavery and the Making of American Capitalism* (New York: Basic Books, 2014).

southern frontier. They spoke the same language as whites and many had converted to Christianity. Some learned how to read and write, although since this was illegal most kept it secret from their white owners.

Slaveholders, for their part, grew ever more anxious about and defensive of the South's racial order in the antebellum era. This derived in part from the clear fact that the American South was increasingly isolated in maintaining slavery in the early nineteenth century. In addition to the gradual emancipation programs of many northern states, slavery had been forbidden in the Northwest Territory. Britain abolished the slave trade in 1807 and ended slavery in 1833. France outlawed slavery in 1794. (Napoleon re-instated it during his reign; it was abolished a second, final time in 1848). Britain, France, and the northern states in the United States continued to turn profits from trading in slave-produced commodities, the cotton market in particular. But slavery as an institution was forbidden, a fact that made their southern planter partners increasingly skittish and defensive.

A number of widely-publicized slave uprisings only added to the conviction of southern whites that their way of life was under siege. In 1791, a revolution on the French colony of Saint Domingue resulted in the abolition of slavery on the Caribbean island and the creation of the first free black republic, Haiti. The Haitian Revolution was the most successful slave rebellion in history, and it horrified southern whites. No doubt it helped inspire the men in Henrico County to plan their own uprising. Though they failed, their attempt terrified white Virginians. A generation later, another Virginia uprising did succeed, at least partly. During the Nat Turner Rebellion in 1831, fifty-five whites were killed, many as they slept. This only deepened slaveholders' insecurities and their desire to be vigilant in controlling African Americans—and not just in Virginia. In response to Nat Turner's Rebellion, southern states passed a series of laws that made the system of slavery even more restrictive. Manumission statutes grew far more rigid. In Mississippi, each manumission required a special act of the state legislature, and Virginia mandated the outmigration of any freed slave. It became illegal even for owners to teach their slaves to read. Compulsory slave patrols policed the southern countryside, acting as sheriff, judge, and jury if they found a slave away from his or her owner without written permission. Postmasters searched the mails for banned abolitionist literature.

Aware of the tremendous obstacles and perils of trying to overthrow their enslavers, African Americans relied on other, more subtle forms of resistance. Instructions were forgotten, tools broken, meals burned, and illnesses feigned. Maintaining their own religious traditions that rejected the white enslavers' constant refrain of obedience empowered African Americans, too, as did preserving family ties, oral traditions, and cultural values. The creation of thriving black cultures under slavery gave lie to a foundational element of slaveholders' world view, which sought to dehumanize people and turn them into machines of production (and, in the case of women, reproduction).

Despite—or perhaps because of—the changing world around them, slaveholding southerners also went to great lengths to justify preserving their "peculiar institution." By the 1830s, gone was the founding generation's lament about slavery being a necessary evil. Now, white southerners promoted slavery as a positive good—for blacks and whites alike—that they intended to preserve at any cost. Law, economics, science, theology, and history were all mustered in defense of slaveholding. Prominent proslavery advocate George Fitzhugh argued that African Americans were so inferior to whites that, if freed, "gradual but certain extermination would be their fate." "Our negroes," he further insisted, "are confessedly better off than any free laboring population in the world." In an 1837 speech before the U.S. Senate, famous South Carolina politician John C. Calhoun pronounced slavery ennobling to the South and maintained the institution "is indispensible to the peace and happiness of both" blacks and whites. Southerners argued that slavery was a more humane system than northern capitalism—which, of course, worked in tandem with southern commercial agriculture. They insisted that enslaved African Americans were fed, clothed, sheltered, and cared for when they were ill and aged, whereas factory workers were paid pitifully low wages and then discarded when they were no longer useful. Furthermore, many white southerners bragged that slavery introduced "barbarous" Africans to "civilized" American ways, including

to Christianity.[7] Here they carefully ignored the many ways in which African Americans turned Christianity into a liberation theology.

In such an atmosphere, in which many of the South's intellectual efforts went into defending slavery, dissent and freedom of thought could not thrive. White southerners who disagreed with the proslavery agenda remained silent, were cowed into submission, or decided to leave the region. The antebellum South became increasingly a defensive, insular echo chamber: white politicians, preachers, writers, and physicians—everyone in positions of authority—shared the same perspective, set on defending racial slavery and the "southern way of life."

White southerners without enough money to enslave African Americans still benefited from the institution. Even the poorest white person enjoyed a social status superior to all African Americans. Slavery created a racial divide in the South that superseded class divisions and promoted white solidarity. As historian Edmund S. Morgan elegantly argued in his magisterial study of slavery and freedom in early Virginia, all white men could

7. George Fitzhugh, *Sociology for the South: Or the Failure of Free Society* (Richmond: A. Morris, 1854), in Paul Finkelman, ed., *Defending Slavery: Proslavery Thought in the Old South, A Brief History with Documents* (Boston: Bedford/St. Martin's, 2003), 190. Fitzhugh, *Cannibals All! Or Slaves Without Masters*, in Finkelman, ed., *Defending Slavery*, 199. John C. Calhoun, "Speech on the Reception of Abolition Petitions, Delivered in the Senate, February 6th, 1837," in Richard R. Crallé, ed., *Speeches of John C. Calhoun, Delivered in the House of Representatives and in the Senate of the United States* (New York: D. Appleton, 1853), reprinted in Finkelman, ed., *Defending Slavery*, 58.

imagine themselves free and equal because they would never be black and enslaved.[8] Fear of black uprisings also led many non-slaveholders to fall in line with their planter neighbors, participating in slave patrols and voting for proslavery politicians. Some whites believed that emancipation would bring them into direct economic competition with blacks, which, they assumed, would drive down wages. Forgotten was how slavery discouraged economic diversification and widened the wealth gap between the region's large planters and everyone else. Racial power seemed to matter more to poor white southerners than their own economic interests.

Non-slaveholding whites—who represented the majority of the South's population—thus propped up the institution of racial slavery. The proportion of white southern families who owned slaves actually declined in the nineteenth century, from one-third in 1830 to roughly one-fourth by 1860. Moreover, nearly three-fourths of these slaveholders owned fewer than ten slaves. Slaveholders, then, were a distinct minority of the white southern population, and those men who owned large plantations and hundreds of slaves were an exceedingly small group. But because they maintained the solid support of their non-slaveholding neighbors, elite slaveholders controlled the region and became incredibly wealthy.[9]

8. Edmund S. Morgan, *American Slavery, American Freedom: The Ordeal of Colonial Virginia* (New York: W.W. Norton, 1975).
9. For non-elite slaveholding families, see Stephanie McCurry, *Masters of Small Worlds: Yeoman Households, Gender Relations, and*

Compared to the oceans of ink that white southerners spilled to insist that their slaves were happy and their region a thriving success, evidence of the perceptions of enslaved African Americans is exceedingly limited. Given the restrictive nature of the slave system, the relative paucity of literary sources is hardly surprising. Literacy was discouraged if not outright illegal, so most slaves never learned to read and write. Even those who did often lacked the wherewithal to preserve their writings over generations. And before the mid-twentieth century, relatively few archives sought to acquire African American manuscript materials. The creation and preservation of African American sources, then, was very challenging.

The major exception to this pattern can be found in the writings of slaves who escaped to the North and published accounts of their experiences with abolitionist presses. Those printed essays and books survived over time, preserving black voices for modern readers. The most famous of these ex-slave narratives was written by Frederick Douglass. In this chapter, you will read excerpts from three other writers, less well known than Douglass's but no less revealing.

John Thompson and Harriet Jacobs both escaped slavery in the South and fled North to reveal their heartbreaking stories, whereas Solomon Northup, a free black man from New York, was kidnapped and sold into slavery in the South. Only once he returned to his home was he able to tell about

the Political Culture of the South Carolina Low Country (New York: Oxford University Press, 1995).

his ordeal. (In 2013, Northup's book became the subject of an Academy Award winning movie, *Twelve Years a Slave.*) The excerpts you are reading from these books must be understood on two levels. The written accounts chronicle each person's experiences with bondage. The published narratives also represent a particular kind of challenge to slavery. These authors and their publishers were abolitionists: they advocated for the immediate end of the institution of slavery and equal citizenship for African Americans.

The men and women who sued for their freedom and for damages in the courts of St. Louis, Missouri, were fighting a more individual battle, rather than the systemic one waged by abolitionist writers and publishers.[10] The context of their cases was significant. Suing for freedom and/or damages for unlawful imprisonment required of litigants a nuanced understanding of complex legal structures. That St. Louis was a river town, a center of interstate commerce, and bordered by the free state of Illinois was crucial. Those circumstances gave African Americans greater mobility and access to lawyers and the courts—at least far more so than most enslaved people living in the rural South. Like the ex-slave narratives, the depositions in these freedom suits

hold multiple meanings. On one level, they are first-person accounts of African American men and women about their ordeal under slavery. They also expose the blurred lines between slave and free states and the illegal lengths to which enslavers would go to control and profit from African Americans. And, because of the court cases that produced the depositions, they represent another way of resisting enslavement.

The third kind of evidence included in this chapter introduces the issue of historical memory. Certainly the three writers who escaped slavery were recalling their experiences from memory, as were the litigants in St. Louis. But the ex-slave interviews you are reading were conducted decades after the Civil War. In the 1930s, the U.S. government created the Federal Writers' Project, one of many New Deal efforts to get Americans employed by hiring them for public works projects. The Works Progress Administration (WPA), which ran the Federal Writers' Project, hired men and women to travel all over the South, interviewing African Americans and accumulating more than two thousand narratives from ex-slaves in every southern state except Louisiana. These materials are housed in the Library of Congress in Washington, DC, and available through the Library's open access website.

Most of the men and women interviewed by WPA employees were remembering their childhood experiences with slavery. Some drew on family stories and folk traditions to supplement their own memories. These sources derived from personal recollection and oral tradition must be used with imagination

10. Historian Kelly Marie Kennington recently published an excellent article exploring these cases: "Law, Geography, and Mobility: Suing for Freedom in Antebellum St. Louis," *Journal of Southern History* 80 (August 2014): 575–604. For small slaveholders in border states, see also Diane Mutti Burke, *On Slavery's Border: Missouri's Small Slaveholding Households, 1815–1865* (Athens: University of Georgia Press, 2010).

and care. In particular, you will want to think about how the passage of time and changing circumstances shaped memory. Woven though all these stories are hints at the ways in which enslaved African Americans survived and resisted the brutal system of racial slavery.

◆

The Method

Historians must always seek to understand the context and the limitations of their evidence. In the Federal Writers' Project, most of the former slaves were in their eighties or nineties (quite a few were older than one hundred) at the time they were interviewed. In other words, most of the interviewees had been children or young people in 1860. It is important to know that although some of the WPA workers conducting the interview were African Americans, the overwhelming majority were white. The 1930s was a violent period in southern history: "Jim Crow" segregation, lynching, the KKK. It was dangerous, then, for African Americans to be too trusting or too forthcoming with white strangers asking questions about the South's racial past. Keep in mind, too, that while many of the people interviewed had moved to another location or a different state after the Civil War, many others still resided in the same county as their family's former enslavers.

As historian Ira Berlin pointed out in his edited collection of slave narratives, former enslaved African Americans were often patronized and sometimes intimidated by white interviewers.[11] Once in a while, the actual interviews were written up in a stereotypical black dialect form (we have included examples of this) and occasionally the content itself was edited by the interviewers. Eventually the Federal Writers' Project issued directives to stop these practices. Berlin also notes that many, perhaps most, of the men and women interviewed did not fear retaliation and were eager to tell their stories. Some people were very forthcoming, whereas others answered obliquely or indirectly when the interviewers' questions touched on sensitive racial issues. For example, they might say that they were treated alright but then tell about other situations where slaves were brutalized.

Like all historical evidence, ex-slave narratives have both strengths and weaknesses. They are firsthand reports that, when carefully evaluated, can provide insight into the last years of slavery in the United States from the viewpoint of slaves themselves. Some of the stories or anecdotes may not actually be true, but they still convey a great deal about the perceptions of former enslaved people. Apocryphal stories can, in fact, reveal larger truths about African American experiences and culture. Therefore, you will need to pull meaning from these narratives, inferring what the interviewee meant and believed as well as what he or she said.

11. Ira Berlin et al., eds. *Remembering Slavery* (New York: New Press, 1998).

Practice the same attention to historical context and critical analysis of evidence in your reading of the book excerpts and the court records. The narratives of Solomon Northup, John Thompson, and Harriet Jacobs were all published in the North, close together in time (1853, 1856, 1861), and through abolitionist networks. But as you read each account, keep in mind the differences between the three writers' experiences. Harriet Jacobs (who used the pen name Linda Brent) was twenty-nine years old when she ran away in 1842, but her narrative was not published until the beginning of the Civil War. Throughout her story, Jacobs used fictitious names and places to protect those who helped her and to conceal the escape route she used. Jacobs was self-educated, she wrote her own book, and she was widely read in the nineteenth century. Her narrative continues to be a popular teaching text today. John Thompson represents a very different kind of slave narrative. He did not become famous, like Jacobs, and little is known about his life aside from the information contained in his narrative. After he escaped to Philadelphia, Thompson feared he might be returned to slavery, so he took to the seas. He worked for several years in the whaling industry, traveling the world before contributing his story to an abolitionist press in Massachusetts in 1856. Solomon Northup—like some of the St. Louis litigants—was a free black man. In 1841, he went to Washington, DC, where slavery was legal, and was kidnapped and sold into slavery in the South. Northup wrote his harrowing account after finally making his way home to New York, and he lectured widely about his ordeal, though he never achieved the renown of Jacobs. He disappeared entirely from the historical record a few years after publishing his narrative, and the circumstances of his death remain unknown.

The most famous of the St. Louis freedom suits was brought in 1847 by Dred and Harriet Scott, who sued for their freedom after being taken by their owner to regions of the United States where laws prohibited slavery. Their case eventually made it all the way to the U.S. Supreme Court, where Chief Justice Roger Taney wrote the majority opinion, deciding against the Scotts and denying African Americans all citizenship rights. Taney's opinion inflamed the already volatile divisions between the North and South and is widely understood to have been a milestone in the build-up to the Civil War. The famous Scott case and the largely unknown materials from the four cases you will read below numbered among hundreds of freedom suits filed in the St. Louis Circuit Court in the early nineteenth century. (Records of 286 cases have survived.) Not unlike the WPA interviews—though not to that degree—the voices of African American plaintiffs are filtered through whites, in this instance through attorneys who recorded their story and presented their case in court. Slightly more women than men sued for their freedom, though the reasons for this are not clear. African American women who prevailed in freedom suits could pass their status on to their children, so that may have been an important factor. Or perhaps lawyers and judges sympathized more with women than men and agreed to hear their cases more often. What is clear is that the Missouri law enabling all these lawsuits was designed not to encourage challenges to slavery but rather to prevent legally free blacks from being kidnapped into slavery—individuals like Solomon Northup. But increasingly in the 1830s and 1840s, enslaved African Americans used the law to their own ends. The case materials you are reading are divided between individuals who sued for unlawful imprisonment—free blacks illegally held as slaves—and those who were enslaved but sought freedom because of residence in free states or territories. This is an important part of the context of their suits and worthy of your consideration.

As you examine each source, jot down enough notes to allow you to recall that evidence later. Also, perhaps in a separate column, write down the important context of each source. For example, who is the audience? How does the medium (interview, court record, published book) shape the message? After you have examined each piece of evidence, look back over your notes. What forms of resistance stand out? How does gender, place, and time shape individuals' opportunities and actions?

◆

The Evidence

Sources 1 through 14 excerpted from *Born in Slavery: Slave Narratives from the Federal Writers' Project, 1936–1938*, Library of Congress, http://memory.loc.gov/ammem/snhtml

1. Hog-Killing Time.[12]

I remember Mammy told me about one master who almost starved his slaves. Mighty stingy, I reckon he was.

Some of them slaves was so poorly thin they ribs would kinda rustle against each other like cornstalks a-drying in the hot winds. But they gets even one hog-killing time, and it was funny too, Mammy said.

They was seven hogs, fat and ready for fall hog-killing time. Just the day before old master told off they was to be killed something happened to all them porkers. One of the field boys found them and come a-telling the master: "The hogs is all died, now they won't be any meats for the winter."

When the master gets to where at the hogs is laying, they's a lot of Negroes standing round looking sorrow-eyed at the wasted meat. The master asks: "What's the illness with 'em?"

12. Oklahoma Narratives, Volume 13, Josie Jordan, age 75.

"Malitis," they tells him, and they acts like they don't want to touch the hogs. Master says to dress them anyway for they ain't no more meat on the place.

He says to keep all the meat for the slave families, but that's because he's afraid to eat it hisself account of the hogs' got malitis.

"Don't you-all know what is malitis?" Mammy would ask the children when she was telling of the seven fat hogs and seventy lean slaves. And she would laugh, remembering how they fooled old master so's to get all them good meats.

"One of the strongest Negroes got up early in the morning," Mammy would explain, "long 'fore the rising horn called the slaves from their cabins. He skitted to the hog pen with a heavy mallet in his hand. When he tapped Mister Hog 'tween the eyes with the mallet, 'malitis' set in mighty quick, but it was a uncommon 'disease,' even with hungry Negroes around all the time."

2. The Old Parrot.[13]

The mistress had an old parrot, and one day I was in the kitchen making cookies, and I decided I wanted some of them, so I tooks me out some and put them on a chair and when I did this the mistress entered the door. I picks up a cushion and throws [it] over the pile of cookies on the chair and mistress came near the chair and the old parrot cries out, "Mistress burn, Mistress burn." Then the mistress looks under the cushion and she had me whupped but the next day I killed the parrot, and she often wondered who or what killed the bird.

3. The Coon and the Dog.[14]

Every time I think of slavery and if it done the race any good, I think of the story of the coon and dog who met. The coon said to the dog, "Why is it you're so fat and I am so poor, and we is both animals?" The dog said: "I lay round Master's house and let him kick me and he gives me a piece of bread right on." Said the coon to the dog: "Better, then, that I stay poor." Them's my sentiment. I'm lak the coon, I don't believe in 'buse.

---

13. Kentucky Narratives, Volume 7, Sophia Word, age 99.
14. Oklahoma Narratives, Volume 7, Stephen McCray, age 88.

4. The Partridge and the Fox.[15]

A partridge en a fox 'greed ter kill a beef. Dey kilt en skinned hit. B'fo dey
divide hit de fox said, "Mah wife seze sen' her sum beef fer soup." So he tuck
a piece ob hit en carried hit down de hill, den kum back en said, "Mah wife
wants mo' beef fer soup." He kep dis up 'til all de beef wuz gon' 'cept de libber.
De fox cum back, en de partridge seze, "Now let's cook dis libber en both ob
us eat hit." De partridge cooked de libber, et hits parts rite quick, en den fell
ovuh like hit wuz sick. De fox got skeered en said dat beef ez pizen, en he
ran down de hill en started bringin' de beef back. En w'en he brought hit all
back, he lef', en de partridge had all de beef.

5. The Rabbit and the Tortoise.[16]

I wan' to tell you one story 'bout de rabbit. De rabbit and de tortus had
a race. De tortus git a lot of tortuses and put 'em 'long de way. Ever now
and den a tortus crawl 'long de way, and de rabbit say, "How you now, Br'er
Tortus?"And he say, "Slo' and sho', but my legs very short." When dey git
tired, de tortus win 'cause he dere, but he never run the race, 'cause he had
tortuses strowed out all 'long the way. De tortus had other tortuses help him.

6. Same Old Thing.[17]

The niggers didn't go to the church building; the preacher came and preached
to them in their quarters. He'd just say, "Serve your masters. Don't steal
your master's turkey. Don't steal your master's chickens. Don't steal your
master's hogs. Don't steal your master's meat. Do whatsomever your master
tells you to do." Same old thing all the time.

7. Freedom.[18]

I been preachin' the Gospel and farmin' since slavery time. I jined the church
mos' 83 year ago when I was Major Gaud's slave and they baptises me in
the spring branch clost to where I finds the Lord. When I starts preachin'

15. Tennessee Narratives, Volume 15, Cecelia Chappel, age 102.
16. Texas Narratives, Volume 16, Reverend Lafayette Prince, age unknown.
17. Arkansas Narratives, Volume 2, Lucretia Alexander, age 89.
18. Texas Narratives, Volume 16, Anderson Edwards, age ca. 93.

I couldn't read or write and had to preach what massa told me and he say tell them niggers iffen they obeys the massa they goes to Heaven but I knowed there's something better for them, but daren't tell them 'cept on the sly. That I done lots. I tells 'em iffen they kepps prayin' the Lord will set 'em free.

8. Prayers.[19]

My master used to ask us chillun, "Do your folks pray at night?" We said "No," 'cause our folks had told us what to say. But the Lawd have mercy, there was plenty of that goin' on. They'd pray, "Lawd, deliver us from under bondage."

9. Buck Brasefield.[20]

Dey was pretty good to us, but ole Mr. Buck Brasefiel', what had a plantation 'jining us'n, was so mean to his'n that 'twan't nothin' for 'em to run away. One nigger Rich Parker, runned off one time an' whilst he gone he seed a hoodoo man, so when he got back Mr. Brasefiel' tuck sick an' stayed sick two or three weeks. Some of de darkies tole him, "Rich been to de hoodoo doctor." So Mr. Brasefiel' got up outten dat bed an' come a-yellin' in the fiel', "You thought you had ole Buck, but by God he rose agin." Dem niggers was so skeered, dey squatted in the fiel' jes' lack partridges, and some of 'em whispered, "I wish to God he had-a died."

10. Family Life Remembered.[21]

"My father was sold to another man for seventeen hundred dollars. My mother was sold for twenty hundred. I heard them say that so much that I never will forget it."

"I think my father's parents got beat to death in slavery. Grandfather on my mother's side was tied to a stump and whipped to death. He was double jointed and no two men could whip him. They wanted to whip him because he wouldn't work. That was what they would whip any one for."

19. Arkansas Narratives, Volume 2, Talitha Lewis, age 86.
20. Alabama Narratives, Volume 1, Jake Green, age 85.
21. Arkansas Narratives, Volume 2, Ishe Webb, age ca. 78.

11. Forbidden Knowledge.[22]

None of us was 'lowed to see a book or try to learn. Dey say we git smarter den dey was if we learn anything, but we slips around and gits hold of dat Webster's old blue back speller and we hides it 'til 'way in de night and den we lights a little pine torch, and studies that spellin' book. We learn it too. I can read some now and write a little too.

Dey wasn't no church for de slaves, but we goes to de white folks arbor on Sunday evenin' and a white man he gits up dere to preach to de niggers. He say, "Now I takes my text, which is, nigger obey your master and your mistress, 'cause what you git from dem here in dis world am all you ev'r goin' to git, 'cause you jes' like de hogs and de other animals—when you dies you ain't no more, after you been throwed in dat hole." I guess we believed dat for a while 'cause we didn' have no way findin' out different. We didn' see no Bibles.

12. Broken Families.[23]

I seen chillun sold off and de mammy not sold, and sometimes de mammy sold and a little baby kept on de place and given to another woman to raise. Dem white folks didn't care nothing 'bout how de slaves grieved when dey tore up a family.

13. Burning in Hell.[24]

We was scart of Solomon and his whip, though, and he didn't like frolickin'. He didn't like for us niggers to pray, either. We never heared of no church, but us have prayin' in the cabins. We'd set on the floor and pray with our heads down low and sing low, but if Solomon heared he'd come and beat on the wall with the stock of his whip. He'd say, "I'll come in there and tear the hide off you backs." But some the old niggers tell us we got to pray to Gawd that he don't think different of the blacks and the whites. I know that Solomon is burnin' in hell today, and it pleasures me to know it.

22. Texas Narratives, Volume 16, Jenny Procter, age ca. 87
23. Oklahoma Narratives, Volume 13, Katie Rowe, age 88.
24. Texas Narratives, Volume 16, Mary Reynolds, age ca. 100.

14. Marriage.[25]

After while I taken a notion to marry and massa and missy marries us same as all the niggers. They stands inside the house with a broom held crosswise of the door and we stands outside. Missy puts a li'l wreath on my head they kept there and we steps over the broom into the house. Now, that's all they was to the marryin'. After freedom I gits married and has it put in the book by a preacher.

Source 15 from Solomon Northup, *Twelve Years a Slave: Narrative of Solomon Northup, a Citizen of New-York, Kidnapped in Washington City in 1841, and Rescued in 1853, from a Cotton Plantation Near the Red River, in Louisiana* (Miller, Orton & Mulligan, 1853), pp. 109–115.

15. Excerpt from Solomon Northup, *Twelve Years a Slave.*

. . . As the day began to open, Tibeats came out of the house to where I was, hard at work. He seemed to be that morning even more morose and disagreeable than usual. He was my master, entitled by law to my flesh and blood, and to exercise over me such tyrannical control as his mean nature prompted; but there was no law that could prevent my looking upon him with intense contempt. I despised both his disposition and his intellect. I had just come round to the keg for a further supply of nails, as he reached the weaving-house.

"I though I told you to commence putting on weather-boards this morning," he remarked.

"Yes, master, and I am about it," I replied.

"Where?" he demanded.

"On the other side," was my answer.

He walked round to the other side, examined my work for a while, muttering to himself in a fault-finding tone.

"Didn't I tell you last night to get a keg of nails of Chapin?" he broke forth again.

"Yes, master, and so I did; and overseer said he would get another size for you, if you wanted them, when he came back from the field."

Tibeats walked to the keg, looked a moment at the contents, then kicked it violently. Coming towards me in a great passion, he exclaimed,

25. Texas Narratives, Volume 16, Mary Reynolds, age ca. 100.

"G—d d—n you! I thought you *knowed* something."

I made answer: "I tried to do as you told me, master. I didn't mean anything wrong. Overseer said— " But he interrupted me with such a flood of curses that I was unable to finish the sentence. At length he ran towards the house, and going to the piazza, took down one of the overseer's whips. The whip had a short wooden stock, braided over with leather, and was loaded at the butt. The lash was three feet long, or thereabouts, and made of raw-hide strands.

At first I was somewhat frightened, and my impulse was to run. There was no one about except Rachel, the cook, and Chapin's wife, and neither of them were to be seen. The rest were in the field. I knew he intended to whip me, and it was the first time any one had attempted it since my arrival at Avoyelles. I felt, moreover, that I had been faithful—that I was guilty of no wrong whatever, and deserved commendation rather than punishment. My fear changed to anger, and before he reached me I had made up my mind fully not to be whipped, let the result be life or death.

Winding the lash around his hand, and taking hold of the small end of the stock, he walked up to me, and with a malignant look, ordered me to strip.

"Master Tibeats," said I, looking him boldly in the face, "I will *not*." I was about to say something further in justification, but with concentrated vengeance, he sprang upon me, seizing me by the throat with one hand, raising the whip with the other, in the act of striking. Before the blow descended, however, I had caught him by the collar of the coat, and drawn him closely to me. Reaching down, I seized him by the ankle, and pushing him back with the other hand, he fell over on the ground. Putting one arm around his leg, and holding it to my breast, so that his head and shoulders only touched the ground, I placed my foot upon his neck. He was completely in my power. My blood was up. It seemed to course through my veins like fire. In the frenzy of my madness I snatched the whip from his hand. He struggled with all his power; swore that I should not live to see another day; and that he would tear out my heart. But his struggles and his threats were alike in vain. I cannot tell how many times I struck him. Blow after blow fell fast and heavy upon his wriggling form. At length he screamed— cried murder—and at last the blasphemous tyrant called on God for mercy. But he who had never shown mercy did not receive it. The stiff stock of the whip warped round his cringing body until my right arm ached.

Until this time I had been too busy to look about me. Desisting for a moment, I saw Mrs. Chapin looking from the window, and Rachel standing in the kitchen door. Their attitudes expressed the utmost excitement and alarm. His screams had been heard in the field. Chapin was coming as fast as he could ride. I struck him a blow or two more, then pushed him from me with such a well-directed kick that he went rolling over on the ground.

Rising to his feet, and brushing the dirt from his hair, he stood looking at me, pale with rage. We gazed at each other in silence. Not a word was uttered until Chapin galloped up to us.

"What is the matter?" he cried out.

"Master Tibeats wants to whip me for using the nails you gave me," I replied.

"What is the matter with the nails?" he inquired, turning to Tibeats.

Tibeats answered to the effect that they were too large, paying little heed, however, to Chapin's question, but still keeping his snakish eyes fastened maliciously on me.

"I am overseer here," Chapin began. "I told Platt to take them and use them, and if they were not of the proper size I would get others on returning from the field. It is not his fault. Besides, I shall furnish such nails as I please. I hope you will understand *that*, Mr. Tibeats."

Tibeats made no reply, but, grinding his teeth and shaking his fist, swore he would have satisfaction, and that it was not half over yet. Thereupon he walked away, followed by the overseer, and entered the house, the latter talking to him all the while in a suppressed tone, and with earnest gestures.

I remained where I was, doubting whether it was better to fly or abide the result, whatever it might be. Presently Tibeats came out of the house, and, saddling his horse, the only property he possessed besides myself, departed on the road to Chenyville.

When he was gone, Chapin came out, visibly excited, telling me not to stir, not to attempt to leave the plantation on any account whatever. He then went to the kitchen, and calling Rachel out, conversed with her some time. Coming back, he again charged me with great earnestness not to run, saying my master was a rascal; that he had left on no good errand, and that there might be trouble before night. But at all events, he insisted upon it, I must not stir.

As I stood there, feelings of unutterable agony overwhelmed me. I was conscious that I had subjected myself to unimaginable punishment. The reaction that followed my extreme ebullition of anger produced the most painful sensations of regret. An unfriended, helpless slave—what could I *do*, what could I *say*, to justify, in the remotest manner, the heinous act I had committed, of resenting a *white* man's contumely and abuse. I tried to pray—I tried to beseech my Heavenly Father to sustain me in my sore extremity, but emotion choked my utterance, and I could only bow my head upon my hands and weep. For at least an hour I remained in this situation, finding relief only in tears, when, looking up, I beheld Tibeats, accompanied by two horsemen, coming down the bayou. They rode into the yard, jumped from their horses, and approached me with large whips, one of them also carrying a coil of rope.

"Cross your hands," commanded Tibeats, with the addition of such a shuddering expression of blasphemy as is not decorous to repeat.

"You need not bind me, Master Tibeats, I am ready to go with you anywhere," said I.

One of his companions then stepped forward, swearing if I made the least resistance he would break my head—he would tear me limb from limb— he would cut my black throat—and giving wide scope to other similar expressions. Perceiving any importunity altogether vain, I crossed my hands, submitting humbly to whatever disposition they might please to make of me. Thereupon Tibeats tied my wrists, drawing the rope around them with his utmost strength. Then he bound my ankles in the same manner. In the meantime the other two had slipped a cord within my elbows, running it across my back, and tying it firmly. It was utterly impossible to move hand or foot. With a remaining piece of rope Tibeats made an awkward noose, and placed it about my neck.

"Now, then," inquired one of Tibeats' companions, "where shall we hang the nigger?"

One proposed such a limb, extending from the body of a peach tree, near the spot where we were standing. His comrade objected to it, alleging it would break, and proposed another. Finally they fixed upon the latter.

During this conversation, and all the time they were binding me, I uttered not a word. Overseer Chapin, during the progress of the scene, was walking hastily back and forth on the piazza. Rachel was crying by the kitchen door, and Mrs. Chapin was still looking from the window. Hope died within my heart. Surely my time had come. I should never behold the light of another day— never behold the faces of my children—the sweet anticipation I had cherished with such fondness. I should that hour struggle through the fearful agonies of death! None would mourn for me—none revenge me. Soon my form would be mouldering in that distant soil, or, perhaps, be cast to the slimy reptiles that filled the stagnant waters of the bayou! Tears flowed down my cheeks, but they only afforded a subject of insulting comment for my executioners. . . .

Source 16 from Linda Brent, *Incidents in the Life of a Slave Girl* (New York: Harcourt Brace Jovanovich, 1973).

16. Excerpts from Linda Brent (Harriet Jacobs), *Incidents in the Life of a Slave Girl*.

I wish I were more competent to the task I have undertaken. But I trust my readers will excuse deficiencies in consideration of circumstances. I was born and reared in Slavery; and I remained in a Slave State twenty-seven years. Since I have been at the North, it has been necessary for me to work diligently for my own support, and the education of my children. This has not left me much leisure to make up for the loss of early opportunities to improve myself; and it has compelled me to write these pages at irregular intervals, whenever I could snatch an hour from household duties. . . .

[Brent explains that she hopes her story will help northern women realize the suffering of southern slave women.]

I was born a slave; but I never knew it till six years of happy childhood had passed away. My father was a carpenter, and considered so intelligent and skilful in his trade, that, when buildings out of the common line were to be erected, he was sent for from long distances, to be head workman. On condition of paying his mistress two hundred dollars a year, and supporting himself, he was allowed to work at his trade, and manage his own affairs. His strongest wish was to purchase his children; but, though he several times offered his hard earnings for that purpose, he never succeeded. In complexion my parents were a light shade of brownish yellow, and were termed mulattoes. They lived together in a comfortable home; and, though we were all slaves, I was so fondly shielded that I never dreamed I was a piece of merchandise, trusted to them for safe keeping, and liable to be demanded of them at any moment. I had one brother, William, who was two years younger than myself—a bright, affectionate child. I had also a great treasure in my maternal grandmother, who was a remarkable woman in many respects. . . .

[When Linda Brent was six years old, her mother died, and a few years later the kind mistress to whom Brent's family belonged also died. In the will, Brent was bequeathed to the mistress's five-year-old niece, Miss Emily Flint. At the same time, Linda Brent's brother William was purchased by Dr. Flint, Emily's father.]

My grandmother's mistress had always promised her that, at her death, she would be free; and it was said that in her will she made good the promise.

But when the estate was settled, Dr. Flint told the faithful old servant that, under existing circumstances, it was necessary she should be sold. . . .

[Brent's grandmother, widely respected in the community, was put up for sale at a local auction.]

. . . Without saying a word, she quietly awaited her fate. No one bid for her. At last, a feeble voice said, "Fifty dollars." It came from a maiden lady, seventy years old, the sister of my grandmother's deceased mistress. She had lived forty years under the same roof with my grandmother; she knew how faithfully she had served her owners, and how cruelly she had been defrauded of her rights; and she resolved to protect her. The auctioneer waited for a higher bid; but her wishes were respected; no one bid above her. She could neither read nor write; and when the bill of sale was made out, she signed it with a cross. But what consequence was that, when she had a big heart overflowing with human kindness? She gave the old servant her freedom. . . .

During the first years of my service in Dr. Flint's family, I was accustomed to share some indulgences with the children of my mistress. Though this seemed to me no more than right, I was grateful for it, and tried to merit the kindness by the faithful discharge of my duties. But I now entered on my fifteenth year—a sad epoch in the life of a slave girl. My master began to whisper foul words in my ear. Young as I was, I could not remain ignorant of their import. I tried to treat them with indifference or contempt. The master's age, my extreme youth, and the fear that his conduct would be reported to my grandmother, made him bear this treatment for many months. He was a crafty man, and resorted to many means to accomplish his purposes. . . . The mistress, who ought to protect the helpless victim, has no other feelings towards her but those of jealousy and rage. . . . Even the little child, who is accustomed to wait on her mistress and her children, will learn, before she is twelve years old, why it is that her mistress hates such and such a one among the slaves. . . . She listens to violent outbreaks of jealous passion, and cannot help understanding what is the cause. She will become prematurely knowing in evil things. Soon she will learn to tremble when she hears her master's footfall. She will be compelled to realize that she is no longer a child. If God has bestowed beauty upon her, it will prove her greatest curse. That which commands admiration in the white woman only hastens the degradation of the female slave. . . .

[Afraid to tell her grandmother about Dr. Flint's advances, Brent kept silent. But Flint was enraged when he found out that Brent had fallen in love with a young, free, African American carpenter. The doctor redoubled his efforts to seduce Brent and told her terrible stories about what happened to slaves who tried to run away.]

For a long time, she was afraid to try to escape because of stories such as the one she recounts here.]

In my childhood I knew a valuable slave, named Charity, and loved her, as all children did. Her young mistress married, and took her to Louisiana. Her little boy, James, was sold to a good sort of master. He became involved in debt, and James was sold again to a wealthy slaveholder, noted for his cruelty. With this man he grew up to manhood, receiving the treatment of a dog. After a severe whipping, to save himself from further infliction of the lash, with which he was threatened, he took to the woods. He was in a most miserable condition—cut by the cowskin, half naked, half starved, and without the means of procuring a crust of bread.

Some weeks after his escape, he was captured, tied, and carried back to his master's plantation. This man considered punishment in his jail, on bread and water, after receiving hundreds of lashes, too mild for the poor slave's offence. Therefore he decided, after the overseer should have whipped him to his satisfaction, to have him placed between the screws of the cotton gin, to stay as long as he had been in the woods. This wretched creature was cut with the whip from his head to his feet, then washed with strong brine, to prevent the flesh from mortifying. . . . He was then put into the cotton gin, which was screwed down, only allowing him room to turn on his side when he could not lie on his back. Every morning a slave was sent with a piece of bread and bowl of water, which were placed within reach of the poor fellow. The slave was charged, under penalty of severe punishment, not to speak to him.

Four days passed, and the slave continued to carry the bread and water. On the second morning, he found the bread gone, but the water untouched. When he had been in the press four days and five nights, the slave informed his master that the water had not been used for four mornings, and that a horrible stench came from the gin house. The overseer was sent to examine into it. When the press was unscrewed, the dead body was found partly eaten by rats and vermin. . . .

[Dr. Flint's jealous wife watched his behavior very closely, so Flint decided to build a small cabin out in the woods for Brent, who was now sixteen years old. Still afraid to run away, she became desperate.]

And now, reader, I come to a period in my unhappy life, which I would gladly forget if I could. The remembrance fills me with sorrow and shame. . . . The influences of slavery had had the same effect on me that they had on other young girls; they had made me prematurely knowing, concerning the evil ways of the world. I knew what I did, and I did it with deliberate calculation. . . .

I have told you that Dr. Flint's persecutions and his wife's jealousy had given rise to some gossip in the neighborhood. Among others, it chanced that a white unmarried gentleman had obtained some knowledge of the circumstances in which I was placed. He knew my grandmother, and often spoke to me in the street. He became interested for me, and asked questions about my master, which I answered in part. He expressed a great deal of sympathy, and a wish to aid me. He constantly sought opportunities to see me, and wrote to me frequently. I was a poor slave girl, only fifteen years old.

So much attention from a superior person was, of course, flattering; for human nature is the same in all. I also felt grateful for his sympathy, and encouraged by his kind words. It seemed to me a great thing to have such a friend. By degrees, a more tender feeling crept into my heart. He was an educated and eloquent gentleman; too eloquent, alas, for the poor slave girl who trusted in him. Of course I saw whither all this was tending. I knew the impassable gulf between us; but to be an object of interest to a man who is not married, and who is not her master, is agreeable to the pride and feelings of a slave, if her miserable situation has left her any pride or sentiment. It seems less degrading to give one's self, than to submit to compulsion. There is something akin to freedom in having a lover who has no control over you, except that which he gains by kindness and attachment. A master may treat you as rudely as he pleases, and you dare not speak; moreover, the wrong does not seem so great with an unmarried man, as with one who has a wife to be made unhappy. There may be sophistry in all this; but the condition of a slave confuses all principles of morality, and, in fact, renders the practice of them impossible.

[Brent had two children, Benjy and Ellen, as a result of her relationship with Mr. Sands, the white "gentleman." Sands and Brent's grandmother tried to buy Brent, but Dr. Flint rejected all their offers. However, Sands was able (through a trick) to buy his two children and Brent's brother, William. After he was elected to Congress, Sands married a white woman. William escaped to the North, and Brent spent seven years hiding in the tiny attic of a shed attached to her grandmother's house. Finally, Brent and a friend escaped via ship to Philadelphia. She then went to New York City, where she found work as a nursemaid for a kind family, the Bruces, and was reunited with her two children. However, as a fugitive slave, she was not really safe, and she used to read the newspapers every day to see whether Dr. Flint or any of his relatives were visiting New York.]

But when summer came, the old feeling of insecurity haunted me. It was necessary for me to take little Mary[26] out daily, for exercise and fresh air, and

26. Mary was the Bruces' baby.

the city was swarming with Southerners, some of whom might recognize me. Hot weather brings out snakes and slaveholders, and I like one class of the venomous creatures as little as I do the other. What a comfort it is, to be free to *say* so! . . .

I kept close watch of the newspapers for arrivals; but one Saturday night, being much occupied, I forgot to examine the Evening Express as usual. I went down into the parlor for it, early in the morning, and found the boy about to kindle a fire with it. I took it from him and examined the list of arrivals. Reader, if you have never been a slave, you cannot imagine the acute sensation of suffering at my heart, when I read the names of Mr. and Mrs. Dodge, at a hotel in Courtland Street.[27] It was a third-rate hotel, and that circumstance convinced me of the truth of what I had heard, that they were short of funds and had need of my value, as *they* valued me; and that was by dollar and cents. I hastened with the paper to Mrs. Bruce. Her heart and hand were always open to every one in distress, and she always warmly sympathized with mine. It was impossible to tell how near the enemy was. He might have passed and repassed the house while we were sleeping. He might at that moment be waiting to pounce upon me if I ventured out of doors. I had never seen the husband of my young mistress, and therefore I could not distinguish him from any other stranger. A carriage was hastily ordered; and, closely veiled, I followed Mrs. Bruce, taking the baby again with me into exile. After various turnings and crossings, and returnings, the carriage stopped at the house of one of Mrs. Bruce's friends, where I was kindly received. Mrs. Bruce returned immediately, to instruct the domestics what to say if any one came to inquire for me.

It was lucky for me that the evening paper was not burned up before I had a chance to examine the list of arrivals. It was not long after Mrs. Bruce's return to her house, before several people came to inquire for me. One inquired for me, another asked for my daughter Ellen, and another said he had a letter from my grandmother, which he was requested to deliver in person.

They were told, "She *has* lived here, but she has left."

"How long ago?"

"I don't know, sir."

"Do you know where she went?" "I do not, sir." And the door was closed. . . .

[*Mrs. Bruce was finally able to buy Brent from Mr. Dodge, and she immediately gave Brent her freedom.*]

27. Emily Flint and her husband.

Reader, my story ends with freedom; not in the usual way, with marriage. I and my children are now free! We are as free from the power of slaveholders as are the white people of the north; and though that, according to my ideas, is not saying a great deal, it is a vast improvement in *my* condition. The dream of my life is not yet realized. I do not sit with my children in a home of my own. I still long for a hearthstone of my own, however humble. I wish it for my children's sake far more than for my own. But God so orders circumstances as to keep me with my friend Mrs. Bruce. Love, duty, gratitude, also bind me to her side. It is a privilege to serve her who pities my oppressed people, and who has bestowed the inestimable boon of freedom on me and my children. . . .

[Harriet Jacobs's story was published in 1861, and during the Civil War she did relief work with the newly freed slaves behind Union army lines. For several years after the war ended, she worked tirelessly in Georgia to organize orphanages, schools, and nursing homes. Finally, she returned to the North, where she died in 1897 at the age of eighty-four.]

Source 17 from John Thompson, *"The Life of John Thompson, a Fugitive Slave; Containing His History of 25 Years in Bondage, and His Providential Escape. Written by Himself"* (1856). Documenting the American South Project, 2000. Accessed online Nov. 21, 2009: http://docsouth.unc.edu/neh/thompson/thompson.html

17. Excerpts from John Thompson, *The Life of John Thompson, a Fugitive Slave.*

. . . My mistress and her family were all Episcopalians. The nearest church was five miles from our plantation, and there was no Methodist church nearer than ten miles. So we went to the Episcopal church, but always came home as we went, for the preaching was above our comprehension, so that we could understand but little that was said. But soon the Methodist religion was brought among us, and preached in a manner so plain that the way-faring man, though a fool, could not err therein.

This new doctrine produced great consternation among the slaveholders. It was something which they could not understand. It brought glad tidings to the poor bond-man; it bound up the broken-hearted it opened the prison doors to them that were bound, and let the captive go free.

As soon as it got among the slaves, it spread from plantation to plantation, until it reached ours, where there were but few who did not experience religion. The slaveholders, becoming much alarmed at this strange phenomenon, called a meeting, at which they appointed men to patrol the country, and break up these religious assemblies. This was done, and many a poor victim had his back severely cut, for simply going to a prayer meeting. . . .

. . . MR. W. was a very cruel slave driver. He would whip unreasonably and without cause. He was often from home, and not unfrequently three or four weeks at a time, leaving the plantation, at such times, in care of the overseer. When he returned, he sometimes ordered all the slaves to assemble at the house, when he would whip them all round; a little whipping being, as he thought, necessary, in order to secure the humble submission of the slaves.

Sometimes he forced one slave to flog another, the husband his wife; the mother her daughter; or the father his son. This practice seemed very amusing to himself and his children, especially to his son, John, who failed not to walk in his father's footsteps, by carrying into effect the same principle, until he became characteristically a tyrant.

When at home from school, he would frequently request his grandmother's permission, to call all the black children from their quarters to the house, to sweep and clear the yard from weeds, &c., in order that he might oversee them. Then, whip in hand, he walked about among them, and sometimes lashed the poor little creatures, who had on nothing but a shirt, and often nothing at all, until the blood streamed down their backs and limbs, apparently for no reason whatever, except to gratify his own cruel fancy.

This was pleasing to his father and grandmother, who, accordingly, considered him a very smart boy indeed! Often, my mother, after being in the field all day, upon returning at night, would find her little children's backs mangled by the lash of John Wagar, or his grandmother; for if any child dared to resist the boy, she would order the cook to lash it with a cowhide, kept for that purpose.

I well remember the tears of my poor mother, as they fell upon my back, while she was bathing and dressing my wounds. But there was no redress for her grievance, she had no appeal for justice, save to high heaven; for if she complained, her own back would be cut in a similar manner.

Sometimes she wept and sobbed all night, but her tears must be dried and her sobs hushed, ere the overseer's horn sounded, which it did at early dawn, lest they should betray her. And she, unrefreshed, must shake off her dull slumbers, and repair, at break of day, to the field, leaving her little ones to a similar, or perhaps, worse fate on the coming day, and dreading a renewal of her own sorrows the coming evening. Great God, what a, succession of crimes! Is there no balm in Gilead; is there no physician there, that thy people can be healed? . . .

. . . After I had learned to read, I was very fond of reading newspapers, when I could get them. One day in the year 1830, I picked up a piece of old newspaper containing the speech of J. Q. Adams, in the U. S. Senate, upon a petition of the ladies of Massachusetts, praying for the abolition of slavery in the District of Columbia. This I kept hid away for some months, and read it until it was so worn that I could scarce make out the letters.

While reading this speech, my heart leaped with joy. I spent many Sabbaths alone in the woods, meditating upon it. I then found out that there was a place where the negro was regarded as a man, and not as a brute; where he might enjoy the "inalienable right of life, liberty, and the pursuit of happiness"; and where he could walk unfettered throughout the length and breadth of the land.

These thoughts were constantly revolving in my mind, and I determined to see, ere long, the land from whence echoed that noble voice; where man acknowledged a difference between his brother man and a beast; and where I could "worship God under my own vine and fig tree, with none to molest or make afraid."

Little did Mr. Adams know, when he was uttering that speech, that he was "opening the eyes of the blind"; that he was breaking the iron bands from the limbs of one poor slave, and setting the captive free. But bread cast upon the waters, will be found and gathered after many days. . . .

. . . At the plantation where I lived two years previously, I became acquainted with three slaves, who had now determined to make an effort to gain their freedom, by starting for the free States. They came down to see me, and try to induce me to go with them, they intending to start in about three weeks; but they exacted from me a promise of secrecy in regard to the whole matter. I had not as yet fully made up my mind to make an attempt for my freedom, therefore did not give a positive promise to accompany them. I had known several, who, having made the attempt, had failed, been brought back, whipped, and then sold far to the South. Such considerations somewhat discouraged me from making the attempt.

As the time drew near for them to start, they came again to know my decision. I told them that I had consulted my mother, whose fears for my success were so great, that she had persuaded me not to go. These three friends were very religious persons, one of them being a Methodist preacher. He, in particular, urged me very strongly to accompany them, saying that he had full confidence in the surety of the promises of God, who had said that heaven and earth should pass away, before one jot of his word should fail; that he had often tried God, and never knew him to fail; consequently he believed he was able to carry him safely to the land of freedom, and accordingly he was determined to go. Still I was afraid to risk myself on such uncertain promises; I dared not trust an unseen God.

This visit to me was on Sunday, and they had planned to start the Saturday night following, and travel the next Sunday and Monday. It was not uncommon for slaves to go away on Saturday and not return until the following Tuesday, feigning sickness as an excuse, though this pretence not unfrequently subjected them to a flogging. So that very little alarm was felt for a slave's absence until Wednesday, unless his previous conduct had excited suspicion. . . . I well remember the evening of their departure. It was a beautiful night, the moon poured a flood of silver light, and the stars shone brilliantly upon their pathway, seeming like witness of God's presence, and an encouragement that he would guide them to their journey's end.

After they had gone, I began to regret that I had so much distrusted God, and had not accompanied them, and these regrets weighed so heavily upon my mind, that I could not rest day or night. . . .

Sources 18–21 are depositions and legal filings from "Freedom Suits Case Files, 1814–1860," Circuit Court Case Files, Office of Circuit Court Clerk-St. Louis, Missouri State Archives-St. Louis. Accessible online at http://stlcourtrecords.wustl.edu/about-freedom-suits-series.php.

18. John Singleton, November 1827, Case #23, p. 11.

State of Missouri
County of St. Louis
In the circuit court of St. Louis county, Novr. 1827 Term

John Singleton, a free man of color, complains of Alexander Scott and Robert Lewis of a plea of trespass; For that the said Alexander Scott and Robert Lewis, on the twenty seventh day of August, in the year of our Lord Eighteen hundred and twenty seven, with force and arms, made an assault in and upon the body of him the said John Singleton, to wit, at the county of St. Louis in the state of Missouri, and then & there beat, bruised and ill treated him the said John, and then and there imprisoned him the said John, and kept and detained him in prison for a long time, to wit, for the span and term of Eight days then next following, and still keeps and detains him in prison, without any reasonable or probable cause whatsoever, contrary to the laws of the land, and against the will of the said John, and other wrongs to the said John then and there did, against the peace and dignity of the state; And the said plaintiff owns, that before and at the time of the committing the said grievances he was and still is a free person, and that the said defendants then & there held and detained him, the plaintiff, &

still hold & detain him in slavery; wherefore the said plaintiff saith he is injured and hath sustained damages in the sum of five hundred dollars, and therefore he brings his suit, & c.

19. Nelly Richards, July 1831, Case #2, pp. 2 and 5.

To the Hon. Judge of the Circuit Court & of the Third Judicial Circuit,
Saint Louis County
State of Missouri

Your Petitioner, Nelly Richards represents to this Honourable Court that she was born in Charles County Maryland, lived there until she was fourteen years old the property of Kitty Middleton at whose death she was left free, after the death of Kitty Middleton her daughter sent the Petitioner to Virginia Fauquier County to William Sewel the Husband of Kitty Middleton's daughter, about four years since the said William Sewel moved with his Family to Indiana and the Town of Indianapolis, where your Petitioner was allowed freedom by the Judgment of the Court of that State, that after that the said Sewel removed your Petitioner to Louisville Kentucky and brought her from that place to the City of Saint Louis That your Petitioner is Twenty four years old.

Your Petitioner states that she is still held in slavery by the said William Sewel in the County of Saint Louis and State of Missouri where she is advised and believes that she is entitled to her freedom and therefore your petitioner prays that she may be permitted to sue in forma pauperis[28] to establish her right thereto and that such other and further orders may be made in the premises as the Law directs and as may seem meet and proper to this Hon. Court.

St. Louis County Circuit Court
of the Term of July 1831

State of Missouri
Saint Louis County

To wit Nelly Richards, a woman of colour, who by permission of the Court sues in forma paupiris, complains of William Sewel. For that on the first day of August in the Year 1830, the said William Sewel made an assault on the said Nelly Richards to wit, at the City within the County of Saint Louis and State of Missouri; and then

28. This is a Latin term, meaning in the form of a pauper. Before 1845, Missouri state law held that all people, regardless of income level, should have equal access to the courts. Judges could and routinely did waive court costs for individuals such as Nelly Richards. In 1845 the Missouri legislature ended this practice and required litigants to prove they could cover their own court costs. This was very much in line with the general pattern of making slavery even more restrictive in the 1840s and 1850s.

and there seized, and laid hold of the said Nelly Richards, and with great force and violence, pulled and dragged about her the said Nelly Richards, and then and there struck the said Nelly Richards a great many violent blows and strokes, and then and there imprisoned the said Nelly Richards, and kept and detained her in prison there without any reasonable or probable cause whatsoever for a long space of time to wit for the space of six Months then next following contrary to law and against the will of the said Nelly whereby she the said Nelly Richards was then and there not only greatly bruised and wounded but was thereby greatly exposed and her life endangered to wit at the City of Saint Louis aforesaid and within the said County And the said Nelly Richards avers that before and at the time of committing the said grievances she was & still is a Free Person and that the defendant William Sewel held and detained her, and still holds and detains her, in slavery to wit at the County of Saint Louis aforesaid, and other wrongs to the said Nelly Richards then and there did, against the peace of the State and to the damage of the said Nelly Richards of Five hundred dollars and therefore she brings suit.

20. Peter, November 1841, Case #84, pp. 2 and 4.

To the Honorable Bryan Mullanssky Judge of Circuit Court within and for the County of St. Louis and State of Missouri:

Respectfully represents and complains, your petitioner, Peter, a colored man, that he is held in slavery, unlawfully and against right as he believes, by John Richardson of the County of St. Louis, under the following circumstances.

In the Spring of the year 1833, he was the lawful slave of said Richardson, and was by him taken to Dubuque in the Territory of Iowa and there worked for his master in the business of mining, at or about said period. That he has remained in said place for a space of about Eight years, by and with the consent and direction of the said Richardson. That said Territory is a portion of the United States in which slavery is not allowed by the laws of the United States, and therefore your petitioner believes he is fully entitled to his freedom.

Wherefore he prays the Honorable Court, that an order may be granted, allowing the petitioner to sue in the Circuit Court of St. Louis County, as a poor person, to establish his right to freedom; that counsel may be assigned him; that he have reasonable liberty to attend his counsel and the Court, as occasion may require; that he be not removed out of the jurisdiction of the Court; and that he be not subjected to any severity on account of his application for freedom.

And as in duty bound will ever pray,
Peter

In St. Louis Circuit Court
November Term A.D. 1841

Peter (a colored man) vs. John Richardson   Trespass for false imprisonment

Peter, a colored man, plaintiff in this suit, by his Attorneys, complains of John Richardson defendant of a plea of trespass—

For that the defendant heretofore, to wit, on the first day of June in the year of our Lord one thousand eight hundred and thirty three, in Dubuque in the Territory of Iowa to wit in the County of St. Louis and State of Missouri, with force and arms made an assault on said plaintiff and then and there beat, bruised and ill-treated him, and then and there imprisoned him and kept him in prison without any reasonable or probable cause whatever for a long space of time, to wit for the space of one year then next following, contrary to the laws of the State of Missouri and against the will of the plaintiff, and other wrongs to the said plaintiff then and there did against the peace of the State of Missouri to the damage of the said plaintiff in the sum of One Thousand Dollars.

And the said plaintiff avers that before and at the time of the committing of the grievances aforesaid by the said defendant, the said plaintiff was and still is a free person, and that the defendant held and still holds him in slavery.

Wherefore he brings suit by his Attorneys,
J. Davis

21. George Johnson, November 1852, Case # 36, pp. 1, 3–4.

State of Missouri
County of St. Louis

St. Louis Circuit Court.
April Term. 1852.

To the Hon. Circuit Court of St. Louis County and State of Missouri, your petitioner George Johnson, humbly complaining, respectfully represents to your honorable Court that he is a free man of color, and that he is now claimed and held as a slave by one Henry Moore, a citizen of Missouri, who has now your petitioner confined in the trading yard of B. W. Lynch of this City, and he is not allowed to see his friends or counsel. Your petitioner further states the following to be the grounds on which his claim to freedom is founded:

To wit—that he was born of free colored parents in Fayette County in the State of Pennsylvania, and that he has remained free from his birth to the present time, never having owed service nor belonged to any person whatever.

Your petitioner further states that, he has resided a free man of color in the State of Missouri for the last eight years.

Your petitioner further states that, by reason of his said free birth by his free parents, he feels that he is entitled to his freedom, and prays the Court to permit him to sue, as a poor person, for his freedom, and, until such suits shall be decided, to allow him free access to his counsel and the Court, and to prevent him from being removed beyond the jurisdiction of this Court.

George Johnson a free man of color vs. Henry Moore

In the St. Louis Circuit Court
April Term 1852

George Johnson the Plff in the above entitled case states that he is a free man of color and as such entitled in law and equity to his freedom, that he was born in the county of Fayette in the State of Pennsylvania of free colored parents on or about the Eighth day of January in the year of our lord Eighteen hundred and twenty six which said state of Pennsylvania was on the day and year aforesaid a free state in which the institution of slavery did not exist by the laws of said state or by the laws of the Federal Government of the united states of America and at the time of Plff's birth his parents were free colored citizens of the state of Pennsylvania, and the Plff further states that by reason and virtue of his said birth and nativity in the state of Pennsylvania he is entitled to his freedom. Nevertheless the plff states that on or about the first day of May, 1841 he came to the state of Missouri and was on the Twenty sixth day of May in the year Eighteen hundred and fifty two forcibly seized and held in custody and close confinement by Henry Moore the defendant who claims the plff as his lawful slave and that the said deft has since the seizure of the Plff held him confined in the trading yard of B. W. Lynch a negro trader in the City of St. Louis, the Plff further states that before and at the time of the committing of the grievances by the deft he was and still is a free person and that the deft held and still holds him in slavery. He therefore prays the court to grant him Judgment of Liberation and declare him to be a free man.

George Johnson, by his attys
Nelson & Dedman

George Johnson being duly sworn states that the foregoing petition and the matters therein stated are true.

✦

Questions to Consider

The evidence in this chapter falls into three categories of accounts created by African Americans about slavery: interviews conducted in the 1930s with former slaves (sources 1–14); excerpts from published books written by Solomon Northup, Harriet Jacobs, and John Thompson (sources 15–17); claims presented by African American plaintiffs in freedom suits (sources 18–21).

Since the varied kinds of evidence also contain a number of subtopics, framing the documents around themes could be helpful. You might even find it useful to re-organize the materials according to theme. For example:

What mechanisms of control did slaveholders attempt to employ?
In what ways did African Americans directly resist enslavement?
In what ways did African Americans subtly challenge enslavement?
What role did religion play in the lives of enslaved African Americans?
What role did family and community play in the lives of enslaved African Americans?
How did gender shape perceptions and experiences of slavery?
How important was stage of life in shaping perceptions and experiences under slavery?
How important was place of residence?

Once you have a strong grasp of the themes directly discussed in the sources, begin to analyze the sources themselves. Think about what is unsaid. Particularly with the WPA interviews, but with the published memoirs, too, keep in mind the importance of historical memory. As you will know from our own lives, some experiences make a deep imprint that time cannot erase. At the same time, family stories can sometimes take on a life of their own, revealing emotional truths but distorting specifics. How did the passage of time and distance from the immediate experience of slavery likely shape recollections?

Reflect as well on the importance of audience. Jacobs, Northup, and Thompson wrote their autobiographies for northern readers in a critical period of national divisions over the future of slavery. Harriet Jacobs worked as an abolitionist, and she believed her writings would contribute to that political cause. Northup gave lectures before abolitionist audiences with a similar expectation. By no means does the anti-slavery commitment of any of these three writers invalidate their work. But historians should bear in mind when analyzing these sources that they were written with a particular audience in mind, which might shape what was told, how it got told, and what might have been left out of the story. Likewise, the depositions of African Americans suing in the courts addressed a particular audience and required a distinct kind of reporting on experiences with enslavers and understanding of the laws in both slave and free states.

You should also think about how place and time influenced resistance as well as the kinds of stories African Americans told about their experiences. The most obvious place to look for geographic variations is in the court depositions. One of the challenges before judges—and now before you—centered on sorting out when African Americans moved into free states or territories. Keep in mind with all of these sources which states these men and women lived in and what kinds of work they did, because both shaped opportunities for resisting slavery as well as obstacles to achieving freedom. African Americans in St. Louis, with legal access to federal courts, were in a much different position, for example, than individuals working on cotton plantations in rural Alabama. Furthermore, some of the plaintiffs were born into free black families while others gained their freedom over time

and by varied means. Compare, too, the accounts of John Thompson and Harriet Jacobs, who were enslaved from birth and fled North to escape, with Solomon Northup, who was born free in the North and kidnapped and carried South before escaping. And contrast the memories of slaves emancipated after Confederate defeat with those who fled or sued for their freedom. How do the writings and memories of individuals who successfully escaped slavery in the antebellum era compare with those emancipated after the Civil War?

As you work your way through the primary sources, reading closely and remaining attentive to such matters, you will see the many ways men and women challenged and resisted enslavement while also recognizing the lengths to which enslavers went to preserve their profitable and brutal "peculiar institution."

Epilogue

Even before the Civil War formally ended, thousands of African Americans began casting off the shackles of slavery. Some ran away to meet the advancing U.S. Army; after 1863, 200,000 black men enlisted in the U.S. military. African American soldiers represented nearly 10 percent of the nation's fighting forces. Casualties were high—roughly one-third of the African American soldiers who saw action were wounded or killed—and

their desertion rate was lower than the U.S. Army as a whole. Twenty-one African Americans won the Congressional Medal of Honor for heroic service during the Civil War. As men took to the battlefield, many families migrated into cities, where they hoped to find work and new opportunities. Others stayed on the land, expecting to become free-holding farmers. At the end of the war, African Americans quickly established their own churches, independent of the racist preaching that marked antebellum services. Knowing the power of education in preserving freedom and autonomy, adults joined children in enrolling in schools they established in partnership with the Freedmen's Bureau. And for decades, African Americans searched for lost kin, seeking reunions with spouses, children, and siblings long sold away.

Generations of white southerners had dreaded the violence they predicted would accompany black liberation: that fear lay behind their reactions to uprisings like the thwarted rebellion in Richmond, Virginia, in 1800. As it turned out, African Americans did not seek revenge against their white enslavers. They wanted a new start and an equal stake in the country they had built by their labor and sacrifices.

Reconstruction, achieved through military occupation of the rebellious states, temporarily addressed many of the former slaves' ambitions—particularly those of African American men. Ratification of three Constitutional Amendments guaranteed a permanent end to slavery, equal protection under the law for all citizens, and voting rights. As a result, black men participated in politics and served in Reconstruction governments. African American delegates to the South Carolina state legislature outnumbered whites, and Blanche Bruce and Hiram Revels, both African American men, represented Mississippi in the U.S. Senate.

In 1865, Massachusetts senator Charles Sumner proposed that the federal government confiscate the land of former slaveholding planters and distribute it to former slaves. Sumner was hardly alone in recognizing the consequence of independent landholding for African American families. The idea of reparations seemed not only just but also in the long-term best interest of the nation, for it would have fostered more economic opportunity and equality and therefore encouraged more social and political stability. But the U.S. Congress rejected the idea of reparations, and that choice left most southern blacks without the wherewithal to achieve economic independence. Former enslavers kept their land and with it their control over the southern economy. Without their own land, African Americans, alongside poor whites, soon found themselves forced into sharecropping for the old planter class. The system was corrupt and exploitative. By the late 1870s, the Ku Klux Klan, working as a paramilitary wing of the Democratic Party in the South, ushered in a period of racial terrorism and swept out the Republican Reconstruction state governments. This "Redemption" of the South was marked by systemic racial violence, "Jim Crow" segregation laws, and the persistence of a cotton-based economy—all of which led to pervasive black disfranchisement and poverty. Nearly a hundred years would pass before the unfinished revolution of securing African American rights was resurrected by a cohort of southern ministers led by Dr. Martin Luther King, Jr.

Fueled by the Civil Rights Movement of the 1950s and 1960s, scholars began to explore African American history, using not only print sources like the ones you read in this chapter but also folk music, religious practices, oral traditions, and artifacts. This rich diversity of sources inspired scholars to undertake new approaches to engaging evidence: anthropological methods, for example, and theoretical frameworks. As a result, historians have been able to reconstruct the lives and thoughts of people once considered unknowable. Their innovative approaches to scholarship influenced the methods and evidence used by historians in many other subfields, broadening and enriching the discipline of history.

Caring for the Sick and Wounded: Female Nurses in the American Civil War

The Problem

Two days following the surrender of Fort Sumter after a thirty-three-hour Confederate bombardment, President Abraham Lincoln called 75,000 militiamen into national service for ninety days to put down an insurrection "too powerful to be suppressed by the ordinary course of judicial proceedings." Along with Lincoln, most Americans in the North and South believed the military actions would be quick and relatively bloodless.[1]

As General-in-Chief of the Union Army, Gen. Winfield Scott, a veteran of both the War of 1812 and the Mexican-American War, vigorously opposed what he considered the rash decision of sending raw and untrained militiamen into immediate action. But Scott could not hold back the popular and political onslaught. For one thing,

Americans' conception of warfare was romantic and glamorous. Second, many in the North believed that a quick, effective strike would bring southern Unionists out into the open and cause the new Confederate government (that had just moved to Richmond) to collapse. Finally, Union regiments were piling up in Baltimore and Washington, and with little or nothing to do would misbehave *en masse*. One member of the 75th New York Regiment lamented that "tonight not 200 men are in camp. Capt. Catlin, Capt. Hurburt, Lt. Cooper, and one or two other officers are under arrest. A hundred men are drunk, a hundred more at houses of prostitution." Thus Gen. Scott was overruled and President Lincoln approved a Union attack into Virginia, and on July 16 a Union force of a hastily assembled and amateur army of around 34,000 men under Gen. Irwin McDowell (who had never led troops in battle) marched out of Washington and toward Manassas Junction in Virginia.

1. For President Lincoln's proclamation, see Roy P. Basler, ed., *The Collected Works of Abraham Lincoln* (New Brunswick, NJ: Rutgers University Press, 1953), vol. 4, pp. 331–332.

"You are green, it is true," confessed the President to one of the generals, "but they are green also; you are all green alike."[2]

What was intended by the Union to be the battle that would break the rebels' spirit instead turned into a chaotic rout of green Federal troops who suffered what people at the time thought was an appalling 2,645 casualties against the Confederates' 1,981. In New York, Mrs. Maria Lydig Daly (1824–1894), a strong Union supporter, mourned in her diary, "Never in my life did I feel as badly as when I saw this fearful, disgraceful news. . . . It will prolong the war another year, if not three. . . ." Indeed, what most northerners thought would be a ninety days' war ultimately turned out to be even longer than Maria Daly feared.[3]

No one could have predicted the terrible toll that the four-year war would have on both the North and the South. The number of sick and wounded soldiers forced both the Union and the Confederacy to construct hospitals or appropriate older buildings for that purpose. Although they first resisted using women as nurses (relying instead on soldiers unfit for duty), both were forced to recruit women to serve in the Civil War hospitals. At first, men were convinced that women would not volunteer for what would be very difficult and grisly work, but both sides were surprised when probably more than 10,000 women came forth to answer the call (undoubtedly several applicants were rejected). They came from all walks of life, almost all of them untrained. Not a few of these female nurses knew of the courageous service of British nurse Florence Nightingale's work in the Crimean War of 1853–1856. Her book *Notes on Nursing* was published in the United States in 1860 and was avidly read by many women on both sides.[4]

Your task in this chapter is twofold. By reading and analyzing the first-person accounts of Union and Confederate nurses in the Evidence section of this chapter, answer the following two questions: **How did women in Civil War hospitals change the popular notions of American nursing and of American women themselves? In what ways did nursing change**

2. For popular opinion and political pressure on Scott, see James M. McPherson, *Battle Cry of Freedom: The Civil War Era* (New York: Oxford University Press, 1988), pp. 333–335. For the popular conception of warfare, the behavior of the 75th New York Regiment, and Lincoln's comment on green soldiers, see *ibid.,* pp. 329, 332, 336.
3. For Union and Confederate casualties, see Stewart Brooks, *Civil War Medicine* (Springfield, IL: Charles C. Thomas, 1966), p 132. For Daly's doleful prediction, see Maria Lydig Daly, *Diary of a Union Lady, 1861–1865,* ed. Harold Earl Hammond (New York: Funk and Wagnalls, 1962), p. 39. For his part, Gen. McDowell reported that the "larger part of the men are a confused mob, entirely demoralized." Bruce Catton, *The Coming Fury,* vol. 1 in *The Centennial History of the Civil War* (Garden City, NY: Doubleday, 1961), p. 463.

4. Although Lincoln used the term "civil war" in his Gettysburg Address, most northerners referred to the conflict as the "War of Rebellion," while southerners called it the "War Between the States." The term "Civil War" was adopted later. For Florence Nightingale's influence, see Jane E. Schultz, *Women at the Front: Hospital Workers in Civil War America* (Chapel Hill: Univ. of North Carolina Press, 2004), pp. 47, 50, 54, 169–170: Drew Gilpin Faust, *Mothers of Invention: Women of the Slaveholding South in the American Civil War* (Chapel Hill: Univ. of North Carolina Press, 1996), p. 92.

◆ CHAPTER 10

Caring for the Sick
and Wounded:
Female Nurses
in the American
Civil War

those women who took up the challenge?

Some of the women who volunteered as nurses became well-known to later generations: author Louisa May Alcott (*Little Women*, 1868 & 1869), founder of the American Red Cross Clara Barton, heroine of the Underground Railroad Harriet Tubman, abolitionist Sojourner Truth, philanthropist Sally Louisa Tompkins, and others. And yet, even as most of the several thousand nurses who labored in Civil War hospitals have been forgotten, in their own time they were revered by the men and boys they served and who never forgot them.

◆

Background

By the nineteenth century, the United States was the least militarized of all Western societies. For the most part, the nation's foes were small and generally weak—Native American tribes and their confederacies, a mere fraction of the British armed forces, and the disorganized and anemic Mexican army. In Europe, however, the emergence of absolute monarchies in the seventeenth and eighteenth centuries required comparatively enormous standing armies to centralize political and economic authority, expand the kingdoms into genuine nation-states, and check the power of the regional nobles. By the 1630s, the Spanish armies numbered 300,000, while in France Louis XIV needed over 400,000 to dominate Europe. And by 1812, the self-crowned Emperor of France Napoleon Bonaparte had assembled a French army of 880,000, roughly 630,000 of whom invaded Russia, the largest force Europe had ever seen.[5]

Napoleon was able to accomplish this because he had sown the seeds of *nationalism* in France, a contagious germ that he carried into many of the regions he conquered. Mercenary soldiers were abandoned in favor of citizen armies who fought for their country, not their monarch or their regional nobleman. Uniforms were introduced to bind the warriors together, and the civilian populations became participants in what might have been called "total war" for "their" nation. Perhaps the person who best expressed this was French army officer Lazare Carnot

---

5. For absolutism, see Jacques Barzun, *From Dawn to Decadence: 1500 to the Present, 500*

Years of Western Cultural Life (New York: Harper Collins, 2000), part II, chapter 10, pp. 239–259; Merry E. Wiesner, et al. *Discovering the Western Past: A Look at the Evidence* (Stamford, CT: Cengage Learning, 2008), vol. 2, chapter 3. Of the roughly 630,000 who invaded Russia, 400,000 died of battle casualties, starvation, and exposure, and 200,000 were taken prisoner. It was the end of what was called the "Grand Army." For the Grand Army, see John Keegan, *A History of Warfare* (New York: Knopf, 1993), p. 352; John Keegan and Richard Holmes, *Soldiers: A History of Men in Battle* (New York: Viking Penguin, 1985), p. 227.

(1753–1823), who drafted the French Act of August 23, 1793:

> From now until the enemy has been harried out of the land, all young men will fight. Married men will forge arms and cart supplies, women will make tents and help in hospitals. Nobody will hire substitutes. Civil servants will remain at their posts. Male citizens aged 18 to 25 who are single and childless will march first.[6]

Thus, in some ways absolutist European nations were harbingers of things to come across the ocean.

For their part, however, since colonial times Americans had been suspicious of large standing armies, forces that could create tyrannies and act to take away the people's "natural rights." In America's War of Independence, in 1778 Gen. George Washington's Continental Army numbered only 16,782 men, and was the largest body of regular troops ever assembled under the American banner. And as late as early 1861, the U.S. army numbered only around 16,000, most of them stationed in Indian territory. Not surprisingly, casualties were light. In the War of 1812, Americans suffered only 5,877 casualties and some years later in the Mexican-American War the total casualties were 12,876.[7]

In place of a standing army, Americans preferred a militia of citizens who could be called out from their farms and shops to protect communities, a state, or later a nation. As states rewrote their constitutions during and immediately after the War for Independence, every state constitution prohibited peacetime standing armies and asserted the need to preserve citizen control of the military. Thus, soon after the ratification of the new U.S. Constitution in 1788, a series of amendments were enacted, one of which stated that "A well regulated Militia being necessary to the society of a free State, the right of the people to keep and bear Arms, shall not be infringed." Even so, over the years the musters and drills of the state militias became more social than military events. And when militias were called out, often they were worse than ineffective.[8]

By Manassas Junction, however, it was clear to both Union and Confederate leaders that Napoleon-type massive citizen armies would be needed, and needed over an extended period of time, to crush their opponents. And while on the surface it would appear that almost all the statistical

---

6. For Carnot, see Barzun, *From Dawn to Decadence,* pp. 434–435.

7. For Washington's Continental Army, see Christopher Ward, *The War of the Revolution* (NY: Macmillan Co., 1952), vol. 2, p. 594. For the size of the U.S. Army in 1861, see John Keegan, *The American Civil War: A Military History* (New York: Alfred A. Knopf, 2009), p. 39. For the War of 1812 and Mexican-American War casualties, see Richard B. Morris, ed., *Encyclopedia of American History*

(NY: Harper & Brothers, 1961 ed.) pp. 152 & 208. At the siege of Yorktown in late 1781, Lord Cornwallis's British army of around 8,000 faced a combined force of 8,845 American and 7,800 French rank and file. Ward, *War of the Revolution,* vol. 2, pp. 886–887.

8. For an excellent discussion of the Second Amendment to the Constitution, see Saul Cornell, ed., *Whose Right to Bear Arms Did the Second Amendment Protect?* (Boston: Bedford/St. Martin's, 2000), esp. pp. 9–16. For one example of the militia in battle, see Walter R. Borneman, *1812: The War That Forged a Nation* (New York: Harper Collins, 2004), pp. 74–75.

◆ CHAPTER 10

Caring for the Sick
and Wounded:
Female Nurses
in the American
Civil War

advantages favored the Union (population, industrial output, naval strength, banking capital, railroad mileage, etc.), the South also had certain assets that, if used wisely, might well even the odds. Perhaps the most important was the geographical and psychological advantages of fighting a *defensive* war over a very large terrain (750,000 square miles). If the South's military leadership, that many contemporaries believed was superior to that of the North, could make use of that asset, then the Confederacy would not actually have to *win* the conflict but instead only fight on until the Union, politically divided as it was, might simply give up and allow the Confederacy to secede in peace. Finally, the South's "cotton diplomacy" might cause both England and France to recognize the Confederacy as a legitimate nation and offer crucial economic, naval, and even military aid. In that way, the Confederacy hopefully could imitate many of the advantages of the Patriots in their own War for Independence to which they often compared themselves. Thus, as Confederate General P.G.T. Beauregard claimed, "No people ever warred for independence with more relative advantages than the Confederacy. . . ." And so the war must be fought, with massive European-style armies on battlefields often soaked in the blood of both sides.[9]

Therefore, the Union and the Confederacy undertook to fight what turned out to be the "largest and longest war of the nineteenth century," engaging each other in 2,196 separate battles in which "huge armies faced each other, firing as they advanced until one or the other gave ground." Mobile artillery often left gaping holes in the ranks and cavalry attacks often rolled up infantry flanks or terrorized the rank and file. For their part, the infantry often used muskets that fired minie balls—rifle bullets designed with hollow bases that expanded when fired, causing terrible, often fatal wounds.[10]

As one might expect, the number of casualties was horrifying. Recent research by historian J. David Hacker has shown that the number of deaths caused by battles and diseases has been underestimated by approximately twenty percent. He has estimated that the total deaths for both sides were close to 761,000, 58 percent of which were Union deaths and 42 percent were Confederate deaths. That statistic would mean that roughly "one in ten northern white men of military age in 1860 died as a result of the war and 200,000 white women were widowed." In her superb book, *This Republic of Suffering: Death*

9. For comparative advantages, see David Donald, ed., *Why the North Won the Civil War* (Baton Rouge: Louisiana State University Press, 1960) and Emory M. Thomas *The Confederacy as a Revolutionary Experience* (Columbia: University of South Carolina Press, 1971). For Beauregard's comment, see Richard N. Current, "God and the Strongest

Battalions," in *Why the North Won the Civil War*, p. 5.

10. For the "largest and longest" claim, see Keegan and Holmes, *Soldiers*, p. 94. For infantry tactics, see Keegan, *A History of Warfare*, p. 352; Philip A. Kalisch and Beatrice J. Kalisch, *The Advance of American Nursing* (Boston: Little, Brown and Co., 2nd ed. 1986), pp. 54–55. For the minie ball (invented by French army officer Claude Etienne Minié), see Sister Mary Denis Maher, *To Bind Up the Wounds: Catholic Sister Nurses in the U.S. Civil War* (New York: Greenwood, 1989), p. 46.

and the *American Civil War* (2008), historian Drew Gilpin Faust has shown that the appalling number of fatalities profoundly changed the ways in which Americans viewed and dealt with death.[11]

While the number of battle deaths was appalling, the numbers of sick and wounded were *over twice* the totals of those killed in battle or died of disease. Living in close proximity, Union and Confederate soldiers suffered from typhoid, diarrhea, dysentery, measles, and other communicable diseases. In a letter to his mother, one New York soldier suffering from diarrhea claimed that "within the last few days I have passed everything through me except my hat." Earlier, during the summer of 1861, 8,617 soldiers of the Confederate Army of the Potomac (one in seven) suffered from measles while 650 of the Third Tennessee Regiment's 1,000 soldiers had the same malady. And a few months before that, the Louisiana Seventh Regiment reported that 645 of the 920 soldiers suffered from illnesses that made them unfit for combat.[12]

Indeed, it is clear that medical officers of both sides were almost totally unprepared to deal with the flood of sick and wounded. Writing at the end of the war, U.S. Surgeon General Dr. William Hammond stated that the Civil War "was fought at the end of the medical Middle Ages." Agreeing with Hammond, a former Confederate physician lamented, "We did not do the best we would, but the best we could."[13]

As for surgeons, both Union (12,000) and Confederate (3,236) surgeons for the most part were poorly trained, had almost never treated a bullet wound and did not know about wound infections, were unfamiliar with anesthetics (Union surgeons used *over one million gallons of whiskey*), and had never performed an amputation (Union surgeons performed over 29,000). Almost none were licensed, as most states did not require state approval to practice medicine. In Cincinnati, Ohio, Joseph Buchanan of the Eclectic Medical Institute sold literally hundreds of medical diplomas by mail.[14]

---

11. See J. David Hacker, "A Census-Based Account of the Civil War Dead," in *Civil War History*, vol. 57 (2011), pp. 307–348. The number of deaths (441,380 for the Union and 370,000 for the Confederacy) was computed by the author using the same percentages used earlier by those who estimated the total deaths as around 620,000. If anything, Confederate deaths were undercounted due to destruction of records and purposeful undercounting to maintain morale in the last years of the war.
12. For diseases, see Kalisch and Kalisch, *The Advance of American Nursing*, p. 58. For measles in Confederate ranks, see Nancy Schurr, "Inside the Confederate Hospital: Community and Conflict During the Civil War" (Unpub. Ph.D. diss., University of Tennessee, 2004), p. 1. For the 7th Louisiana, see Terry L. Jones, "Brother Against Microbe," in *New York Times,* October 26, 2012. For the

New York soldier, see Margaret Humphreys, *Marrow of Tragedy: The Health Crisis of the American Civil War* (Baltimore: The Johns Hopkins Univ. Press, 2013), p. 27. For spreading diseases, drinking cups were passed from soldier to soldier (the drinking straw was not invented until 1888). See *ibid.,* p. 9.
13. For Hammond's claim, see *The Smithsonian Civil War: A Visual History* (Washington: Smithsonian Institution, 2011), p. 205. For the southern physician, see Jones, "Brother Against Microbe."
14. For the number of surgeons, see Glenna R. Schroeder-Lein, *Encyclopedia of Civil War Medicine* (Armonk, N.Y.: M.E. Sharpe, 2008), p. 220. On bullet wounds, 94 percent of all wounds were caused by minie balls. See Maher, *To Bind Up the Wounds,* p. 46. For whiskey, see *ibid.,* p. 48 and Humphreys, *Marrow of Tragedy,* p. 26. For Union amputations, see Stewart T. Brooks,

✦ CHAPTER 10

Caring for the Sick
and Wounded:
Female Nurses
in the American
Civil War

Before the Civil War, almost every sick or wounded person was treated at home. As for hospitals, they were generally avoided, as they were viewed as *lazarettos* (places for people with infectious diseases) or as combinations of prisons, poorhouses, and places to shut up immoral people. But the enormous numbers of sick and wounded required the establishment of places where people could be treated in order to send them back to the front. By the end of the war, there were 204 Union hospitals and 150 Confederate hospitals, around 30 of them in Richmond alone. Some were small, like the Robertson Hospital in Richmond with 20 beds while others were large, like the Chimborazo Hospital with places for approximately 4,000 and which treated around 75,000 during the war. Desertions were problems at almost all the hospitals and guards were posted to deal with drunkards, fights, and deserters. And since few people were familiar with French scientist Louis Pasteur's germ theory, probably as many men contracted illnesses in the hospitals as were those who were cured of them.[15]

At the beginning of the war, almost all the nurses were males: convalescing soldiers, invalids, or others unfit to serve, and the care they provided was minimal. Some were better, as was journalist and poet Walt Whitman, who years later wrote a series of newspaper columns that later were collected into a book. But the desperate need for nurses forced the Union and later the Confederacy to enlist female volunteers. In 1861, the U.S. Sanitary Commission turned to internationally known reformer Dorothea Dix to recruit female nurses. And in spite of the fact that before the war female nurses were regarded as "individuals of the lower classes," women of all stations eagerly volunteered to serve. In her criteria for admission as nurses, Dix required that the applicant "must be over thirty years of age, plain looking [so as to avoid men's advances], dressed in brown or black without ornaments of any sort, and be in strong health and excellent personal habits, persons of experience, good conduct, neatness, sobriety, and industry." Under Dix's direction, the Sanitary Commission recruited and admitted 3,214. Many contemporaries observed that Dix was not easy to get along with. Cornelia Hancock, a nurse, said that Dix "is a self-sealing can of horror tied up with a red tape" and Maria Lydig Daly, a New York Unionist, said she was "a deaf and despotic maiden of uncertain age." Difficult she may have been, but effective she doubtless was.[16]

Civil War Medicine (Springfield, IL: Charles C. Thomas, 1966), p. 127. On the selling of diplomas, see W.F. Bynum, *et al., The Western Medical Tradition* (Cambridge: Cambridge Univ. Press, 2006), p. 214.

15. For desertions, see Humphreys, *Marrow of Tragedy,* pp 23, 269. For guards see *ibid.*, p. 269. For Pasteur, see Bynum, *The Western Medical Tradition*, pp. 104, 125.

16. For Whitman's collected columns, see the moving *Memoranda During the War*, ed., Peter Coviello (New York: Oxford University Press, 2004). For Dix, see Kalisch and Kalisch, *The Advance of American Nursing*, pp. 56–57, Brooks, *Civil War Medicine*, p. 54, and Deborah Judd and Kathleen Sitzman, *A History of American Nursing* (Burlington, MA: Jones and Bartlett, 2nd ed., 2014), pp. 97–100. For unkind views of Dix, see Cornelia Hancock, *South After Gettysburg: Letters of Cornelia Hancock from the Army of the Potomac, 1863–1865* (Philadelphia: University of Pennsylvania Press, 1937), p. 131. *Diary of a Union*

At first, most of the surgeons opposed female nurses in "their" hospitals, citing their almost universal lack of training and the fact that they were "too delicate" to withstand the rigors of hospital work. For his part, Confederate physician William Owen ordered that "no more women or flies to be admitted into the Confederate Hospital in Lynchburg, Virginia." On the Union side, according to one Federal matron, "Many surgeons . . . were determined by a systematic course of ill-treatment toward women to drive them from the service." But, as you will see as you read selections from their memoirs or letters, female nurses generally performed well and offered services that the vast majority of male nurses either could not or would not do.[17]

The Method

Of the approximately 10,000 female nurses who served in the Union and Confederate armies or hospitals (9,000 Union, 1,000 Confederate), only 347 women wrote accounts of their work and only 69 of those accounts were published as books. To be sure, nurses' exploits also appeared in veterans' war memories. Even so, we cannot be sure how typical the nurses' or veterans' accounts actually were.[18]

Of those nurses who did write accounts, most of them seem to have been aware of the popular conception of hospital nursing as "appropriate only for individuals of the lower classes." At the same time, nurses also confronted the general image of "female delicacy" that should discourage women from this grim work. As you will see, many of the nurses' memoirs were written to challenge both these stereotypes.[19]

It is possible that some of the nurses would not have written about their experiences if they hadn't been contacted by professional publishers. Others, however, were eager to tell of the patriotic service that had been rendered by themselves and their sisters. And still others, like the Confederate nurse Kate Cumming, hoped to make some money to recoup their diminished fortunes. Almost none, however, made much money from their accounts, the most

Lady, ed. Harold Earl Hammond (New York: Funk and Wagnalls, 1962), p. 72.
17. It is true that the vast majority of nurses were barely trained, but significant exceptions were the Roman Catholic Sisters who were both trained and well-organized. At least 617 Sisters served in either Union or Confederate hospitals. See Maher, *To Bind Up the Wounds,* p. 70. for Owen's nasty order, see Schurr, "Inside the Confederate Hospital," p. 61. For the myth of "female delicacy," see Livinia L. Dock and Isabel Maitland Stewart, *A Short History of Nursing, From the Earliest Times to the Present Day* (New York: G.P. Putnam's Sons, 1920), p. 117. For the charge of one Federal matron, see Brooks, *Civil War Medicine,* p. 54.
18. For these statistics, see Shultz, *Women at the Front,* pp. 220, 232–237.

19. For these stereotypes, see Faust, *Mothers of Invention,* pp. 92–93; Dock and Stewart, *A Short History of Nursing,* p. 117.

◆ CHAPTER 10

Caring for the Sick
and Wounded:
Female Nurses
in the American
Civil War

dramatic exception being Sarah Emma Edmonds (1841–1898), whose volume *Nurse and Spy in the Union Army* sold approximately 175,000 copies and was still in print in 1900. Several people accused Edmonds of writing fiction in order to become wealthy, a charge she vehemently denied.[20]

Remember that your assignment in this chapter is to (1) determine the ways in which women nurses on Civil War battlefields and in hospitals changed the popular notions of American nursing and of American women themselves and (2) understand the ways in which nursing changed those women who took up the challenge. As you read each of the ten selections by nurses, keep that dual task in mind. It would be very helpful if you made a chart to organize and recall the points the nurses made.

After you analyze the ten nurses' selections and complete your chart, use your chart to offer some generalizations concerning both parts of the assignment. In some cases, you will have to read between the lines to see how each selection can be used to complete the two parts of the assignment.

As you have seen, each selection also contains a *great deal more* information to answer some other question you may want to answer. For example:

1. How does each selection show a *change* in the author over the time she served?
2. How did each nurse deal with male medical personnel (patients, surgeons, stewards, etc.)?
3. What were the nurses' views of African Americans (soldiers, hospital workers, freedmen and women, etc.)?
4. Were there any other opinions or observations that you think are important enough to mention?

Take notes on questions 1 through 4 *and* any other questions you have asked and use column 4 in your chart for these.

Finally, Source 11 is a song that was extremely popular among both Union and Confederate soldiers. That song could be called an obvious example of *Romanticism*. How would you define that term? Does that song tell you anything about soldiers and the nurses who cared for them? Explain.

Name	Ways in which women nurses in the Civil War helped to change the stereotypes of the American nurses	Ways in which nursing changed those women who worked on battlefields and in hospitals	Other important observations found in the nurses' accounts

20. See Schultz, *Women at the Front*, p. 227, and Elizabeth D. Leonard's introduction to a new edition of the book titled *Memoirs of a Soldier, Nurse, and Spy: A Woman's Adventure in the Union Army* (DeKalb, IL: Northern Illinois Univ. Press, 1999), xiii–xxii.

The Evidence

Source 1 from L[ouisa] M[ay] Alcott, *Hospital Sketches* (Boston: James Redpath, 1863), pp. 1–2, 31–32, 55–61, 91–92.[21]

1. Louisa May Alcott's *Hospital Sketches*

"I want something to do."

This remark being addressed to the world in general, no one in particular felt it their duty to reply; so I repeated it to the smaller world about me, received the following suggestions, and settled the matter by answering my own inquiry, as people are apt to do when very much in earnest.

"Write a book," quoth the author of my being.

"Don't know enough, sir. First live, then write."

"No thank you, ma'am, ten years of that is enough."

"Take a husband like my Darby, and fulfil your mission," said sister Joan, home on a visit.

"Can't afford expensive luxuries, Mrs. Coobiddy."

"Turn actress, and immortalize your name," said sister Vashti, striking an attitude.

"I won't."

"Go nurse the soldiers," said my young brother, Tom, panting for "the tented field."

"I will."

So far, very good. Here was the will—now for the way. . . .

"They've come! they've come! hurry up, ladies—you're wanted."

"Who have come? the rebels?"

This sudden summons in the gray dawn was somewhat startling to a three days' nurse like myself, and, as the thundering knock came at our door, I sprang up in my bed, prepared

"To gird my woman's form,
And on the ramparts die."

if necessary, but my room-mate took it more coolly, and, as she began a rapid toilet, answered my bewildered question,—

21. Louisa May Alcott volunteered as a nurse at age 30 and began writing articles about her experiences for *Commonwealth* magazine. Extremely popular, her articles were combined into a book in 1863. For *Hospital Sketches* she took the pen-name Tribulation Periwinkle. Her novel *Little Women* (1868, 1869) brought her considerable success, and she continued to write until her death in 1888.

◆ CHAPTER 10

Caring for the Sick
and Wounded:
Female Nurses
in the American
Civil War

"Bless you, no child; it's the wounded from Fredericksburg; forty ambulances are at the door, and we shall have our hands full in fifteen minutes."

"What shall we have to do?"

"Wash, dress, feed, warm and nurse them for the next three months, I dare say. Eighty beds are ready, and we were getting impatient for the men to come. Now you will begin to see hospital life in earnest, for you won't probably find time to sit down all day, and may think yourself fortunate if you get to bed by midnight. Come to me in the ball-room when you are ready; the worst cases are always carried there, and I shall need your help."

So saying, the energetic little woman twirled her hair into a button at the back of her head, in a "cleared for action" sort of style, and vanished, wrestling her way into a feminine kind of pea-jacket as she went. . . .

"Come, my dear, begin to wash as fast as you can. Tell them to take off socks, coats and shirts, scrub them well, put on clean shirts, and the attendants will finish them off, and lay them in bed."

If she had requested me to shave them all, or dance a hornpipe on the stove funnel, I should have been less staggered; but to scrub some dozen lords of creation at a moment's notice, was really—really—-. However, there was no time for nonsense, and, having resolved when I came to do everything I was bid, I drowned my scruples in my washbowl, clutched my soap manfully, and, assuming a business-like air, made a dab at the first dirty specimen I saw, bent on performing my task *vi et armis* [with force and arms] if necessary. I chanced to light on a withered old Irishman, wounded in the head, which caused that portion of his frame to be tastefully laid out like a garden, the bandages being the walks, his hair the shrubbery. He was so overpowered by the honor of having a lady wash him, as he expressed it, that he did nothing but roll up his eyes, and bless me, in an irresistible style which was too much for my sense of the ludicrous; so we laughed together, and when I knelt down to take off his shoes, he "flopped" also and wouldn't hear of my touching "them dirty craters. May your bed above be aisy darlin', for the day's work ye are doon!" . . .

[Alcott eventually made friends with one of the wounded, named John.]

A most attractive face he had, framed in brown hair and beard, comely featured and full of vigor, as yet unsubdued by pain; thoughtful and often beautifully mild while watching the afflictions of others, as if entirely forgetful of his own. His mouth was grave and firm, with plenty of will and courage in its lines, but a smile could make it as sweet as any woman's; and his eyes were child's eyes, looking one fairly in the face, with a clear, straightforward glance, which promised well for such as placed their faith in him. He seemed to cling to life, as if it were rich in duties and delights, and he had learned the secret of content. The only time I saw his composure disturbed, was when my surgeon brought another to examine John, who scrutinized their faces with an anxious look, asking of the elder: "Do you think I shall pull through, sir?" "I hope so, my man."

[The next night the doctors confessed to Louisa that "There's not the slightest hope" for John. "He won't last more than a day or two." Louisa admitted that "I could have sat down on the spot and cried heartily, if I had not learned the wisdom of bottling up one's tears." She met John again.]

"Do you ever regret that you came, when you lie here suffering so much?"

"Never, ma'am; I haven't helped a great deal, but I've shown I was willing to give my life, and perhaps I've got to; but I don't blame anybody, and if it was to do over again, I'd do it. I'm a little sorry I wasn't wounded in front; it looks cowardly to be hit in the back, but I obeyed orders, and it don't matter in the end, I know."

Poor John! it did not matter now, except that a shot in front might have spared the long agony in store for him. He seemed to read the thought that troubled me, as he spoke so hopefully when there was no hope, for he suddenly added:

"This is my first battle; do they think it's going to be my last?"

"I'm afraid they do, John."

It was the hardest question I had ever been called upon to answer; doubly hard with those clear eyes fixed on mine, forcing a truthful answer by their own truth. He seemed a little startled at first, pondered over the fateful fact a moment then shook his head, with a glance at the broad chest and muscular limbs stretched out before him:

"I'm not afraid, but it's difficult to believe all at once. I'm so strong it don't seem possible for such a little wound to kill me."

"Shall I write to your mother, now?" I asked, thinking that these sudden tidings might change all plans and purposes; but they did not; for the man received the order of the Divine Commander to march with the same unquestioning obedience with which the soldier had received that of the human one, doubtless remembering that the first led him to life, and the last to death.

"No, ma'am; to Laurie just the same; he'll break it to her best, and I'll add a line to her myself when you get done."

So I wrote the letter which he dictated, finding it better than any I had sent; for, though here and there a little ungrammatical or inelegant, each sentence came to me briefly worded, but most expressive; full of excellent counsel to the boy, tenderly bequeathing "mother and Lizzie" to his care, and bidding him good bye in words the sadder for their simplicity. He added

✦ CHAPTER 10

Caring for the Sick
and Wounded:
Female Nurses
in the American
Civil War

a few lines, with steady hand, and, as I sealed it, said, with a patient sort of sigh, "I hope the answer will come in time for me to see it."

To me, the saddest sight I saw in that sad place, was the spectacle of a grey-haired father, sitting hour after hour by his son, dying from the poison of his wound. The old father, hale and hearty; the young son, past all help, though one could scarcely believe it; for the subtle fever, burning his strength away, flushed his cheeks with color, filled his eyes with lustre, and lent a mournful mockery of health to face and figure, making the poor lad comelier in death than in life. His bed was not in my ward; but I was often in and out, and, for a day or two, the pair were much together, saying little, but looking much. The old man tried to busy himself with book or pen, that his presence might not be a burden; and once, when he sat writing, to the anxious mother at home, doubtless, I saw the son's eyes fixed upon his face, with a look of mingled resignation and regret, as if endeavoring to teach himself to say cheerfully the long good bye. And again, when the son slept, the father watched him, as he had himself been watched; and though no feature of his grave countenance changed, the rough hand, smoothing the lock of hair upon the pillow, the bowed attitude of the grey head, were more pathetic than the loudest lamentations. [T]he son died; and the father took home the pale relic of the life he gave, offering a little money to the nurse, as the only visible return it was in his power to make her; for, though very grateful, he was poor. Of course, she did not take it, but found a richer compensation in the old man's earnest declaration:

"My boy couldn't have been better cared for if he'd been at home; and God will reward you for it, though I can't."

But more interesting than officers, ladies, mules, or pigs, were my colored brothers and sisters, because so unlike the respectable members of society I'd known in moral Boston.

Here was a genuine article—no, not the genuine article at all, we must go to Africa for that—but the sort of creatures generations of slavery have made them: obsequious, trickish, lazy and ignorant, yet kind-hearted, merry-tempered, quick to feel and accept the least token of the brotherly love which is slowly teaching the white hand to grasp the black, in this great struggle for the liberty of both the races.

I had not been there a week, before the neglected, devil-may-care expression in many of the faces about me, seemed an urgent appeal to leave nursing white bodies, and take some care for these black souls. Much as the lazy boys and saucy girls tormented me, I liked them, and found that any show of interest or friendliness brought out the better traits which live in the most degraded and forsaken of us all. . . .

The nurses were willing to be served by the colored people, but seldom thanked them, never praised, and scarcely recognized them in the street; whereat the blood of two generations of abolitionists waxed hot in my veins, and, at the first opportunity, proclaimed itself, and asserted the right of free speech. . . .

Happening to catch up a funny little black baby, who was toddling about the nurses' kitchen, one day, when I went down to make a mess for some of my men, a Virginia woman standing by elevated her most prominent features, with a sniff of disapprobation, exclaiming:

"Gracious, Miss P.! how can you? I've been here six months, and never so much as touched the little toad with a poker."

"More shame for you, ma'am," responded Miss P.; and, with the natural perversity of a Yankee, followed up the blow by kissing "the toad," with ardor. . . .

Source 2 from Cornelia Hancock, *South After Gettysburg: Letters of Cornelia Hancock from the Army of the Potomac, 1803–1865,* ed. Henrietta Stratton Jaquette (Philadelphia: Univ. of Pennsylvania Press, 1937), pp 4–5, 10, 17–18.[22]

2. Cornelia Hancock (1839–1926)

We arrived in the town of Gettysburg on the evening of July sixth, three days after the last day of battle. We were met by Dr. Horner, at whose house we stayed. Every barn, church, and building of any size in Gettysburg had been converted into a temporary hospital. We went the same evening to one of the churches, where I saw for the first time what war meant. Hundreds of desperately wounded men were stretched out on boards laid across the high-backed pews as closely as they could be packed together. The boards were covered with straw. Thus elevated, these poor sufferers' faces, white and drawn with pain, were almost on a level with my own. I seemed to stand breast-high in a sea of anguish.

The townspeople of Gettysburg were in devoted attendance, and there were many from other villages and towns. The wounds of all had been dressed at least once, and some systematic care was already established. Too inexperienced to nurse, I went from one pallet to another with pencil,

22. Cornelia Hancock was a Quaker from New Jersey whose application to be a nurse was rejected by Dorothea Dix because she was too young and attractive. She found another way to become a nurse and began her service at Gettysburg. After the war, she opened a school for African Americans in Mount Pleasant, S.C.

◆ CHAPTER 10

Caring for the Sick
and Wounded:
Female Nurses
in the American
Civil War

paper, and stamps in hand, and spent the rest of that night in writing letters from the soldiers to their families and friends. To many mothers, sisters, and wives I penned the last message of those who were soon to become the "beloved dead."

Learning that the wounded of the Third Division of the Second Corps, including the 12th Regiment of New Jersey, were in a Field Hospital about five miles outside of Gettysburg, we determined to go there early the next morning, expecting to find some familiar faces among the regiments of my native state. As we drew near our destination we began to realize that war has other horrors than the sufferings of the wounded or the desolation of the bereft. A sickening, overpowering, awful stench announced the presence of the unburied dead, on which the July sun was mercilessly shining, and at every step the air grew heavier and fouler, until it seemed to possess a palpable horrible density that could be seen and felt and cut with a knife. Not the presence of the dead bodies themselves, swollen and disfigured as they were, and lying in heaps on every side, was as awful to the spectator as that deadly, nauseating atmosphere which robbed the battlefield of its glory, the survivors of their victory, and the wounded of what little chance of life was left to them.

As we made our way to a little woods in which we were told was the Field Hospital we were seeking, the first sight that met our eyes was a collection of semi—conscious but still living human forms, all of whom had been shot through the head, and were considered hopeless. They were laid there to die and I hoped that they were indeed too near death to have consciousness. Yet many a groan came from them, and their limbs tossed and twitched. The few surgeons who were left in charge of the battlefield after the Union army had started in pursuit of Lee had begun their paralyzing task by sorting the dead from the dying, and the dying from those whose lives might be saved; hence the groups of prostrate, bleeding men laid together according to their wounds.

There was hardly a tent to be seen. Earth was the only available bed during those first hours after the battle. A long table stood in this woods and around it gathered a number of surgeons and attendants. This was the operating table, and for seven days it literally ran blood. A wagon stood near rapidly filling with amputated legs and arms; when wholly filled, this gruesome spectacle withdrew from sight and returned as soon as possible for another load. So appalling was the number of the wounded as yet unsuccored, so helpless seemed the few who were battling against tremendous odds to save life, and so overwhelming was the demand for any kind of aid that could be given quickly, that one's senses were benumbed by the awful responsibility that fell to the living. Action of a kind hitherto unknown and unheard of was needed here and existed here only. . . .

It took nearly five days for some three hundred surgeons to perform the amputations that occurred here, during which time the rebels lay in a dying condition without their wounds being dressed or scarcely any food. If the rebels did not get severely punished for this battle, then I am no judge. We have but one rebel in our camp now; he says he never fired his gun if he could help it, and, therefore, we treat him first rate. One man died this morning. I fixed him up as nicely as the place will allow; he will be buried this afternoon. We are becoming somewhat civilized here now and the men are cared for well. . . .

There are many sights here, but the most melancholy one is to see the wounded come in in a long train of ambulances after night fall. I must be hardhearted though, for I do not feel these things as strangers do. What is the war news? I do not know the news at all. I never read the papers now, which is a slight change for me. I look at it in this way that I am doing all a woman can do to help the war along, and, therefore, I feel no responsibility. If people take an interest in me because I am a heroine, it is a great mistake for I feel like anything but a heroine. . . .

I have no doubt that most people think I came into the army to get a husband. It is a capital place for that, as there are very many nice men here, and all men are required to give great respect to women. There are many good-looking women here who galavant around in the evening, and have a good time. I do not trouble myself much with the common herd. There is one man who is my right-hand man; he is about nineteen years old—is a hospital steward and will do anything to accommodate. . . .[23]

Source 3 from Charlotte McKay, *Stories of Hospitals and Camp* (Freeport, NY: Books for Libraries Press, 1876), pp. 167–168, 176, 182–183.[24]

3. Charlotte McKay (1818–1894)

Living in an encampment of freed people affords one a rare opportunity of observing the general effects of slavery. Here the monster "being dead, yet speaketh," through thousands of prisoners come up out of the prison-house,

23. More than a few nurses made this complaint. Harriet Eaton, a nurse from Boston, was pursued ardently by a captain, a colonel, a major, and a surgeon. She wrote, "I am weary with this continual beau hunting, lady seeking, joking, laughing community." Schultz, *Women at the Front,* p. 90. Similar complaints were made by Kate Cumming and Phoebe Pember concerning charges made by *other women* as to why they were nurses. *Ibid.,* pp. 51–52.
24. Charlotte McKay served as a nurse in a Union military hospital after the deaths of her husband and child. After the war, she stayed on as a nurse to freedmen.

✦ CHAPTER 10

Caring for the Sick
and Wounded:
Female Nurses
in the American
Civil War

and his ugly apparition stalks in broad daylight, revealed in all its hideous proportions.

Here are seen men and women, literally children of a hundred years, whose intellects have been dwarfed and held down by the hard hand of oppression; and here, young women, comely in person, refined in feeling, sensitive in nature, bearing on their bodies the marks of the master's lash, administered by his own hand, and he at once their father and the father of their children. As I walk about the encampment, I often look into the little hut where poor old Si Gillis, nearly blind, sits before his lonely hearth, holding out his hands to the fire, as if to obtain a little of its warmth were his only remaining earthly consolation. He is very tall, though now bent by the weight of years; his features are regular, and he must once have had a noble physique.

"How old are you, uncle?"

"Eighty-three years old, madam."

"Were you a free man before the war?"

"Oh, no, madam. I've been a slave, a dead slave, all my life."

"Would not your master take care of you after you had served him so long?"

"No, madam; he always worked me hard, and kept me hard, and at last he died himself. If he'd a' lived, he'd a' made me knock as long as I could a' knocked, and then he'd a' shoved me off with a piece of bread, only enough to keep me from starving—just as he did my brother, who was a hundred years old when he died, and had been a slave all his life."

"Did you have a family, uncle?"

"Yes, madam; I had children, and grand-children, and great grand-children, but they were all sold away from me; and I don't know where one of them is but my daughter that lives in Petersburg, and she's a cripple." . . .

The representatives of the Freedmen's Bureau in this department are doing for them all that they can; the National Freedman's Relief Association is doing all it can; friends in England have done much by sending quantities of stout under-garments; and yet, such is their destitution and suffering, that I doubt if to most of these poor humans, whose "masters were *worser* to them after the war began, and so they done runned away," the exchange is not a leap "from the frying-pan into the fire." They are, in general, willing to work, but the old slavocracy will not employ them if it can possibly do without, and they have a horror of going North. Still, of the five or six hundred collected in and about this encampment, only about one hundred and fifty draw Government rations, the remainder contriving in some way to subsist themselves.

"Did you have a good master in North Carolina?" I asked of a carpenter who was making some repairs on my quarters. "Yes, madam; as the general run of them goes in that country, I can't say but I did." "Would you not have done better to stay with him?" "Oh, no, indeed, madam. I'm bound to believe I can do better to have my own labor. To earn a hundred dollars for another man, and not get a hundred cents for yourself, is poor business."

Walking around their quarters, and looking into their little huts, one sees pitiable signs of destitution and suffering, but hears no desire to return to the old masters. . . .

[McKay came across an African American mother whose son was named Jefferson Davis.]

"Why in the world," I asked of a sensible woman, who was calling her boy "Jeff Davis," across the way, "did you give that name to your child?" "I didn't want to call him so, missus; but ole master named him, and I couldn't help it; I wanted to call him Thomas." "You had better change it now, and not compel him to bear that name through life. He will be ashamed of it when he grows up." "Yes, missus; I think I'll call him Thomas Grant." . . .

Source 4 from Sarah A. Palmer, *The Story of Aunt Becky's Army Life* (New York: New York Printing Co, 1871), pp. 1–3, 23, 118.[25]

4. Sarah A. Palmer (1830–1908)

It is no record of bloody battles which these pages are opened to detail; neither do I purpose [sic] to depict the horrible scenes of carnage which made the "Sunny South" one red field of flame: only to show one weak woman's work amongst the sufferers gathered up from those dreadful slaughter-plains, and those driven in sick and exhausted from the unwonted exposure in camp and march, this work of recording is begun.

Standing firm against the tide of popular opinion; hearing myself pronounced demented—bereft of usual common sense; doomed to the horrors of an untended death-bed—suffering torture, hunger, and all the

25. Sarah Palmer was from Ithaca, N.Y. and served as a nurse with the 109th Regiment of New York Volunteers. After the war, she remarried and moved to Des Moines, Iowa. During the Spanish-American War (1898), she helped to raise funds for medical supplies for Iowa soldiers.

◆ CHAPTER 10

Caring for the Sick
and Wounded:
Female Nurses
in the American
Civil War

untold miseries of a soldier's fate; above the loud echoed cry, "It is no place for woman," I think it was well that no one held a bond over me strong enough to restrain me from performing my plain duty, fulfilling the promise which I made my brothers on enlistment, that I would go with them down to the scene of conflict, and be near when sickness or the chances of battle threw them helpless from the ranks.

I found it *was* a place for woman. All of man's boasted ingenuity had been expended to devise terrible engines with which to kill and maim God's own image; and if war was right, it was right for woman to go with brothers, and husbands, and sons, that in the time of peril the heart might not faint with the thought of an untended death-bed in the crowded hospitals, where no hand but the rough soldier's should close the dead staring eyes.

It was something to brave popular opinion, something to bear the sneers of those who loved their ease better than their country's heroes, and who could sit down in peace and comfort at home, while a soldier's rations, and a soldier's tent for months and years made up the sum of our luxurious life.

Had there been more women to help us, many a brave man, whose bones moulder beneath the green turf of the South, would have returned to bless the loved ones left in the dear old home behind him. But all alone, while the shadow of the valley of death was fast stealing over the numbing senses, his spirit went back, and his white lips murmured words which the beloved so far away would have given worlds to hear; and we heard them, but could not repeat them from the dying lips.

It is past and gone. The long agony is over, and the nation breathes free. Yet hardly a heart or home but holds the remembrance of some brave one, near and dear, who gave his life to save his country's honor. . . .

Dying men looked into my face beseechingly, and I could give them no hope. They called for wife, and mother, and child in the swift workings of delirium, but no wife, or mother, or child could stand by the death-bed, to hear, as I heard, the dying words. . . .

One of seventeen years, who was mortally wounded through the lungs, sent a messenger for me one day, having heard my name spoken by some of his comrades, and I hastened to his ward. Very cheerfully he asked me how many hours I thought he could live, and I said, "You may live a day, and perhaps longer," for it was useless and cruel to deceive when they themselves knew that death hovered near them.

He only sighed, and turned his face away for a moment, then asked me brightly if I would play checkers with him, adding, "It will bring home back clearer to me than anything else, for my sister played with me the last evening we spent at home—and we used to be so happy together." . . .

Source 5 from John R. Brumgardt, ed., *Civil War Nurse: The Diary and letters of Hannah Ropes* (Knoxville: Univ. of Tennessee Press, 1980), pp. 73, 93, 107–108, 113, 115.[26]

5. Hannah Ropes (1809–1863)

Today we send off fifty men. Not half of them are able to go, but that is of no account to one head surgeon, who cares no more for a private than for a dog. Dr. Hays was a prince of a youth; but he would marry, and so had to go away. We upon the whole have had goodish men to rule over us. Still, between surgeons, stewards, nurses and waiters, the poor men in all the hospitals barely escape with life or clothes or money.

The head surgeon was also a new man, tall, stiff, thin, light hair, whity blue eyes, and whity yellow complexion, glasses on eyes, and a way of looking out at the end of his glasses at you, surreptitiously, if I may use so big a word. He was young and I took to him. He was ignorant of hospital routine; ignorant of life outside of the practice in a country town, in an interior state, a weak man with good intentions, but puffed up with the gilding on his shoulder straps. If he had not been weak, and it had been my style to make a joke at the expense of others, there was a fine chance here; but he was safe at my hands, for he *was* weak, and I am strong in the knowledge at least which comes with age. And it is likely that in some way even this man, made giddy with an epaulette [epaulet was a shoulder ornament on a military uniform, sometimes to designate rank], will learn that God has made the private and officer of one equality, so far as the moral treatment of each other is concern. . . .

Dr. Clark[27] was put in charge. He was a man of small powers, a great idea of the dignity inherent in *straps*—talked large. The new steward who came in was a Frenchman, without principle, and rather large brain. Such a state of things as two months brought about you can hardly conceive. The men were starved, the clothes were stolen, the rations were stolen.

[While she was absent the chaplain came in and relieved his mind]

"When shall we be rid of this tyranny? The boys are suffering with cold; I begin to think Brother Ottman and myself have been remiss in duty. We ought to have moved in this matter before, for this is a Godless man, I am convinced, a Godless man. Now here are two hundred people besides

---

26. Ropes's letters and journal were donated to the Univ. of California, Riverside beginning in 1957. Hannah Ropes (1809–1863) was a New England reformer and abolitionist who served as a Union nurse until January 1863 when she died of pneumonia.
27. Dr. A.M. Clark was in charge of Union Hospital from September 16 to November 8, 1862.

◆ CHAPTER 10

Caring for the Sick
and Wounded:
Female Nurses
in the American
Civil War

assistants made miserable through the power of this man. It must not be, indeed it must not!"

"Well, why don't you go enter a complaint?"

"I hate to do it. I hate to badger a fox when he is run into his hole, and though he talks at the table in his usual pompous style we know where he has been and who can place him there again." The chaplain fidgeted on his chair with a mind disturbed from its calm, scholarly thoughtfulness, and unable to find in the wisdom of the schools a precedent to act from. Indeed, I was looking at him with surprise that he had spoken so plainly and decidedly, because when he was questioned by the man of law, sent out by Stanton, he seemed like one who had left his thoughts in his study from which he had been summoned. And I had not forgotten my disappointment at the want of clearness in his testimony. I think through all this troubled water the men have been much less clear in the sense of right than the women have. Is it that they hate to give up one of their own club to the law? Certainly, if ever there was a case demanding prompt action, it was this. . . .

It [culminated] in the thrusting of one of the boys into a dark hole in the cellar.[28] As you may believe, it did not take me long to go in to Washington to Stanton,[29] who very promptly arrested the steward and sent him to the Old Capitol [Prison]. The day following, Dr. Clark was also arrested and placed in limbo at the same quarters! Stanton behaved splendidly. The prompt action startled all the doctors and the stewards in the District. Dr. [Clemens?] tried to have me removed. Stanton said it should not be done, and ordered him to go to the "front." We now are having peaceable times with Dr. Stipp for head surgeon. The men have enough to eat; the clothes are washed in the back room of the small house, where a huge boiler is set. . . .

The blacks are able and ready to free themselves; they only wait for legitimate "orders" to do it. Our chaplain is a Virginian, from its south line, a remarkable scholar, and a driven refugee from his home. He assured me that there is no telegraph so quick to communicate as the black race from one end of the country to the other. . . .

This is God's war, in spite of uncertain generals, in spite of ill success; in spite of our own unworthiness; the cause is that of the human race, and must prevail. Let us work then with a good heart, here and at home. We are all scholars in the same school. Having failed to learn in prosperity, we ought to be glad of the Divine Mercy which gives us another chance in the upheaving of all social comforts and necessities.

28. The new steward dug a hole in the basement and thrust soldiers into it for punishment.
29. Secretary of War Edwin Stanton. Ropes knew him from their days as reformers and she had no difficulty gaining access to him.

Now is the judgment of this world. Each man and woman is taking his or her measure. As it is taken even so must it stand—it will be recorded. The activities of war quicken into life every evil propensity as well as every good principle.

No soul now can stand on neutral ground. Between truth and error there surges and foams a great gulf, but a *respectably* dressed crowd line the shore of dishonesty! Let *us* be *loyal* and *true,* then if the great world never hears a word about us one shall not fear, even though the waves of war's uncertain tide swallow us in the general wreck! . . .

Source 6 from Susie King Taylor, *Reminiscences of My Life in Camp with the 33rd U.S. Colored Troops, Late 1st S.C. Volunteers,* ed. Patricia W. Romero (Princeton: Markus Wiener, 1994; orig. pub. 1902), pp. 107, 119–120, 135–136.[30]

6. Susie King Taylor (1848–1912)

On February 28, 1865, the remainder of the regiment were ordered to Charleston, as there were signs of the rebels evacuating that city. Leaving Cole Island, we arrived in Charleston between nine and ten o'clock in the morning, and found the "rebs" had set fire to the city and fled, leaving women and children behind to suffer and perish in the flames. The fire had been burning fiercely for a day and night. When we landed, under a flag of truce, our regiment went to work assisting the citizens in subduing the flames. It was a terrible scene. For three or four days the men fought the fire, saving the property and effects of the people, yet these white men and women could not tolerate our black Union soldiers, for many of them had formerly been their slaves; and although these brave men risked life and limb to assist them in their distress, men and even women would sneer and molest them whenever they met them. . . .

My dear friends! Do we understand the meaning of war? Do we know or think of that war of '61? No, we do not, only those brave soldiers, and those who had occasion to be in it, can realize what it was. I can and shall never forget that terrible war until my eyes close in death. The scenes are just as fresh in my mind to-day as in '61. I see now each scene,—the roll-call, the drum tap, "lights out," the call at night when there was danger from the enemy, the double force of pickets, the cold and rain. How anxious I would be,

30. Susie King Taylor began her service with the First South Carolina Volunteers as a laundress, but soon became a nurse. She was the only African American woman to publish a memoir of her wartime experience. After the war, she moved to Boston.

◆ CHAPTER 10

Caring for the Sick
and Wounded:
Female Nurses
in the American
Civil War

not knowing what would happen before morning! Many times I would dress, not sure but all would be captured. Other times I would stand at my tent door and try to see what was going on, because night was the time the rebels would try to get into our lines and capture some of the boys. It was mostly at night that our men went out for their scouts, and often had a hand to hand fight with the rebels, and although our men came out sometimes with a few killed or wounded, none of them ever were captured.

We do not, as the black race, properly appreciate the old veterans, white or black, as we ought to. I know what they went through, especially those black men, for the Confederates had no mercy on then; neither did they show any toward the white Union soldiers. I have seen the terrors of that war. I was the wife of one of those men who did not get a penny for eighteen months for their services, only their rations and clothing. . . .

I look around now and see the comforts that our younger generation enjoy, and think of the blood that was shed to make these comforts possible for them, and see how little some of them appreciate the old soldiers. My heart burns within me, at this want of appreciation.[31] There are only a few of them left now, so let us all, as the ranks close, take a deeper interest also, and remember that it was through the efforts of these veterans that they and we older ones enjoy our liberty today.

Living here in Boston[32] where the black man is given equal justice, I must say a word on the general treatment of my race, both in the North and South, in this twentieth century. I wonder if our white fellow men realize the true sense or meaning of brotherhood? For two hundred years we had toiled for them; the war of 1861 came and was ended, and we thought our race was forever free from bondage, and that the two races could live in unity with each other, but when we read almost every day of what is being done to my race by some whites in the South, I sometimes ask, "Was the war in vain? Has it brought freedom, in the full sense of the word, or has it not made our condition more hopeless?"

In this "land of the free" we are burned, tortured, and denied a fair trial, murdered for any imaginary wrong conceived in the brain of the negro-hating white man. There is no redress for us from a government which promised to protect all under its flag. It seems a mystery to me. They say, "One flag, one nation, one country indivisible." Is this true? Can we say this truthfully, when one race is allowed to burn, hang, and inflict the most horrible torture

31. Susie King Taylor almost surely was present in Boston on May 31, 1897 when the memorial honoring the 54th Massachusetts Regiment and Colonel Robert Gould Shaw was unveiled. Eighty-five veterans of the 54th, along with veterans of other African American regiments took part in the ceremony.
32. This section was added to her memoirs some years later.

weekly, monthly, on another? No, we cannot sing, "My country 'tis of thee, Sweet land of Liberty"! It is hollow mockery. The Southland laws are all on the side of the white, and they do just as they like to the negro, whether in the right or not.

Source 7 from *A Confederate Nurse: The Diary of Ada W. Bacot, 1860-1863* (Columbia, SC: Univ. of South Carolina Press, 1994), pp. 71, 104, 111, 1178, 147, 154, 169–170, 175.[33]

7. Ada W Bacot (1832–1911)

There was another death at the Monticello[34] last night, quite a boy, a melancholy case, he was very much frightened, & I'm told wept nearly all day yesterday. I am so very sorry I did not know it, I would have gone to him & tryed to ease his last moments. I havent a doubt he was some mothers pride, & perhaps her only prop & stay in this world tis too sad. Dr. Rembert tells me that pneumonia is taking off hundreds. It is even more fatal than Typhoid fever. Tis too too sad. . . .

This has indeed been a day of work, instead of rest. There was so much to do this morning that I couldent get to church. Marie was too unwell to get down to dinner, I came up directly after I had finished mine to try & get her to take a cup of hot coffee, which she did, soon after I went to the window upon hearing the car whistle, I saw Dr. Rembert a little while after coming this way with a sick soldier, a perfect stream of them followed some looking very weak & scarcely able to move along twenty of the worst off were taken to the Monticello. 16 have been put on my two wards, some of them very ill, we did not know they were to be up today so nothing was redy for them, however it did not take long to make beds for them as every thing was at hand & every one redy to help[.] Good kind hearted Miss Reynolds soon had plenty of good soup & bread in rediness, & helped us distribute it to the poor hungry creatures. Then there was punch, poultices, & plasters to be made & put on I did not rest from 1/2 3 until 7. I told some of the young men whom I have been nursing, that they must help me now that I had so much to do. O, yes maam they all said in a breath, we will do any thing for

33. Ada Bacot's unpublished diary was sold to the South Caroliniana Library in 1964. She was born on the Roseville plantation in South Carolina, and married her second cousin Thomas Bacot in 1851, who was killed by the plantation's overseer in 1856. Her father and all her brothers served in the Confederate army, and she volunteered as a nurse before the war broke out.
34. Monticello was a hospital established in Charlottesville, Virginia by the South Carolina Hospital Aid Association. See Bacot Diary, p. 26n.

◆ CHAPTER 10

Caring for the Sick
and Wounded:
Female Nurses
in the American
Civil War

you. We can never do too much for you. Tis very gratifing to me to hear all this. I thank God I have been able to do any thing to relieve the sufferings of any of our brave soldiers. Not one of the men who came in today was a South Carolinian. Though I am glad to do what I can for the men of other states I am sorry that our own men should suffer for attention. I have no doubt there are many Carolinians suffering for the very attentions we are bestowing on these men from other states. Our men are out of our reach here having fallen back from these lines. More rain tonight, Marie & myself took our tea up here, we were to[o] fatigued to go down when we got in. . . .

It has been raining nearly all the afternoon, I went to tea feeling very gloomy & homesick, I noticed Dr. McIntosh ait nothing & looked sad. I wondered what could be the matter when we got up from the tea table he left the room, Dr. Rembert wrote on a slip of paper & handed it to me, "This was to be McIntosh's wedding night you must excuse him." As soon as I read it I felt as if I could have wept, poor fellow, he feels it deeply. I left the little party down stairs to come & write him a note of sympathy. It had escaped my mind that this was the night fixed upon for his marriage until Dr. Rembert reminded me of it. I showed Marie the note, she laughed & made great fun of my thinking of writing to the Doctor; but said she would take him the note, which she did. Mr. Hicks sleeps in the house tonight he came in after we had finished tea. Tonight ends another month, who can tell what the history of the next may be. Mr. Barnwell drew up a gloomy picture of the state of affairs as they now exist at the dinner table today. Davis seems to have lossed every friend he had by his obstinacy & self will. Mr. B. even said he thought it would be a na[t]ional blessing if [President Jefferson] Davis were to die. I firmly believe God will deliver our beloved country yet. A hard strugle we will have for our independence but I believe he will cary us through. Both Marie & Esse have retired, & the light is anoying them, so I must make redy to follow them. . . .

I found Logan very much worse this morning, he asked me to read to him again, which I did, I remained with him as much as I could all the morning, reading & talking to him he told me he was near his end & that he was very happy perfectly resigned to the will of God. I never saw a dieing person so perfectly in their mind, about noon he asked to see a minister, I sent for Mr. Early who lives just across the street, he came instantly, & prayed for the poor sufferer. I was standing by the bed weeping[.] Logan said do not weep for me, I am going to rest, I am perfectly willing to die, I do not suffer as much as you think. When he spoak of his mother, he said she was good & would be rejoiced to hear he had died a christian. He thanked all who had done any thing for him, his eyes rested on me all the time, he told Mr. Early

I had done for him as if he were my son[.] I have never witnessed such a death bed in the hospital, I had to leave him for a little while I go back now, I doubt if he still lives. . . .

Most of the wounds are doing finely[.] I could not go to the hospital until after ten this morning as I was again unable to get down to breakfast. Poor Sturgess got me to write to his wife for him, he has lost his right hand & yet he bears it with so much fortitude & manliness[.] I can scarcely bear to go into the hospital now the wounds are begining to smell terably, we try to keep it as clean & nice as possible, but seems to me a dreadful poisonous smell hangs about the whole house. Some times when the wind is in this direction we can even smell it over here. Little Arthur has been quite sick all day, both the doctor & Mrs. R. are very uneasy about him, I think it one of the most miserable climates I ever knew of for children. Old Willie left today, very quietly, she did not say goodbye to any of us. Mr. Mills got home just before we went to tea he found his brother, but could not move him, he is comfortably cared for in a private house & has a friend staying with him. We have no idea of the suffering many a poor man lyes down by the roadside & dies with out [a] friend to close his eyes even. I am too sick to write any more, this is certainly a most disgusting desiese. . . .

Not one of [us] attended the sale to day, last night about two oclock Capt. Mallory came up to Dr. Macs room to ask him to go out to a place about six miles in the country where the cars had met with an accident. It seems two cows were on the track causing the engine to be thrown from the track pulling five of the first cars after it. They were thrown down a very steep embankment crushing them all to pieces & killing & wounded many of the soldiers in them. Dr. McIntosh discribed it as a most horrable scene, he heard the wounded crying & groaning with their wounds long before he reached the place. Many of the unfortunate victims were lying around large fires made on the side of the road while the dead were scattered here & there among the men. . . .

When Dr. Poellnitz came in to dinner I noticed he had been taking something. He talked a great deal to Dr. Harrold which is not usual & talked about his own private affairs which I did not suppose he would do if he had been in his right mind[.] I was sitting with Fannie just before the tea bell rang talking & laughing, when I heard some one come to the front door & try to get in. The door was locked & he kicked & banged away until Jane went to open it. It was Dr. P. he was so drunk he could scarcely stand, when Jane opened the door she invited him in but he stood there bowing with his hands in his pockets & said he would not come in until he knew why the door was locked, so Jane left the door open & came in to the room she had bearly

✦ CHAPTER 10

Caring for the Sick
and Wounded:
Female Nurses
in the American
Civil War

shut the door when he began to call Jane at the top of his voice, finding she did not go to him he stagered in & went to his room. Poor Mrs. P. she has the sympathy of the household. She could not come to her tea, Dr. Paten called after tea to see Dr. P. but he was not fit to receive him. . . .

Poor little woman I feel very much for her, to have to travle with an intoxicated husband is anything but pleasant. . . .

Source 8 from Fannie A. Beers, *Memories: A Record of Personal Experience and Adventure During Four Years of War* (Philadelphia: J. B. lippincott, 1891), pp. 61, 63, 85, 177, 187, 200–201.[35]

8. Fannie A. Beers (1832–1894)

I noticed few male nurses. Perhaps half a dozen women met us at the doors of different wards, jauntily dressed, airily "showing off" their patients, and discoursing of their condition and probably chances of life, in a manner utterly revolting to me. I caught many a glance of disgust bent upon them by the poor fellows who were thus treated as if they were stocks or stones. These women were, while under the eye of the surgeon, obsequious and eager to please, but I thought I saw the "lurking devil in their eyes," and felt sure they meant mischief. . . .

I found a man who had been brought in several days before, suffering from excessive drinking. Not being able to obtain whiskey, he had managed to get hold of a bottle of turpentine emulsion from a table in the hall, and had drank the whole. Dr. Minor and I worked for hours with this unfortunate and hoped he would recover, but other patients required looking after, and during my absence whiskey was smuggled in to him, of which he partook freely. After that, nothing could save his life. A patient suffering agonies from gastritis was also placed under my special charge. I was to feed him myself, and avoid giving water, except in the smallest quantities. I did my best, but he grew worse, and just in time I found under his pillow a canteen full of water, which had been procured for him by the woman who attended in his ward. . . .

35. Fannie Amelia Dimon was born in Connecticut. She met and married Augustus Beers, a student at Yale College, then moved to New Orleans. When her husband volunteered for service in the Confederate army, Fannie Beers became a nurse attached to the Louisiana Light Infantry and became one of the best-known Confederate nurses. She died in a New York hospital on April 14, 1893.

Returning to my patients in the church about noon, I found a change for the better in many cases; in others it was but too evident that days, even hours, were numbered. Two soldiers in particular attracted my attention. One was an Irishman, of an Alabama regiment, the other from Arkansas. The Irishman was fast passing away, and earnestly desired to see a priest. There was none nearer than twelve miles. One of our foragers, himself a Roman Catholic, volunteered to go for him and by permission of Dr. McAllister rode off through the snow, returning after nightfall to report that Father _____ had been called in another direction, and would not return home until the next day. Finding the poor fellow, though almost too far gone to articulate, constantly murmuring words of prayer, I took his prayer-book and read aloud the "Recommendation of a soul departing," also some of the preceding prayers of the "Litany for the dying." He faintly responded, and seemed to die comforted and satisfied. Afterwards I never hesitated to use the same service in like cases. . . .

How often I have marshalled into the hospital wards mothers and wives, who for the sake of some absent loved one had come from homes many miles away, to bring some offering to the sick. Timid, yet earnest women, poorly dressed, with sunbrowned faces and rough hands, yet bearing in their hearts the very essence of loving-kindness towards the poor fellows upon whose pale faces and ghastly wounds they looked with "round-eyed wonder" and pity. After a while they would gain courage to approach some soldier whom they found "sort o' favored" their own, to whom they ventured to offer some dainty, would stroke the wasted hand, smooth the hair, or hold to the fevered lips a drink of buttermilk or a piece of delicious fruit. Ah, *how many* times I have watched such scenes! To the warmly-expressed thanks of the beneficiaries they would simply answer, "That is nothing; 'mebbe' somebody will do as much *for mine* when he needs it." . . .

I do not consider myself competent, nor do I wish to criticise the generals who led our armies and who, since the war, have, with few exceptions, labored assiduously to throw the blame of failure upon each other. I have read their books with feelings of intense sorrow and regret,—looking for a reproduction of the glories of the past,—finding whole pages of recrimination and full of "all uncharitableness." For my own part, I retain an unchanged, unchangeable respect and reverence for *all* alike, *believing each to have been a pure and honest patriot, who, try as he might, could not surmount the difficulties which each one in turn encountered.*

A brave, *vindictive* foe, whose superiority in numbers, in arms, and equipment, and, more than all, *rations,* they could maintain indefinitely. And to oppose them, an utterly inadequate force, whose bravery and unparalleled

◆ CHAPTER 10

Caring for the Sick
and Wounded:
Female Nurses
in the American
Civil War

endurance held out to the end, although hunger gnawed at their vitals, disease and death daily decimated them....

And when the end came, when the bravest soldiers returned, wretched and despairing, even weeping bitter tears within the faithful arms that sheltered them, the faces which bent above them still bravely smiled. Beloved voices whispered of encouragement and hope, patient hearts assumed burdens under which men fainted and failed.

From the root of patriotism, deeply buried in the hearts of Southern women, sprung a new and vigorous growth. Its tendrils overspread and concealed desolate places; the breath of its flowers filled all the land, stealing over the senses like an invigorating breeze.

"There is life in the old land yet," said men to each other. Let us cherish and develop it. And so, once more each lifted his heavy burden, and finding it unexpectedly lightened, turned to find at his side, no longer a helpless clinging form which should hamper his every step, but a true woman, strong in the love which defied discouragement, "with a heart for any fate," a *helpmeet,* indeed, who hereafter would allow no burden to remain unshared.

Thus faithful to the living, the women of the South never forgot their dead heroes. At first it was impossible to do more than to "keep green" their sacred graves, or to deposit thereon a few simple flowers, but the earliest rays of the sun of prosperity fell upon many a "storied urn and animated bust," raised by tireless love and self-sacrifice, to mark "the bivouac of the dead."...

Source 9 from Kate Cumming, *Kate: The Journal of a Confederate Nurse,* ed. Richard Barksdale Harwell (Baton Rouge: Louisiana State Univ. Press, 1959; orig. pub. 1866), pp. 12–13, 15, 17, 35, 290–292.[36]

9. Kate Cumming (1835–1909)

It seems that the surgeons entertain great prejudice against admitting ladies into the hospital in the capacity of nurses. The surgeon in charge, Dr. Caldwell, has carried this so far that he will not even allow the ladies of the place to visit his patients. These young ladies went over with some milk and bouquets, and were not permitted to present them in person to the patients, but had to give them to the doctor. So they told him they knew

36. Kate Cumming was born in Scotland and moved with her family to Mobile, Alabama as a child. Her family was wealthy and she had never been inside a hospital until she volunteered as a Confederate nurse. After the war, she moved with her father to Birmingham where she was active as a teacher and a church volunteer. Her journal was one of the most popular written by a Confederate nurse.

the reason; he wanted all the *good things* for himself. The doctors, one and all, are getting terrible characters from the ladies; even good Dr. Nott of Mobile is not spared. I only wish that the doctors would let us try and see what we can do! Have we not noble examples of what our women have done? For instance, Mrs. Hopkins, in Virginia, and, I have no doubt, many others. Is the noble example of Miss Nightingale to pass for nothing? I trust not. We need not aspire to be Miss Nightingales, or Mrs. Hopkinses; still we can contribute our "two mites." . . .

I met at the depot Dr. Anderson of Mobile; and was quite amused at a remark which he made to some ladies who were telling him how badly Dr. Caldwell had acted, in not permitting us to visit his hospital. In his usual humorous manner, he said, "What can be expected from an old bachelor, who did not appreciate the ladies enough to marry one?" He also said that he did not think any hospital could get along without ladies. So we have one doctor on our side. . . .

[Cumming arrived at her first field hospital—"As far as the eye could reach, in the midst of all this slop and mud, the white tents of our brave army could be seen through the trees." . . .]

O, if the authors of this cruel and unnatural war could but see what I saw there, they would try and put a stop to it! To think that it is man who is working all this woe upon his fellowman. What can be in the minds of our enemies, who are now arrayed against us, who have never harmed them in any way, but simply claim our own, and nothing more! May God forgive them, for surely they know not what they do. . . .

I sat up all night, bathing the men's wounds, and giving them water. Every one attending to them seemed completely worn out. Some of the doctors told me that they had scarcely slept since the battle. As far as I have seen, the surgeons are very kind to the wounded, and nurse as well as doctor them.

The men are lying all over the house, on their blankets, just as they were brought from the battle-field. They are in the hall, on the gallery, and crowded into very small rooms. The foul air from this mass of human beings at first made me giddy and sick, but I soon got over it. We have to walk, and when we give the men any thing kneel, in blood and water; but we think nothing of it at all. There was much suffering among the patients last night; one old man groaned all the time. He was about sixty years of age, and had lost a leg. He lived near Corinth, and had come there the morning of the battle to see his two sons, who were in the army, and he could not resist shouldering his musket and going into the fight. I comforted him as well as I could. He is a religious man, and prayed nearly all night. . . .

[299]

◆ CHAPTER 10

Caring for the Sick
and Wounded:
Female Nurses
in the American
Civil War

One of the doctors, named Little, of Alabama, told me to-day that he had left his young wife on his plantation, with more than a hundred negroes upon it, and no white man but the overseer. He had told the negroes, before he left, if they desired to leave, they could do so when they pleased. He was certain that no more than one or two would go. . . .

These things are very sad. A few evenings since, Dr. Allen was conversing about the horrors with which we are surrounded. He remarked that it was hard to think that God was just in permitting them. "Shall we receive good at the hands of God, and shall we not receive evil?" We, as a nation, have been so prosperous, that we forget that it was from him that we derived our benefits. He often sends us sorrows to try our faith. He will not send us more than we are able to bear. How patiently the soldiers endure their trials! Who dare say that strength is not given them from on high? Let us do our part, and, whatever happens, not lose trust in him, "for he doeth all things well"; and, in the language of Bishop Wilmer, "May the trials through which we are passing serve to wean us from the world, and move us to set our affections on things above!" "May we bear the rod, and him who hath appointed it!" . . .

[Gen. Lee's Army of Northern Virginia surrendered on April 9, 1865 at Appomattox Court House. The remainder of Confederate troops surrendered on April 18 and May 26. News of the collapse of the Confederacy spread slowly throughout the South.]

Cumming's journal entry of May 15, 1865:

A few days ago a speech was published in the papers, made by [United States] President [Andrew] Johnson to the Indiana delegation [in which he spoke harshly of the South]. It seems to have struck dismay to many a [southern] heart, and if he carries out what he says in it, I am confident the war is not over yet, for I have watched the countenances of some men, who I have been told never favored the war or secession, and I think they expressed a determination that, if there should be another war, they would assist in it, heart and soul.

If President Johnson wants the southern people to be more inimical to the North than even this war has made them, he will carry out the policy indicated in that speech; but, if he wishes the North and South to be united in spirit, as well as in the form, he will adopt another.

"God has implanted a desire to resist oppression in the nature of every man," and "even the smallest worm will turn, being trodden on."

What wound was ever healed by continual irritation[?] Have we not been wounded? God knows how terribly! Grant that we were in the wrong, are we the only people who have erred? . . . We are of the same indomitable race as himself. We have not been conquered, for that would be a disgrace to him, as well as us; but we have been overpowered by numbers, and in no craven spirit would I tell him, for we and all we have are in his power, that forbearance and magnanimity are godlike virtues, while cruelty and revenge characterize the dastard; and that if he wishes to make a name for himself, such as mortal man has never had before, by bringing two such adverse spirits together, in peace and harmony, it will never be done by oppression. History gives us no such examples.

O, if I had the ability to write to him, as did the lamented Bishop Otey to [U.S. Secretary of State William] Seward, at the out-break of the war, and plead with him, in earnest tones, to let dove-eyed peace reign where cruel war has been sole monarch—with the hope that my appeal would not be in vain as was bishop Otey's—how earnestly I would pray to him to have peace, and peace alone, as his sole aim!

God grant that some wise and able advocate may rise in our behalf, and that ere long, peace, with all its blessings, may reign over our now distracted land!

To the people of the South I would also say a few words. Our doom is sealed; we are in the power of the North. Our representative man a prisoner; our armies vanquished—or, those which are not soon will be. Have we done our duty? Have the planters given of the abundance of their harvests to the poor women and children of soldiers who were fighting to save their wealth? But I should not say poor, for that is not the word; none were poor whose husbands, sons, and brothers offered up their lives a sacrifice for liberty! No money can buy such riches.

Have no native southern men remained at home, when their country had need of their strong arms, speculating on what the planters charged so much for, doubly taking the bread out of these same poor, yet rich, soldiers' families' mouths?

Have no native southern quartermasters and commissaries robbed these *poor*, yet *rich* soldiers, who walked boldly up to the cannon's mouth, regardless of consequences? They have starved, gone ragged and bare-footed through burning suns and chilling frosts, while these delinquent commissaries and quartermasters have lived on the best of the land, and worn the finest clothes to be had.

Have the examining surgeons conscientiously worked, sending none to the field but those who were fit for field service? And none who would have served their country better and more effectively had they been left at home to till the ground, thereby making food for the army and themselves?

Have the conscript officers taken none for the army, that the surgeons had discharged some three or four times, and sent them to the field; they dying before it was ever reached?

♦ CHAPTER 10

Caring for the Sick
and Wounded:
Female Nurses
in the American
Civil War

Have the stewards and foragers, in hospitals, never speculated on food sold them, much cheaper by the farmers, because it was for the soldiers and the cause; and have they never robbed the government of the money appropriated by it to buy food for the wounded and sick soldiers?

Have there been no officers, to whose keeping mothers have entrusted their young sons—they promising to guide and protect them; but who, as soon as away from all restraint, forgot all obligations, and took advantage of the position the war had given to them to act the tyrant in a thousand petty ways, inducing many of the men to do what they would otherwise never have thought of?

Have all the young native southerners who cried *secession,* and *war* to the *knife,* before the war broke out, gone into the field when their country was bleeding at every pore?

Have all the Christian and refined women of the South, who had no household duties to attend, gone into the hospitals, nursed the wounded and sick, preparing little delicacies, which no man has ever been able to do, for the poor bed-ridden soldier, who had lost all but honor for his country; and, when his hours were numbered, stood by his bedside when no wife, mother, or sister was there, to soothe his last moments and lift his thoughts to the Cross whereon his Redeemer had died, and to that heaven where he was waiting with open arms to receive the departing spirit?

Have the women of the South never passed by, in disdain, a ragged and wounded soldier, who had suffered more than words can express? In a word, have the women of the South done their whole duty; and can the southern people, as a whole, say they have fully done their duty?

Had we been true to our God and country, with all the blessings of this glorious, sunny land, I believe we could have kept the North, with all her power, at bay for twenty years.

What I would ask now, is for the southern people to look to themselves, forgetting all the wrongs inflicted on us by our foe in the knowledge that we have sinned against each other. I do not mean that we should forget all we have suffered, for that would dishonor the glorious dead. I mean, to stop all useless recriminations. They will do us no good now. Let us look to ourselves; "raise monuments where public virtues bloom." Let us leave the North to itself, with all its isms, to answer for its own sins. I think we have as many as we can see to.

To professed Christians, north and south, I would say, much, very much, depends on you. If you quarrel with each other, in the name of every thing that is good and holy, what will become of us? . . .

Source 10 from Phoebe Yates Pember, *A Southern Woman's Story* (Columbia: Univ. of South Carolina Press, 2002 [orig pub 1879]) pp. 9, 14, 25, 74.[37]

10. Phoebe Yates Pember (1823–1913).

The orders ran somewhat in this fashion: "Chicken soup for twenty—beef tea for forty—tea and toast for fifty." A certain Mr. Jones had expressed his abhorrence of tea and toast, so I asked the nurse why he gave it to him.

He answered that the diet was ordered by the surgeon, but Jones said he would not touch it, for he never ate slops, and so he had eaten nothing for two days.

"Well, what does he wish?"

"The doctor says tea and toast" (reiterating his first remark).

"Did you tell the doctor he would not eat it?"

"*I* told the doctor, and *he* told the doctor."

"Perhaps he did not hear, or understand you."

"Yes, he did. He only said that he wanted that man particularly to have tea and toast, though I told him Jones threw it up regularly; so he put it down again, and said Jones was out of his head, and Jones says the doctor is a fool."

My remark upon this was that Jones could not be so very much out of his head—an observation that entailed subsequent consequences. The habit so common among physicians when dealing with uneducated people, of insisting upon particular kinds of diet, irrespective of the patient's tastes, was a peculiar grievance that no complaint during four years ever remedied. . . .

Daily inspection too, convinced me that great evils still existed under my rule, in spite of my zealous care for my patients. For example, the monthly barrel of whiskey which I was entitled to draw still remained at the dispensary under the guardianship of the apothecary and his clerks, and quarts and pints were issued through any order coming from surgeons or their substitutes, so that the contents were apt to be gone long before I was entitled to draw more, and my sick would suffer for want of the stimulant. There were many suspicious circumstances connected with this *institution;* for the monthly barrel was an institution and a very important one. Indeed, if it is necessary to have a hero for this matter of fact narrative, the whiskey barrel will have to step forward and make his bow.

37. Phoebe Yates Pember was born into a prominent Charleston, S.C. family. She was married to Thomas Pember in 1856, but he died of tuberculosis in 1861. In late 1862, she volunteered to become the chief matron at the huge Chimborazo Hospital in Richmond. She died in Pittsburgh, Pennsylvania in 1913.

✦ CHAPTER 10

Caring for the Sick
and Wounded:
Female Nurses
in the American
Civil War

So again I referred to the hospital bill passed by Congress, which provided that liquors in common with other luxuries, belonged to the matron's department, and in an evil moment, such an impulse as tempted Pandora to open the fatal casket assailed me, and I despatched the bill, flanked by a formal requisition for the liquor. An answer came in the shape of the head surgeon. He declared I would find "the charge most onerous," that "whiskey was required at all hours, sometimes in the middle of the night, and even if I remained at the hospital, he would not like me to be disturbed," "it was constantly needed for medicinal purposes," "he was responsible for its proper application;" but I was not convinced, and withstood all argument and persuasion. He was proverbially sober himself, but I was aware why both commissioned and non-commissioned officers opposed violently the removal of the liquor to my quarters. So, the printed law being at hand for reference, I nailed my colors to the mast, and that evening all the liquor was in my pantry and the key in my pocket. . . .

The mass of patients were uneducated men, who had lived by the sweat of their brow, and gratitude is an exotic plant, reared in a refined atmosphere, kept free from coarse contact and nourished by unselfishness. Common natures look only with surprise at great sacrifices and cunningly avail themselves of the benefits they bestow, but give nothing in return,—not even the satisfaction of allowing the giver to feel that the care bestowed has been beneficial; *that* might entail compensation of some kind, and in their ignorance they fear the nature of the equivalent which might be demanded.

Still, pleasant episodes often occurred to vary disappointments and lighten duties.

"Kin you writ me a letter?" drawled a whining voice from a bed in one of the wards, a cold day in '62.

The speaker was an up-country Georgian, one of the kind called "Goubers" [sic] by the soldiers generally; lean, yellow, attenuated, with wispy strands of hair hanging over his high, thin cheek-bones. He put out a hand to detain me and the nails were like claws.

"Why do you not let the nurse cut your nails?"

"Because I aren't got any spoon, and I use them instead."

"Will you let me have your hair cut then? You can't get well with all that dirty hair hanging about your eyes and ears."

"No, I can't git my hair cut, kase [sic] as how I promised my mammy that I would let it grow till the war be over. Oh, it's onlucky to cut it!"

"Then I can't write any letter for you. Do what I wish you to do, and then I will oblige you."

This was plain talking. The hair was cut (I left the nails for another day), my portfolio brought, and sitting by the side of his bed I waited for further orders. They came with a formal introduction,—"for Mrs. Marthy Brown." . . .

The doctor's dictum was, "No hope: give him anything he asks for;" but five days and nights I struggled against this decree, fed my patient with my own hands, using freely from the small store of brandy in my pantry and cheering him by words and smiles. The sixth morning on my entrance he tamed an anxious eye on my face, the hope had died out of his, for the cold sweat stood in beads there, useless to dry, so constantly were they renewed. What comfort could I give? Only silently open the Bible, and read to him without comment the ever-living promises of his Maker. Glimpses too of that abode where the "weary are at rest." Tears stole down his cheek, but he was not comforted.

"I am an only son," he said, "and my mother is a widow. Go to her, if you ever get to Baltimore, and tell her that I died in what I consider the defense of civil rights and liberties. I may be wrong. God alone knows. Say how kindly I was nursed, and that I had all I needed. I cannot thank you, for I have no breath, but we will meet up there." He pointed upward and closed his eyes, that never opened again upon this world. . . .

Soon after New Year, 1865, some members of the committee on hospital affairs called to see me, desirous of getting some information regarding the use or abuse of liquor, before the bill for the appropriations for the coming year would be introduced. There were doubts afloat as to whether the benefit conferred upon the patients by the use of stimulants counterbalanced the evil effects they produced on the surgeons, who were in the habit of making use of them when they could get them.

The problem was difficult to solve. A case in point had lately come under my observation. A man had been brought into our hospital with a crushed ankle, the cars having run over it. He had been attended to, and the leg put in splints before we had received him, so as he was still heavy and drowsy, possibly from some anodyne administered, the surgeon in attendance ordered him to be left undisturbed. The nurse in a few hours came to me to say that the man was suffering intensely. He had a burning fever, and complained of the fellow leg instead of the injured one. The natural idea of sympathy occurred, and a sedative given which failed in producing any effect. I determined to look at it in spite of orders, his sufferings appearing so great, and finding the foot and leg above and below the splint perfectly well, the thought of examining the fellow leg suggested itself. It was a most shocking sight—swollen, inflamed and purple—the drunken surgeon had set the wrong leg! The pain induced low fever, which eventually assumed a typhoid form, and the man died. With this instance fresh in my memory I hesitated to give any opinion in favor, and yet felt we could not manage without the liquor. However, the appropriation was made.

◆ CHAPTER 10

Caring for the Sick
and Wounded:
Female Nurses
in the American
Civil War

This poor fellow was the most dependent patient I ever had, and though entirely uneducated, won his way to my sympathies by his entire helplessness and belief in the efficacy of my care and advice. No surgeon in the hospital could persuade him to swallow anything in the shape of food unless I sanctioned the order, and a few kindly words, or an encouraging nod would satisfy and please him. His ideas of luxuries were curious, and his answer to my daily inquiries of what he could fancy for food, was invariably the same—he would like some "scribbled eggs and flitters.". . .

Source 11 from Elmer Ruan Coates, "Be My Mother Till I Die" (Philadelphia: Winner & Co., 1863)

11. "Be My Mother Till I Die"

Soon no wicked war will harm me,
Angels bringing peace are nigh;
Ladies, some one be my Mother,
Be my Mother 'till I die.

Ladies, some one be my Mother;
Then 'twill seem that I am home;
I'll imagine I'm a brother,
Hearing each familiar tone.

But I want a mother near me,
With that heaven in her eye;
Ladies, some one be my Mother,
Be my Mother 'till I die.

Long before I was a soldier,
Lone before I fought and bled,
In our cottage all the dear ones
Thus would gather round my bed.
Do not treat me as a stranger;
Let me feel a brother's tie;
One of you I want as Mother,
Be my Mother 'till I die.

Questions to Consider

Although Union and Confederate nurses came from every socio-economic class, with very few exceptions the memoirs were written by middle class and well-to-do women. None had previously been nurses (the exceptions being the Roman Catholic Sisters of Charity), nor were they prepared to see (as Cornelia Hancock put it) "for the first time what war meant." How (if they did) did the authors of the ten selections adjust to the war and battlefield or hospital life? The answers to that question will help you to answer the two *central* questions of this chapter.

What duties were the nurses expected to perform? In *their* view, what was the most difficult duty? How will the answers to those two questions assist you in answering the chapter's *central* questions?

What were the popular images of female nurses before and during the war? Which of the selections deal with those images (including the women's relations with male patients and staff members)? How do those questions help you to answer the two *central* questions?

What were the popular images of African Americans? How did the nurses (including Susie King Taylor) deal with those images?

How did the nurses, both Union and Confederate, deal with women who did not serve? Can the answer to that question help you to answer the chapter's two *central* questions?

Can you devise *other* questions that will help you to answer the chapter's two *central* questions?

In her selection, Cornelia Hancock, who began her nursing career at Gettysburg, noted that the postwar atmosphere "robbed the battlefield of its glory, the survivors of their victory, and the wounded of what little chance of life was left to them." How many of the selections found the war considerably less romantic than did writers and authors of songs, such as Julia Ward Howe's "Battle Hymn of the Republic"? How, if at all, did they express those emotions? How will the answers to these two questions help you in answering the chapter's two *central* questions?

As you analyze the selections and think about the above questions, can you begin to fashion the answers to the chapter's two *central* questions?

Epilogue

For those women who volunteered to serve as Civil War nurses, it almost surely was a life-changing experience. Several women, including Louisa May Alcott, could not stand the daily closeness to agony and death, and resigned after a few weeks or months. For those who stayed the course, however, not

◆ CHAPTER 10

Caring for the Sick
and Wounded:
Female Nurses
in the American
Civil War

only was their service important to the total war effort but at the same time they changed the popular conception of nurses and in turn were changed by it.

The sheer numbers of wounded and diseased soldiers nearly overwhelmed not only the nurses themselves but also the entire Union and Confederate medical systems. Nurses worked very hard to make care more personal, but that was extremely difficult. Judith McGuire, a Confederate nurse at the Robertson Hospital in Richmond, told of her valiant efforts to save a young lad who had been carried to her ward:

> He was watched and nursed during the night, [but] by the break of day he was no more. . . . My heart yearned over him, and my tears fell fast. [He was carried to a cemetery and given a Christian burial] with the lonely word "stranger" carved upon his headstone, [but] he was surely "Somebody's Darling."[38]

In addition, nurses treated soldiers of all classes, men and boys whom many of them might never have met. And some nurses cared equally for white and black soldiers alike, even though hospitals were generally segregated. Emily Elizabeth Parsons treated both white and black patients and tried to establish a training program for African American women. "It

is a difficult task," she wrote, "but one worth trying."[39]

What they all witnessed must have been horrifying. Approximately 94 percent of all wounds came from minie balls, which left gaping holes wherever they hit and made treatment difficult. And amputations, which were universally practiced if a minie ball had struck an arm or leg, had poor survival rates. Roughly 74 percent of all ankle joint amputations proved fatal, as did 83 percent of hip joints and 53 percent of knee joints. Every nurse who wrote of her experiences remembered amputations.[40]

Finally, as noted earlier, disease felled twice as many soldiers as did minie balls. Union soldiers who contracted pneumonia suffered a death rate of 190 per 1,000. For Confederates it was worse: 400 per 1,000. Female nurses worked ceaselessly fighting disease and infection, and the general hospital wards with female administrators had a fatality rate that was half of those wards with men in charge. Yet lack of knowledge of germ theory and how diseases spread made the fight an uphill battle. As noted earlier, it was common for cups of water (or whiskey) to be passed from patient to patient,

---

38. Judith W. McGuire Diary, February 12, 1863, in www.mdgorman.com (Civil War Richmond).

39. *Memoir of Emily Elizabeth Parsons, Published for the Benefit of the Cambridge Hospital* (Boston: Little, Brown, 1880), p. 133.
40. For Union amputations, see Brooks, *Civil War Medicine*, p. 127. Almost all of the records of the Confederate Medical Department were lost in a fire that destroyed most of Richmond in April 1865. See Ira M. Rutkow, *Bleeding Blue and Gray: Civil War Surgery and the Evolution of American Medicine* (New York: Random House, 2005), p. xiii.

and it wasn't until 1888 that the modern drinking straw was invented.[41]

At the end of the war, many nurses found it difficult to return to their pre-war situations. Their work had earned for them status and importance and for years they were thanked and praised by the soldiers they had cared for. As Mary Gardner Holland remembered in her 1895 book *Our Army Nurses,* "How the eyes of the old veterans fill with tears when, at our camp fires, some old lady is introduced, and the presiding officer says, 'Boys, she was an army nurse'." For their part, former nurse Emily Parsons spoke for many of them when she wrote to her mother, "I wonder what I shall do with myself when the war is over. . . . I never can sit and do nothing." Most did return home but became active in charity work, fund-raising for soldiers' monuments, and organizing and participating in soldiers' reunions. Not a few became teachers or joined reform movements. Others found full-time work in the enlarged federal government and still others became active in supporting education for nurses. Emily Parsons wrote, "I never expect to live at home again. . . . Work is my life. I cannot be happy doing nothing."[42]

And yet many of those nurses who served so courageously probably never fully understood or appreciated the contributions they had made, for their role in the Civil War helped to establish nursing as a respectable field for middle class women. In 1868, the American Medical Association recognized nurses by passing a resolution that nursing schools should be attached to hospitals. And for younger women, those nurses held open the possibility of becoming physicians.

Only a handful of women were physicians at the onset of the Civil War. Undoubtedly the most well-known was Dr. Mary Edwards Walker, who put her practice on hold to serve in Union hospitals or on the battlefield. While engaged in that work, she broke with custom when she dressed like a man, complete with trousers. When she was captured by Confederates, a southern officer wrote to his wife that a female doctor was "a thing that nothing but a debased and depraved Yankee Nation could produce." In November 1865, she was awarded the Congressional Medal of Honor. And along with nurses, she paved the way for younger women: by 1880 there were 2,432 women physicians in the United States and by 1900 the nation had more women doctors than any other country.[43]

After the war, a few former Union nurses were granted pensions by

41. Brooks, *Civil War Medicine*, p. 111; Humphreys, *Marrow of Tragedy*, pp. 9, 24.
42. See Mary Gardner Holland, comp., *Our Army Nurses: Interesting Sketches, Addresses, and Photographs* (Boston: H. Wilkins & Co., 1895). p. 11. For Parsons, see Schultz, *Women at the Front*, p. 145; see also *ibid.*, chapter 5.

43. Humphreys, *Marrow of Tragedy*, pp. 57–58, 74; W.F. Bynum, et al., *The Western Medical Tradition, 1800–2000* (Cambridge, UK: Cambridge Univ. Press, 2006), p. 174. For a photograph of Dr. Walker see Humphreys, *Marrow of Tragedy, p. 57.*

♦ CHAPTER 10

Caring for the Sick
and Wounded:
Female Nurses
in the American
Civil War

special acts of Congress. But most were left out. Anna Beers complained to former nurse Mary Ann Bickerdyke, "Are we not all soldiers?" Finally in 1892, Congress passed the Army Nurses Pension Act that guaranteed former Union nurses a monthly pension of $12 (approximately $812 in 2001 U.S. dollars) if they had served for more than six months. Former Confederate nurses were excluded, as were many women who performed nurses' work (like Susie King Taylor) but technically were not listed as nurses but rather as cooks, laundresses, seamstresses, matrons, chambermaids, dining room girls, etc. And many women never applied. As a result, of the roughly 9,000 Union nurses who served for the required length of time, only 2,448 claims were processed and only 600 pensions granted.[44]

Years after the Battle of Gettysburg, the Governor General of Canada asked former Confederate General George Pickett (who led the disastrous "Pickett's Charge" at Gettysburg) "to what he attributed the failure of the Confederates at Gettysburg." Tongue in cheek, Pickett replied, "I've always thought the Yankees had something to do with it."[45]

Pickett may have been correct if he was referring only to the Battle of Gettysburg, where the Union army outnumbered the Confederates by roughly 14,000 and sustained fewer killed, wounded, or missing. But when looking at the total statistics for the Civil War, it is clear that the total Confederate strength was fatally sapped by disease in the ranks. From 1861 to 1865, a disturbing 31 percent of the South's total white male population under the age of 30 died of disease. When added to those who were killed in battle or died from battle wounds, the total number of Confederate deaths was an astounding 57.3 percent of the entire southern white male population under 30.[46] No nation (or would-be nation) could survive after suffering such losses. Not enough medical care, surgeons, hospitals, or nurses could stand for long against a larger and better medically equipped foe.

To be sure, the Union suffered staggering statistics as well. But the United States began the war with over twice as many white males under 30, used a flow of approximately 400,000 foreign-born males to fill the ranks, and after 1862 could count on 180,000 African American men to fight, 21 of whom were awarded the Congressional

44. For Beers' complaint, see Schultz, *Women at the Front,* p. 183. On pensions see *ibid.,* chapter 6. For the numbers of applicants and pensions granted, see Holland, *Our Army Nurses,* p. 11. One reason that only around 25 percent of the claimants actually received pensions was because they could not provide sufficient evidence. *Ibid.* Union nurses who were widows of soldiers already received pensions.
45. See James McPherson's "American Victory, American Defeat," in John D. Fowler, ed., *The Confederate Experience Reader:*

Selected Documents and Essays (New York: Routledge, 2008), p. 405.
46. The statistic clearly is misleading, since many Confederate soldiers—and deaths—were men over 30 with some of them significantly over 30. And yet, if the number of southern white males over 30 is augmented by 100,000 *and* the number of deaths remains constant, the percentage of total Confederate deaths would be just over 47 percent, the statistical majority from disease.

Medal of Honor. Add to that a much larger and better organized medical system with nine times the number of nurses who cared for and treated the wounded, and victory, although it took four bloody years, was almost sure to come. For many, it was not soon enough.

To Our Readers

As you complete this chapter, many of you might be interested in learning more about Civil War medicine and its female nurses.

An excellent place to begin your research would be Frank R. Freemon, *Microbes and Minie Balls: An Annotated Bibliography of Civil War Medicine* (Rutherford, NJ: Fairleigh Dickinson Univ. Press, 1993), which includes listings of 144 primary sources and 93 secondary sources. The number of nurses' memoirs is disappointing, with only around 30 of the 60+ accounts. When Freemon deals with medicine, however, the bibliography is excellent.

Much better for female nurses and hospital workers is Jane Schultz's *Women at the Front,* cited earlier in this chapter. Her book has a very helpful bibliography of 22 pages of published sources.

Published memoirs by both Union and Confederate female nurses have become extremely popular of late, and more than a few of those that were out of print have been recently republished. In addition, computer collections of primary sources have veritably mushroomed and contain many female nurses' accounts that are out of print.

There also are a growing number of biographies of female nurses. On the Union side, perhaps the best-known is Nina Brown Baker's *Cyclone in Calico: The Story of Mary Ann Bickerdyke* (Boston: Little, Brown, 1952). For Confederates, a number of articles and *Google* secondary sources have been written about Sally Louisa Tompkins (1833–1916), who privately founded and nursed in Richmond's Robertson Hospital. When Confederate President Jefferson Davis instituted rules requiring military hospitals be under military command, he sidestepped his own order by commissioning Tompkins as a captain in the Confederate States' Army. Upon her death in 1916, she was buried with full military honors in Virginia's Mathews County. At the centennial of her work in Richmond, a stained glass memorial window was placed in St. James Episcopal Church on Monument Avenue in Richmond, corrrectly named the "City of Monuments."

Another interesting way to study this subject is to choose one hospital with good existing records. Chimborazo Hospital, the Confederacy's largest, has numerous records. State historical journals contain numerous articles on Civil War hospitals, as do *The Journal of Southern History* and *The Journal of American History,* both of which have first-rate indexes. Historical societies will contain unpublished sources.

Almost no male nurses left accounts of their service. The most famous exception was the poet and journalist Walt Whitman (1819–1892), whose *Memoranda During the War* (1875) left

✦ CHAPTER 10

Caring for the Sick
and Wounded:
Female Nurses
in the American
Civil War

a vivid portrait of hospitals around Washington, DC.

Near the end of the nineteenth century, efforts were made to collect the names of Union female nurses before they were lost. One former nurse, Mary Gardner Holland, compiled sketches of almost 100 nurses, collected in the book *Our Army Nurses: Interesting Sketches, Addresses, and Photographs*... (Boston: H. Wilkins & Co., 1895), which was republished in somewhat abbreviated form in 1998.

Enormous photographic and music collections are available in the Library of Congress and the National Archives, some of which have been digitized. The music lyrics can be patriotic and uplifting ("Rally 'Round the Flag, Boys") or terribly sad. Dr. Drew Gilpin

Faust came across what we think is the saddest in the Library Company of Philadelphia: "Oh, Do Not Bury Me Here." You can read it on page 195 of her book *This Republic of Suffering*.

Finally, out-of-print memoirs by Civil War nurses fairly regularly turn up in local as well as college and university libraries. Also, local historical societies contain these prized sources.

The search will be well worth the effort.

For post-war activities of some southern women in honoring the soldiers, see Caroline E. Janney, *Burying the Dead But Not the Past: Ladies' Memorial Associations and the Lost Cause* (Chapel Hill: Univ. of North Carolina Press, 2008).

11

Reconstructing Reconstruction: The Political Cartoonist and American Public Opinion

◆

The Problem

Impoverished, desperate, and nearly forgotten, political cartoonist Thomas Nast had accepted a minor position as a consular official in out-of-the-way Ecuador as a political favor from President Theodore Roosevelt. The fairly undemanding job paid a modest salary, only about one seventh of his total income in 1879 as the United States' most well-known and influential political cartoonist for *Harper's Weekly* in New York City. Four months after his arrival in Guayaquil, Nast died of yellow fever.[1]

In his years at *Harper's Weekly* from 1862 to 1886, Thomas Nast had drawn several hundred cartoons on a vast array of topics: temperance, foreign affairs, presidential elections, anti-Irish immigration, anti-Roman Catholicism, anti-political corruption and political bosses, and many, many others.[2] This chapter, however, will concentrate on Nast's cartoons relating to the post–Civil War Reconstruction of the former Confederacy. Since *Harper's Weekly* was a national periodical with a circulation of around 160,000, many thousands of people were aware of Nast's position on the issues regarding Reconstruction and very likely were influenced by his cartoons.

1. On Nast's death, see Albert Bigelow Paine, *Th. Nast: His Period and His Pictures* (New York: Pearson Publishing, 1904), pp. 561–574; Fiona Deans Halloran, *Thomas Nast: The Father of Modern Political Cartoons* (Chapel Hill: Univ. of North Carolina Press, 2012), pp. 278–281.

2. Paine's biography lists 885 cartoons and illustrations, but this number surely is incomplete. Paine, *Th. Nast,* pp. xvii–xx.

✦ CHAPTER 11

Reconstructing
Reconstruction:
The Political
Cartoonist and
American Public
Opinion

The end of the War of the Rebellion[3] in 1865 left the United States with a host of difficult questions. What should happen to the defeated South? Should the states of the former Confederacy be permitted to take their pre-war places in the Union as quickly and smoothly as possible, with minimum concessions to their northern conquerors? Or should the United States insist on a more drastic reconstruction of the South? Tied to these questions was the thorny constitutional issue of whether the southern states actually had left the Union at all in 1861. But perhaps the most difficult questions the Union's victory raised concerned the status of the former slaves. To be sure, they were no longer in bondage, but should they possess the same rights as whites? Should they be allowed to vote? Should they be assisted in becoming landowners? If not, how would they earn a living? Indeed, while the war settled a number of questions, its conclusion left all Americans with other dilemmas.

In all these questions, public opinion in the victorious North was a critical factor in shaping or altering the federal government's policies designed to reconstruct the South. Earlier democratic reforms (such as universal white male suffrage, rotation in office, the evolution of political campaigns, and so forth) made it unlikely that either the president or Congress could defy public opinion successfully. Yet public opinion can shift with remarkable speed, and political figures forever must be sensitive to its sometimes fickle winds.

Although public opinion is a crucial factor in a democratic republic such as the United States, that same public opinion often can be shaped or manipulated by political figures, interest groups, or the press. In this chapter, you will be examining and analyzing how Thomas Nast, through his cartoons, attempted to influence and shape public opinion in the North. Although Nast certainly was not the only person who sought to do so, many of his contemporaries, friends and foes alike, admitted that his political cartoons ranked among the most powerful opinion shapers during the era of Reconstruction.

Your task in this chapter is to examine and analyze each cartoon in the Evidence section of this chapter to answer the following central question: **In what ways did the cartoons of Thomas Nast reflect and at the same time attempt to sway the national debate over the issues regarding the Reconstruction era?**

3. Many northerners used the term "War of the Rebellion" during and immediately after the war. The official records of the conflict, published by the U.S. Government Printing Office from 1880 to 1901 were titled *The Official Records of the War of the Rebellion*. President Lincoln and others, however, preferred the term "Civil War," that was ultimately adopted. During the war, many southerners referred to the War for Southern Independence, and later to the War Between the States.

Background

Even as political leaders wrestled with the extremely difficult problems of Reconstruction, they also had to deal with issues stemming from the dramatic changes in the United States itself. Although most Americans still made their livings in agriculture, from 1865 to 1873 industrial production increased by 75 percent while the number of manufacturing and construction workers more than doubled. The railroad and the telegraph not only drew people westward but also at the same time were gradually binding the people of the nation together. In the early 1800s, opponents of westward expansion had warned that a larger nation would require a larger and considerably more powerful central government, a prediction that was coming true during and after the Civil War. From roughly 1860 to 1880, the number of civilian employees of the federal government had increased almost sixfold, the number of postal employees had doubled, and federal expenditures had increased from around $67 million to nearly $400 million. In almost every way, the United States was in the process of becoming a new nation.[4]

All of these changes were witnessed and participated in by Americans who were considerably better informed than their grandparents had been. For one thing, by the time of the Civil War nearly all adult white males could vote. Initially, political leaders of the Revolutionary Age had opposed universal suffrage, agreeing with Sir William Blackstone that "such persons [who] are in so mean a situation as to be esteemed to have no will of their own" should not have the privilege of casting ballots.[5] But gradually property and taxpayer restrictions were repealed, in part because nineteenth-century political chieftains feared that the rapidly expanding number of white males who could not vote would lead to dangerous uprisings among the nation's poor—and especially among the urban poor. Also, each evolving political party supported widening of the suffrage because it feared that its rival party might claim credit for doing so. Perhaps, this was not exactly in the spirit of democracy, but it certainly did democratize the electorate.[6]

Widening of the suffrage also led to well-organized and exciting political campaigns, perhaps the first of which was the presidential election of 1840 in which mass parades, campaign signs and buttons, and the widespread circulation of campaign literature were used to influence the voters, most of whom had never voted before. The most effective campaign tactics were carried out by the Whigs. They nominated military hero William Henry Harrison for president and then spread the word that Harrison lived in a log cabin (he didn't) and

4. For statistics, see *Statistical History of the United States, from Colonial Times to the Present* (Stanford, CT: Fairfield Publishers, 1965), pp. 710–711, 718.

5. For Blackstone, see Chilton Williamson, *American Suffrage: From Property to Democracy, 1760–1860* (Princeton: Princeton Univ. Press, 1960), quoted p. 11.

6. On widening of the suffrage, see Alexander Keyssar, *The Right to Vote: The Contested History of Democracy* (New York: Basic Books, rev. ed. 2009), p. 28.

◆ CHAPTER 11

Reconstructing
Reconstruction:
The Political
Cartoonist and
American Public
Opinion

consumed "hard cider" (he didn't). The campaign was successful, as around 80 percent of the qualified electorate actually cast ballots. The new president gave a much-too-long inauguration address in freezing rain and died of pneumonia after only about one month in office.[7]

A better way of maintaining the allegiance of voters was through newspapers and periodicals. In the early days of the republic, most newspapers were financed by political factions. For example, Secretary of State Thomas Jefferson and Secretary of the Treasury Alexander Hamilton both secretly underwrote their respective party's newspapers. Party-backed newspapers continued to slant the news in their own parties' favor.

But even as inventions and technology were revolutionizing American agriculture, industry, transportation, and communications, they were also revolutionizing newspaper and periodical publishing. The establishment of the Associated Press (AP, 1846) and Western Union (1856) allowed news stories to be sent by way of telegraph throughout the nation. At the same time, technological breakthroughs in printing increased the number of copies that could be printed and as a result drove the prices of newspapers and periodicals down. For example, by the 1870s, the *New-York Tribune* could publish an astounding 18,000 newspaper *per hour*. As a result, circulation increased, as did advertising revenue, making it possible for newspapers to become independent of political

parties or factions. The establishment of these independent—and inexpensive—newspapers increased national circulation from 1870 to 1890 by 222 percent. In a word, newspapers and newspaper chains were becoming big business.[8]

Equally prosperous were *weekly* papers that published news stories, editorials, literature, poetry, engraved pictures, and cartoons. By 1860, there were 3,173 weeklies as opposed to only 387 dailies. The weeklies boasted of national audiences and had national circulations that were much higher than the daily newspapers. Two of the most successful were *Frank Leslie's Illustrated Newspaper* (1855) and *Harper's Weekly* (1857). Frank Leslie (orig. Henry Carter) was an Englishman who came to the United States, changed his name, and established several periodicals, the most successful of which was his illustrated newspaper. The name was so successful that when Frank Leslie died in 1880, his widow legally changed her name to Frank Leslie and continued to publish the periodical profitably for years.[9]

Although Leslie's periodical boasted a larger circulation, *Harper's Weekly*

7. On Harrison, see Daniel Walker Howe, *What Hath God Wrought: The Transformation of America, 1815–1848* (New York: Oxford Univ. Press, 2007), pp. 570–571, 589. The number of voters who cast ballots in 1840 was an increase of 63 percent over those of 1836.

8. For statistics, see *Statistical History of the United States*, p. 500. For the publishing of the *Tribune,* see George H. Douglas, *The Golden Age of the Newspaper* (Westport, CT: Greenwood Press, 1999), p. 83. For AP and Western Union, see Jean Folkerts and Dwight Teeter, Jr., *Voices of a Nation: A History of Media in the United States* (New York: Macmillan, 1989). For newspapers as big business, see Douglas, *Golden Age,* p. 82.
9. For the number of weeklies, see Bernard A. Weisberger, *The American Newspaperman* (Chicago: Univ. of Chicago Press, 1961), p. 111. For the comparatively smaller circulation of the dailies, see Frank Luther Mott, *American Journalism: A History* (New York: Macmillan, 3rd ed. 1962), p. 403. On the Leslies, see Douglas, *Golden Age,* p. 185.

became better known. Both, of course, were published weekly and distributed nationally via the telegraph. For its part, *Harper's Weekly* was established by four Harper brothers, none of them actually newspapermen but all of them shrewd business figures. In 1862, they hired Thomas Nast away from the *New York Illustrated News* for $150 per page. It was a wise investment.[10]

Thomas Nast was born in the German Palatinate (one of the German states) in 1840, the son of a musician in the Ninth Regiment Bavarian Band. The family moved to New York in 1846, at which time young Thomas was enrolled in school. An indifferent student, one teacher admonished him, "Go finish your picture. You will never learn to read or figure." After unsuccessfully trying to interest their son in music, his parents ultimately encouraged the development of his artistic talents.

The Nasts were far from wealthy, living in New York's working class Fourth Ward, which was populated principally by immigrants and naturalized citizens (13,244 out of 14,166). The major ethnic group was the Irish, whom Nast hated, possibly because they bullied him and also because they persecuted African Americans, for whom Nast felt considerable sympathy. Finally, although the Nast family was Roman Catholic, Thomas Nast himself disliked the Catholic school in which he was initially enrolled and because he rejected some of the church's teachings. Some years later, after Nast had become a full-time artist and cartoonist, these prejudices would surface.

Thomas Nast went to work for various newspapers and periodicals at the age of fifteen. By 22, he had joined the elite group of cartoonists in New York at the time when their drawings were growing in demand by newspapers and periodicals. On September 3, 1864, *Harper's Weekly* published Nast's drawing "Compromise with the South" (Source 1). The reaction was so successful that *Harper's Weekly* had to print a second run, and the Republican Party printed several thousand copies to distribute as campaign literature. As Nast biographer Fiona Deans Halloran commented, "If ever there was a smash hit in nineteenth-century cartooning, this was it." Success followed success until by the end of the war General Ulysses Grant, when asked who was the foremost figure in civilian life who was developed by the Rebellion, replied, "*I* think, Thomas Nast. He did as much as any one man to preserve the Union. . . ."[11]

As one of Nast's biographers observed, cartoons "straddle the problematic boundary between the elite and the street. . . . [c]onsumed by the rich and poor, the educated and illiterate, . . . cartoons were a popular form of political expression. . . ." It is obvious from his work that Nast was a man of strong feelings and emotions. In his eyes, those people whom he admired possessed no flaws. Conversely, those whom he opposed were, to him, capable of every conceivable villainy. As a result, his characterizations often were terribly unfair, gross distortions of reality and more than occasionally libelous. In his view, however,

10. On the hiring of Nast by *Harper's Weekly,* see Paine, *Th. Nast,* p. 120.

11. On the September 3, 1864 drawing, see Halloran, *Thomas Nast,* p. 59. On Grant see Paine, *Th. Nast,* p. 120.

◆ CHAPTER 11

Reconstructing
Reconstruction:
The Political
Cartoonist and
American Public
Opinion

his central purpose was not to entertain but to move his audience, to make them scream out in outrage or anger, to prod them to action. The selection of Nast's cartoons in this chapter is typical of the body of his work for *Harper's Weekly*: artistically inventive and polished, blatantly slanted, and brimming with indignation and emotion.[12]

Thomas Nast had just begun his career about the same time as the Republican Party was born, and the two formed a mutually profitable alliance that existed for almost three decades. The erosion and ultimate collapse of the Whig Party, which split over the issue of the expansion of slavery, left many Americans without a political affiliation. In 1854, groups of former Whigs, anti-slavery expansionists, nativists, abolitionists, and anti-slavery Democrats gathered in Ripon, Wisconsin to form a new party, adopted the name Republicans, and two years later nominated Col. John C. Frémont for president and former Whig William

L. Dayton of New Jersey for vice president. Democrat James Buchanan won the presidential election but Frémont did surprisingly well by garnering 114 electoral votes to Buchanan's 174. The next presidential election was won by Republican Abraham Lincoln. The secession of the southern states, all of which boasted heavy Democratic majorities, gave the Republicans the dominance of the federal government for years. Nast's pro-Republican loyalties were patently obvious in nearly all his cartoons.[13]

The evidence in this chapter consists of ten cartoons by Thomas Nast that were published in *Harper's Weekly* between September 3, 1864 and December 9, 1876. Your task in this chapter is to examine and analyze each of the ten cartoons to answer the chapter's central question: In what ways did the cartoons of Thomas Nast reflect and at the same time attempt to sway the national debate over the issues regarding the Reconstruction era?

◆

The Method

Almost all of us have laughed at, been informed by, been angered by, or agreed with political cartoons we have seen. Today it is considerably easier to identify the issues, events, and characters portrayed in these cartoons as well as to realize how the cartoonists are hoping to sway his or her "readers." But the political cartoons of Thomas Nast that you will be working with are approximately *140 years old*. How can

you hope to "unpack" (analyze) those subjective artistic works?

To begin with, each of Thomas Nast's political cartoons (as well as those of other artists) usually dealt with one issue or event. Like the authors of editorials that appeared in newspapers and periodicals, cartoonists often had

12. Halloran, *Thomas Nast*, p. 291.

13. Gordon S.P. Kleeberg, *The Formation of the Republican Party as a National Political Organization* (New York: Moods Pub. Co., 1911), pp. 13–50; Gordon H. Mayer, *The Republican Party, 1854–1966*, (New York: Oxford Univ. Press, 1967), chapters 1 through 3.

a distinct *point of view.* Therefore, like the editors of *Harper's Weekly,* Thomas Nast's cartoons were not objective reports of an event or issue.

Examine each cartoon to determine what event or issue was being addressed. Here your text and your instructor will prove to be invaluable. In addition, we have provided some "clues" that will help you to interpret the cartoons. They are in the Evidence section of the chapter.

Once you have decided what event or issue each cartoon was dealing with, then examine the people who were portrayed. Are some of the persons actual characters (such as Presidents Andrew Johnson or Ulysses Grant, etc.) or drawings intended to represent a certain character (a Confederate soldier, a freedman, etc.)? Here again, the "clues" we have provided should help.

Like other political cartoonists, Nast often used *symbols* to make his points, sometimes in the form of an *allegory.* In an allegory, familiar figures are shown in a situation or setting that everyone knows—for example, a setting from the Bible, a children's fairy tale, or another well-known source. For example, a setting in which a tiny president of the United States holding a slingshot and fighting a gigantic man labeled "Congress" would remind viewers of the story of David and Goliath. In that story, the small man won. The message of the cartoon is that the president will triumph in his struggle with Congress.

Other, less complicated symbolism is often used in political cartoons. In Nast's time, as today, the American flag was an important symbol of the ideals of our democratic country, and an olive branch or dove represented the desire for peace. Some symbols have changed, however. Today, the tall, skinny figure we call Uncle Sam represents the United States. In Nast's time, Columbia, a tall woman wearing a long classical dress, represented the United States. Also in Nast's time, an hourglass, rather than a clock, symbolized that time was running out. And military uniforms, regardless of the fact that the Civil War had ended in 1865, were used to indicate whether a person had supported the Union (and, by implication, was a Republican) or the Confederacy (by implication, a Democrat).

Once you have decided what event or issue each cartoon is addressing *and* who the persons in each cartoon are or who or what they represent *and* the meaning of the symbols or the allegory in each cartoon, then you are ready to answer the chapter's central question:

In what ways did the political cartoons of Thomas Nast reflect and at the same time attempt to sway the national debate over the Reconstruction era?

The Evidence

Sources 1 through 10 from *Harper's Weekly. A Journal of Civilization,* September 3, 1864; March 30, 1867; September 5, October 3, 1868; April 13, September 21, 1872; March 14, July 18, 1874; September 2, November 4, 1876. It would be helpful if you used a magnifying glass to discover some of the details in each cartoon.

◆ CHAPTER 11

Reconstructing
Reconstruction:
The Political
Cartoonist and
American Public
Opinion

1. Compromise with the South, September 3, 1864.

2. Amphitheatrum Johnsonianum—"Massacre of the Innocents at New Orleans," March 30, 1867.

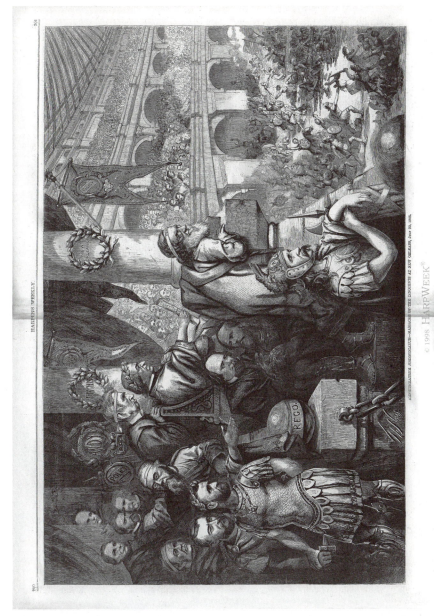

◆ CHAPTER 11

Reconstructing
Reconstruction:
The Political
Cartoonist and
American Public
Opinion

3. "This Is a White Man's Government," September 5, 1868.

4. "The Modern Samson," October 3, 1868.

✦ CHAPTER 11

Reconstructing
Reconstruction:
The Political
Cartoonist and
American Public
Opinion

5. "Republic Is Not Ungrateful," April 13, 1872.

THE REPUBLIC IS NOT UNGRATEFUL.

"It is not what is *charged* but what is *proved* that damages the party defendant. Any one may be accused of the most heinous offenses; the Saviour of mankind was not only arraigned but convicted; but what of it? Facts alone are decisive."—*New York Tribune, March 13, 1872.*

6. "Let Us Clasp Hands over the Bloody Chasm" (Horace Greeley),
   September 21, 1872.

✦ CHAPTER 11

Reconstructing
Reconstruction:
The Political
Cartoonist and
American Public
Opinion

7. "Colored Rule in a Reconstructed (?) State," March 14, 1874.

COLORED RULE IN A RECONSTRUCTED (?) STATE.—[See Page 242.]

(THE MEMBERS CALL EACH OTHER THIEVES, LIARS, RASCALS, AND COWARDS.)

COLUMBIA. "You are Aping the lowest Whites. If you disgrace your Race in this way you had better take Back Seats."

8. "Don't Let Us Have Any More of This Nonsense," July 18, 1874.

◆ CHAPTER 11

Reconstructing
Reconstruction:
The Political
Cartoonist and
American Public
Opinion

9. "Is This a Republican Form of Government? Is This Protecting Life,
Liberty, or Property? Is This the Equal Protection of the Laws?"
September 2, 1876.

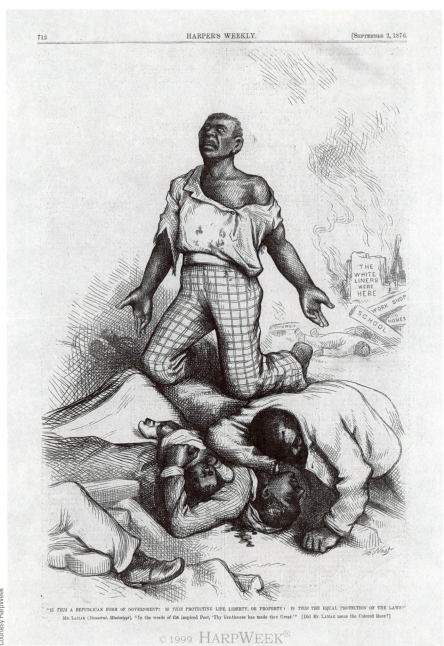

10. "The Solid South Against the Union," November 4, 1876.

◆ CHAPTER 11

Reconstructing
Reconstruction:
The Political
Cartoonist and
American Public
Opinion

11. "Clues."

The following clues are intended to assist you in interpreting the ten cartoons of Thomas Nast (Sources 1 through 10). The "clues" are not arranged in the same order as the cartoons. Also, as you will see, there are more "clues" than there are cartoons. By examining closely the "clues," determine what "clue" (or "clues") can be matched to particular cartoons.

1. Prior to the unofficial adoption of Uncle Sam as the United States' unofficial symbol, the nation's symbol was the woman Columbia, or Miss Liberty (note the Statue of Liberty, a gift from France to the United States in 1884, and the naming of the District of Columbia). She appears in cartoons 1, 5, 7, and 8.

2. Andersonville was a grisly prison camp for Union soldiers located in southwest Georgia. Over 42,000 were held there, over 12,000 of whom died.

3. A Union veteran is attempting to reach a ballot box, but is prevented from doing so by three individuals. "Five Points" is a section of New York City inhabited by lower class Irish. Another man has the initials NBF on his hat and the initials CSA on his belt buckle. The third individual is Horatio Seymour, Democratic nominee for president.

4. The Civil War began in April 1861 with the Confederates firing on Fort Sumter in Charleston harbor.

5. In his acceptance speech at the 1872 Democratic convention liberal editor Horace Greeley used the phrase "Let us clasp hands over the bloody chasm," intended to urge the end of hostile feelings between North and South.

6. In 1864 the Democratic Party convention met in Chicago and passed a resolution calling for immediate efforts to end the war and bring the seceding states back into the Union at any price.

7. South Carolina was one of the three remaining states that were occupied by federal troops. Prior to the 1876 presidential election, a group of white supremacists in Hamburg, S.C., attempted to stop freedmen from voting by destroying their homes, workshops, and schools and killing as many African Americans as they could.

8. Alexander Shepherd was nominated by President Ulysses Grant as governor of the District of Columbia. As it was discovered that Shepherd was corrupt and received bribes for political favors, the Senate refused to confirm his nomination. The President remained loyal to his nominee.

9. On July 30, 1866, a race riot broke out in New Orleans in which several African Americans were killed or wounded. President Johnson's inaction led to the first serious calls for his impeachment and removal.

10. As southern states gradually were permitted to occupy seats in Congress and have presidential electoral votes, the Republican Party feared its national demise. If African Americans would vote for Republicans in state and federal elections, it would be possible for Republicans to retain their strong political positions by carrying some southern states.

11. South Carolina was the only state in which African Americans made up a significant majority of the state legislature during Reconstruction. Much worthwhile was accomplished, but there was also considerable corruption and bad behavior.

12. A woman symbolizing "Southern Democracy" was taking power from the freedmen by overturning their rights to vote. In the background are cheering whites, the five in the first row represent Nathan Bedford Forrest, Robert E. Lee, Horatio Seymour, Francis Blair (an ally of Andrew Johnson), and John T. Hoffman (New York City mayor and ally of the Tweed political machine).

13. Columbia mourns the "Union Heroes, who fell in a Useless War." Useless?

14. As the three men hold back the African American Union veteran from voting, each of them carried a powerful weapon. At the bottom of the cartoon is the following quotation: "We regard the Reconstruction Acts (so called) of Congress as usurpations, and unconstitutional, revolutionary, and void.—Democratic Platform."

15. What is the allegory in Source 4?

16. In Source 7, Columbia scolds the South Carolina legislators: "You are aping the lowest whites. If you disgrace your race in this way you had better take back seats."

17. Ulysses Grant appears in three of the ten cartoons (2, 5, 8). How is he treated in each cartoon?

18. What is the meaning of the two flags in Source 10?

◆

Questions to Consider

As you were instructed earlier, begin by examining each cartoon, answering the following questions:

1. What issue or event is depicted in this cartoon?
2. Who are the principal figures and how is each portrayed? What figures are intended to represent certain groups of individuals?
3. What imagery, symbols, and allegories are used?

With the assistance of your text, your instructor, and the 18 clues at the end of the Evidence section, you should be able to answer the above questions.

As you have discovered, however, Thomas Nast filled his drawings with all kinds of details, details that his "readers" may have easily recognized but that you will not. All of those details direct the "readers" to Nast's subjective opinions that he wanted his "readers" to make their own. To examine and analyze each of Nast's drawings and subjective points will require you to get your magnifying glass and examine the details, not a few of them are in the *backgrounds* of his drawings.

You already have examined and analyzed Source 1, "Compromise with the

◆ CHAPTER 11

Reconstructing
Reconstruction:
The Political
Cartoonist and
American Public
Opinion

South." But have you looked closely at the *flags*? At the *people* in the background?

We already have mentioned that Ulysses Grant is depicted in Source 2, on the lower left of the drawing. Note that he is restraining someone—who is Gen. Philip Sheridan. What was Nast saying about Grant?

In short, every single one of the Thomas Nast cartoons is filled with details, *minutia* if you will, that was intended to guide the "reader" to the point(s) Nast was attempting to make. Examine the background, the feathers on the arrows in Source 5, as well as the statues behind Grant, the sign over the door in source 8, and so forth. Leave no stone unturned.

◆

Epilogue

Undoubtedly, Thomas Nast's work had an important impact on northern opinion of Reconstruction, the Democratic Party, Andrew Johnson, Ulysses Grant, Horace Greeley, Irish-Americans, and a host of other individuals and issues. Yet gradually, northern ardor began to decline as other issues and concerns eased Reconstruction out of the limelight and as it appeared that the crusade to reconstruct the South would be an endless one. Gradually southern Democrats regained control of their state governments, partly through intimidation of black voters and partly through appeals to whites to return the South to the hands of white southerners.[14] Fearing northern outrage and a potential return to Radical Reconstruction, however, on the surface most southern political leaders claimed to accept emancipation and

decried against widespread lynchings and terror against former slaves.

Meanwhile in the North, those Radical Republicans who had insisted on equality for the freemen either were dying or retiring from politics, replaced by conservative Republicans who spoke for economic expansion, industrialism and commerce, and prosperous farmers. For their part, northern Democrats envisaged a political reunion of northern and southern Democrats that could win control of the federal government. Like their Republican counterparts, but for different reasons, northern Democrats had no stomach for assuring freedom and rights to former slaves.

Finally, in the late 1880s, when white southerners realized that the Reconstruction spirit had waned in the North, southern state legislatures began instituting rigid segregation of schools, public transportation and accommodations, parks, restaurants and theaters, elevators, drinking fountains, and so on. Not until the 1950s did those chains begin to be broken.

14. Conservative Democrats regained control of southern state governments in Tennessee and Virginia (1869); Georgia (1872); Alabama, Arkansas, and Texas (1874); Mississippi (1876); North Carolina, South Carolina, Louisiana, and Florida (1877).

Self-Portrait of Thomas Nast, July 24, 1876.

◆ CHAPTER 11

Reconstructing
Reconstruction:
The Political
Cartoonist and
American Public
Opinion

As the reform spirit waned in the later years of Reconstruction, Nast's popularity suffered. The public appeared to tire of his anger, his self-righteousness, and his relentless crusades. Meanwhile newspaper and magazine technology was changing, and Nast had great difficulty adjusting to the new methodology.[15] Finally, the new publisher of *Harper's Weekly* sought to make the publication less political, and in such an atmosphere there was no place for Thomas Nast. His last cartoon for *Harper's Weekly* appeared on Christmas Day of 1886. He continued to drift from job to job, in 1893 briefly owned his own paper, *Nast's Weekly,* which turned out to be a financial disaster, and by 1901 was deeply in debt. It was then that President Roosevelt came to his aid with a minor consular post in Ecuador, where he died four months after his arrival. He was buried in a quiet ceremony in Woodlawn Cemetery in The Bronx, New York.

Although Nast was only sixty-two years old when he died, most of the famous subjects of his cartoons had long predeceased him. William Marcy Tweed, the political boss of New York's Tammany Hall who Nast had helped to bring down, was sentenced to twelve years in prison in late 1873. But "Boss"

Tweed escaped in 1875 and fled to Cuba, where he was apprehended by authorities who identified him with the assistance of a Nast cartoon. He died in prison in 1878.

Nast's hero, Ulysses S. Grant, left the White House in 1877 after an administration marked by corruption and scandal. Not a wealthy man, Grant hurried to finish his memoirs (to provide for his wife Julia) before the throat cancer he had been diagnosed with killed him. He died on July 23, 1885, and was interred in Central Park in New York City, not far from Nast's modest grave. In 1897, a magnificent tomb was dedicated to Grant and his remains were relocated there. When Julia died in 1902, she was laid to rest in what grammatically should be called Grants' Tomb.

Thomas Nast was a pioneer of a tradition and a political art form that remains extremely popular today. As Joel Pett, cartoonist for the Lexington (KY) *Herald-Leader* put it, "If [newspaper publishers] ... sign on to the quaint but true notion that journalism ought to comfort the afflicted and afflict the comfortable, there's no better way to afflict the comfortable than with editorial cartoons."[16] Nast couldn't have said it better himself.

---

15. Nast began drawing his cartoons in soft pencil on wooden blocks that were then prepared by engravers. Around 1880 photomechanical reproduction of ink drawings replaced the older and slower method. J. Chal Vinson, *Thomas Nast, Political Cartoonist* (Athens: University of Georgia Press, 1967), p. 35; and Morton Keller, *The Art and Politics of Thomas Nast* (London: Oxford University Press, 1968), p. 327.

16. Chris Lamb, *Drawn to Extremes: The Use and Abuse of Editorial Cartoons* (New York: Columbia University Press, 2004), p. 238.

CHAPTER

12

History Skills in Action: Designing Your Own Project

◆

The Problem

Some history classes using *Discovering the American Past* culminate in an individually chosen research project, while others teach students the essential skills and historical understanding to succeed in later research-based courses. All history teachers want to instill in students a love of history and a desire to keep learning. And many students become curious about a question or subject and want to discover more of the American past on their own. If, for whatever reason, you decide to undertake your own historical research, **how do you choose a project**?

◆

Background

There are many guidebooks for developing clear historical writing as well as reference books explaining the mechanics of historical research: how to take notes, organize citations, and structure arguments. Your professor or the history department at your school may also provide students with style manuals, such as *The Chicago Manual of Style*, that explain how to cite primary and secondary sources. But the starting point for historical research and writing begins with a question you want to answer, a topic you want to explore. This chapter builds on the historical detective skills you've developed by using *Discovering the American Past* to help you imagine your own research project.

History is a discipline that can remain a lifelong passion and pursuit even if your vocation turns out to be in business, for example, or a medical field or the arts. You likely know people in your family or community who read history for pleasure or research history as a hobby. History enthusiasts also volunteer at historical sites, join re-enactor groups, build their own artifact collections, and write stories and books based on their explorations of the past. Even if you don't spark to history at quite that level, you will surely find the skills of historical research invaluable to your intellectual and career pursuits. Weighing all relevant sources, critically evaluating evidence, and developing thoughtful interpretations

[335]

of complex issues are life skills that you learn through history class.

Because of the digital revolution, never before has conducting historical research been so accessible. Online resources like ancestory.com have made exploring individual family history much quicker and more rewarding. Digital history projects managed by the Library of Congress and National Archives allow Americans free and immediate access to some of the nation's richest and most meaningful historical records.[1] At these websites, you can listen to early sound recordings, study photographs and artifacts, and read everything from personal letters to international treaties. Universities also fund digital humanities projects that make studying the past more democratically available than ever before. The Avalon Project of the Yale University Law School, for example, the Rotunda collections through the University of Virginia Press, and the National Historical Geographic Information System at the University of Minnesota are marvelous examples of digital humanities projects that inspire greater curiosity and understanding of American history.[2]

Through your "brick and mortar" college or university library and at nearby public libraries and historical sites, you can enjoy ready access to even more materials for researching America's past. Local archives, historical societies, and museums will have rare manuscript materials like the freedom suits in St. Louis or the diaries of Civil War nurses. It is a singular thrill to sit in an archive and hold the actual diary

a nurse wrote while caring for patients in 1863 or read an 1831 deposition in the lawyer's own handwriting.

The preceding chapters have given you examples of the many sources used by historians: personal letters and diaries and memoirs, newspapers and magazines, law and court cases, statistics, cartoons, sermons, novels, and government documents. But this book is also limited in what we can share with teachers and students. Sound recordings, documentary films, and artifacts cannot easily—or in some cases even possibly—be presented in a print reader. But libraries and archives hold all kinds of such sources, as well as art books and published plays and television shows and news footage. Your university library also likely buys access to some fee-based databases. Our favorites include Early American Imprints and Early English Books Online, both of which are amazing and of the highest scholarly standards and word searchable. Like many other databases, these two require paid subscriptions.

It is easy to forget in our point-and-click age how expensive curating and housing historical sources can be. Digital projects are very, very expensive to launch and maintain, and so fees for use are often essential. Different libraries make different choices about which databases to purchase, but your university library certainly has subscriptions to several, bringing archives from around the country or even the globe to your campus—and even your computer. As one revolutionary leader said of his age, "The world is a wonder."

1. www.loc.gov and www.archives.gov.
2. The Avalon project at www.avalon.law.yale.edu contains a remarkable number and range of documents in law, history, and diplomacy. The American Founding Era collection at Rotunda (www.upress.virginia.edu/rotunda)

offers access to the decades-long magisterial documentary edition projects of leading members of the founding generation, as well as new "born digital" projects. Through the Minnesota NHGIS site (www.nhgis.org), users can access, explore, and create their own research using U.S. census materials.

Access does not equal ease, however. The challenge before historians is not so much *where* to find *information*—we are flooded with it—but *how* to acquire *knowledge*.

◆

The Method

The foundation for designing your own project is asking a question. This is deceptively simple and requires much more work than you might initially think. The research you conduct should be aimed at answering a central question, and the question must be two things at once: *interesting* to you and *significant* to the historian's craft.

No historian would dispute that diplomatic history is an important field. How nations interact with one another, how they negotiate treaties, settle boundaries, establish trading relations, and reconcile disputes—such matters are self-evidently significant. Similarly, you will find a consensus among historians that studying the evolution of women's citizenship is vital to understanding U.S. history. But not everyone is interested in studying foreign relations or gender history.

On the other hand, some of us find our own family history fascinating. Or we might be curious about our hometown or enjoy collecting memorabilia from an earlier era. Such topics might or might not be historically significant. There is an imprecise line between antiquarianism and historical research. Just because something was in the past does not make it historically meaningful.

Your professor can help guide you toward historical significance. You will find reflecting on your class notes and the readings in previous chapters of this book helpful on that score. What kinds of issues get emphasized in lectures and discussions? What larger connections are drawn to move from information to meaning?

If you have an idea about a project you want to research, ask this important question: *So what?* This is perhaps the most important question you can ask when researching history and a great guide to ensuring your project has historical significance.

Only you can know if a project is personally interesting. Independent research, unlike weekly readings or taking class notes, requires a high level of self-motivation. If you are not genuinely interested in the question you ask, you will likely struggle to develop a thoughtful answer.

To start, review the chapters in this book you've worked through so far as well as your notes from class lectures and discussions. What topics did you find most engaging? Which ones did you enjoy least? Remember that no one—even the most passionate researcher or teacher—connects with everything in history. Give yourself permission to think critically about your experiences in class.

Now reflect on your answers to these questions. Are there any common themes among the topics you liked most? Is there a specific era that you'd like to learn more about? Were you drawn to a particular place or group of people or event? For the topics that interested you least, was that because of the kinds of sources you read? Would you rather have read about the medical training of nurses instead of their wartime experiences? Would sermons from Puritan ministers have been more intriguing than the Hutchinson trial transcript? Or, did you find the period or the place or the particular people uninteresting?

Were there topics that you wanted to learn more about that we mentioned but did not explore? Perhaps you wondered about what exactly happened in the Stono Rebellion or during the Stamp Act Crisis. Maybe you wanted to know more about another part of the presidencies of Thomas Jefferson or Andrew Jackson.

If you are very intentional about asking a question that intrigues you and is historically significant, then the remainder of your individually driven research will be far more enriching and productive.

◆

The Evidence

The evidence for your project will be both primary (firsthand sources created in the period under consideration) and secondary (interpretive works by historians who have considered similar or related questions). Research projects rely more heavily on primary sources, with secondary works framing and contextualizing the interpretation of those sources. The "Background" section of each chapter in *Discovering the American Past* provides such context to the "Evidence" section, which is the center of each chapter.

You should be very mindful of asking a question and choosing an evidentiary base that can be fully considered in the amount of time you have to research and write. For class assignments, you will want to be equally attentive to page length requirements. Students are often nervous about writing an original work of ten or twenty pages and think, "I can never do that." If you choose your project wisely—if you ask an important and engaging question—you will likely face the opposite situation: trying to fit your ideas and evidence within the boundaries of length and time. For research outside of class, you may find it useful to seek out a mentor,

a faculty member or a classmate, to help you work through the planning of your project. Research and writing are often very solitary undertakings, but the best work occurs in a community, with classmates and teachers sharing ideas and giving feedback. If your historical curiosity takes you past the semester and the classroom, think about reaching out to an archivist or librarian who helped you, a relative or neighbor who loves history, or friends on social media. Love of history tends to be infectious, after all.

Make certain the evidence required to answer your question is accessible. If you don't have a car on campus, don't plan a project that requires travel to an archive, even if it is nearby. Don't depend on databases that are only temporarily available. Sometimes historians can get short-term free access to fee-based databases or digital projects. Some digital projects are permanent, but others are temporary—like museum exhibits. You may have access to digital materials through your hometown library but not on your college campus. Be very mindful of all these considerations. Research always requires returning to the documents—as you doubtless learned while working through the preceding chapters.

So, make certain that you have reliable, long-term access to your primary sources.

Digital projects are great, but don't forget the rich opportunities available through published primary sources in your library. Published primary sources are often annotated. That is, historians who have transcribed the primary sources for print also include footnotes identifying individuals and events, clarifying the meanings of words or ideas, and offering invaluable context to the primary source. This is especially useful for apprentice historians like you and your classmates. Immediate access on your computer to primary sources is not nearly so beneficial if you don't understand the larger context of those materials. Outstanding models of published primary sources include documentary editorial projects funded by major American universities and the National Historical Publications and Records Commission (NHPRC). Their projects include the papers of Thomas Jefferson, Frederick Douglass, Lucretia Mott, Harriet Jacobs, and Andrew Jackson and are of the highest scholarly standard. NHPRC publications represent an ideal place for beginning historians to research primary sources.[3]

A word of warning about selecting both digital and print sources: know the source of your source. Always make sure to vet your evidence with your professor or, for independent research, a professional historian. Sources can be edited and otherwise manipulated to fit a particular ideological agenda. If you rely on such sources, your project will be flawed at its foundation. You can trust materials you find at the National Archives or the Library of Congress; primary sources published or digitally managed by a reputable university press; or databases maintained by a respected company like Readex (which manages Early American Imprints).

Finally, as you seek out sources to answer your question, the evidence you discover may actually lead you to refine your central question or consider a new question. For example, you might start out wanting to learn more about the presidency of Thomas Jefferson and stumble across the letters President Jefferson wrote his grandchildren. Or, you might be curious about protests against the Stamp Act and, in reading the press coverage of events, decide to explore newspaper publishing in colonial America. Be open to changes in ideas driven by evidence and your own curiosity.

Questions to Consider

Still not sure about what question you might like to investigate? We will give you a few ideas to consider. But, as you've hopefully done in prior chapters of *Discovering the American Past*, challenge yourself to go beyond our questions to design and answer your own.

3. For NHPRC-funded projects, visit www.archives.gov/nhprc/

Did Chapter 1 inspire you to want to learn more about how Indian and English religious views shaped their encounters in colonial Virginia? If so, you will find nearly all the firsthand accounts written by early colonists at the Virtual Jamestown website (www.virtualjamestown.org). There you can explore, too, ideas about land, warfare, foodways, and trade. If other topics about early Virginia intrigued you, you can investigate the "starving times" in 1609–1610, the collapse of the Virginia Company and royal takeover, Bacon's Rebellion in 1676, and Virginia's evolving legal code.

Do you know why the founding generation so quickly and significantly changed the U.S. Constitution by adopting ten amendments in the first Congress? The project *The Documentary History of the Ratification of the Constitution*, published by the Wisconsin Historical Society, offers a remarkable range of evidence from the ratification debates in the various states, where Anti-federalist objections to the exclusion of guaranteed citizens' rights led to pressure for a federal Bill of Rights. James Madison's *Notes on the Debates in the Federal Convention* reveals the conversations in the Philadelphia Convention about the design of the Constitution. The records of the first federal Congress are available through the Library of Congress.

Perhaps you wanted to better understand the complicated ties and tensions between women's rights advocates and abolitionists in antebellum America. Why did some feminists encourage passage of the Fourteenth Amendment and others oppose it? Why did some abolitionists support the Seneca Falls movement and others did not? The NHPRC supports publication of the Frederick Douglass Papers, which would be of great use to investigating these questions. And the writings of Elizabeth Cady Stanton, Susan Anthony, and many other early feminists are available in print, too. Some of Stanton and Anthony's writings are also available through Rutgers University at http://ecssba.rutgers.edu.

Maybe Thomas Nast made you eager to explore print culture in the Civil War era. In addition to political cartoons, mid-nineteenth-century Americans had a popular new media form: photography. You can explore how nineteenth-century American civilians saw war for the first time because photographic images of Civil War soldiers and battlefields are available through the Library of Congress. Photographers also captured families and civic groups, enslaved African Americans at work, and cityscapes.

◆

Epilogue

Once you've decided on a question and found the evidence necessary to present a thoughtful answer, you are ready to analyze that evidence and present your project. Before the digital revolution, that always meant writing your ideas down on paper. But now, the opportunities for sharing historical research are much wider. Depending on your project, it might make sense to create a website, a multimedia presentation, or a documentary short film. Just as you were imaginative about asking a question and exploring evidence, think broadly about how your historical knowledge can be shared with others.

Consider also how the historical skills you've acquired in this class and the knowledge you've gained from your own reading and research can transcend the classroom and your college experience. Might you make history a lifelong passion and pursuit?